Computer Algorithms:
Design, Analysis and Applications

Computer Algorithms:
Design, Analysis and Applications

Edited by Aaron Armstrong

CLANRYE
INTERNATIONAL
www.clanryeinternational.com

Clanrye International,
750 Third Avenue, 9th Floor,
New York, NY 10017, USA

ISBN: 978-1-63240-925-6

Cataloging-in-Publication Data

Computer algorithms : design, analysis and applications / edited by Aaron Armstrong.
p. cm.
Includes bibliographical references and index.
ISBN 978-1-63240-925-6
1. Computer algorithms. 2. Computer programming. I. Armstrong, Aaron.
QA76.9.A43 C66 2020
005.1--dc23

For information on all Clanrye International publications
visit our website at www.clanryeinternational.com

Contents

Preface

This book has been a concerted effort by a group of academicians, researchers and scientists, who have contributed their research works for the realization of the book. This book has materialized in the wake of emerging advancements and innovations in this field. Therefore, the need of the hour was to compile all the required researches and disseminate the knowledge to a broad spectrum of people comprising of students, researchers and specialists of the field.

A computer algorithm is a set of instructions for performing calculation, data processing or automated reasoning. An initial state and input is provided, after which the algorithm proceeds through a succession of finite states to produce a final state and output. Algorithms may be classified on the basis of their implementation into recursive algorithm, logical algorithm, deterministic or non-deterministic algorithm, etc. They may also be classified as divide and conquer algorithm, search algorithm, randomized algorithm, etc. depending on the design paradigm or methodology. The study and analysis of algorithms is an important area of computer science. Algorithmic analysis is required to determine how much of a particular resource is required for a given algorithm. It is usually practiced without the implementation of a specific programming language. Most algorithms are applied on hardware/software platforms in which their algorithmic efficiency is evaluated using real code. For fast, interactive and commercial or scientific usage, algorithm efficiency is vital. The topics included in this book on computer algorithms are of utmost significance and bound to provide incredible insights to readers. Also included herein is a detailed explanation of the various aspects of the design, analysis and applications of algorithms. This book, with its detailed analyses and data, will prove immensely beneficial to professionals and students involved in this area at various levels.

At the end of the preface, I would like to thank the authors for their brilliant chapters and the publisher for guiding us all-through the making of the book till its final stage. Also, I would like to thank my family for providing the support and encouragement throughout my academic career and research projects.

Editor

A Robust Watermarking Scheme based on Maximum Wavelet Coefficient Modification and Optimal Threshold Technique

Chunlei Li, Xiaowei Song, Zhoufeng Liu, Aihua Zhang, and Ruimin Yang

School of Electronic and Information Engineering, Zhongyuan University of Technology, Zhengzhou 450007, China

Correspondence should be addressed to Chunlei Li; lichunlei1979@sina.com

Academic Editor: René Cumplido

Digital watermarking has received extensive attention as a new method for copyright protection. This paper proposes a robust watermarking algorithm based on maximum wavelet coefficient modification and optimal threshold technique. The medium wavelet coefficients are randomly permutated according to a secret key and divided into subgroups. We modify the maximum wavelet in each subgroup according to the embedded watermark bits, which can effectively resist attacks. During the extraction process, an optimal threshold value calculated by iterative computation is used to extract the watermark from the watermarked image under different attacks, without using the original image or watermark. Numerous experiments are conducted to evaluate the watermarking performance. Experimental results demonstrate the superiority of our scheme on robustness against content-preserving operations and incidental distortions such as JPEG compression, Gaussian noise, median filter, resizing, cropping, and sharpening.

1. Introduction

Currently, with rapid growth of the Internet and digital media, large amounts of media data are transmitted through the Internet due to its convenience and amazing speed. Digital media content and copyright are confronted with great challenges. Many researchers are aware of the importance of copyright protection, image authentication, and so forth, and they have great interest in applying watermarking scheme into digital multimedia for copyright protection [1, 2]. One of the most important branches in digital watermarking community is robust watermarking, which aims at achieving robustness, imperceptibility, and high security simultaneously [3–7].

However, the robustness and imperceptibility are contradictory to each other, and thus a good embedding scheme is required to achieve an appropriate trade-off between them. Basically, the watermark can be embedded in either the spatial domain or the transform domain. The former embeds a watermark into the host image by directly modifying the pixel value of the host image [8–10]. In contrast, the latter firstly performs the domain transformation and then embeds watermarks by modifying the coefficients in the

transform domain. In general, watermarking in transform domain is more robust than the one in spatial domain. In the past decades, a lot of watermarking algorithms have been developed in transform domain, for example, discrete cosine transforms (DCT) [11] and discrete wavelet transforms (DWT) [12].

Comparing DWT for JPEG2000 with DCT for JPEG, DWT has merits such as no blockiness, fast processing time, and high compression ability [13]; the robust watermarking scheme based on DWT has attracted great interest.

Wavelet-based watermarking scheme can be classified into two categories: wavelet tree-based watermarking methods and block-based DWT watermarking methods. The wavelet tree-based watermarking methods are generally using the energy difference among grouped wavelet coefficients for invisible watermark embedding and extraction [14–22]. Wang and Lin [14] grouped two wavelet trees into a so-called supertree, and each bit is embedded into two supertrees. The two trees exhibit a large statistical difference after one of the two trees is quantized with respect to a quantization index, which will be used for watermark extraction. Lien and Lin [15] improved Wang's method by using four trees to represent two watermark bits in order to improve visual quality. Wu and Huang [16] embedded the watermark into the supertrees by structure-based quantization method. According to watermark bits, the supertrees will be quantized into a significant structure. Compared to the unquantized supertree, the quantized version has strong statistical character in energy distribution, which can be used to extract watermark bits. In [19], wavelet trees are classified into two clusters using the distance vector to denote binary watermark bits and the two clusters exhibit a sufficiently large statistical difference based on the distance vector, a difference which is then used for subsequent watermark extraction. Tsai [21] enhanced the security of wavelet tree quantization watermarking scheme by adopting the chaotic system. Run et al. [22] embedded a watermark bit in the maximum wavelet coefficient of a wavelet; this is different from those in [14–16] which use two trees to embed a watermark bit. And the embedding method modifies the magnitude of the significant difference between the two largest wavelet coefficients in a wavelet tree to improve the robustness of the watermarking.

On the other hand, some researches embed a watermark using block-based DWT [23–31]. Davoine [23] proposed the watermarking methods based on the triplets and rectangular blocks of significant wavelet coefficients. Zhang et al. [24] divided the original image into blocks and transformed them into a DWT domain. The watermark is embedded by using the mean and the variance of a subband to modify the wavelet coefficient of a block. Khelifi et al. [25] proposed an adaptive blind watermarking method based on DWT. The host image is separated into nonoverlapping blocks classified as uniform or nonuniform blocks using a JND-based classifier. The watermark is embedded in the high subband of each block according to its classification. In [26–28], the block-based watermarking in the wavelet domain is proposed. They applied the significant difference between the first and second greatest coefficients to distinguish the bipolar watermark. Verma and Jha [29] Improved significant difference-based watermarking technique using lifting wavelet coefficients. In [30], the embedding algorithm hides a watermark bit in the low-low (LL) subband of a target nonoverlap block of the host image by modifying a coefficient of U component on SVD version of the block. A blind watermark extraction is designed using a trained SVR to estimate original coefficients. Subsequently, the watermark bit can be computed using the watermarked coefficient and its corresponding estimate coefficient. Sahraee and Ghofrani [31] propose a robust blind watermarking algorithm based on quantization of distance among wavelet coefficients for copyright protection. The authors divided wavelet coefficients into some blocks and obtained the first, second, and third maximum coefficients in each block. Then, the first and second maximum coefficients are quantized according to binary watermark bits. Using the block-based watermarking, the watermark can be extracted without using the original image or watermark.

The above-mentioned methods focused on locating the significant DWT component as embedding candidates and formulate appropriate strategy to modulate them without raising perceptual distortion. However, watermark extraction scheme is also critical for watermarking methods. In this paper, we propose a robust watermarking scheme based

on maximum wavelet coefficient modification and optimal threshold technique. The medium wavelet coefficients are randomly permutated and divided into nonoverlapped groups based on a private key. In each group, the largest two coefficients in a block are called significant coefficients and their difference is called significant difference. We modify the maximum wavelet coefficients to guarantee that the significant difference between watermark bit 0 and watermark bit 1 exhibits a large energy difference. During the extraction process, an optimal threshold value calculated by iterative computation is used to extract the watermark from the watermarked image under different attacks, without using the original image or watermark.

The remainder of the paper is organized as follows. In Section 2, we give an overview of DWT significant difference quantization based watermarking methods proposed by Lin et al. [26]; in Section 3, the details of our proposed robust watermarking algorithms are given; in Section 4, the experimental results and analysis are presented; and finally Section 5 concludes the proposed scheme.

2. Watermarking Method Based on Significant Difference of Wavelet Coefficient Quantization

Locating the significant coefficients embedding and adopting appropriate strategy to modulate them without raising perceptual distortion are two critical issues for DWT based watermarking methods. Compared with previous work, the methods based on group significant wavelet coefficients proposed by Lin et al. [26] can blindly find the permutation of significant coefficients and modulate the maximum to provide good watermarking robustness. The proposed method can be described as follows.

The proposed method in Lin et al. [26] firstly transforms the host image into wavelet domain by 3-L wavelet transform (DWT). Then LH3 which is more significant than HL3 is used for embedding watermarks. Every seven consecutive coefficients in LH3 subband are grouped into a block, and a secret key is then utilized to randomly select N_w blocks to embed the watermark bits $W = \{w_k \in \{0, 1\} \mid k = 1, 2, \ldots, N_w\}$. The quantization method is to adjust the significant difference (the difference between the first and second largest coefficients) to represent the binary watermark. If the embedding watermark bit is 1, then $\max_k$ is modified as $\max_k'$ as:

$$
\max_k'
= \begin{cases} \max_k + Q, & \text{if } (\max_k - \sec_k) < \text{maxium}\,(\varepsilon, Q) \\ \max_k, & \text{otherwise,} \end{cases} \quad (1)
$$

where $\max_k$ is the largest coefficient and $\sec_k$ is the second largest coefficient in the kth block. ε is the average significant difference of all N_w blocks and Q is the embedding strength. Otherwise, if the watermark bit is 0, the embedding equation is described as

$$
\max_k' = \sec_k. \quad (2)
$$

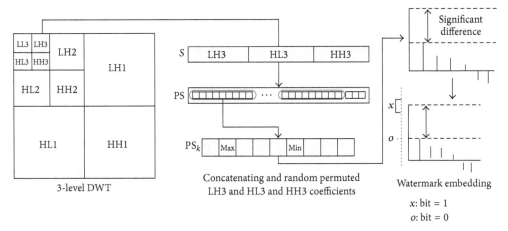

FIGURE 1: Watermark bits embedding.

The difference between watermark bits "0" and "1" is significant after embedding. In order to extract watermark bits W, a statistic difference is analyzed by (3) to find a threshold τ; it depends on the ratio between two watermark symbols:

$$\tau = \left\lfloor \frac{1}{N_w \alpha} \sum_{j=1}^{N_w \alpha} \delta_j \right\rfloor, \quad (3)$$

where $\delta_1 \leq \delta_2 \leq \cdots \leq \delta_j$ are ordered significant difference and α $(0 < \alpha \leq 1)$ is an empirical trade-off parameter and is sensitive to the ratio of two kinds of binary watermark bits. When the two kinds of binary watermark bits are equiprobable, α is set to 0.9.

Next, watermark information bits w_k are extracted by comparing the significant difference with the threshold τ, and it can be described as follows:

$$w_i = \begin{cases} 1, & \text{if } \left(\max_k' - \sec_k'\right) \geq \tau \\ 0, & \text{otherwise.} \end{cases} \quad (4)$$

The normalized correlation coefficient (NC) is calculated using the original watermark w_i and the extracted watermark w_i' to judge the existence of watermark, and it can be defined as follows:

$$\text{NC}\left(W, W'\right) = \frac{1}{N_w} \sum_{j=1}^{N_w} w_j w_j'. \quad (5)$$

The value is compared with a threshold value ρ. If $\text{NC} \geq \rho$, and it demonstrated that the extracted watermark is existing [26]; otherwise, it does not. When N_w is 512, the false positive error is 1.03×10^{-7} and ρ is set to 0.23.

3. The Proposed Robust Watermarking Scheme

In Lin et al. [26], each watermark bit is embedded into a block consisting of consecutive seven coefficients of HL3 subband. However, Meerwald et al. [33] pointed out that an attacker can analyze the property of embedding method and destroy the watermark. In this paper, the coefficients are selected from three subbands (HL3, LH3, and HH3) and then grouped into blocks after random permutation. A watermark bit is embedded into a coefficient group by improving maximum wavelet coefficient modification. Moreover, both the watermarked image quality and security can be achieved simultaneously. Finally, watermark extraction can be converted to threshold segmentation, and then an optimal threshold calculated by iterative computation is adopted to efficiently extract watermarks.

3.1. Watermark Embedding. In order to improve security of the proposed method, a random sequence is generated by utilizing the logistic chaotic map to encrypt the generated watermarks $W = \{w_i, \ i = 1, 2, \ldots, N_w\}$ [34]:

$$y_{n+1} = \lambda y_n \left(1 - y_n\right), \quad (6)$$

where $3.57 < \lambda \leq 4$ and $0 < y_0 \leq 0.5$. This sequence is nonperiodic, nonconvergent, and very sensitive to the initial value y_0; thus, the secret key k_1 is formulated as follows: $k_1 = \{\lambda, y_0\}$. We set λ and y_0 to 3.78 and 0.43, respectively. Then we binarize this sequence to a binary string s_j ($j = 1, 2, \ldots, N_w$) $\in \{0, 1\}$. Exclusive-OR operation is used to encrypt information bits by using

$$ew_i = w_i \oplus s_i, \quad i = 1, 2, \ldots, N_w. \quad (7)$$

Figure 1 illustrates the watermark embedding process. We firstly apply three-level wavelet decomposition into the original host image with size of 512×512 and select LH3, HL3, and HH3 subbands as embedding candidates. Three groups of 64×64 midfrequency coefficients are converted into 4096-dimension sequences, respectively. Thereafter, we concatenate the sequences into a single sequence S with 12288 coefficients. To enhance the security of the system, the sequence S is permuted as PS by using the secret key k_2. The permuted sequence PS is divided into N_w subgroups denoted as PS $= \text{PS}_k$, $k = 1, 2, \ldots, N_w$, where N_w is the number of watermark bits. We embed one bit for each group.

Dither modulation scheme is an improvement of the original uniform QIM (quantization index modulation) algorithm proposed by Chen and Wornell [35]. Applying dither modulation in watermark embedding process can tackle the quantization noise; it has two advantages: first, a pseudorandom dither vector can reduce quantization artifacts and get a perceptually superior quantized content. Second, the private key based dither vector can be secretly shared by the embedder and extractor and thus improve the system security.

Therefore, we improve the embedding method in Lin et al. [26] by adopting dither modulation scheme. And the embedding process can be described as follows:

(1) Generate the pseudorandom dither vectors $d[k, w_k]$ according to another private key k_3. $d[k, 0]$ is randomly generated from $[-Q/4, Q/4]$, and $d[k, 1]$ is generated using the following equation:

$$d[k, 1] = \begin{cases} d[k, 0] + \dfrac{Q}{4}, & d[k, 0] \geq 0 \\[2mm] d[k, 0] - \dfrac{Q}{4}, & \text{otherwise,} \end{cases} \qquad (8)$$

where T is embedding strength set by embedder.

(2) Embed the watermark bit by modifying the maximum wavelet in each subgroup. If a watermark bit 1 is embedded, we quantize $\max_i$ with Q and dither vectors $d[k, 1]$ as shown in (7):

$$\max_i^{\text{new}} = \begin{cases} \sec_i + Q + d[k, 1], & \text{if } \max_i - \sec_i < Q \\[2mm] \max_i + d[k, 1], & \text{otherwise,} \end{cases} \qquad (9)$$

where $\sec_i$ is the second largest coefficient, $\max_i$ is the largest coefficient in subgroup PS_i, and $\max_i^{\text{new}}$ is denoted as the new maximum value. If the difference between $\max_i$ and $\sec_i$ is smaller, we need an extra parameter Q and $d[k, 1]$ to do quantization. Otherwise, the difference is obvious and we only use $d[k, 1]$ to do quantization.

On the other hand, if a block is embedded with a watermark bit 0, $\max_i$ is quantized as follows:

$$\max_i^{\text{new}} = \sec_i + d[k, 0]. \qquad (10)$$

Finally, we recover the watermarked coefficients to original positions by k_2 and apply inverse wavelet transform to obtain the final watermarked image.

Algorithm 1 (watermark embedding).

Input. It includes an original image and watermark W.

Output. It includes a watermarked image with size of 512 × 512:

(1) Encrypt watermarks using (7).

(2) Apply three-level wavelet decomposition to the host image and select LH3, HL3, and HH3 subbands as embedding candidates.

(3) Concatenate the three subbands coefficient sequences into a single sequence S, and then randomly permute S using secret key k_2 to get PS.

(4) Equally split PS into N_w coefficient groups PS_i.

(5) Generate the dither vectors $d[k, 0]$ and $d[k, 1]$ using (8).

(6) Embed the watermark bit w_i into the ith group, $i = 1, 2, \ldots, N_w$ using (9) or (10).

(7) Recover the watermarked coefficients, and apply inverse wavelet transform to get the watermarked image.

3.2. Watermark Extraction. In the proposed method, either an original image or an original watermark is not required for the extraction process. The difference between the largest coefficient and the second coefficient is used to extract watermark. If watermarked image keep unaltered, the difference is less than $Q/4$ for embedding "0"; on the other hand, the difference is above $3/4Q$ for embedding "1." Therefore, watermark extraction can be converted into threshold segmentation. For a coefficient group, when the significant difference is satisfied with $d_i > T$, where $d_i = (\max_i' - \sec_i')$; there is a large probability that a watermark bit 1 was embedded; otherwise, a watermark bit 0 was embedded, where T is an optimal threshold obtained by iterations.

First, the differences are segmented into two parts. Then the mean value of the two parts is, respectively, computed. The average of the two mean values is taken as an updated threshold to iteratively segment the differences until the process converges. The process can be described as follows.

(1) Calculate the initial threshold T_0 ($k = 0$) by

$$T_0 = \frac{d_{\min} + d_{\max}}{2}, \qquad (11)$$

where $d_{\min}$ and $d_{\max}$ are, respectively, the minimum and the maximum value of the differences.

(2) Split the differences via threshold T_k ($k = 0, 1, \ldots,$) into two parts of R_1 and R_2, and it can be written as

$$\begin{aligned} R_1 &= \{d_i \mid d_i \geq T_k\}, \\ R_2 &= \{d_j \mid 0 \leq d_j < T_k\}. \end{aligned} \qquad (12)$$

(3) Calculate the mean value of R_1 and R_2:

$$Z_1 = \sum_{i=1}^{N_L} \frac{d_i}{N_L},$$

$$Z_2 = \sum_{j=1}^{N_H} \frac{d_j}{N_H}, \qquad (13)$$

N_L is the number of the differences which are less than T_k, and N_H is the number of the differences which are larger than T_k.

(4) Update threshold T_{k+1}:

$$T_0 = \frac{Z_1 + Z_2}{2}. \qquad (14)$$

(5) If $|T_{k+1} - T_k| < \delta$ (δ is a predetermined small value), end the iteration; otherwise go to Step (2).

After generating the optimal threshold T, the watermark bit can be extracted as

$$b_i = \begin{cases} 1, & \text{if } \left(\max_i' - \sec_i'\right) \geq T \\[2mm] 0, & \text{otherwise.} \end{cases} \qquad (15)$$

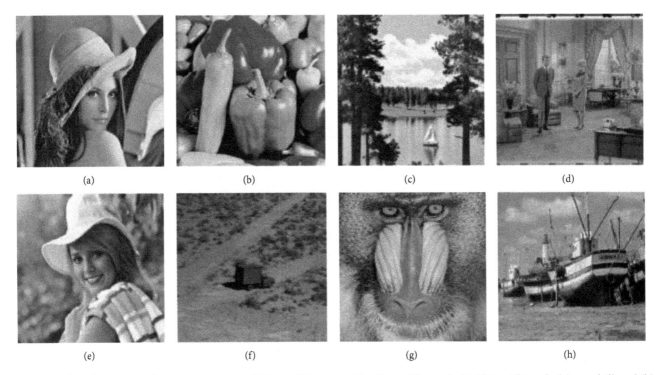

FIGURE 2: Selected images used in our experiment. (a) Lena, (b) pepper, (c) sailboat, (d) couple, (e) Elaine, (f) trunk, (g) mandrill, and (h) ship (all images are from USC-SIPI).

Algorithm 2 (watermark extraction).

Input. It includes a watermarked image.

Output. It includes a binary watermark sequence:

(1) A 512×512 watermarked image is decomposed using the 3-level DWT; select LH3, HL3, and HH3 subbands to extract watermarks.

(2) Concatenate the three subbands coefficient sequences into a single sequence S, and then randomly permute S using secret key k_2 to get PS as we have done in embedding procedure.

(3) Equally split PS into N_w coefficient groups PS_i.

(4) Get the values of $\max_i' - \sec_i'$ for each coefficient group.

(5) Calculate an optimal threshold value using (11)–(14).

(6) Extract the watermark bits using (15).

4. Experimental Results and Analysis

Cohen-Daubechies-Fauraue (CDF) 9/7 wavelet is a biorthogonal wavelet and has better energy compaction and lower computational cost, and it is selected as a part of the JPEG2000 standard. Therefore, CDF 9/7 wavelet is used for watermark embedding in our method. Meantime, twenty eight-bit gray scale images of size 512×512 from the USC-SIPI database [36] are used for evaluating watermarking performance, and the selected eight images are presented in Figure 2.

TABLE 1: Embedding strength versus PSNR and SSIM.

Q	10	20	30	40	50	60	70	80
PSNR (dB)	48.75	46.57	45.18	44.23	43.19	42.17	41.81	41.79
SSIM	0.99	0.99	0.98	0.98	0.98	0.98	0.97	0.97

For making comparisons with our method and the other watermarking methods [14, 26, 27, 32], random binary sequences of the same length $N_w = 512$ with equal ratio of "0" and "1" are employed as watermarks. Therefore, a watermark bit can be embedded into a coefficient group with size 24 in our method.

4.1. Embedding Distortion Assessment. To measure the embedding distortion between original image and its watermarked image, the peak signal-to-noise ratio (PSNR) and structural similarity index (SSIM) are adopted in this paper, in which, the definition of SSIM is as follows:

$$\text{SSIM}(x, y) = \frac{\left(2u_x u_y + C_1\right)\left(2\sigma_{xy} + C_2\right)}{\left(\mu_x^2 + \mu_y^2 + C_1\right)\left(\sigma_x^2 + \sigma_y^2 + C_2\right)}. \quad (16)$$

Table 1 presents the PSNR and SSIM for different embedding strength Q. By increasing the embedding strength, imperceptibility decreases. Thus, a trade-off is made in selecting the suitable quantization step. Generally, the PSNR values are above 40 dB often which corresponds to almost invisible differences. In this paper, we set the quantization step to 60, PNSR is up to 42 dB, and SSIM is 0.98.

TABLE 2: Embedding strength versus PSNR and SSIM.

	10	15	20	25	30	40	50	70	90
WTQ [14] (39.6 dB)	—	—	—	—	0.24	0.37	0.49	0.75	1
SDWCQ [26] (42.2 dB)	0.42	0.56	0.70	0.80	0.86	0.94	0.97	1	1
MWCQ [27] (41.5 dB)	0.35	0.52	0.69	0.81	0.85	0.92	0.95	0.96	0.99
SD-QIM [32] (43.3 dB)	0.39	0.72	0.91	0.96	0.98	0.99	1	1	1
Our method (42.2 dB)	0.61	0.84	0.96	0.99	0.99	1	1	1	1

TABLE 3: Comparisons of robustness against JPEG2000 compression.

	0.1	0.125	0.15	0.2	0.25	0.3	0.4	0.5	0.6
WTQ [14] (39.6 dB)	—	—	—	—	—	0.25	0.36	0.48	0.61
SD-QIM [32] (43.3 dB)	0.35	0.56	0.61	0.63	0.84	0.99	0.99	0.99	1
Our method (42.2 dB)	0.59	0.88	0.93	0.96	0.99	0.99	1	1	1

TABLE 4: Comparisons of robustness against incidental manipulation.

	Media (3 × 3)	Media (5 × 5)	Resizing (0.5)	Cropping (25%)	Sharpening	Gauss
WTQ [14] (39.6 dB)	0.51	—	—	—	0.46	0.64
SDWCQ [26] (42.2 dB)	0.88	0.74	0.86	0.70	0.99	0.86
MWCQ [27] (41.5 dB)	0.90	0.76	0.88	0.66	0.97	0.88
SD-QIM [32] (43.3 dB)	0.94	0.42	0.98	0.87	0.21	1
Our method (42.2 dB)	0.96	0.62	0.93	0.91	0.91	0.99

4.2. Robustness Assessment. To evaluate the robustness quantitatively, normalized correlation coefficient is adopted, and it is described as follows:

$$\text{NC}\left(W, W'\right) = \frac{W \cdot W'}{\|W\| \cdot \|W'\|}, \qquad (17)$$

where W is the original watermark, w' is the extracted watermark, and $\| \cdot \|$ denotes the ζ_2 norm. In this equation, if we map watermark "0" to "−1", we can get $\|W\| \cdot \|W'\| = \sqrt{\sum_{k=1}^{N_w} w_k^2 \cdot \sum_{k=1}^{N_w} (w_k')^2} = N_w$. Then, (17) can be rewritten as the following equation:

$$\text{NC}\left(W, W'\right) = \frac{W \cdot W'}{N_w} = \frac{1}{N_w} \sum_{k=1}^{N_w} w_k \cdot w_k'. \qquad (18)$$

Thereafter, we evaluate the robustness against the common image processing operations and incidental distortions such as lossy compression and noise. First, the robustness of our method under JPEG compression is compared with other methods. Twenty images are selected in our experiment, and the average value for NC is adopted for comparison. The experimental results are presented in Table 2. And the image quality metrics and NC values of other methods are collected from the original papers. From Table 2, we can observe that our method has the best robustness while keeping a high fidelity. Nearly all 512 bits can be accurately extracted when the quality factor is up to 25. Even when the QF decrease to 10, nearly 60% watermark bits can be correctly extracted, which demonstrates a significant advantage over other methods.

Since our method is designed within the DWT domain, it has natural robustness to the DWT quantization based JPEG2000 compression. And the comparing results are presented in Table 3. From the comparison, we can see that our method has advantages over classical DWT based methods. Next, the robustness against the miscellaneous attacks is presented in Table 4. For the cropping attack, the pixel in the 25% area of the whole watermark image in the upper left is set to zeros. For the resizing attack, the watermarked images are downsampled by a scale factor 0.5 and afterward interpolated to original resolution for watermark extraction. For the median filter, the 3 × 3 and 5 × 5 window sizes are used in the experiments. For the sharpening attack, the convolving mask is created from the negative of the Laplacian filter with parameter alpha equal to 0.2. For the Gaussian filter, it is zero mean noise with 0.005 variances. From Table 4, we can conclude that our proposed method is robust to these attacks.

5. Conclusions

In this paper, a robust watermarking scheme based on maximum wavelet coefficient modification and optimal threshold technique is proposed. The main advantages are threefold: (1) security is enhanced by randomly permuting coefficients among a group and image robustness is improved by embedding the watermark in the largest coefficient inside a subgroup by significant difference parity quantization; (2) the adopted dither quantization method can efficiently take control of watermarking distortions and correctly extract the watermarks under various attack conditions; (3) an optimal threshold value is used to extract the watermark from the watermarked image under different attacks, without using the original image or watermark. Comparison results with WTQ SDWCQ, MWCQ, and SD-QIM methods prove that the proposed method can provide better robustness toward a large variety of attacks while keeping relative high fidelity and capacity. In the future work, introducing HVS models for adaptive quantization of the significant amplitude coefficients is the main focus.

Conflict of Interests

The authors declare that there is no conflict of interests regarding the publication of this paper.

Acknowledgments

This work was supported by the National Natural Science Foundation of China (nos. 61202499, 61379113, 61440031, and 60902063), the Project of Henan Provincial Key Science and Technology Research (nos. 142102210578, 132300410163, and 142300410042), and Plan for Scientific Innovation Talent of Henan Province (124100510015).

References

[1] I. J. Cox, J. Kilian, F. T. Leighton, and T. Shamoon, "Secure spread spectrum watermarking for multimedia," *IEEE Transactions on Image Processing*, vol. 6, no. 12, pp. 1673–1687, 1997.

[2] W. Zeng and B. Liu, "A statistical watermark detection technique without using original images for resolving rightful ownerships of digital images," *IEEE Transactions on Image Processing*, vol. 8, no. 11, pp. 1534–1548, 1999.

[3] J.-L. Liu, D.-C. Lou, M.-C. Chang, and H.-K. Tso, "A robust watermarking scheme using self-reference image," *Computer Standards & Interfaces*, vol. 28, no. 3, pp. 356–367, 2006.

[4] R. Liu and T. Tan, "An SVD-based watermarking scheme for protecting rightful ownership," *IEEE Transactions on Multimedia*, vol. 4, no. 1, pp. 121–128, 2002.

[5] L.-T. Ko, J.-E. Chen, H.-C. Hsin, Y.-S. Shieh, and T.-Y. Sung, "Haar-wavelet-based just noticeable distortion model for transparent watermark," *Mathematical Problems in Engineering*, vol. 2012, Article ID 635738, 14 pages, 2012.

[6] B.-Z. Li and Y.-P. Shi, "Image watermarking in the linear canonical transform domain," *Mathematical Problems in Engineering*, vol. 2014, Article ID 645059, 9 pages, 2014.

[7] J. Lu, T. Qu, and H. R. Karimi, "Novel iris biometric watermarking based on singular value decomposition and discrete cosine transform," *Mathematical Problems in Engineering*, vol. 2014, Article ID 926170, 6 pages, 2014.

[8] M. Kutter, F. Jordan, and F. Bossen, "Digital watermarking of color images using amplitude modulation," *Journal of Electronic Imaging*, vol. 7, no. 2, pp. 326–332, 1998.

[9] M. Kutter and S. Winkler, "A vision-based masking model for spread-spectrum image watermarking," *IEEE Transactions on Image Processing*, vol. 11, no. 1, pp. 16–25, 2002.

[10] Y.-S. Juang, L.-T. Ko, J.-E. Chen, Y.-S. Shieh, T.-Y. Sung, and H. C. Hsin, "Histogram modification and wavelet transform for high performance watermarking," *Mathematical Problems in Engineering*, vol. 2012, Article ID 164869, 14 pages, 2012.

[11] M. Barni, F. Bartolini, V. Cappellini, and A. Piva, "A DCT-domain system for robust image watermarking," *Signal Processing*, vol. 66, no. 3, pp. 357–372, 1998.

[12] D. Kundur and D. Hatzinakos, "A robust digital image watermarking method using wavelet-based fusion," in *Proceedings of the International Conference on Image Processing*, vol. 3, pp. 544–547, 1997.

[13] M. Rabbani and R. Joshi, "An overview of the JPEG 2000 still image compression standard," *Signal Processing: Image Communication*, vol. 17, no. 1, pp. 3–48, 2002.

[14] S.-H. Wang and Y.-P. Lin, "Wavelet tree quantization for copyright protection watermarking," *IEEE Transactions on Image Processing*, vol. 13, no. 2, pp. 154–165, 2004.

[15] B. K. Lien and W. H. Lin, "A watermarking method based on maximum distance wavelet tree quantization," in *Proceedings of the 19th Conference on Computer Vision, Graphics and Image Processing*, 2006.

[16] G.-D. Wu and P.-H. Huang, "Image watermarking using structure based wavelet tree quantization," in *Proceedings of the 6th IEEE/ACIS International Conference on Computer and Information Science (ICIS '07)*, pp. 315–319, IEEE, July 2007.

[17] M.-J. Tsai and C.-L. Lin, "Constrained wavelet tree quantization for image watermarking," in *Proceedings of the IEEE International Conference on Communications (ICC '07)*, pp. 1350–1354, IEEE, June 2007.

[18] M.-J. Tsai, C.-T. Lin, and J. Liu, "A wavelet-based watermarking scheme using double wavelet tree energy modulation," in *Proceedings of the 15th IEEE International Conference on Image Processing (ICIP '08)*, pp. 417–420, IEEE, San Diego, Calif, USA, October 2008.

[19] W.-H. Lin, Y.-R. Wang, and S.-J. Horng, "A wavelet-tree-based watermarking method using distance vector of binary cluster," *Expert Systems with Applications*, vol. 36, no. 6, pp. 9869–9878, 2009.

[20] R. Shijie and S. Xin, "A wavelet-tree-based watermarking method using fast ICA," in *Proceedings of the 2nd International Symposium on Computational Intelligence and Design (ISCID '09)*, vol. 2, pp. 162–164, IEEE, Changsha, China, December 2009.

[21] M. J. Tsai, "Security enhancement by adopting the chaotic system for wavelet tree based digital image watermarking," in *Proceedings of the 16th IEEE International Conference on Image Processing (ICIP '09)*, pp. 3661–3664, IEEE, November 2009.

[22] R.-S. Run, S.-J. Horng, W.-H. Lin, T.-W. Kao, P. Fan, and M. K. Khan, "An efficient wavelet-tree-based watermarking method," *Expert Systems with Applications*, vol. 38, no. 12, pp. 14357–14366, 2011.

[23] F. Davoine, "Comparison of two wavelet based image watermarking schemes," in *Proceedings of the International Conference on Image Processing (ICIP '00)*, vol. 3, pp. 682–685, IEEE, Vancouver, Canada, September 2000.

[24] G. Zhang, S. Wang, and Q. Wen, "An adaptive block-based blind watermarking algorithm," in *Proceedings of the 7th International Conference on Signal Processing (ICSP '04)*, pp. 2294–2297, IEEE, August 2004.

[25] F. Khelifi, A. Bouridane, F. Kurugollu, and A. I. Thompson, "An improved wavelet-based image watermarking technique," in *Proceedings of the IEEE Conference on Advanced Video and Signal Based Surveillance (AVSS '05)*, pp. 588–592, IEEE, Como, Italy, 2005.

[26] W.-H. Lin, S.-J. Horng, T.-W. Kao, P. Fan, C.-L. Lee, and Y. Pan, "An efficient watermarking method based on significant difference of wavelet coefficient quantization," *IEEE Transactions on Multimedia*, vol. 10, no. 5, pp. 746–757, 2008.

[27] W.-H. Lin, Y.-R. Wang, S.-J. Horng, T.-W. Kao, and Y. Pan, "A blind watermarking method using maximum wavelet coefficient quantization," *Expert Systems with Applications*, vol. 36, no. 9, pp. 11509–11516, 2009.

[28] Y.-R. Wang, W.-H. Lin, and L. Yang, "An intelligent watermarking method based on particle swarm optimization," *Expert Systems with Applications*, vol. 38, no. 7, pp. 8024–8029, 2011.

[29] V. S. Verma and R. K. Jha, "Improved watermarking technique based on significant difference of lifting wavelet coefficients," *Signal, Image and Video Processing*, 2014.

[30] H.-H. Tsai, Y.-J. Jhuang, and Y.-S. Lai, "An SVD-based image watermarking in wavelet domain using SVR and PSO," *Applied Soft Computing*, vol. 12, no. 8, pp. 2442–2453, 2012.

[31] M. J. Sahraee and S. Ghofrani, "A robust blind watermarking method using quantization of distance between wavelet coefficients," *Signal, Image and Video Processing*, vol. 7, no. 4, pp. 799–807, 2013.

[32] B. Ma, Y. Wang, C. Li, Z. Zhang, and D. Huang, "A robust watermarking scheme based on dual quantization of wavelet significant difference," in *Proceedings of the Pacific-Rim Conference on Multimedia (PCM '12)*, 2012.

[33] P. Meerwald, C. Koidl, and A. Uhl, "Attack on watermarking method based on significant difference of wavelet coefficient quantization," *IEEE Transactions on Multimedia*, vol. 11, no. 5, pp. 1037–1041, 2009.

[34] J. Zhang, L. Tian, and H.-M. Tai, "A new watermarking method based on chaotic maps," in *Proceedings of the IEEE International Conference on Multimedia and Expo (ICME '04)*, vol. 2, pp. 939–942, IEEE, Taipei, Taiwan, June 2004.

[35] B. Chen and G. W. Wornell, "Quantization index modulation: a class of provably good methods for digital watermarking and information embedding," *IEEE Transactions on Information Theory*, vol. 47, no. 4, pp. 1423–1443, 2001.

[36] The USI-SIPI image database, volume 3, http://sipi.usc.edu/database/.

2

Cross-Layer Control with Worst Case Delay Guarantees in Multihop Wireless Networks

Shu Fan and Honglin Zhao

Communication Research Center, Harbin Institute of Technology, Harbin 150080, China

Correspondence should be addressed to Honglin Zhao; hlzhao@hit.edu.cn

Academic Editor: Vinod Sharma

The delay guarantee is a challenge to meet different real-time requirements in applications of backpressure-based wireless multihop networks, and therefore, researchers are interested in the possibility of providing bounded end-to-end delay. In this paper, a new cross-layer control algorithm with worst case delay guarantees is proposed. The utility maximization algorithm is developed using a Lyapunov optimization framework. Virtual queues that ensure the worst case delay of nondropped packets are designed. It is proved through rigorous theoretical analyses and verified by simulations that the time average overall utility achieved by the new algorithm can be arbitrarily close to the optimal solution with finite queue backlogs. The simulation results evaluated with Matlab show that the proposed algorithm achieves higher throughput utility with fewer data dropped compared with the existing work.

1. Introduction

With the exponential increase in wireless multihop networks in the last two decades, increasingly sophisticated approaches that target resource allocation, congestion control, routing, and scheduling have been developed. Among the various policies that have been developed, the backpressure scheduling/routing policy, which was first proposed in the seminal work by Tassiulas and Ephremides [1], is a promising scheme because of its optimal throughput characteristic. Cross-layer algorithms that provide throughput utility optimal operation guarantees for different network structures can be designed by applying the Lyapunov optimization technique and by combining the backpressure scheme with flow control [2]. The flow controller at the transport layer ensures that the admitted rate injected into the network layer lies within the network capacity region. In recent works, spectrum sharing and pricing mechanisms [3], energy management [4], and social selfishness of users [5] have been considered in backpressure-based cross-layer algorithms. Cross-layer algorithms have also been combined with MAC (Media Access Control) layer [6], TCP (Transmission Control Protocol) layer [7], and application layers [8].

Besides throughput utility, end-to-end delay is another important long-term performance metric of the backpressure style algorithms, and it is crucial to many essential applications. As applications with real-time requirements are being developed, it is necessary to design backpressure-based algorithms that provide bounded worst case delay guarantees. Backpressure algorithms usually bear poor delay performance mainly attributed to the following three reasons. First, the slow startup process to form a stable queue backlog gradient from the source to the destination causes large initial end-to-end delay. Second, unnecessarily long or looped paths form owing to the fluctuation of the queue backlog. Finally, the absence of consistent backpressure towards the destination can cause large latency in networks with short-lived or low-rate flows. In [9], average delay bounds are derived for one-hop wireless networks using maximal scheduling. In [10], the delay bounds in wireless ad hoc networks are studied using backpressure scheduling with either one-hop or multihop traffic flows. In [11], the authors propose a cross-layer algorithm providing average end-to-end delay guarantees. These prior works can only provide bounds on the overall average delay via Little's Theorem, except for individual sessions. There are several works aiming to reduce end-to-end delay for individual sessions. In [12], a virtual queue-based gradient is established for nodes. In [13], the authors develop a delay-aware cross-layer algorithm using a novel link-rate allocation strategy and a regulated scheduling policy. A hop-count based queuing structure is used in [14] to provide a worst case hop count to the destination. However, these works fail to provide explicit end-to-end delay guarantees. Deterministic worst case delay guarantees are derived from the algorithm in [15] which uses explicit delay information from the head-of-line packet at each queue in one-hop networks. Considering both one-hop and multihop wireless networks, [16] designs an opportunistic scheduling scheme that guarantees a bounded worst case delay for each session. Our paper is mostly related to the study in [16]. However, different from [16], our algorithm consists of two phases and the persistent service virtual queue [16] is redesigned.

The key contributions of this paper can be summarized as follows.

(i) The paper proposes a two-phase algorithm which can provide a bound on the worst case end-to-end delay of individual sessions by designing a novel virtual delay queue structure.

(ii) By transforming the stochastic control problem into a deterministic optimization problem using the Lyapunov drift-plus-penalty technique, we design a joint congestion control, routing, and scheduling algorithm.

(iii) The performance in terms of utility optimality and network stability of the algorithm is demonstrated with rigorous theoretical analyses. It is shown that the proposed algorithm can achieve a time average throughput utility that can be arbitrarily close to the optimal value, with queue backlogs being bounded by constants.

The remainder of this paper is organized as follows. Section 2 introduces the system model and problem formulation. In Section 3, the algorithm is designed using Lyapunov optimization. The performance analyses of the proposed algorithm are presented in Section 4. The simulation results are given in Section 5. Conclusions are provided in Section 6.

2. Network Model and Problem Formulation

2.1. Network Model. Consider a multihop wireless network consisting of several nodes. Let the network be modeled by a directed connectivity graph $G(N, L)$, where N is the set of nodes and $(i, j) \in L$ represents a unidirectional wireless link between node i and node j which is in the transmission range of i. Let M be the set of unicast sessions m between source-destination pairs in the network. N_s is the set of source nodes s_m and N_d is the set of destination nodes d_m of session m. Packets from the source node traverse multiple wireless hops before arriving at the destination node.

The system is assumed to run in a time-slotted fashion. Nodes in the network communicate using only one channel. $a_{nj}(t) \in \{0, 1\}$ is used to indicate whether link (n, j) is used to transmit packets in time slot t. $a_{nj}(t) = 1$ implies that the link is scheduled. In this model, scheduling is subjected to the following constraints:

$$\sum_{j:(n,j)\in L} \alpha_{nj}(t) + \sum_{i:(i,n)\in L} \alpha_{in}(t) \leq 1, \tag{1}$$

$$\alpha_{nj}(t) + \sum_{k\in N}\sum_{l} \alpha_{kl}(t) \leq 1, \tag{2}$$

where node l is in the transmission range of n and $O(n)$ denotes the set of nodes with $(n, i) \in L$. $I(n)$ denotes the set of nodes with $(j, n) \in L$. Constraint (1) implies that each node is equipped with only one radio, and thus, it can either transmit or receive data at any given time. Constraint (2) states that a node transmitting packets will interfere with the data receptions of the nodes in its transmission range.

2.2. Virtual Queue at the Transport Layer. $A_m(t) \in [0, A_{\max}^{(m)}]$ denotes the arrival rate of session m injected into the transport layer from the application layer at the source node and $A_{\max}^{(m)}$ is the maximum arrival rate of session m. $r_m(t) \in [0, A_m(t)]$ is the admitted rate of session m injected into the network layer. $\eta_m(t) \in [0, A_{\max}^{(m)}]$ is an auxiliary variable known as the virtual input rate. The virtual queue at the transport layer of source node s_m of session m is denoted by Y_m that is updated as follows:

$$Y_m(t+1) = \max\{Y_m(t) - r_m(t), 0\} + \eta_m(t). \tag{3}$$

If each virtual queue Y_m is guaranteed to be stable, according to the necessity and sufficiency for queue stability [17], it is apparent that $\overline{\eta_m} \leq \overline{r_m}$, where the time average value of time-varying variable $x(t)$ is denoted by $\overline{x} = \lim_{t\to\infty}(1/t)\sum_{\tau=0}^{t-1} E(x(\tau))$. Therefore, the lower bound of $\overline{r_m}$ can be derived from $\overline{\eta_m}$ which can be calculated.

2.3. Data Queue at the Network Layer. The data backlog queue for session m at the network layer of node n is denoted by $Q_n^{(m)}(t)$. In each slot t, the queue is updated as

$$Q_n^{(m)}(t+1)$$
$$= \max\left\{Q_n^{(m)}(t) - \sum_{i\in O(n)} \mu_{ni}^{(m)}(t) - D_n^{(m)}(t), 0\right\} \tag{4}$$
$$+ \sum_{j\in I(n)} \mu_{jn}^{(m)}(t) + 1_{\{n=s_m\}} r_m(t),$$

where $\mu_{ni}^{(m)}(t)$ is the amount of data of session m to be forwarded from node n to i in time slot t. $1_{\{n=s_m\}}$ is an indicator function that denotes 1 if $n = s_m$ and 0 otherwise. In addition, $\sum_{m\in M} \mu_{ni}^{(m)}(t)$ must not be greater than $\mu_n^{\max,out}$. $D_n^{(m)} \in [0, D_{\max}]$ represents the number of packets of session m that are dropped by node n in slot t. The optimization of $\mu_{ni}^{(m)}(t)$ is the routing decision. As assumed in [18], in this paper, the transmission capacity of any link is set to be 1.

Therefore, $\mu_{ni}^{(m)}(t)$ is either 0 or 1, and it can not be greater than $Q_n^{(m)}(t)$, which is denoted as

$$\mu_{ni}^{(m)}(t) \in \left\{0, \min\left\{Q_n^{(m)}(t), 1\right\}\right\}, \tag{5}$$

$$\forall (n, i) \in L, \ n \neq d_m, \ m \in M,$$

and $\sum_{m \in M} \mu_{ni}^{(m)}(t) = \alpha_{ni}(t), \forall (n, i) \in L$, can also be derived. The actual amount of packets of session m dropped in slot t can be defined as

$$\widetilde{D_n^{(m)}}(t) = \min\left\{Q_n^{(m)}(t) - \mu_n^{(m)}(t), D_n^{(m)}(t)\right\}. \tag{6}$$

2.4. Persistent Service Virtual Queue. The ϵ-persistent service queue designed in [16] can ensure bounded worst case delay for general types of utility functions. We denote this queue by $G_n^{(m)}$, and in each slot, the queue is updated as

$$G_n^{(m)}(t+1) = \max\left\{G_n^{(m)}(t) + 1_{\{Q_n^{(m)}(t)>0\}}\right.$$

$$\cdot \left(\epsilon - \sum_{i \in O(n)} \mu_{ni}^{(m)}(t)\right) - D_n^{(m)}(t) - 1_{\{Q_n^{(m)}(t)=0\}} \tag{7}$$

$$\left. \cdot \mu_n^{\max,\text{out}}, 0\right\}.$$

From the algorithm in [16] we find that $G_n^{(m)}$ is used in decision of resource allocation and packet dropping. Since in most slots $Q_n^{(m)}(t) > 0$, $G_n^{(m)}$ may increase fast. According to the packet drop decision algorithm, high value of ϵ-persistent service queue leads to serious packets drop. Therefore, the fast increase of $G_n^{(m)}$ leads to dropping of packets and this results in a significant drop in throughput utility.

In this paper, we redesign the ϵ-persistent service queue that is denoted by $Z_n^{(m)}$. In each slot t, the queue is updated as

$$Z_n^{(m)}(t+1) = \max\left\{Z_n^{(m)}(t) + \epsilon_1 \cdot 1_{\{Q_n^{(m)}(t)>Q_{n,\text{standard}}^{(m)}\}}\right.$$

$$+ \epsilon_2 \cdot 1_{\{Q_n^{(m)}(t) \leq Q_{n,\text{standard}}^{(m)}\}} - D_n^{(m)}(t) \tag{8}$$

$$\left. - \sum_{i \in O(n)} \mu_{ni}^{(m)}(t), 0\right\},$$

where $\epsilon_1 > \epsilon_2 > 0$. ϵ_1 and ϵ_2 are constants. $Q_{n,\text{standard}}^{(m)}$ is a constant value that is calculated in phase I of the algorithm which will be given in Section 3. Initial backlog $Z_n^{(m)}(0)$ is supposed to be 0.

$Q_{n,\text{standard}}^{(m)}$ is the time average of length of queue of session m in node n. According to (8), $Z_n^{(m)}$ increases fast only when $Q_n^{(m)}(t) > Q_{n,\text{standard}}^{(m)}$, and thus $Z_n^{(m)}$ should grow slower than $G_n^{(m)}$. According to the packet drop decision algorithm, the number of packets dropped in our new algorithm should

decrease and throughput should increase, compared with the algorithm in [16].

Any algorithm that maintains bounded $Q_n^{(m)}(t)$ and $Z_n^{(m)}(t)$ ensures persistent service with bounded worst case delay, as shown in Theorem 1.

Theorem 1 (worst case delay). *For all time slots $t \in \{0, 1, 2, \ldots\}$ and all sessions $m \in M$, suppose that the algorithm can ensure*

$$Q_n^{(m)}(t) \leq Q_n^{(m),\max},$$

$$Z_n^{(m)}(t) \leq Z_n^{(m),\max}, \tag{9}$$

where $Q_n^{(m),\max}$ and $Z_n^{(m),\max}$ are finite upper bounds for $Q_n^{(m)}(t)$ and $Z_n^{(m)}(t)$, respectively. Assuming First Input First Output (FIFO) service, the worst case delay of the nondropped data at node n is bounded by the constant $W_n^{(m),\max}$, which is given as

$$W_n^{(m),\max} = \left\lceil \frac{\left(Q_n^{(m),\max} + Z_n^{(m),\max}\right)}{\epsilon_2} \right\rceil, \tag{10}$$

where $\lceil x \rceil$ denotes the smallest integer that is greater than or equal to x.

Proof. Fix any slot $t \geq 0$, and let $A_n^{(m)}(t)$ represent the data that arrives at queue $Q_n^{(m)}$ on slot t. As the service is FIFO, the data $A_n^{(m)}(t)$ is placed at the end of the queue $Q_n^{(m)}$ on slot $t+1$. We want to prove that all of the data $A_n^{(m)}(t)$ departs queue $Q_n^{(m)}$ on or before slot $t + W_n^{(m),\max}$. We prove this in three cases.

Case 1. If $Q_n^{(m)}(\tau) > Q_{n,\text{standard}}^{(m)}$ for all $\tau \in \{t+1, \ldots, t+W_n^{(m),\max}\}$, the following can be derived

$$Z_n^{(m)}(\tau+1) \geq Z_n^{(m)}(\tau) + \epsilon_1 - \sum_{i \in O(n)} \mu_{ni}^{(m)}(\tau)$$

$$- D_n^{(m)}(\tau). \tag{11}$$

Summing the above over $\tau \in \{t+1, \ldots, t+W_n^{(m),\max}\}$ yields

$$Z_n^{(m)}\left(t+1+W_n^{(m),\max}\right) - Z_n^{(m)}(t+1)$$

$$\geq \epsilon_1 \cdot W_n^{(m),\max}$$

$$- \sum_{\tau=t+1}^{t+W_n^{(m),\max}} \left[\sum_{i \in O(n)} \mu_{ni}^{(m)}(\tau) + D_n^{(m)}(\tau)\right]. \tag{12}$$

For $Z_n^{(m)}(t+1+W_n^{(m),\max}) \leq Z_n^{(m),\max}$, (12) can be rearranged to yield

$$\epsilon_1 \cdot W_n^{(m),\max} - Z_n^{(m),\max}$$

$$\leq \sum_{\tau=t+1}^{t+W_n^{(m),\max}} \left[\sum_{i \in O(n)} \mu_{ni}^{(m)}(\tau) + D_n^{(m)}(\tau)\right]. \tag{13}$$

According to (10), $W_n^{(m),\max}$ is the smallest integer that is greater than or equal to $(Q_n^{(m),\max} + Z_n^{(m),\max})/\epsilon_2$. Therefore, we can get $W_n^{(m),\max} \geq (Q_n^{(m),\max} + Z_n^{(m),\max})/\epsilon_2$, and we can derive

$$\epsilon_1 \cdot W_n^{(m),\max} - Z_n^{(m),\max}$$
$$\geq Q_n^{(m),\max} + Z_n^{(m),\max} - Z_n^{(m),\max} = Q_n^{(m),\max}. \tag{14}$$

Then, the following can be derived:

$$\sum_{\tau=t+1}^{t+W_n^{(m),\max}} \left[\sum_{i \in O(n)} \mu_{ni}^{(m)}(\tau) + D_n^{(m)}(\tau) \right] \geq Q_n^{(m),\max} \tag{15}$$
$$\geq Q_n^{(m)}(t+1).$$

Equation (15) means that all the data in queue $Q_n^{(m)}$ on slot $t+1$ (including all of the data $A_n^{(m)}(t)$ which arrives at $Q_n^{(m)}$ on slot t) can depart the queue on or before the slot $t + W_n^{(m),\max}$. Therefore, in the condition of $Q_n^{(m)}(\tau) > Q_{n,\text{standard}}^{(m)}$ for all $\tau \in \{t+1, \ldots, t+W_n^{(m),\max}\}$, the worst case delay of nondropped data at node n is bounded by

$$W_{n,\text{Case 1}}^{(m),\max} = \left\lceil \frac{\left(Q_n^{(m),\max} + Z_n^{(m),\max} \right)}{\epsilon_2} \right\rceil. \tag{16}$$

Case 2. If $Q_n^{(m)}(\tau) \leq Q_{n,\text{standard}}^{(m)}$ for all $\tau \in \{t+1, \ldots, t+W_n^{(m),\max}\}$, the following can be derived:

$$Z_n^{(m)}\left(t+1+W_n^{(m),\max}\right) - Z_n^{(m)}(t+1)$$
$$\geq \epsilon_2 \cdot W_n^{(m),\max}$$
$$- \sum_{\tau=t+1}^{t+W_n^{(m),\max}} \left[\sum_{i \in O(n)} \mu_{ni}^{(m)}(\tau) + D_n^{(m)}(\tau) \right]. \tag{17}$$

Similar to Case 1, the bound of the worst case delay of nondropped data at node n in Case 2 is derived as

$$W_{n,\text{Case 2}}^{(m),\max} = \left\lceil \frac{\left(Q_n^{(m),\max} + Z_n^{(m),\max} \right)}{\epsilon_2} \right\rceil. \tag{18}$$

Case 3. If $Q_n^{(m)}(\tau) > Q_{n,\text{standard}}^{(m)}$ in n_1 slots of $\tau \in \{t+1, \ldots, t+W_n^{(m),\max}\}$ and $Q_n^{(m)}(\tau) \leq Q_{n,\text{standard}}^{(m)}$ in n_2 slots of $\tau \in \{t+1, \ldots, t+W_n^{(m),\max}\}$ and if we also have $n_1 + n_2 = W_n^{(m),\max}$, the following can be derived:

$$Z_n^{(m)}\left(t+1+W_n^{(m),\max}\right) - Z_n^{(m)}(t+1)$$
$$\geq \epsilon_1 \cdot n_1 + \epsilon_2 \cdot n_2$$
$$- \sum_{\tau=t+1}^{t+W_n^{(m),\max}} \left[\sum_{i \in O(n)} \mu_{ni}^{(m)}(\tau) + D_n^{(m)}(\tau) \right]. \tag{19}$$

Let $\epsilon_* = (\epsilon_1 \cdot n_1 + \epsilon_2 \cdot n_2)/ W_n^{(m),\max}$; we can get

$$Z_n^{(m)}\left(t+1+W_n^{(m),\max}\right) - Z_n^{(m)}(t+1)$$
$$\geq \epsilon_* \cdot W_n^{(m),\max}$$
$$- \sum_{\tau=t+1}^{t+W_n^{(m),\max}} \left[\sum_{i \in O(n)} \mu_{ni}^{(m)}(\tau) + D_n^{(m)}(\tau) \right]. \tag{20}$$

It is easy to derive $\epsilon_2 < \epsilon_* < \epsilon_1$. Similar to Case 1, the bound of the worst case delay of nondropped data at node n in Case 3 is

$$W_{n,\text{Case 3}}^{(m),\max} = \left\lceil \frac{\left(Q_n^{(m),\max} + Z_n^{(m),\max} \right)}{\epsilon_2} \right\rceil. \tag{21}$$

Considering the three cases above, the worst case delay of the nondropped data at node n is bounded by the constant $W_n^{(m),\max}$, which is given as

$$W_n^{(m),\max} = \left\lceil \frac{\left(Q_n^{(m),\max} + Z_n^{(m),\max} \right)}{\epsilon_2} \right\rceil. \tag{22}$$

□

2.5. Throughput Utility Optimization Problem. Similar to the design of the utility function in [16], let $U_m(\cdot)$ be strictly concave, twice differentiable, and nondecreasing utility function with $U_m(0) = 0$. $\bar{r} = (\overline{r_m}, m \in M)$ denotes the throughput of the network. Λ is the capacity region of the network [17]. Then, the throughput utility maximization problem $P1$ can be defined as follows:

$$\max \quad \sum_{m \in M} U_m\left(\overline{r_m}\right) - \sum_{m \in M} \sum_{n \in N} \beta_m \overline{d_n^{(m)}}, \tag{23}$$

$$\text{s.t.} \quad \bar{r} \in \Lambda, \tag{24}$$

$$(1), (2), (5), \tag{25}$$

where $\overline{d_n^{(m)}}$ is the time average value of $D_n^{(m)}(t)$. β_m is the maximum slope of the utility function $U_m(x)$. Constraint (24) means that the network stability is guaranteed.

3. Dynamic Algorithm via Lyapunov Optimization

The Lyapunov optimization technique is applied to solve $P1$. $Q_n^{(m)}$ ($\forall n \in N, m \in M$), Y_m ($\forall m \in M$), and $Z_n^{(m)}$ ($\forall n \in N, m \in M$) are used in the dynamic algorithm. Let $\Theta(t) = [Q(t), Y(t), Z(t)]$ be the network state vector in time slot t. Define the Lyapunov function as

$$L(\Theta(t)) = \frac{1}{2} \left[\sum_{m \in M} (Y_m(t))^2 + \sum_{n \in N} \sum_{m \in M} \left(Q_n^{(m)}(t) \right)^2 \right.$$
$$\left. + \sum_{n \in N} \sum_{m \in M} \left(Z_n^{(m)}(t) \right)^2 \right]. \tag{26}$$

The conditional Lyapunov drift in time slot t is

$$\Delta(\Theta(t)) = E\{L(\Theta(t+1)) - L(\Theta(t)) \mid \Theta(t)\}. \quad (27)$$

To maximize a lower bound for $\sum_{m \in M} U_m(\overline{r_m}) - \sum_{m \in M} \sum_{n \in N} \beta_m \overline{d_n^{(m)}}$, the drift-plus-penalty function can be defined as

$$\Delta_V(\Theta(t)) = \Delta(\Theta(t)) - VE\left\{ \sum_{m \in M} U_m(\eta_m(t)) \right.$$

$$(28)$$

$$\left. - \sum_{m \in M} \sum_{n \in N} \beta_m D_n^{(m)}(t) \mid \Theta(t) \right\},$$

where V is the weight of the utility defined by the user. The following inequality can be derived:

$$E\{\Delta_V(\Theta(t))\} \le B - \Psi_1(t) - \Psi_2(t) - \Psi_3(t) - \Psi_4(t)$$

$$+ \sum_{n \in N} \sum_{m \in M} Z_n^{(m)} \cdot \epsilon_1, \quad (29)$$

where $\Psi_1(t)$, $\Psi_2(t)$, $\Psi_3(t)$, and $\Psi_4(t)$ can be evaluated as follows:

$$\Psi_1(t) = \sum_{m \in M} [V \cdot U_m(\eta_m(t)) - Y_m(t) \cdot \eta_m(t)],$$

$$\Psi_2(t) = \sum_{m \in M} r_m(t) \cdot [Y_m(t) - Q_n^{(m)}(t) \cdot 1_{\{n=s_m\}}],$$

$$\Psi_3(t) = \sum_{n \in N} \sum_{m \in M} \sum_{i \in O(n)} \mu_{ni}^{(m)}(t) \quad (30)$$

$$\cdot [Q_n^{(m)}(t) - Q_i^{(m)}(t) + Z_n^{(m)}(t)],$$

$$\Psi_4(t) = \sum_{n \in N} \sum_{m \in M} D_n^{(m)}(t)$$

$$\cdot [Q_n^{(m)}(t) + Z_n^{(m)}(t) - V \cdot \beta_m].$$

B is a constant and satisfies

$$B \ge \frac{1}{2} \sum_{m \in M} [(\eta_m(t))^2 + (r_m(t))^2] + \frac{1}{2}$$

$$\cdot \sum_{m \in M} \sum_{n \in N} \left[\left(\sum_{j \in I(n)} \mu_{jn}^{(m)}(t) + 1_{\{n=s_m\}} r_m(t) \right)^2 \right.$$

$$(31)$$

$$+ \left(\sum_{i \in O(n)} \mu_{ni}^{(m)}(t) + D_n^{(m)}(t) \right)^2 + \frac{1}{2} \sum_{m \in M} \sum_{n \in N} \left[\epsilon_1 \right.$$

$$\left. - \sum_{i \in O(n)} \mu_{ni}^{(m)}(t) - D_n^{(m)}(t) \right]^2,$$

according to $0 \le \eta_m(t) \le A_{\max}^{(m)}$, $0 \le r_m(t) \le A_{\max}^{(m)}$, $\mu_{ni}^{(m)}(t) \in \{0,1\}$, and $0 \le D_n^{(m)}(t) \le D_{\max}$, and ϵ_1 is a constant value and the constant B must exist.

The algorithm CCWD is based on the drift-plus-penalty framework [17] and the main design principle of the algorithm is to minimize the right-hand side of (29). The algorithm includes two phases.

Phase I. Choose a sufficiently large T. From time $t = 0, \ldots, T-1$, run the algorithm proposed in [16] using $Q_n^{*(m)}(t)$ as the size of data queues. Set $Q_{n,\text{standard}}^{(m)}$ to be $(1/T) \sum_{\tau=0}^{T-1} Q_n^{*(m)}(\tau) + \rho$, where ρ is a constant.

Phase II. This phase includes five components.

Source Rate Control. For each session $m \in M$ at source node s_m, the admitted rate $r_m(t)$ is chosen to solve

$$\max \quad r_m(t) \cdot [Y_m(t) - Q_n^{(m)}(t) \cdot 1_{\{n=s_m\}}], \quad (32)$$

$$\text{s.t.} \quad 0 \le r_m(t) \le A_m(t). \quad (33)$$

Problem (32) is a linear optimization problem, and if $Y_m(t) > Q_{s_m}^{(m)}(t)$, $r_m(t)$ is set to be $A_m(t)$; otherwise it is set to be zero.

Virtual Input Rate Control. For each session $m \in M$ at source node s_m, the virtual input rate $\eta_m(t)$ is chosen to solve

$$\max \quad V \cdot U_m(\eta_m(t)) - Y_m(t) \cdot \eta_m(t), \quad (34)$$

$$\text{s.t.} \quad 0 \le \eta_m(t) \le A_{\max}^{(m)}. \quad (35)$$

Since the utility function $U_m(\cdot)$ is strictly concave and twice differentiable, (34) is a concave maximization problem with linear constraint. $\eta_m(t)$ can be chosen by

$$\eta_m(t) = \max\left\{ \min\left\{ U_m'^{-1}\left(\frac{Y_m(t)}{V} \right), A_{\max}^{(m)} \right\}, 0 \right\}, \quad (36)$$

where $U_m'^{-1}(\cdot)$ is the inverse function of $U_m'(\cdot)$ that is the first-order derivative of $U_m(\cdot)$. Since the utility function $U_m(\cdot)$ is strictly concave and twice differentiable, $U_m'(\cdot)$ must be a monotonic function, and therefore, $U_m'^{-1}(\cdot)$ must exist.

Joint Routing and Scheduling. At the node $n \in N$, routing and scheduling decisions $\mu_{ni}^{(m)}(t)$ for each session $m \in M$ can be made by solving the following:

$$\max \quad \sum_{n \in N} \sum_{m \in M} \sum_{i \in O(n)} \mu_{ni}^{(m)}(t) \cdot [Q_n^{(m)}(t) - Q_i^{(m)}(t) + Z_n^{(m)}(t)], \quad (37)$$

$$\text{s.t.} \quad (1), (2), (5). $$

First, for each link (n, i), the session m^* for link (n, i) can be chosen as

$$m^* = \underset{m \in M}{\arg\max} \left\{ Q_n^{(m)}(t) - Q_i^{(m)}(t) + Z_n^{(m)}(t) \right\}. \quad (38)$$

The weight of link (n, i) is defined as $w_{ni} = Q_n^{(m^*)}(t) - Q_i^{(m^*)}(t) + Z_n^{(m^*)}(t)$. Therefore, the joint routing and scheduling problem can be reduced to the following:

$$\max \quad \sum_{n \in N} \sum_{i \in O(n)} \mu_{ni}^{(m^*)}(t) \cdot w_{ni}, \quad (39)$$

$$\text{s.t.} \quad (1), (2), (5). \quad (40)$$

Transmission rates $\mu_{ni}^{(m^*)}(t)$ are chosen based on (39) which is a tough problem. The solution requires global knowledge and a centralized algorithm.

Packet Drop Decision. For each session $m \in M$ and each node $n \in N$, choose $D_n^{(m)}$ to solve

$$\max \quad \left[Q_n^{(m)}(t) + Z_n^{(m)}(t) - V \cdot \beta_m \right] \cdot D_n^{(m)}(t), \quad (41)$$

$$\text{s.t.} \quad 0 \le D_n^{(m)}(t) \le D_{\max}. \quad (42)$$

Problem (41) is a linear optimization problem, and if $Q_n^{(m)}(t) + Z_n^{(m)}(t) > V \cdot \beta_m$, $D_n^{(m)}(t)$ is set to be $D_{\max}$; otherwise it is set to be zero.

Update of Queues. $Y(t)$, $Q(t)$, and $Z(t)$ are updated using (3), (4), and (8) in each time slot.

4. Performance Analysis

Theorem 2 (bounded queues). *Assume that $D_{\max} \ge \max\{\epsilon_1, A_{\max}^{(m)} + \mu_n^{\max,in}\}$ holds, where $\mu_n^{\max,in}$ denotes the maximal amount of packets that node n can receive from other nodes in one slot. Then under the algorithm CCWD, all queues are bounded for all $t \ge 0$ as follows:*

$$Q_n^{(m)}(t) \le Q_n^{(m),\max},$$

$$Z_n^{(m)}(t) \le Z_n^{(m),\max}, \quad (43)$$

$$Y_m(t) \le Y^{(m),\max}$$

provided that these inequalities hold at $t = 0$. The queue bounds are given by

$$Y^{(m),\max} = V \cdot \beta_m + A_{\max}^{(m)},$$

$$Q_n^{(m),\max} = V \cdot \beta_m + \mu_n^{\max,in} + 1_{\{n=s_m\}} \cdot A_{\max}^{(m)}, \quad (44)$$

$$Z_n^{(m),\max} = V \cdot \beta_m + \epsilon_1.$$

Proof. The theorem is proved by induction.

(1) According to the induction principle, if $Y_m(t) \le Y^{(m),\max}$ holds for all t and supposing that $Y_m(t) \le Y^{(m),\max}$ for time slot t, it should also hold for time slot $t + 1$. If $Y_m(t) \le V \cdot \beta_m$, then $Y_m(t+1) \le V \cdot \beta_m + A_{\max}^{(m)} = Y^{(m),\max}$, because Y_m can increase by at most $A_{\max}^{(m)}$ in one slot. If $V \cdot \beta_m < Y_m(t) \le Y^{(m),\max}$, because β_m is the maximum slope of the utility function $U_m(x)$, we have

$$V \cdot U_m\big(\eta_m(t)\big) - Y_m(t) \cdot \eta_m(t)$$

$$\le V \cdot U_m(0) + V \cdot \beta_m \cdot \eta_m(t) - Y_m(t) \cdot \eta_m(t)$$

$$= V \cdot U_m(0) + \eta_m(t) \cdot \big(V \cdot \beta_m - Y_m(t)\big) \quad (45)$$

$$\le V \cdot U_m(0) = 0$$

with equality holding only if $\eta_m(t) = 0$. Because $\eta_m(t) = 0$ when $Y_m(t) > V \cdot \beta_m$, $Y_m(t)$ can not increase in the next

slot according to (3). Thus $Y_m(t + 1) \le Y_m(t) \le Y^{(m),\max}$. Then $Y_m(t) \le Y^{(m),\max}$ for all t is proved.

(2) According to the induction principle, if $Q_n^{(m)}(t) \le Q_n^{(m),\max}$ holds for all t and supposing that $Q_n^{(m)}(t) \le Q_n^{(m),\max}$ for time slot t, it should also hold for time slot $t + 1$. If $Q_n^{(m)}(t) \le V \cdot \beta_m$, then

$$Q_n^{(m)}(t + 1) \le Q_n^{(m)}(t) + \sum_{j \in I(n)} \mu_{jn}^{(m)}(t) + 1_{\{n=s_m\}} r_m(t)$$

$$\le V \cdot \beta_m + \mu_n^{\max,in} + 1_{\{n=s_m\}} \cdot A_{\max}^{(m)} \quad (46)$$

$$= Q_n^{(m),\max}.$$

If $V \cdot \beta_m < Q_n^{(m)}(t) \le Q_n^{(m),\max}$, $D_n^{(m)}(t)$ is set to be $D_{\max}$ according to the packet drop decision algorithm. Because $D_{\max} \ge \max\{\epsilon_1, A_{\max}^{(m)} + \mu_n^{\max,in}\}$, then

$$Q_n^{(m)}(t + 1) \le Q_n^{(m)}(t) - D_{\max} + A_{\max}^{(m)} + \mu_n^{\max,in} \quad (47)$$

$$\le Q_n^{(m)}(t) \le Q_n^{(m),\max}.$$

Then $Q_n^{(m)}(t) \le Q_n^{(m),\max}$ for all t is proved.

(3) According to the induction principle, if $Z_n^{(m)}(t) \le Z_n^{(m),\max}$ holds for all t and supposing that $Z_n^{(m)}(t) \le Z_n^{(m),\max}$ for time slot t, it should also hold for time slot $t + 1$. If $Z_n^{(m)}(t) \le V \cdot \beta_m$, then

$$Z_n^{(m)}(t + 1) \le Z_n^{(m)}(t) + \epsilon_1 \le V \cdot \beta_m + \epsilon_1 = Z_n^{(m),\max}. \quad (48)$$

If $V \cdot \beta_m < Z_n^{(m)}(t) \le Z_n^{(m),\max}$, $D_n^{(m)}$ is set to be $D_{\max}$ according to the packet drop decision algorithm. Because $D_{\max} \ge \max\{\epsilon_1, A_{\max}^{(m)} + \mu_n^{\max,in}\}$, then

$$Z_n^{(m)}(t + 1) \le Z_n^{(m)}(t) - D_{\max} + \epsilon_1 \le Z_n^{(m)}(t) \quad (49)$$

$$\le Z_n^{(m),\max}.$$

Then $Z_n^{(m)}(t) \le Z_n^{(m),\max}$ for all t is proved. $\square$

Theorem 3 (algorithm performance). *One has $\varphi(t) = \sum_{m \in M} U_m(r_m(t)) - \sum_{m \in M} \sum_{n \in N} \beta_m D_n^{(m)}(t)$. Define $\varphi^*(t) = \sum_{m \in M} U_m(r_m^*) - \sum_{m \in M} \sum_{n \in N} \beta_m D_n^{*(m)}$ to be the optimal value of $\varphi(t)$ subject to constraints (1), (2), and (5), where r_m^* and $D_n^{*(m)}$ are the solutions to maximize $\varphi(t)$. One can have $\sum_{m \in M} U_m(\overline{r_m}) - \sum_{m \in M} \sum_{n \in N} \beta_m \overline{d_n^{(m)}} \ge \varphi^*(t) - B/V$.*

Proof. The drift-plus-penalty function (28) satisfies

$$
\Delta \left(\Theta \left(t \right) \right) - V \cdot E \left\{ \sum_{m \in M} U_m \left(\eta_m \left(t \right) \right) \right.
$$

$$
\left. - \sum_{m \in M} \sum_{n \in N} \beta_m D_n^{(m)} \left(t \right) \mid \Theta \left(t \right) \right\} \leq B - V
$$

$$
\cdot E \left\{ \sum_{m \in M} U_m \left(\eta_m \left(t \right) \right) \right.
$$

$$
\left. - \sum_{m \in M} \sum_{n \in N} \beta_m D_n^{(m)} \left(t \right) \mid \Theta \left(t \right) \right\} + \sum_{m \in M} Y_m \left(t \right)
$$

$$
\cdot E \left\{ \eta_m \left(t \right) - r_m \left(t \right) \mid \Theta \left(t \right) \right\} + \sum_{m \in M} \sum_{n \in N} Q_n^{(m)} \left(t \right) \tag{50}
$$

$$
\cdot E \left\{ \sum_{j \in I(n)} \mu_{jn}^{(m)} \left(t \right) - \sum_{i \in O(n)} \mu_{ni}^{(m)} \left(t \right) + 1_{\{n = s_m\}} r_m \left(t \right) \right.
$$

$$
\left. - D_n^{(m)} \left(t \right) \mid \Theta \left(t \right) \right\} + \sum_{m \in M} \sum_{n \in N} Z_n^{(m)} \left(t \right) \cdot E \left\{ \epsilon_1 \right.
$$

$$
\left. - \sum_{i \in O(n)} \mu_{ni}^{(m)} \left(t \right) - D_n^{(m)} \left(t \right) \mid \Theta \left(t \right) \right\},
$$

where B is a constant value. According to Theorem 4.5 in [17] and Lemmas 5.6 and 5.7 in [19], the following inequality can be derived from (50):

$$
\Delta \left(\Theta \left(t \right) \right) - V
$$

$$
\cdot E \left\{ \sum_{m \in M} U_m \left(\eta_m \left(t \right) \right) - \sum_{m \in M} \sum_{n \in N} \beta_m D_n^{(m)} \left(t \right) \mid \Theta \left(t \right) \right\}
$$

$$
\leq B - V
$$

$$
\cdot E \left\{ \sum_{m \in M} U_m \left(r_m^* \right) - \sum_{m \in M} \sum_{n \in N} \beta_m D_n^{*(m)} \mid \Theta \left(t \right) \right\} \tag{51}
$$

$$
- \delta_1 \cdot \sum_{m \in M} Y_m \left(t \right) - \delta_2 \cdot \sum_{n \in N} \sum_{m \in M} Q_n^{(m)} \left(t \right) - \delta_3
$$

$$
\cdot \sum_{n \in N} \sum_{m \in M} Z_n^{(m)} \left(t \right),
$$

where $\delta_1, \delta_2, \delta_3 > 0$. Inequality (51) can be transformed to the exact form specified by Theorem 5.4 in [19]. According to

Theorem 5.4 in [19] and the condition $\overline{\eta_m} \leq \overline{r_m}$, the following inequality can be derived:

$$
\sum_{m \in M} U_m \left(\overline{r_m} \right) - \sum_{m \in M} \sum_{n \in N} \beta_m \overline{d_n^{(m)}}
$$

$$
\geq \sum_{m \in M} U_m \left(\overline{\eta_m} \right) - \sum_{m \in M} \sum_{n \in N} \beta_m \overline{d_n^{(m)}}
$$

$$
\geq \sum_{m \in M} U_m \left(r_m^* \right) - \sum_{m \in M} \sum_{n \in N} \beta_m D_n^{*(m)} - \frac{B}{V} \tag{52}
$$

$$
= \varphi^* \left(t \right) - \frac{B}{V}.
$$

Inequality (52) implies that the overall throughput utility achieved by the algorithm in this paper is within a constant gap from the optimum value. □

5. Simulation

In the simulations, the commonly used greedy maximal scheduling (GMS) method is used for schedulable link set generation for each algorithm under comparison. This method is widely used for implementing backpressure-based centralized algorithms under sophisticated networks [20].

5.1. Simulation Setup. For simulations, a network with 20 nodes randomly distributed in a square of 1600 m^2 is considered. A transmission is successful if a receiver is within the transmission range of its sender and outside the range of other concurrent senders. The transmission or interference range of a node is 15 m. There are four unicast sessions with randomly chosen sources and destinations. Data of each session is injected into the transport layer with the same rate in each slot at the source nodes. Parameter V is set as $V = [500 \quad 1000 \quad 1500 \quad 2000]$. The throughput utility function is $U(x) = \log(x + 1)$. Simulations are run in Matlab R2014a. The simulation time of phase I lasts 30000 time slots. The simulation time of phase II lasts 50000 time slots. All initial queue sizes are set to be 0 and the default values are set as follows: $D_{\max} = 3$, $\beta_m = 1$, $A_{\max}^{(m)} = 2$, $\mu_n^{\max,\text{in}} = \mu_n^{\max,\text{out}} = 1$, $\epsilon_1 = 2$, $\epsilon_2 = 1$, and $\rho = 0$.

5.2. Performance Comparison. In this section, the performance of CCWD is compared with that of an existing method called NeelyOpportunistic, which too can provide bounded worst case delay. NeelyOpportunistic is proposed in [16]. The throughput utilities and the time average number of dropped packets achieved by CCWD and NeelyOpportunistic are compared in Figures 1 and 2, respectively. V is set to be 1000. The data arrival rate is set to be from 0.2 packets to 1 packet per time slot. In Figure 1, the utility achieved by CCWD is higher than that of NeelyOpportunistic. Figure 2 shows that fewer packets get dropped using CCWD than with NeelyOpportunistic. According to the packet drop decision algorithm, high value of ϵ-persistent service queue leads to serious packets drop. As mentioned in Section 2.4, the virtual queue of CCWD being redesigned in this paper grows slower

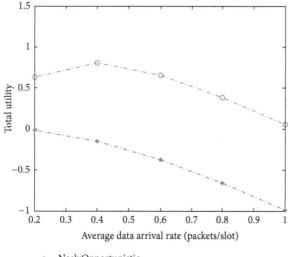

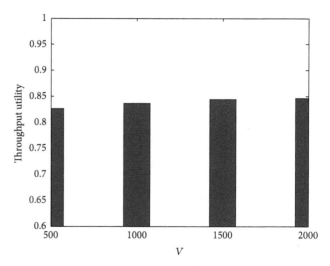

FIGURE 3: Throughput utility versus V.

FIGURE 1: Throughput utility versus average data arrival rate.

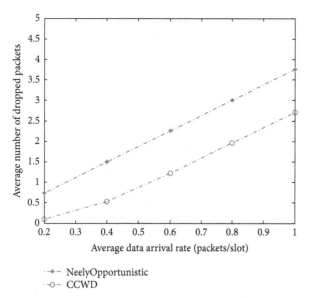

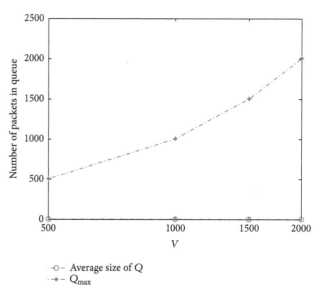

FIGURE 4: Time average size of Q versus V.

FIGURE 2: Time average number of dropped packets versus average data arrival rate.

than the virtual queue of NeelyOpportunistic. Therefore, the virtual queue structure in NeelyOpportunistic leads to more serious packet drop and lower throughput utility.

5.3. Impact of V. According to the analyses in Section 4, with the increase of V, the utility achieved by CCWD can be arbitrarily close to the optimal value with an increase in the length of queues that is linear in V. The data arrival rate $A_m(t)$ is set to be 0.4 packets per time slot. Since the utility function is concave and nondecreasing, the optimal value of throughput utility should be $N_{\text{session}} \cdot \log(1 + A_m(t))$, where N_{session} is the number of sessions. N_{session} is 4 in this section. In this simulation, optimal throughput utility should be 1.34. Figure 3 shows that the utility value is increased with an

increasing V. According to (44), it is easy to calculate $Y^{(m),\max}$, $Q^{(m),\max}$, and $Z^{(m),\max}$. In this section, since the maximum arrival rate $A_{\max}^{(m)}$ of each session is set to be 2 and the throughput utility function of each session is uniform, $Y_{\max}$, $Q_{\max}$, and $Z_{\max}$ can also be calculated using (44). In Figures 4, 5, and 6, V is increased from 500 to 2000 and on a log base 10 scale. From Figures 4, 5, and 6, we can learn that the time average sizes of Q, Y, and Z all increase approximately proportionally with the increase of V and are not larger than the bounds given in Theorem 2. The simulation results show a match between the simulations and the theoretical analyses.

6. Conclusions

This paper proposed a two-phase throughput utility maximization algorithm which provides worst case delay guarantees using a new ϵ-persistent virtual queue for multihop

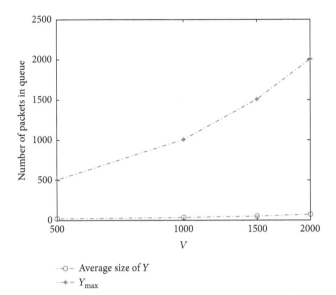

FIGURE 5: Time average size of Y versus V.

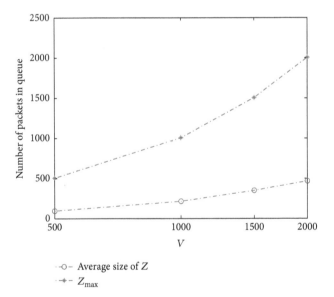

FIGURE 6: Time average size of Z versus V.

wireless networks. Throughput utility optimality of the algorithm is demonstrated with rigorous theoretical analyses. This algorithm ensures that queues are bounded by constants. Compared with existing works, the algorithm presented in this paper performs better in terms of utility and data dropped. The plan for the future work is to combine this proposed algorithm with applications requiring limited delay.

Competing Interests

The authors declare that they have no competing interests.

Acknowledgments

This work was supported by the National Natural Science Foundation of China under Grant no. 2013CB329003, the National Natural Science Foundation of China under Grant no. 61307016, and Natural Science Foundation of Liaoning Province under Grant no. 2014020193.

References

[1] L. Tassiulas and A. Ephremides, "Stability properties of constrained queueing systems and scheduling policies for maximum throughput in multihop radio networks," *IEEE Transactions on Automatic Control*, vol. 37, no. 12, pp. 1936–1948, 1992.

[2] M. J. Neely, E. Modiano, and C.-P. Li, "Fairness and optimal stochastic control for heterogeneous networks," *IEEE/ACM Transactions on Networking*, vol. 16, no. 2, pp. 396–409, 2008.

[3] H. X. Li, C. Wu, Z. P. Li, and F. C. M. Lau, "Socially-optimal multi-hop secondary communication under arbitrary primary user mechanisms," in *Proceedings of the IEEE INFOCOM*, pp. 1717–1725, IEEE, Turin, Italy, April 2013.

[4] Z. Liu, X. Y. Yang, P. Zhao, and W. Yu, "Energy-balanced backpressure routing for stochastic energy harvesting WSNs," in *Proceedings of the 10th International Conference on Wireless Algorithm, Systems, and Applications*, pp. 767–777, August 2013.

[5] H. Li, W. Huang, C. Wu, Z. Li, and F. C. M. Lau, "Utility-maximizing data dissemination in socially selfish cognitive radio networks," in *Proceedings of the 8th IEEE International Conference on Mobile Ad-Hoc and Sensor Systems (MASS '11)*, pp. 212–221, Valencia, Spain, October 2011.

[6] L. Jiang and J. Walrand, "A distributed CSMA algorithm for throughput and utility maximization in wireless networks," *IEEE/ACM Transactions on Networking*, vol. 18, no. 3, pp. 960–972, 2010.

[7] H. Seferoglu and E. Modiano, "TCP-aware backpressure routing and scheduling," in *Proceedings of the IEEE Information Theory and Applications Workshop (ITA '14)*, pp. 1–9, San Diego, Calif, USA, February 2014.

[8] E. Anifantis, E. Stai, V. Karyotis, and S. Papavassiliou, "Exploiting social features for improving cognitive radio infrastructures and social services via combined MRF and back pressure cross-layer resource allocation," *Computational Social Networks*, vol. 1, article 4, 2014.

[9] M. J. Neely, "Delay analysis for maximal scheduling with flow control in wireless networks with bursty traffic," *IEEE/ACM Transactions on Networking*, vol. 17, no. 4, pp. 1146–1159, 2009.

[10] L. B. Le, K. Jagannathan, and E. Modiano, "Delay analysis of maximum weight scheduling in wireless ad hoc networks," in *Proceedings of the 43rd Annual Conference on Information Sciences and Systems (CISS '09)*, pp. 389–394, Baltimore, Md, USA, March 2009.

[11] D. Xue and E. Ekici, "Delay-guaranteed cross-layer scheduling in multihop wireless networks," *IEEE/ACM Transactions on Networking*, vol. 21, no. 6, pp. 1696–1707, 2013.

[12] Z. Jiao, B. Zhang, W. Gong, and H. Mouftah, "A virtual queue-based back-pressure scheduling algorithm for wireless sensor networks," *Eurasip Journal on Wireless Communications and Networking*, vol. 2015, article 35, 2015.

[13] H. Z. Xiong, R. Li, A. Eryilmaz, and E. Ekici, "Delay-aware cross-layer design for network utility maximization in multihop networks," *IEEE Journal on Selected Areas in Communications*, vol. 29, no. 5, pp. 951–959, 2011.

[14] L. Ying, S. Shakkottai, and A. Reddy, "On combining shortest-path and back-pressure routing over multihop wireless networks," in *Proceedings of the 28th Conference on Computer Communications (IEEE INFOCOM '09)*, pp. 1674–1682, Rio de Janeiro, Brazil, April 2009.

[15] M. J. Neely, "Delay-based network utility maximization," in *Proceedings of the IEEE International Conference on Computer Communications (INFOCOM '10)*, San Diego, Calif, USA, March 2010.

[16] M. J. Neely, "Opportunistic scheduling with worst case delay guarantees in single and multi-hop networks," in *Proceedings of the IEEE INFOCOM*, pp. 1728–1736, IEEE, Shanghai, China, April 2011.

[17] M. J. Neely, *Stochastic Network Optimization with Application to Communication and Queueing Systems*, Morgan & Claypool Publishers, 2010.

[18] A. Cammarano, F. L. Presti, G. Maselli, L. Pescosolido, and C. Petrioli, "Throughput-optimal cross-layer design for cognitive radio ad hoc networks," *IEEE Transactions on Parallel and Distributed Systems*, vol. 26, no. 9, pp. 2599–2609, 2015.

[19] L. Georgiadis, M. J. Neely, and L. Tassiulas, "Resource allocation and cross-layer control in wireless networks," *Foundations and Trends in Networking*, vol. 1, no. 1, pp. 1–144, 2006.

[20] Z. Jiao, Z. Yao, B. Zhang, and C. Li, "NBP: an efficient network-coding based backpressure algorithm," in *Proceedings of the IEEE International Conference on Communications (ICC '13)*, pp. 1625–1629, Budapest, Hungary, June 2013.

3

An Algorithm of Traffic Perception of DDoS Attacks against SOA based on Time United Conditional Entropy

Yuntao Zhao,[1,2] Hengchi Liu,[1] and Yongxin Feng[1]

[1]*School of Information Science and Engineering, Shenyang Ligong University, Shenyang 110159, China*
[2]*College of Information Science and Engineering, Northeaster University, Shenyang 110819, China*

Correspondence should be addressed to Yongxin Feng; fengyongxin@263.net

Academic Editor: Jun Bi

DDoS attacks can prevent legitimate users from accessing the service by consuming resource of the target nodes, whose availability of network and service is exposed to a significant threat. Therefore, DDoS traffic perception is the premise and foundation of the whole system security. In this paper the method of DDoS traffic perception for SOA network based on time united conditional entropy was proposed. According to many-to-one relationship mapping between the source IP address and destination IP addresses of DDoS attacks, traffic characteristics of services are analyzed based on conditional entropy. The algorithm is provided with perception ability of DDoS attacks on SOA services by introducing time dimension. Simulation results show that the novel method can realize DDoS traffic perception with analyzing abrupt variation of conditional entropy in time dimension.

1. Introduction

With the development of network technology, Distributed Denial of Service [1] (DDoS) attack has become a huge threat to today's network service and has aroused great concern in various countries around the world. DDoS attack being easy to implement and difficult to guard and track has become the most common network attack techniques, which has a serious impact on the efficiency of network and service [2]. According to statistics, the number of DDoS attacks continued to rise in recent years. From the latest survey released by the Akamai who is the world's largest CDN service provider, the number of DDoS attacks doubled in the second quarter of 2015. In 4 January 2016, HSBC suffered an unknown DDoS attack, which causes the system to crash and service to interrupt for two days. And a Distributed Reflection Denial of Service (DRDoS) attack is becoming an important novel form [3]. DRDoS is a method by which the hacker uses modified source address to produce a large number of forgery requests instead of directly attacks. A lot of forgery requests will point to the attacked node that would crash due to resource exhaustion at last. In the application layer DDoS attacks gradually shifted the target from the

network bandwidth to the server resources of application. With the growth of service-oriented architecture (SOA) and web technology, the attacks in application layer are more destructive.

SOA is an architectural pattern in computer software design in which application components provide services to other components via a communications protocol, typically over a network. The principles of service-orientation are independent of any vendor, product, or technology [4]. Because SOA which has flexible, open, and extensible characteristic is widely used, there is also increasingly great concern over a large number of DDoS attacks against SOA. Jung et al. [5] analyze the difference between the application layer DDoS and Flash Crowd. Lu et al. [6] puts forward the request path and access time of the web server to distinguish between attack flow and normal one. Zhou et al. [7] analyze the characteristics of average access time and page request sequence. Those researchers realize perception of attack with the statistics comparison of normal users and abnormal users.

In this paper, a novel method to traffic perception of the DDoS attack based on SOA is proposed. Because SOA registration centers carry a mass of data traffic that is from many service nodes, it is difficult to distinguish between

DDoS traffic and Flash Crowd (legal flow or normal traffic) on SOA registration centers. In order to effectively perceive the DDoS attacks and distinguish it from Flash Crowd, the time dimension of conditional entropy is considered. The instantaneous jump of conditional entropy is calculated and statistical in the setting time slot, which leads to the sudden traffic from DDoS attacks in the time dimension while normal traffic is smooth. The simulation results show that the algorithm is able to effectively perceive the traffic changes caused by DDoS attacks against SOA.

2. The Vulnerability of SOA under DDoS Attacks

SOA has increasingly popular in all areas of application and rapid developed. A large number of businesses, organizations, government departments, and agencies are setting up and developing their own SOA network. Modern society relies heavily on computer network system under the SOA architecture, which makes it very important to ensure the security of computer and network systems. Otherwise, it will cause not only the waste of manpower and material, but also the loss of competitive advantage, company confidential documents to be stolen. So how to enhance the security of SOA systems and network systems has become the focus of world attention.

Among all the forms of attacks against SOA, the most prominent ones are DDoS attacks. With network systems under SOA with rapid response, distributed collaboration, and reuse of services and other features, it has also undertaken a series of management and security risks brought by public service, especially from DDoS attacks in the process of information exchange.

Under DDoS attacks the vulnerability of SOA is mainly reflected in the following three aspects.

(1) SOA is a central network structure with the registration center as its core. SOA service registration, publish, query, subscription, and so on must go through the service registration center. Once the center suffered from DDoS attacks, the performance of whole network is severely reduced and even the system is paralyzed.

The registration center is taken as the central platform of SOA service release and query, which connects service providers and demanders as shown in Figure 1. So the registration center is more vulnerable to DDoS attacks. It has become a bottleneck and barriers to services system under rapid development of SOA.

(2) In order to maintain the compatibility and extensibility of the cross platform systems, lightweight transport protocols are generally used for SOA, such as SOAP protocol, which can be compatible with and bind to a variety of upper layer protocols. The lightweight protocol is easy to build DDoS attack samples and vulnerable to attacks.

(3) SOA has the characteristics of service integration and data sharing, which inevitably open interface and expose data formats of service models to providers and demanders. This makes the SOA message easy to be monitored, intercepted, and analyzed. An attacker can extract useful information from the acquisition of the SOA message and then launches DDoS attacks.

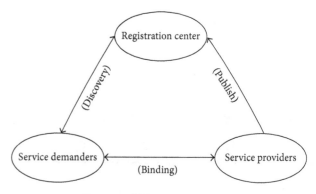

FIGURE 1: SOA system structure.

Therefore, due to the features such as the central structure, lightweight protocols, and services open, SOA is more vulnerable to DDoS attacks. The perception method of DDoS attacks against SOA, especially registration center of SOA, should be studied.

3. Traffic Perception Method of DDoS Attack Based on Entropy

The most prominent feature of DDoS attacks is the large increase in traffic. And traffic perception means are the most common method to detect DDoS attacks. Xiao et al. [8] carried out the classification of DDoS attack in application layer. According to the authenticity of the host to submit the request, DDoS attack in the application layer is divided into real URL request attacks and forgery ones. The former can be further divided into repeated use of a single URL or of multiple URL.

In terms of information theory, entropy is a measure of uncertainty of the random variable. The conditional entropy [9] represents the uncertainty of the second random variable Y in terms of known first random variables X.

Define information entropy of variable Y as

$$H(Y) = \sum_i p(y_i) \log_2 (p(y_i)). \tag{1}$$

Among them, $p(y_i)$ is the prior probability of each component of variable Y.

The variables X and Y of the conditional entropy are defined as

$$H(Y \mid X) = \sum_j p(x_j) \sum_i p(y_i \mid x_j) \log_2 (p(y_i \mid x_j)). \tag{2}$$

Among them, $p(y_i \mid x_j)$ is x_j about y_i of posterior probability.

4. An Algorithm of Traffic Perception of DDoS Attack against SOA

4.1. Principle. With *sip* and *dip*, respectively, representing the source address and destination address, $H(sip \mid dip)$ is defined as the conditional entropy that is consistent with multiple to single map of DDoS attacks. The formula directly reflects the divergence and disorder from *sip* to *dip*. By sampling the network data stream, we set the total number of packets arriving at a sampling period as S. The packets from different source address are set to $\{sip_i \mid i = 1, 2, \ldots, N\}$, and those from different destination addresses are set to $\{dip_i \mid i = 1, 2, \ldots, N\}$. By the definition of M-dimensional matrix $A[M]$, $A[i]$ is the number of packets of the destination address. We define N-M-dimensional matrix $B[M] : B[i]$ to represent the number of packet source addresses as sip_i and the destination address as dip_i. Equation (3) can be obtained:

$$H\left(sip \mid dip\right)$$

$$= -\sum_j p\left(dip_j\right) \sum_i p\left(sip_i \mid dip_j\right) \log_2\left(p\left(sip_i \mid dip_j\right)\right) \quad (3)$$

$$= -\sum_{j=1}^{M} \frac{A[j]}{S} \sum_{i=1}^{N} \frac{B[i][j]}{A[j]} \log_2\left[\frac{B[i][j]}{A[j]}\right].$$

In the above formula, $p(dip_j)$ represents the proportion of the number of packets arriving at dip_j in S, which is the total number of packets arriving at a sampling period. And the expression of $p(sip \mid dip_j)$ represents the proportion of the number of packets arriving at dip_j from sip_i in the total number of packets dip_j.

The relation between *sip* and *dip* of DDoS attacks is many-to-one mapping relationship. The more dispersed the source address, the greater the value of conditional entropy of $H(sip \mid dip)$. Conditional entropy is able to detect DDoS attack under normal circumstances and network environment. Also conditional entropy can reflect the traffic growth of DDoS attacks. But in the SOA systems, the detection method on the usual conditional entropy is not able to find abnormal traffic of DDoS attacks, especially in registration center of SOA. Because in the legal flow (Flash Crowd), the service registration center still has a strong many-to-one mapping relationship, the value of the conditional entropy will become very large. Therefore, it is difficult to distinguish Flash Crowd and the flow of DDoS attacks only by the conditional entropy.

In this paper, the novel method of instantaneous transition of condition entropy is able to make up for this shortfall by introducing timeline Z. In a short time, the emergence of a range of regional conditional entropy change, which can help to determine the occurrence of abnormal traffic of DDoS attacks, makes the SOA anomaly traffic aware method become efficient.

4.2. Select the Test Data Set. In this paper, three data sets are used in the experiment, including an attack data set, a normal flow data set and the set of SOA registration center traffic. The first two sets come from MIT Lincoln Laboratory in the 2000 DDoS data set LLDoS1.0 [10]. With the TCP flood attack traffic, the packets of source address and destination address of attack are randomly generated carrying flag ACK. Another SOA data set is from the laboratory network structures of typical SOA applications. The computers run in a shared

LAN environment of 100 Mbps. A typical system consists of SOA applications from eight computers. IP addresses are from 10.166.178.101 ~ 10.166.178.108. IP address of application system of SOA registry center is 10.166.178.105. When multiple publishers simultaneously release services, the data is sampled from network traffic. In order to test the proposed method on perception capability of the small-scale attacks, under normal flow selected nodes suddenly launched a large data flow attack, which makes the registry center be denial of service. The experimental environment adopts the real source address and the fixed destination port. WIRESHARK software is used to capture the entire packets in all process on the LAN.

4.3. Experiment Result. In this paper, experiments are conducted on three data sets by conditional entropy method. 500 traffic samples are collected in each cycle time, starting from the fiftieth samples to calculate the value of the conditional entropy. And the conditional entropy is recalculated each additional 10 samples. With the advance of time, each distribution of conditional entropy is, respectively, sought out. The traffic matrix is generated based on the previous 50 samples of LLDoS1.0 data set. The matrix reflects features of many-to-one on 50 samples. There are 50 source addresses and 3 destination address.

By (3) the conditional entropy can be calculated as shown in Figure 2.

Then the distribution of conditional entropy can be obtained on the flow of normal data set as shown as Figure 3.

Finally, a kind of typical applications in SOA registration center for publishing services with the previous experimental environments is tested. The difference is that services from multiple nodes simultaneously release to a single node, which belongs to the normal process of interaction with many-to-one way. When attackers send a large number of data packets in an instant by DDoS method, the target node received abnormal traffic. The traffic data is statistical and analyzed to obtain value of conditional entropy, which helps us to judge its unusual traffic. The experimental results are shown in Figure 4.

Through the introduction of conditional entropy on axis Z, the instantaneous transition to study of the distribution of conditional entropy can be drawn as shown in Figure 5.

By extracting conditional entropy in time dimension, it can generate instantaneous jump of entropy condition shown in Figure 6.

4.4. Analysis of the Experimental Results. As shown, by comparison of Figures 2 and 3, we can see that the value of conditional entropy is relatively large by the attack data sets calculated, which is much larger than the value of 5, while the normal flow is calculated in 0 to 1 range. This reflects the definition of entropy: the greater the value of the conditional entropy, the stranger the uncertainty of the source address. The conditional entropy is able to effectively distinguish the DDoS attack traffic from normal traffic in non-SOA architecture.

Under the normal flow of SOA, there is many-to-one mapping relation between the source address (service

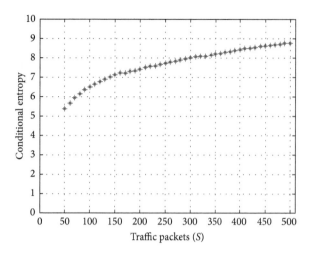

FIGURE 2: Conditional entropy on LLDoS1.0 attack set.

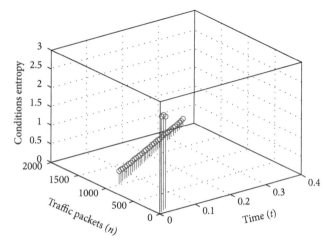

FIGURE 5: Three-dimensional plot of conditions entropy of DDoS on SOA.

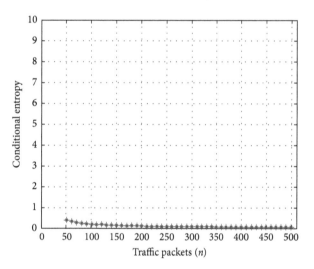

FIGURE 3: Condition entropy on normal traffic set.

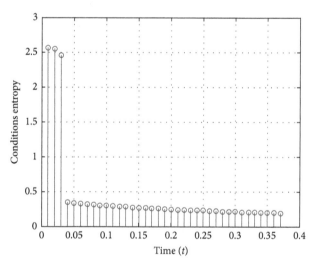

FIGURE 6: Instantaneous jump of conditional entropy on DDoS attacks.

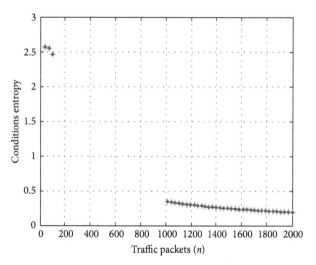

FIGURE 4: Conditional entropy of DDoS traffic on SOA publishing service.

provider and service demander) and destination address (service registry center). Therefore, the normalized SOA architecture also has a higher value of the conditional entropy. From Figures 3, 4, and 5 in the first half part of the curve it can be seen that in normal SOA architecture the value of entropy condition is about 2.5, far greater than the normal flow of non-SOA framework (entropy is far less than 1). If the traditional flow entropy method is used, it would produce a miscarriage of justice where the reasonable, legitimate traffic of SOA is interpreted as attack traffic. Therefore, the time dimension is referenced to the calculation of the conditional entropy and an algorithm of time united conditional entropy is used to distinguish the DDoS attacks. From Figures 3, 4, and 5 it can be seen that when DDoS attacks occur, the conditional entropy changes from a larger value of a sudden small. This is because the DDoS attack makes the traffic from the source to the destination node suddenly increase, while the number of source addresses is not significantly increased. The value of $p(sip \mid dip_j)$ (the proportion of the number of packets arriving at dip_j from sip_i in the total number of packets dip_j) becomes larger; that is, the system becomes more ordered. Therefore, conditional entropy becomes smaller. The instantaneous jump of conditional entropy makes DDoS attacks be effectively perceived, while the normal traffic is smooth. The simulation results show that the algorithm is able to effectively perceive the traffic changes caused by DDoS attacks against SOA.

5. Conclusions

The traffic perception of DDoS attacks is an important supplement to traditional network security. It plays an indispensable role in protecting network security. Due to the wide application of SOA architecture, the abnormal behavior perception method of DDoS attacks against SOA is urgently needed. Conditional entropy instantaneous jump perception method provides such a way with finding DDoS attacks behavior under SOA based network system. It is believed that the novel algorithm with instantaneous jump perception will greatly improve the performance of the current abnormal detection for DDoS attacks against SOA.

Competing Interests

The authors declare that there is no conflict of interests regarding the publication of this article.

Acknowledgments

This work was supported by China Postdoctoral Science Foundation (2016M590234) and the Open Foundation of Key Laboratory of Shenyang Ligong University (4771004kfs32).

References

[1] Z. Y. Yuan, *Distributed Denial of Service Attack Tracking Technology Research*, Central South University, Changsha, China, 2009.

[2] S. Rajesh, "Protection from application layer DDoS attacks for popular websites," *International Journal of Computer and Electrical Engineering*, vol. 5, no. 6, pp. 555–558, 2013.

[3] G. Chen, *DDoS Attacking Countermeasures*, Xi'an University of Electronic Science and Technolog, Xi'an, China, 2005.

[4] Chapter 1: Service Oriented Architecture (SOA), May 2014, https://msdn.microsoft.com.

[5] J. Jung, B. Krishnamurthy, and M. Rabinovich, "Flash crowds and denial of service attacks: characterization and implications for CDNs and web sites," in *Proceedings of the 11th International Conference on World Wide Web (WWW '02)*, pp. 293–304, Honolulu, Hawaii, USA, 2002.

[6] Y. L. Lu, Y. Zhang, and C. L. Sun, "Distributed denial rebound analysis and prevention service," *Computer Engineering*, vol. 2, article 22, 2004.

[7] W. Zhou, L. N. Wang, H. G. Zhang, and J. M. Fu, "A new DDoS attacks and countermeasures," *Computer Application*, vol. 1, article 144, 2003.

[8] J. Xiao, X.-C. Yun, and Y.-Z. Zhang, "Defend against application-layer distributed denial-of-service attacks based on session suspicion probability model," *Chinese Journal of Computers*, vol. 33, no. 9, pp. 1713–1724, 2010.

[9] C. F. Yang, G. Wang, and J. H. Si, "Construction of a new generation of enterprise application integration based on SOA," *Computer Applications and Software*, no. 10, 2005.

[10] MIT Lincoln Laboratory, 2000, http://www.ll.mit.edu/ideval/data/2000data.html.

4

Compressive Imaging of Moving Object based on Linear Array Sensor

Changjun Zha,[1,2] **Yao Li,**[2] **Jinyao Gui,**[2] **Huimin Duan,**[2] **and Tailong Xu**[2]

[1]*Key Laboratory of Intelligent Computing & Signal Processing, Ministry of Education, Anhui University,*
 No. 3 Feixi Road, Hefei 230039, China
[2]*Department of Electronic Information and Electrical Engineering, Hefei University, No. 99 Jinxiu Road, Hefei 230601, China*

Correspondence should be addressed to Changjun Zha; 11586292@qq.com

Academic Editor: Raj Senani

Using the characteristics of a moving object, this paper presents a compressive imaging method for moving objects based on a linear array sensor. The method uses a higher sampling frequency and a traditional algorithm to recover the image through a column-by-column process. During the compressive sampling stage, the output values of the linear array sensor are multiplied by a coefficient that is a measurement matrix element, and then the measurement value can be acquired by adding all the multiplication values together. During the reconstruction stage, the orthogonal matching pursuit algorithm is used to recover the original image when all the measurement values are obtained. Numerical simulations and experimental results show that the proposed compressive imaging method not only effectively captures the information required from the moving object for image reconstruction but also achieves direct separation of the moving object from a static scene.

1. Introduction

In practical situations, objects that are observed moving across borders or uninhabited regions could be either human or animal, and there are considerable differences between their profiles [1, 2]. Large numbers of research results have indicated that it is feasible to determine which objects are human and which are animal based on these differences, but the current research is generally concerned with the acquisition and recognition of the object profile image [3–8]. For image acquisition, the most common method is the use of a linear array sensor to acquire the moving object image [9–11], but the acquired image is relatively simple and cannot show the object in greater detail, meaning that it is difficult to distinguish between similar actions on different objects. Therefore, how to obtain higher-resolution images when using only a small number of sensors has become a question that is worthy of exploration.

As one of the most important research fields in compressive sensing, compressive imaging can capture a small number of measurements to be used for image reconstruction, and the most typical compressive imaging is the single-pixel camera [12–14]. To acquire compressive measurements, the camera uses a single pixel and a spatial light modulator. However, before the single-pixel camera can capture all required measurements, the scene must be in a static state or state of only slight change [15]; otherwise, the original image cannot be reconstructed. In addition, at borders or in uninhabited regions, we only care about the moving object in the monitored region and do not require a static scene. However, the reconstructed image using the single-pixel camera contains both the object and the scene, and elimination of the static scene and realization of moving object compressive sampling are subjects that require further study. To solve this problem using a combination of a linear array sensor and the theory of compressive sensing, this paper proposes a compressive imaging method for moving objects based on compressive sensing. Theoretical analyses and experimental results demonstrate the effectiveness of the proposed method.

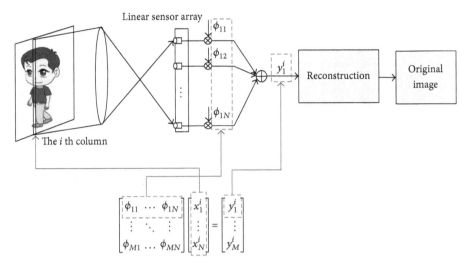

FIGURE 1: Compressive imaging system based on linear array sensor.

This paper is organized as follows. Section 2 introduces the principle of compressive sensing. Section 3 describes our proposed compressive imaging scheme in detail, and experimental results are provided in Section 4. Section 5 contains a summary of this paper and gives our conclusions.

2. Theory of Compressive Sensing

Consider a one-dimensional sparse signal $\mathbf{x} \in \mathbf{R}^N$, which can be represented as a linear combination of the columns of $\mathbf{\Psi} \in \mathbf{R}^{N \times N}$:

$$\mathbf{x} = \mathbf{\Psi}\theta. \qquad (1)$$

If only k ($k \ll N$) values are nonzero in the vector $\theta \in \mathbf{R}^N$, then θ is the sparse representation of $\mathbf{x}$ in the domain $\mathbf{\Psi}$. For the sparse signal reconstruction problem, θ can be estimated by minimizing the l_1-norm with the measurement matrix $\mathbf{\Phi} \in \mathbf{R}^{M \times N}$ ($M \ll N$) and the measurements $\mathbf{y} = \mathbf{\Phi}\mathbf{x} \in \mathbf{R}^M$:

$$\hat{\theta} = \arg\min \quad \|\theta\|_1,$$
$$\text{s.t.} \quad \mathbf{y} = \mathbf{\Phi}\mathbf{\Psi}\theta. \qquad (2)$$

Finally, the original signal $\mathbf{x}$ can be reconstructed using the coefficient vector $\hat{\theta}$, which satisfies l_1-minimization [16, 17]; that is,

$$\mathbf{x} = \mathbf{\Psi}\hat{\theta}. \qquad (3)$$

In practice, when taking the effects of noise into account, (3) can be rewritten as

$$\hat{\theta} = \arg\min \quad \|\theta\|_1,$$
$$\text{s.t.} \quad \|\mathbf{y} - \mathbf{\Phi}\mathbf{\Psi}\theta\|_2 \leq \varepsilon, \qquad (4)$$

where ε is the error tolerance [18–20].

For static objects, each projection measurement contains the same original information [15], but this does not apply for a moving object. We present a novel compressive imaging method to achieve compressive sampling of moving objects in the next section.

3. Compressive Imaging System for Moving Object

Figure 1 shows the proposed compressive imaging system for moving objects based on a linear array sensor. Unlike single-pixel cameras, the system captures the moving object image measurements through a column-by-column process. The measurement is based on the inner product of the row vector $\phi_m = [\phi_{m1} \ \phi_{m2} \ \cdots \ \phi_{mN}] \in \mathbf{R}^N$ ($1 \leq m \leq M$) of the measurement matrix $\mathbf{\Phi}$ and the output values of the linear array sensor.

Assume here that the image of the moving object is expressed as $\mathbf{X} = [\mathbf{x}^1, \mathbf{x}^2, \ldots, \mathbf{x}^N] \in \mathbf{R}^{N \times N}$. We use the measurement matrix $\mathbf{\Phi} \in \mathbf{R}^{M \times N}$ ($M \ll N$) to capture compressive measurements of the ith column vector $\mathbf{x}^i = \left[x_1^i \ \cdots \ x_N^i\right]^T \in \mathbf{R}^N$ of the image $\mathbf{X}$. Based on the theory of compressive sensing, these measurements can be expressed as $\mathbf{y}^i = \mathbf{\Phi}\mathbf{x}^i$; that is,

$$\mathbf{y}^i = \begin{bmatrix} y_1^i \\ \vdots \\ y_M^i \end{bmatrix} = \mathbf{\Phi}\mathbf{x}^i = \begin{bmatrix} \phi_{11} & \cdots & \phi_{1N} \\ \vdots & \ddots & \vdots \\ \phi_{M1} & \cdots & \phi_{MN} \end{bmatrix} \begin{bmatrix} x_1^i \\ \vdots \\ x_N^i \end{bmatrix}$$
$$= \begin{bmatrix} \phi_1\mathbf{x}^i \\ \vdots \\ \phi_M\mathbf{x}^i \end{bmatrix} = \begin{bmatrix} \phi_1 \\ \vdots \\ \phi_M \end{bmatrix} \mathbf{x}^i, \qquad (5)$$

where $\mathbf{y}^i \in \mathbf{R}^M$ ($M \ll N$) and $\phi_m = [\phi_{m1} \ \phi_{m2} \ \cdots \ \phi_{mN}] \in \mathbf{R}^N$ ($1 \leq m \leq M$). During the compressive sampling stage, each row of the measurement matrix obtains a single measurement. When this measurement is obtained, the next row of the measurement matrix is used as the output coefficient of the sensor group. In this way, M measurements of the ith column vector of the image are obtained.

Because the object is in a state of motion, each of the rows ϕ_m ($1 \leq m \leq M$) of the measurement matrix samples

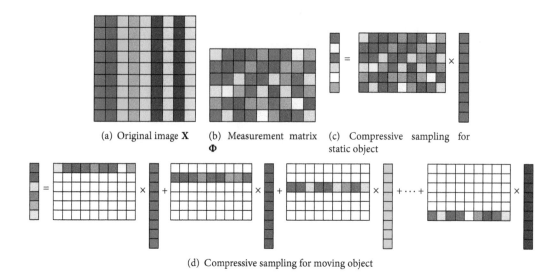

(a) Original image **X**   (b) Measurement matrix   (c) Compressive sampling for
                               Φ   static object

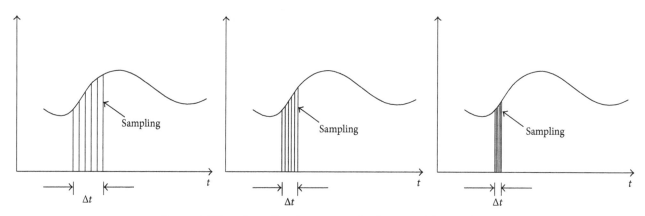

(d) Compressive sampling for moving object

FIGURE 2: Compressive sampling of static and moving states.

FIGURE 3: Effect of sampling frequency on the diversity of the samples.

different columns of the target image, as shown in Figure 2. Therefore, (5) should be rewritten as

$$\mathbf{y}^i = \begin{bmatrix} y_1^i \\ \vdots \\ y_M^i \end{bmatrix} = \begin{bmatrix} \boldsymbol{\phi}_1 \mathbf{x}^{i_1} \\ \vdots \\ \boldsymbol{\phi}_M \mathbf{x}^{i_M} \end{bmatrix}. \tag{6}$$

In general, the vectors $\mathbf{x}^{i_1}, \mathbf{x}^{i_2}, \ldots, \mathbf{x}^{i_M}$ $(1 \le m \le M)$ are not equal, which means that the original image cannot be reconstructed from measurements that do not contain the same information.

In a real situation, when a person or an animal passes through the sensors' field of view, the velocity is always limited. Therefore, we could capture M effective measurements $\mathbf{y}^i = \begin{bmatrix} y_1^i & \cdots & y_M^i \end{bmatrix}^T$ of the ith column vector $\mathbf{x}^i = \begin{bmatrix} x_1^i & \cdots & x_N^i \end{bmatrix}^T$ by using a higher sampling frequency. If we assume that the object's average velocity is v and the sensors'

sampling frequency is f, then within a short time Δt, the number of measurements M can be expressed as

$$M = f \cdot \Delta t. \tag{7}$$

From (7), we see that when M is fixed, Δt becomes smaller and smaller as the sensors' sampling frequency f increases, and the differences among the M columns $\{\mathbf{x}^{i_1}, \mathbf{x}^{i_2}, \ldots, \mathbf{x}^{i_M}\}$ in the range of Δt also become smaller, as shown in Figure 3. Assuming that the vector acquired in Δt corresponds to the ith column vector $\mathbf{x}^i$ of the original image, then the column vectors $\{\mathbf{x}^{i_1}, \mathbf{x}^{i_2}, \ldots, \mathbf{x}^{i_M}\}$ that were captured using the higher sampling frequency can be represented as

$$\mathbf{x}^{i_1} = \mathbf{x}^i + \boldsymbol{\varepsilon}_1,$$

$$\mathbf{x}^{i_2} = \mathbf{x}^i + \boldsymbol{\varepsilon}_2,$$

$$\vdots$$

$$\mathbf{x}^{i_M} = \mathbf{x}^i + \boldsymbol{\varepsilon}_M, \tag{8}$$

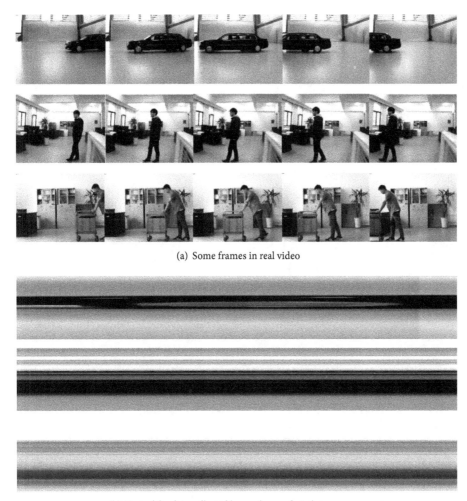

(a) Some frames in real video

(b) Part of the data collected by a column of pixels in a camera

FIGURE 4: Real video and images.

where $\boldsymbol{\varepsilon}_1, \boldsymbol{\varepsilon}_2, \ldots, \boldsymbol{\varepsilon}_M$ are the error vectors. By combining (6) with (8), we obtain

$$
\mathbf{y}^i = \begin{bmatrix} y_1^i \\ \vdots \\ y_M^i \end{bmatrix} = \begin{bmatrix} \boldsymbol{\phi}_1 \mathbf{x}^{i_1} \\ \vdots \\ \boldsymbol{\phi}_M \mathbf{x}^{i_M} \end{bmatrix} = \begin{bmatrix} \boldsymbol{\phi}_1 \left(\mathbf{x}^i + \boldsymbol{\varepsilon}_1 \right) \\ \vdots \\ \boldsymbol{\phi}_M \left(\mathbf{x}^i + \boldsymbol{\varepsilon}_M \right) \end{bmatrix}
$$

$$
= \begin{bmatrix} \boldsymbol{\phi}_1 \mathbf{x}^i \\ \vdots \\ \boldsymbol{\phi}_M \mathbf{x}^i \end{bmatrix} + \begin{bmatrix} \boldsymbol{\phi}_1 \boldsymbol{\varepsilon}_1 \\ \vdots \\ \boldsymbol{\phi}_M \boldsymbol{\varepsilon}_M \end{bmatrix} = \boldsymbol{\Phi} \mathbf{x}^i + \boldsymbol{\varepsilon}, \tag{9}
$$

where

$$
\boldsymbol{\varepsilon} = \begin{bmatrix} \boldsymbol{\phi}_1 \boldsymbol{\varepsilon}_1 \\ \vdots \\ \boldsymbol{\phi}_M \boldsymbol{\varepsilon}_M \end{bmatrix}. \tag{10}
$$

At this point, the ith column vector $\mathbf{x}^i$ of the original image can be reconstructed using (4), which indicates that the entire image of the moving object can be obtained by merging all of the reconstructed columns.

For a static scene, the sensors acquire compressive measurements from the same column of the scene image. Thus, all of the columns of the reconstructed image are the same, and the reconstructed scene image is no longer the static scene that we can see.

To facilitate a clearer description, we assume that no moving objects are passing through the sensor's field of view. The reconstructed column is then expressed as $\mathbf{x}^r = \begin{bmatrix} x_1^r & x_2^r & \cdots & x_N^r \end{bmatrix}^T \in \mathbf{R}^N$, and the reconstructed image can be represented as

$$
\widehat{\mathbf{X}} = \begin{bmatrix} \mathbf{x}^r & \mathbf{x}^r & \cdots & \mathbf{x}^r \end{bmatrix} = \begin{bmatrix} x_1^r & x_1^r & \cdots & x_1^r \\ x_2^r & x_2^r & \cdots & x_2^r \\ \vdots & \vdots & \vdots & \vdots \\ x_N^r & x_N^r & \cdots & x_N^r \end{bmatrix}, \tag{11}
$$

where $\widehat{\mathbf{X}} \in \mathbf{R}^{N \times N}$. From (11), we can see that the reconstructed scene is a texture image. In other words, the static

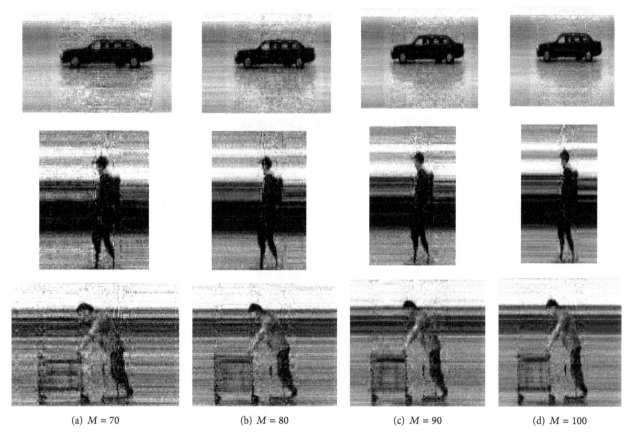

(a) $M = 70$ (b) $M = 80$ (c) $M = 90$ (d) $M = 100$

FIGURE 5: Reconstruction of images.

scene can be eliminated using the proposed compressive imaging method.

4. Simulation Experiment and Analysis

To verify the validity of the proposed method, a single column pixel of an industrial camera is used to capture the data from a moving object. The number of single column pixels is 120 and the camera's frame rate is 150 fps. Some frames of the real video and a portion of the collected data under different motions and different backgrounds are shown in Figure 4.

Assuming that the sparsity level of each column in the original image is $K = 30$, then the numbers of measurements M are 70, 80, 90, and 100, which represent the total numbers of 58.3%, 66.7%, 75%, and 83.3%, respectively; we then adopt the orthogonal matching pursuit algorithm to reconstruct the original image and obtain the results shown in Figure 5.

As shown in Figure 5, the proposed compressive imaging system can reconstruct the image of a moving object. Different from Figure 4(a), the reconstructed image contains only the moving object. It is clear that the reconstruction quality improves as the number of measurements increases.

5. Conclusions

When a traditional single-pixel camera captures compressive measurements, the scene is required to remain in a state of rest. This paper proposed a compressive imaging method for a moving object, where the method generally adopts a higher sampling frequency to capture the measurements of the moving object through a column-by-column process. The results of simulations and real data experiments show that our method can reconstruct the image of a moving object and can separate the moving object from a static scene. Therefore, the proposed method is of practical significance for application to the monitoring of borders or uninhabited regions.

Competing Interests

The authors declare that they have no competing interests.

Acknowledgments

This work is supported by the Anhui Provincial Natural Science Foundation (no. 1508085QF118), the Hefei University Science Foundation (no. 2014xk06), the Key Projects of Research and Development Foundation of Hefei University (no. 14KY02ZD), and the Opening Foundation of Key Laboratory of Intelligent Computing & Signal Processing (Anhui University), Ministry of Education.

References

[1] D. J. Russomanno, E. M. Carapezza, M. Yeasin, E. Jacobs, M. Smith, and S. Sorower, "Sparse detector sensor: profiling

experiments for broad-scale classification," in *Proceedings of the Unattended Ground, Sea, and Air Sensor Technologies and Applications X*, vol. 6963 of *Proceedings of SPIE*, Orlando, Fla, USA, March 2008.

[2] C. Zha and T. Xu, "Multiple feature sample classification via joint sparse representation," *Journal of Computational Information Systems*, vol. 11, no. 14, pp. 5125–5133, 2015.

[3] D. J. Russomanno, S. Chari, E. L. Jacobs, and C. Halford, "Near-IR sparse detector sensor for intelligent electronic fence applications," *IEEE Sensors Journal*, vol. 10, no. 6, pp. 1106–1107, 2010.

[4] S. Chari, C. Halford, E. Jacobs, F. Smith, J. Brown, and D. Russomanno, "Classification of humans and animals using an infrared profiling sensor," in *Unattended Ground, Sea, and Air Sensor Technologies and Applications XI*, vol. 7333 of *Proceedings of SPIE*, Orlando, Fla, USA, April 2009.

[5] D. Russomanno, S. Chari, and C. Halford, "Sparse detector imaging sensor with two-class silhouette classification," *Sensors*, vol. 8, no. 12, pp. 7996–8015, 2008.

[6] R. K. Reynolds, S. Chari, and D. J. Russomanno, "Embedded real-time classifier for profiling sensors and custom detector configuration," in *Ground/Air Multisensor Interoperability, Integration, and Networking for Persistent ISR II*, vol. 8047 of *Proceedings of SPIE*, Orlando, Fla, USA, April 2011.

[7] A. Galvis and D. J. Russomanno, "Advancing profiling sensors with a wireless approach," *Sensors*, vol. 12, no. 12, pp. 16144–16167, 2012.

[8] J. Hossen, E. L. Jacobs, and S. Chari, "Real-time classification of humans versus animals using profiling sensors and hidden Markov tree model," *Optical Engineering*, vol. 54, no. 7, Article ID 073102, 2015.

[9] D. J. Russomanno, S. Chari, K. Emmanuel, E. Jacobs, and C. Halford, "Testing and evaluation of profiling sensors for perimeter security," *ITEA Journal*, vol. 31, no. 1, pp. 121–130, 2010.

[10] R. B. Sartain, K. Aliberti, T. Alexander et al., "Long-wave infrared profile feature extractor (PFx) sensor," in *Proceedings of the Unattended Ground, Sea, and Air Sensor Technologies and Applications XI*, vol. 7333 of *Proceedings of SPIE*, Orlando, Fla, USA, April 2009.

[11] S. Chari, E. L. Jacobs, and D. Choudhary, "Pyroelectric linear array sensor for object recognition," *Optical Engineering*, vol. 53, no. 2, Article ID 023101, 2014.

[12] D. Takhar, J. N. Laska, M. B. Wakin et al., "A new compressive imaging camera architecture using optical-domain compression," in *Computational Imaging IV*, vol. 6065 of *Proceedings of SPIE*, San Jose, Calif, USA, January 2006.

[13] M. F. Duarte, M. A. Davenport, D. Takbar et al., "Single-pixel imaging via compressive sampling," *IEEE Signal Processing Magazine*, vol. 25, no. 2, pp. 83–91, 2008.

[14] P. T. Boufounos and R. G. Baraniuk, "1-Bit compressive sensing," in *Proceedings of the 42nd Annual Conference on Information Sciences and Systems (CISS '08)*, pp. 16–21, Princeton, NJ, USA, March 2008.

[15] I. Noor and E. L. Jacobs, "Adaptive compressive sensing algorithm for video acquisition using a single-pixel camera," *Journal of Electronic Imaging*, vol. 22, no. 2, Article ID 021013, 2013.

[16] S. S. Chen, D. L. Donoho, and M. A. Saunders, "Atomic decomposition by basis pursuit," *SIAM Journal on Scientific Computing*, vol. 20, no. 1, pp. 33–61, 1998.

[17] D. L. Donoho, M. Elad, and V. N. Temlyakov, "Stable recovery of sparse overcomplete representations in the presence of noise,"

IEEE Transactions on Information Theory, vol. 52, no. 1, pp. 6–18, 2006.

[18] E. J. Candès, J. Romberg, and T. Tao, "Robust uncertainty principles: exact signal reconstruction from highly incomplete frequency information," *IEEE Transactions on Information Theory*, vol. 52, no. 2, pp. 489–509, 2006.

[19] E. J. Candès, J. K. Romberg, and T. Tao, "Stable signal recovery from incomplete and inaccurate measurements," *Communications on Pure and Applied Mathematics*, vol. 59, no. 8, pp. 1207–1223, 2006.

[20] J. A. Tropp and A. C. Gilbert, "Signal recovery from random measurements via orthogonal matching pursuit," *IEEE Transactions on Information Theory*, vol. 53, no. 12, pp. 4655–4666, 2007.

5

Anomaly Detection for Aviation Safety based on an Improved KPCA Algorithm

Xiaoyu Zhang, Jiusheng Chen, and Quan Gan

College of Electronics, Information & Automation, Civil Aviation University of China, Tianjin 300300, China

Correspondence should be addressed to Xiaoyu Zhang; xy_zhang@cauc.edu.cn

Academic Editor: R. Aguilar-López

Thousands of flights datasets should be analyzed per day for a moderate sized fleet; therefore, flight datasets are very large. In this paper, an improved kernel principal component analysis (KPCA) method is proposed to search for signatures of anomalies in flight datasets through the squared prediction error statistics, in which the number of principal components and the confidence for the confidence limit are automatically determined by OpenMP-based K-fold cross-validation algorithm and the parameter in the radial basis function (RBF) is optimized by GPU-based kernel learning method. Performed on Nvidia GeForce GTX 660, the computation of the proposed GPU-based RBF parameter is 112.9 times (average 82.6 times) faster than that of sequential CPU task execution. The OpenMP-based K-fold cross-validation process for training KPCA anomaly detection model becomes 2.4 times (average 1.5 times) faster than that of sequential CPU task execution. Experiments show that the proposed approach can effectively detect the anomalies with the accuracy of 93.57% and false positive alarm rate of 1.11%.

1. Introduction

In a flight, onboard Quick Access Recorder (QAR) and Flight Data Recorder (FDR) can record more than 600 parameters sampled at 1 Hz. Typical FDR and QAR parameters are acquired from the propulsion system, avionics system, landing gear, cockpit switches position, control surfaces, and other critical systems. Due to the complexity of flight conditions and aircraft systems, there are a large number of abnormalities that are often unclear. Detecting precursors of aviation safety incidents based on anomalies detection of FDR and QAR data from aircraft is becoming more and more important for pilots and airline safety management teams. Once these anomalies are detected, the additional contextual information of historical flight data is needed to determine the frequency of anomalies occurrence.

Bay and Schwabacher [1] proposed a distance-based anomaly detection method called Orca. The distance metric was used to detect abnormal points. The output from Orca was a distance score representing the average distance to its k-nearest neighbors. Higher score meant more anomalies since the nearest neighbors were farther away. Iverson et al. [2] developed a health monitoring software called Inductive

Monitoring System (IMS). Clustering method was used to analyze system data; a higher composite distance value was adopted to detect anomaly data.

Recently, kernel methods were applied to flight data analysis. Das et al. [3] developed a multiple kernel anomaly detection (MKAD) algorithm which could work with heterogeneous datasets including both continuous and discrete sample sequences. MKAD could detect some significant anomalies from real aviation operational data. The major advantage of MKAD was that it could detect potential safety anomalies in both discrete streams and continuous streams.

Smart et al. [4] presented a two-phase novelty detection approach to locate abnormalities of flight data in the descent phase. Compared with the mixture of Gaussians and K-means, the support vector machine (SVM) provided the best detection rate and identified obstacle abnormalities with higher accuracy.

Kernel principal component analysis (KPCA) algorithm was used by Cho et al. [5] for fault identification in process monitoring. There were two significant problems for anomaly detection in the KPCA-based method: computation performance and adaptability. For the KPCA-based method, the kernel matrix was defined for the principal component feature extraction and analysis. However, computing the associated kernel matrices required $O(n^3)$ computational complexity, where n was the size of the training data, which limited the applicability of these methods for large dataset. Because the parameter in the kernel function, the number of principal components, and the confidence for the confidence limit should be set before anomaly detection by KPCA method, the adaptability of the KPCA method was largely limited.

To solve problems of KPCA, many extended methods were developed including fast iterative KPCA (FIKPCA) [6], adaptive KPCA [7, 8], and multiscale KPCA [9]. The adaptive KPCA [7] could flexibly track the change of external environment or sample data. However, the model should be updated with real-time data, which affected the real-time diagnosis with increasing data. In [8], the number of principal components and squared prediction error (SPE) confidence limit were obtained by experience.

The method proposed in this paper is based on KPCA and aims at anomaly detection in the flight. In order to analyze vast amounts of flight data, the anomaly detection algorithm should be effectively accelerated. The rest of this paper is organized as follows. In Section 2, classical KPCA algorithm is introduced. Section 3 introduces the improved KPCA algorithm used to optimize key parameters such as the parameter of the radial basis function (RBF), the number of principal components, and the SPE confidence limit. Experimental results and performance evaluation of the proposed anomaly detection model are given in Section 4.

2. Kernel Principal Component Analysis

KPCA is one of kernel-based learning methods, which is the extension of principal component analysis (PCA) in the nonlinear area. Basic KPCA method is introduced as follows [5–11].

Given the training set $D = \{(\mathbf{x}_i, y_i), i = 1, \ldots, n\}$, $\mathbf{x}_i \in R^d$, $i = 1, 2, \ldots, n$ is the training data with zero mean, $y_i = \{+1, -1\}$, $i = 1, 2, \ldots, n$ is the class label, and the sample covariance matrix $\mathbf{C}$ in the feature space is expressed as

$$\mathbf{C} = \frac{1}{n}\sum_{i=1}^{n}\phi\left(\mathbf{x}_i\right)\phi\left(\mathbf{x}_i\right)^{\mathrm{T}}, \qquad (1)$$

where $\phi(\cdot)$ is a nonlinear mapping function. The principal component can be obtained by

$$\mathbf{Cv} = \lambda\mathbf{v} = \frac{1}{n}\sum_{i=1}^{n}\left\langle\phi\left(\mathbf{x}_i\right), \mathbf{v}\right\rangle\phi\left(\mathbf{x}_i\right), \qquad (2)$$

where $\langle\mathbf{x}, \mathbf{y}\rangle$ denotes the dot product of $\mathbf{x}$ and $\mathbf{y}$, $\mathbf{v} \neq \mathbf{0}$ is the eigenvector, and $\lambda > 0$ is the corresponding eigenvalue. The $\mathbf{v}$ corresponding to the largest λ is the first principal component, and the $\mathbf{v}$ corresponding to the smallest λ is the last principal component. The eigenvector $\mathbf{v}$ can be expressed as

$$\mathbf{v} = \sum_{i=1}^{n}\alpha_i\phi\left(\mathbf{x}_i\right). \qquad (3)$$

To obtain coefficients α_i, $i = 1, \ldots, n$, defining the kernel matrix $\mathbf{K}$ of $n \times n$, the elements in the matrix are determined by $K_{ij} = \phi(\mathbf{x}_i)^{\mathrm{T}}\phi(\mathbf{x}_j) = \kappa(\mathbf{x}_i, \mathbf{x}_j)$, where $\kappa(\mathbf{x}_i, \mathbf{x}_j)$ is the inner product of $\mathbf{x}_i$ and $\mathbf{x}_j$. In this paper, the kernel matrix $\mathbf{K}$ is calculated through RBF kernel function, which is adopted as follows:

$$\kappa\left(\mathbf{x}_i, \mathbf{x}_j\right) = \exp\left(-\beta\left\|\mathbf{x}_i - \mathbf{x}_j\right\|^2\right), \quad 0 < \beta < +\infty, \qquad (4)$$

where β is the parameter of RBF. The coefficient $\boldsymbol{\alpha}$ can be obtained by

$$n\lambda\boldsymbol{\alpha} = \mathbf{K}\boldsymbol{\alpha}, \quad \boldsymbol{\alpha} = \left[\alpha_1, \ldots, \alpha_n\right]^{\mathrm{T}}. \qquad (5)$$

The centered kernel matrix $\overline{\mathbf{K}}$ can be calculated by

$$\overline{\mathbf{K}} = \mathbf{K} - \mathbf{EK} - \mathbf{KE} + \mathbf{EKE}, \qquad (6)$$

where matrix $\mathbf{E} = (1/n)\begin{bmatrix} 1 & \cdots & 1 \\ \vdots & \ddots & \vdots \\ 1 & \cdots & 1 \end{bmatrix} \in R^{n \times n}$.

Assuming $\phi(\mathbf{x}_{\mathrm{new}})$ is a nonlinear mapping function that projects the new data $\mathbf{x}_{\mathrm{new}} \in R^d$ from the original space to the feature space, the projection from $\phi(\mathbf{x}_{\mathrm{new}})$ onto the eigenvector $\mathbf{v}_l$, $l = 1, 2, \ldots, p$; $1 \leq p \leq n$ can be obtained by

$$\mathbf{t}_l = \left\langle\mathbf{v}_l, \phi\left(\mathbf{x}_{\mathrm{new}}\right)\right\rangle = \sum_{i=1}^{n}\alpha_i^l\left\langle\phi\left(\mathbf{x}_i\right), \phi\left(\mathbf{x}_{\mathrm{new}}\right)\right\rangle$$
$$= \sum_{i=1}^{n}\alpha_i^l\kappa\left(\mathbf{x}_i, \mathbf{x}_{\mathrm{new}}\right). \qquad (7)$$

The number of principal components can influence the detection rate and computational complexity. In the anomaly detection model, the cumulative percent variance theory [8] is adopted to calculate the number of principal components:

$$\mathrm{CPV}\left(p\right) = \frac{\sum_{i=1}^{p}\lambda_i}{\sum_{i=1}^{n}\lambda_i} \geq \gamma, \qquad (8)$$

where γ is the threshold of principal components and p is the number of principal components.

SPE statistic is adopted to detect abnormal flight data in this paper. In [11], SPE is expressed as follows:

$$\mathrm{SPE} = \left\|\phi\left(\mathbf{x}\right) - \hat{\phi}_p\left(\mathbf{x}\right)\right\|^2 = \left\|\hat{\phi}_n\left(\mathbf{x}\right) - \hat{\phi}_p\left(\mathbf{x}\right)\right\|^2$$
$$= \sum_{i=1}^{n}t_i^2 - \sum_{i=1}^{p}t_i^2. \qquad (9)$$

The confidence limit for SPE is calculated through its approximate distribution [11]:

$$\mathrm{SPE}_\eta \sim g\chi_h^2, \qquad (10)$$

where η is the confidence degree of χ^2 distribution, $g = b/2a$, $h = 2a^2/b$, a is the estimated mean of the SPE, and b is the estimated variance of the SPE.

3. Improved KPCA Anomaly Detection Model

To improve the computation efficiency of KPCA-based method, an improved KPCA method based on parallel computing is proposed, where the RBF parameter is calculated

> *Input.* $D = \{(\mathbf{x}_i, y_i),\ i = 1,\ldots,n\} \in R^d \times Y,\ Y = \{+1, -1\}$: the training set
> *Output.* $\beta^* \in R$: the optimal RBF parameter
> (1) $\mathbf{X} = \{\mathbf{x}_1, \ldots, \mathbf{x}_n\}$
> (2) $\Omega_{ij} = -\|\mathbf{x}_i - \mathbf{x}_j\|^2,\ i, j = 1,\ldots,n$
> (3) $\widetilde{\mathbf{K}}_{ij} = \begin{cases} 1, & \text{if } y_i = y_j \\ 0, & \text{if } y_i \neq y_j \end{cases}$
> (4) **repeat**
> (5) $J_\beta = \dfrac{1}{2}\sum\limits_{i=1}^{n}\sum\limits_{j=1}^{n}(\widetilde{\mathbf{K}}_{ij} - \mathbf{K}_{ij})^2$
> (6) $\nabla_\beta J = \sum\limits_{i=1}^{n}\sum\limits_{j=1}^{n}\|\mathbf{x}_i - \mathbf{x}_j\|^2(\widetilde{\mathbf{K}}_{ij} - \mathbf{K}_{ij})\mathbf{K}_{ij}$
> (7) $\beta = \beta - \delta\nabla_\beta J$
> (8) **until** convergence

ALGORITHM 1: Gradient descent algorithm for obtaining the optimal RBF parameter.

on GPU and implemented by CUDA [12], and the number of principal components and the confidence for the confidence limit are determined via parallel K-fold cross-validation by OpenMP [13].

3.1. RBF Parameter Computation by CUDA. Because the structure of the training data in the feature space is determined by the chosen kernel function, inappropriate choice of parameter of kernel function will seriously affect the detection performance. In this paper, an optimized method for calculating the parameter of the RBF kernel function is proposed based on the training data.

Two important properties of the RBF kernel are $\kappa(\mathbf{x}, \mathbf{x}, \beta) = 1$ and $0 < \kappa(\mathbf{x}, \mathbf{z}, \beta) \leq 1$. The optimization of the RBF parameter β can be achieved by following properties [14]:

(1) For samples in the same class, the RBF kernel $\kappa(\mathbf{x}_i, \mathbf{x}_j, \beta) \approx 1$ if $y_i = y_j$.

(2) For samples in different classes, the RBF kernel $\kappa(\mathbf{x}_i, \mathbf{x}_j, \beta) \approx 0$ if $y_i \neq y_j$.

The optimal RBF parameter β^* is obtained by solving the following optimization problem [15]:

$$\min_{\beta > 0}\ J(\beta) \equiv \left\|\widetilde{\mathbf{K}} - \mathbf{K}\right\|_2^2 = \frac{1}{2}\sum_{i=1}^{n}\sum_{j=1}^{n}\left(\widetilde{\mathbf{K}}_{ij} - \mathbf{K}_{ij}\right)^2, \quad (11)$$

where $\widetilde{\mathbf{K}}$ is a constant matrix $\widetilde{\mathbf{K}} = (\widetilde{\mathbf{K}}_{ij})_{i,j=1}^{n}$ with entries

$$\widetilde{\mathbf{K}}_{ij} = \begin{cases} 1, & \text{if } y_i = y_j \\ 0, & \text{if } y_i \neq y_j. \end{cases} \quad (12)$$

$\mathbf{K}$ is the kernel matrix $\mathbf{K} = (\mathbf{K}_{ij})_{i,j=1}^{n}$ with entries

$$\mathbf{K}_{ij} = \kappa\left(\mathbf{x}_i, \mathbf{x}_j\right) = \exp\left(-\beta\left\|\mathbf{x}_i - \mathbf{x}_j\right\|^2\right),$$
$$i, j = 1,\ldots,n. \quad (13)$$

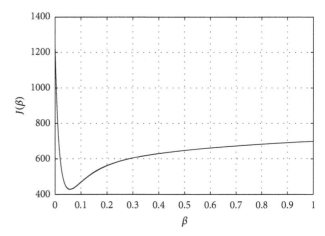

FIGURE 1: Schematic illustration of the function $J(\beta)$.

The schematic illustration of function $J(\beta)$ is shown in Figure 1. The horizontal axis represents the RBF parameter β and the vertical axis represents the corresponding $J(\beta)$. The graph shows that there is only one minimum value which is the optimal RBF parameter value in the proposed method.

The optimal RBF parameter β^* is obtained via gradient descent [16]. The partial derivative of function $J(\beta)$ is expressed as

$$\frac{\partial}{\partial\beta}J(\beta) = \sum_{i=1}^{n}\sum_{j=1}^{n}\left\|\mathbf{x}_i - \mathbf{x}_j\right\|^2\left(\widetilde{\mathbf{K}}_{ij} - \mathbf{K}_{ij}\right)\mathbf{K}_{ij}. \quad (14)$$

The iterative formula of gradient descent is expressed as follows:

$$\beta = \beta - \delta\nabla_\beta J, \quad (15)$$

where $\nabla_\beta J$ is the partial derivative of function $J(\beta)$ and δ is the learning step. The gradient descent algorithm for obtaining the optimal RBF parameter is given in Algorithm 1.

Input. $D = \{(\mathbf{x}_i, y_i), \ i = 1, \ldots, n\} \in R^d \times Y, \ Y = \{+1, -1\}$: the training set

Output. $\beta^* \in R$: the optimal RBF parameter

(1) $\mathbf{X} = \{\mathbf{x}_1, \ldots, \mathbf{x}_n\}$

(2) $\Omega_{ij} = -\|\mathbf{x}_i - \mathbf{x}_j\|^2, \ i, j = 1, \ldots, n$

(3) $\widetilde{\mathbf{K}}_{ij} = \begin{cases} 1, & \text{if } y_i = y_j \\ 0, & \text{if } y_i \neq y_j \end{cases}$

(4) Transfer Ω from CPU to GPU

(5) Transfer $\widetilde{\mathbf{K}}$ from CPU to GPU

(6) **repeat**

(7)   (GPU) $J_\beta = \dfrac{1}{2} \sum_{i=1}^{n} \sum_{j=i}^{n} (\widetilde{\mathbf{K}}_{ij} - \mathbf{K}_{ij})^2$

(8)   (GPU) $\nabla_\beta J = \sum_{i=1}^{n} \sum_{j=i}^{n} \|\mathbf{x}_i - \mathbf{x}_j\|^2 (\widetilde{\mathbf{K}}_{ij} - \mathbf{K}_{ij})^2 \mathbf{K}_{ij}$

(9) $\beta = \beta - \delta \nabla_\beta J$

(10) **until** convergence

ALGORITHM 2: GPU code of gradient descent algorithm for obtaining the optimal RBF parameter.

The approach is executed with the sequential algorithm on CPU. When the amount of sample increases, computation time increases rapidly. If the dimension of the kernel matrix is 8350, the total computation time increases to 1106 s. The computation of lines (5) and (6) in Algorithm 1 is implemented through level 2 for-loop, so it is better to perform them on GPU. The optimal RBF parameter β^* is obtained by a parallel algorithm on GPU which replaces overlapped ones by the sequential CPU algorithm. The GPU code of the gradient descent algorithm for obtaining the optimal RBF parameter is given in Algorithm 2.

If kernel matrix $\mathbf{K}$ is transferred from GPU to CPU in each step of the convergence loop, the data transfer becomes an acceleration bottleneck. To reduce the amount of transferred data, we focus on the structure of matrices Ω and $\widetilde{\mathbf{K}}$ as described in lines (2) and (3) of Algorithm 2.

The matrix Ω and matrix $\widetilde{\mathbf{K}}$ do not change with the optimal RBF parameter β^* in each step of the convergence loop; the transfer of matrices Ω and $\widetilde{\mathbf{K}}$ is necessary only in the initialization. In addition, Ω and $\widetilde{\mathbf{K}}$ are symmetric matrices. Thus, it is necessary to transfer upper triangular part of matrices Ω and $\widetilde{\mathbf{K}}$ from CPU to GPU. The size of the transferred data in Algorithm 2 on lines (4) and (5) is $((n + 1) \times n)/2$, respectively.

3.2. Parameters γ and η Computation by OpenMP. To make the anomaly detection model more accurate, the number of principal components and the confidence for the confidence limit are determined via K-fold cross-validation [20].

The K-fold cross-validation process randomly splits $\mathbf{D}$ into K disjointed parts with almost equal size $D_1, \ldots, D_K$. At each kth fold, $\mathbf{D}_k$ $(k = 1, \ldots, K)$ and $\mathbf{D}^{(-k)} = \mathbf{D} - \mathbf{D}_k$ are used as the test dataset and the training dataset. To assess the performance of the K-fold cross-validation, the balanced error rate matrix is utilized. The balanced error rate (BER) [4] is given by

$$\text{BER} = \text{FPR} + \text{FNR}, \qquad (16)$$

where false positive rate (FPR) denotes the percentage of incorrectly identified normal flight data and false negative rate (FNR) denotes the percentage of incorrectly identified abnormal flight data

The threshold of principal components γ and the confidence for the confidence limit η are confirmed according to a fivefold cross-validation with $\log_2^{1-\gamma} \in \{-7, -6, \ldots, -1\}$ and $\log_2^{1-\eta} \in \{-7, -6, \ldots, -1\}$. The K-fold cross-validation process can be exploited by loop-level parallelism which executes loop iterations across multiple processors concurrently. The execution time can be reduced significantly. The OpenMP-based K-fold cross-validation algorithm for obtaining optimal parameters γ^* and η^* is given in Algorithm 3.

4. Numerical Experiments and Discussions

The performance evaluation of the proposed algorithm in the CPU-GPU heterogeneous environment is given in this section. For the GPU algorithm, i7-3770 CPU with Nvidia GTX 660 is used, and the bandwidth is about 144.2 GB/s. For the CPU algorithm i7-3770@3.40 GHz CPU with 8 GB SDRAM is used. Synthetic datasets [3] are used in the experiment, which include 300 flights, each flight with 1000 sample points. In this paper, fault type I in the synthetic data is used to access the performance of the improved KPCA. The specifications of the experiment environment are listed in Table 1.

4.1. Computation Performance. Experiment results are showed in Figures 2, 3, and 4. Figure 2 shows the dimension of the kernel matrix, elapsed time for computing the parameter of RBF function on GPU and CPU, and speedup achieved by the parallel code over the sequential code. Figure 3 shows the breakdown of elapsed time for computing the parameter of RBF function on GPU. Figure 4 shows the dimension of the kernel matrix, elapsed time for computing the K-fold cross-validation process, and speedup achieved by the parallel code over the sequential code.

Input. $\mathbf{D} = \{(\mathbf{x}_i, y_i),\ i = 1, \ldots, n\} \in R^d \times Y,\ Y = \{+1, -1\}$: the training set, K: const of K-fold
Output. γ^*, η^*: optimal parameters
(1) Partiton($\mathbf{D}, K$)
(2) #pragma omp parallel for schedule (dynamic)
(3) **for** $i = 1$ to K **do**
(4) $\mathbf{T} = \mathbf{D} - \mathbf{D}_i$
(5)   **for** $m = 1$ to 7 **do**
(6)   **for** $n = 1$ to 7 **do**
(7)   Training($\mathbf{T}, \gamma_m, \eta_n$)
(8)   Testing($\mathbf{D}_i, \gamma_m, \eta_n$)
(9) $\text{BER}_{m,n} = \text{FPR}_{m,n} + \text{FNR}_{m,n}$
(10)   **end for**
(11)   **end for**
(12) **end for**

ALGORITHM 3: OpenMP-based K-fold cross-validation algorithm for obtaining optimal parameters γ^* and η^*.

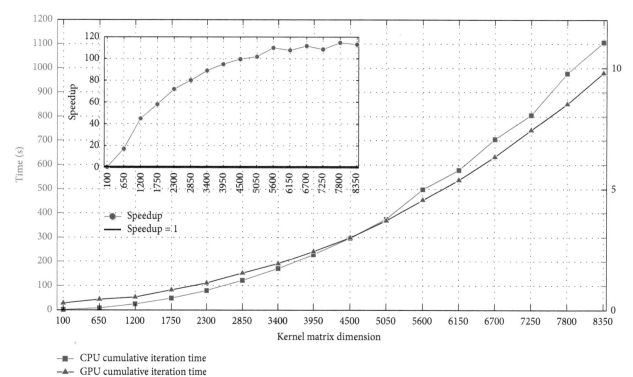

FIGURE 2: Elapsed time and speedup for RBF parameter computation on GPU and CPU.

TABLE 1: Specifications of the experiment environment.

CPU	Intel(R) Core(TM) i7-3770 (3.4 GHz, 4 core) Memory: DDR3 SDRAM 8 GB
GPU	NVIDIA GeForce GTX 660 Memory: GDDR5 2 GB
Software	CUDA Toolkit 5.0 [12] OpenMP 2.0 [13] Armadillo 4.0 [17] mlpack-1.0 [18], using the data load function and gradient descent function gsl 1.8 [19], using the gsl_cdf_chisq_Pinv function

As shown in Figure 2, the speedup on GPU code is larger than 100 when the dimension of the kernel matrix is larger than 5050. Elapsed time on GPU is slower than that on CPU with small dimension of kernel matrix, but faster with large kernel matrix dimension. When the dimension of kernel matrix is 100, the elapsed time on GPU is up to 2.3 times slower than that on CPU. However, it is up to 112.9 times faster on GPU than that on CPU while the dimension of kernel matrix is 8350. The reason is that when kernel matrix dimension is small, the synchronization cost for parallelism on GPU is larger than that needed on CPU and the data transfer between the CPU and GPU becomes the accelerating

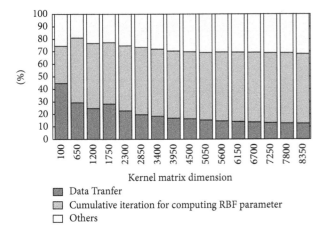

FIGURE 3: Breakdown of elapsed time for RBF parameter computation on GPU.

bottleneck. When the dimension of the kernel matrix is small, the computation cost of the exponentiation and addition arithmetic is negligible on CPU, and the effective acceleration by parallel processing cannot offset the data transfer time between the CPU and GPU.

As shown in Figure 3, the ratio of time taken up by "Data Transfer" and "Others" is relatively high for small-dimension kernel matrix. As the dimension of the kernel matrix becomes larger, computation cost becomes higher, and almost all the elapsed time is spent on exponentiation and addition arithmetic for RBF parameter computation, so the time for data transfer is relatively reduced.

The time for "Data Transfer" is significantly lower than that in other processes when the dimension of the kernel matrix is larger. For large-dimension kernel matrices, the occupancy of "Data Transfer" is less than 15%. In other words, data transfer does not become the acceleration bottleneck and the size of data transferred between the CPU and GPU is effectively reduced in the proposed GPU-based method, especially for large-dimension matrices.

As shown in Figure 4, the running time of the parallel algorithm and the sequential algorithm increases quickly when the kernel matrix dimension increases. When the dimension of the kernel matrix is 100, the parallel algorithm is 1.8 times faster than the sequential algorithm; when the dimension of the kernel matrix is 500, it is up to 2.4 times faster, but 1.1 times slower when the dimension of the kernel matrix is 1500. The reason is that the OpenMP-based parallel algorithm needs to synchronize among multiple processors. In this case, when kernel matrix dimension is large, the synchronization cost on parallel algorithm becomes higher than that needed on sequential algorithm.

4.2. Detection Performance. In the synthetic datasets [3], a set of Gaussian distributions was defined for each continuous parameter. The continuous parameters would draw from their defined distribution at each time step. The statistical distribution of each continuous parameter is shown in Figure 5. It can be clearly seen that the statistical distribution

of each continuous parameter follows Gaussian distribution, and favorable results are obtained by normal probability density function.

The initial training data number (including normal sample and abnormal sample), the test sample number, the best parameters, the detection rate (DR), FNR, and FPR are listed in Table 2. The continuous parameters are decomposed for three layers through Daubechies-4 (DB4) wavelet. Wavelet coefficients of the third layer are used to reconstruct high-frequency bands and scaling coefficients of the third layer are used to reconstruct low-frequency bands. Then, the feature parameter vector is constructed by the high-frequency and low-frequency bands of the continuous parameters. DR denotes the percentage of correctly identified abnormal flight data, FPR denotes the percentage of incorrectly identified normal flight data, and FNR denotes the percentage of incorrectly identified abnormal flight data. From the result, when normal sample is 1000 and abnormal sample is 266, DR is up to 93.57% with FPR of 1.11%.

4.3. Comparison of Some Detection Methods. Two kinds of kernel-based fault detection methods, one-class support vector machine (OCSVM) [21] and improved KPCA, are compared, and results are listed in Table 3. For both algorithms, the number of initial samples and testing samples are 1266 (1000 normal samples and 266 abnormal samples) and 10000, respectively.

For OCSVM, parameter v of OCSVM is searched in $\{0.01k, 0.1k\}$, where $k = 1, 2, \ldots, 9$, and parameter β of the RBF kernel is searched in 2^{2k-1}, where $k = -7, -6, \ldots, 3$. The parameters v and β are selected by fivefold cross-validation. LIBSVM is used for OCSVM detection model training [22].

For improved KPCA, parameter β of the RBF kernel is adjusted by the gradient descent algorithm, which is given in Algorithm 1. The parameters γ and η are searched according to a fivefold cross-validation with $\log_2^{1-\gamma} \in \{-7, -6, \ldots, -1\}$ and $\log_2^{1-\eta} \in \{-7, -6, \ldots, -1\}$, respectively.

From Table 3, it can be clearly seen that the FPR of the improved KPCA fault detection method is better than that of OCSVM. But the DR and FNR of OCSVM fault detection method are better than those of the improved KPCA. Considering DR, FNR, and FPR, the detection performance of the improved KPCA fault detection method is more favorable compared to that of OCSVM.

5. Conclusion

Kernel method is often used in anomaly detection in the field of aviation safety. The computation performance is the main problem in aviation data analysis domain. In this paper, an improved KPCA solution is proposed for efficient anomaly detection. The RBF parameter is optimized by GPU and OpenMP-based K-fold cross-validation is adopted for training KPCA anomaly detection model. The experiment was performed with i7-3770 CPU and Nvidia GTX 660. Results show that RBF parameter computation accelerates up

TABLE 2: Detection performance by the improved KPCA method.

| Training data | | | | | | |
Normal sample number	Abnormal sample number	Test sample number	Best Parameters	DR (%)	FNR (%)	FPR (%)
600	266	10000	$\beta = 0.031, \alpha = 0.75, \eta = 0.9921875$	93.52	6.48	1.16
800	266	10000	$\beta = 0.0245, \alpha = 0.5, \eta = 0.9921875$	93.77	6.23	0.91
1000	266	10000	$\beta = 0.0201, \alpha = 0.5, \eta = 0.9921875$	93.57	6.43	1.11
1200	266	10000	$\beta = 0.0173, \alpha = 0.5, \eta = 0.9921875$	93.41	6.59	1.27
1400	266	10000	$\beta = 0.031, \alpha = 0.75, \eta = 0.9921875$	93.47	6.53	1.21
1600	266	10000	$\beta = 0.0508, \alpha = 0.5, \eta = 0.9921875$	94.34	5.66	0.34

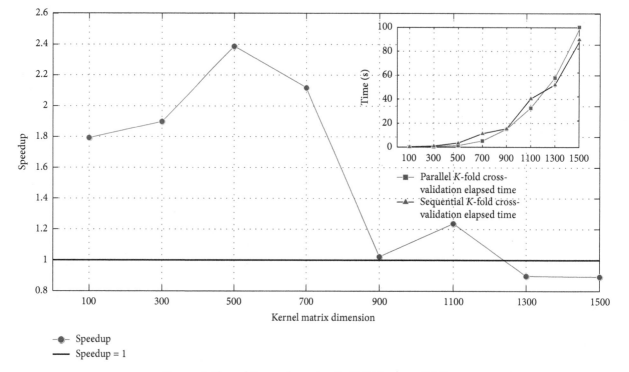

FIGURE 4: Elapsed time and speedup for K-fold cross-validation.

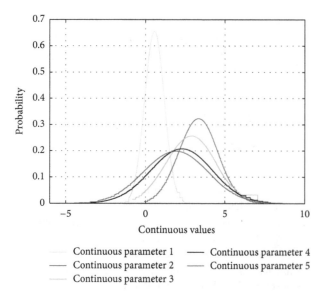

FIGURE 5: Statistical distribution of continuous parameters.

TABLE 3: Comparison of different methods.

Algorithm	DR (%)	FNR (%)	FPR (%)
OCSVM	94.55	5.45	21.57
Improved KPCA	93.57	6.43	1.11

to 112.9 times (average 82.6 times) faster by GPU than that by sequential CPU, and training KPCA anomaly detection model accelerates up to 2.4 times (average 1.5 times) faster by OpenMP K-fold cross-validation than that by sequential CPU execution.

Conflicts of Interest

The authors declare that they have no conflicts of interest.

Acknowledgments

This work was jointly funded by the National Natural Science Foundation of China (Grant no. 61603395) and the National

Natural Science Foundation of China and the Civil Aviation Administration of China (Grants nos. U1433103 and U1533017). The authors would like to express their gratitude for the support provided.

References

[1] S. D. Bay and M. Schwabacher, "Mining distance-based outliers in near linear time with randomization and a simple pruning rule," in *Proceedings of the 9th ACM SIGKDD International Conference on Knowledge Discovery and Data Mining (KDD '03)*, pp. 29–38, ACM, August 2003.

[2] D. L. Iverson, R. Martin, M. Schwabacher et al., "General purpose data-driven system monitoring for space operations," *Journal of Aerospace Computing, Information and Communication*, vol. 9, no. 2, pp. 26–44, 2012.

[3] S. Das, B. L. Matthews, A. N. Srivastava, and N. C. Oza, "Multiple kernel learning for heterogeneous anomaly detection: algorithm and aviation safety case study," in *Proceedings of the 16th ACM SIGKDD International Conference on Knowledge Discovery and Data Mining (KDD '10)*, pp. 47–55, July 2010.

[4] E. Smart, D. Brown, and J. Denman, "A two-phase method of detecting abnormalities in aircraft flight data and ranking their impact on individual flights," *IEEE Transactions on Intelligent Transportation Systems*, vol. 13, no. 3, pp. 1253–1265, 2012.

[5] J.-H. Cho, J.-M. Lee, S. W. Choi, D. Lee, and I.-B. Lee, "Fault identification for process monitoring using kernel principal component analysis," *Chemical Engineering Science*, vol. 60, no. 1, pp. 279–288, 2005.

[6] W. Liao, A. Pizurica, W. Philips, and Y. Pi, "A fast iterative kernel PCA feature extraction for hyperspectral images," in *Proceedings of the 17th IEEE International Conference on Image Processing (ICIP '10)*, pp. 1317–1320, IEEE, Hong Kong, September 2010.

[7] M. Ding, Z. Tian, and H. Xu, "Adaptive kernel principal analysis for online feature extraction," *World Academy of Science, Engineering and Technology*, vol. 59, pp. 288–293, 2009.

[8] J. Ni, C. Zhang, and S. X. Yang, "An adaptive approach based on KPCA and SVM for real-time fault diagnosis of HVCBs," *IEEE Transactions on Power Delivery*, vol. 26, no. 3, pp. 1960–1971, 2011.

[9] Y. Zhang and C. Ma, "Fault diagnosis of nonlinear processes using multiscale KPCA and multiscale KPLS," *Chemical Engineering Science*, vol. 66, no. 1, pp. 64–72, 2011.

[10] B. Schölkopf, A. Smola, and K.-R. Müller, "Nonlinear component analysis as a kernel eigenvalue problem," *Neural Computation*, vol. 10, no. 5, pp. 1299–1319, 1998.

[11] J.-M. Lee, C. Yoo, S. W. Choi, P. A. Vanrolleghem, and I.-B. Lee, "Nonlinear process monitoring using kernel principal component analysis," *Chemical Engineering Science*, vol. 59, no. 1, pp. 223–234, 2004.

[12] NVIDIA, *CUDA Toolkit 5.0 Library*, 2012, https://developer.nvidia.com/cuda-toolkit-50-archive.

[13] OpenMP Architecture Review Board, *OpenMP Application Program Interface, V. 2.0*, OpenMP Architecture Review Board, 2002.

[14] C.-H. Li, C.-T. Lin, B.-C. Kuo, and H.-S. Chu, "An automatic method for selecting the parameter of the RBF kernel function to support vector machines," in *Proceedings of the 30th IEEE International Geoscience and Remote Sensing Symposium (IGARSS '10)*, pp. 836–839, IEEE, Honolulu, Hawaii, USA, July 2010.

[15] X. Zhang, Z. Wu, J. Chen, and M. Yue, "An adaptive KPCA approach for detecting LDoS attack," *International Journal of Communication Systems*, vol. 30, no. 4, pp. 1–11, 2017.

[16] L. Bottou, "Large-scale machine learning with stochastic gradient descent," in *Proceedings of COMPSTAT'2010*, pp. 177–186, Physica, 2010.

[17] C. Sanderson, "Armadillo: an open source C++ linear algebra library for fast prototyping and computationally intensive experiments," Technical Report Version, NICTA, Sydney, Australia, 2010.

[18] R. R. Curtin, J. R. Cline, N. P. Slagle et al., "MLPACK: a scalable C++ machine learning library," *The Journal of Machine Learning Research*, vol. 14, no. 1, pp. 801–805, 2013.

[19] M. Galassi, J. Davies, J. Theiler et al., *GNU Scientific Library Reference Manual*, 2015, http://www.gnu.org/software/gsl.

[20] C. Hu, B. D. Youn, and P. Wang, "Ensemble of data-driven prognostic algorithms with weight optimization and k-fold cross validation," in *Proceedings of the ASME International Design Engineering Technical Conferences and Computers and Information in Engineering Conference (IDETC/CIE '10)*, pp. 1023–1032, American Society of Mechanical Engineers, August 2010.

[21] B. Schölkopf, R. Williamson, A. Smola, J. Shawe-Taylor, and J. Platt, "Support vector method for novelty detection," in *Advances in Neural Information Processing Systems—NIPS 1999*, pp. 582–588, MIT Press, 1999.

[22] C.-C. Chang and C.-J. Lin, "LIBSVM: a library for support vector machines," *ACM Transactions on Intelligent Systems and Technology*, vol. 2, no. 3, article 27, 2011.

6

An Improved Harmony Search Algorithm for Power Distribution Network Planning

Wei Sun and Xingyan Chang

Department of Business Administration, North China Electric Power University, Baoding 071003, China

Correspondence should be addressed to Xingyan Chang; changxi2013@163.com

Academic Editor: Ping Feng Pai

Distribution network planning because of involving many variables and constraints is a multiobjective, discrete, nonlinear, and large-scale optimization problem. Harmony search (HS) algorithm is a metaheuristic algorithm inspired by the improvisation process of music players. HS algorithm has several impressive advantages, such as easy implementation, less adjustable parameters, and quick convergence. But HS algorithm still has some defects such as premature convergence and slow convergence speed. According to the defects of the standard algorithm and characteristics of distribution network planning, an improved harmony search (IHS) algorithm is proposed in this paper. We set up a mathematical model of distribution network structure planning, whose optimal objective function is to get the minimum annual cost and constraint conditions are overload and radial network. IHS algorithm is applied to solve the complex optimization mathematical model. The empirical results strongly indicate that IHS algorithm can effectively provide better results for solving the distribution network planning problem compared to other optimization algorithms.

1. Introduction

Distribution network planning can reduce the probability of blackouts, reduce transmission loss, and improve power quality, so that it is an important part of power distribution automation system. The main task of distribution network planning is to optimize network structure and find the optimal expansion scheme of power distribution network. The distribution network planning problem consists of minimizing investment and operation cost of the objective function subject to technical constraints, such as overload, voltage drop, and radial network. Distribution network expansion planning is a complex and large scale combinatorial optimization problem; the classical mathematical methods cannot perform satisfactorily for solving it [1–4]. Modern metaheuristic methods, such as Genetic Algorithm (GA), Particle Swarm Optimization (PSO), and Ant Colony System (ACS), are used recently to solve the distribution network planning problem and have achieved some results. However, the heuristic algorithms mentioned above have some defects: GA is a stochastic search algorithm for global optimization

problems. It can reduce the difficulty of solving distribution network planning which is a nonlinear, multiconstraint, and multiobjective problem [5]. But in the practical application of the distribution network planning, it always falls into local optimum prematurely and converging slowly; there may even be infeasible solutions; PSO is a classic biological intelligence algorithm and has some advantages over other similar optimization techniques such as PSO which is easier to implement and there are fewer parameters to adjust, but it is prone to premature convergence [6]; ACS is a swarm intelligence algorithm based on distributed parallel search mechanism. It has strong robustness, but it also has some defects such as long calculation time, prone to stagnation and premature convergence [7, 8].

HS algorithm is a heuristic search algorithm for global optimization, which has been recently developed in an analogy with music improvisation process where musicians in an ensemble continue to polish their pitches in order to obtain better harmony [9]. The algorithm has the advantages of simple concept and model, easy implementation, less adjustable parameters, and quick convergence. However, when to solve the complex optimization problems, the standard HS algorithm still has some defects such as premature convergence. According to the defects of the standard algorithm and characteristics of distribution network planning, this paper proposed an improved harmony search (IHS) algorithm with the mechanism for dynamically adjusting parameters. We apply IHS algorithm to solve power distribution network planning. The simulation of example obviously shows that the solution is superior to that of other optimization algorithms.

2. Mathematical Model of Distribution Network Planning

In this paper, the model of distribution network planning adopts the objective function to minimize comprehensive costs per year, including the line investment expenses, the depreciation and maintenance costs, and the running year electrical energy loss expense. Considering overload constraints and radial network structure constraints, the objective function can be described as follows [10]:

$$\min f(x) = \begin{cases} \sum_{i=1}^{n} \left(C_{1i} T_i x_i + C_{2i} \tau_{\max i} \Delta P_i \right) + M_1 \times L, \\ \qquad \text{when the network is radial} \\ M_2, \quad \text{else,} \end{cases} \tag{1}$$

where $f(x)$ is the cost per year of distribution network planning; $C_{1i} = \gamma_i + \partial_i$, γ_i is the rate of return on investment; ∂_i is annual depreciation rate of equipment; T_i is the total investment for the ith newly built line; X is n-dimensional decision vectors; $X = (x_1, x_2, \ldots, x_n)$ is the n transmission lines which is to be elected in the optimization problem. x_i is the element of X, $x_i = 1$ when the ith line is newly built, and $x_i = 0$ otherwise; C_{2i} is unit power price; $\tau_{\max i}$ is annual maximum load utilization hours; $\Delta P_i = (P_i^2 + Q_i^2) R_i / U_i^2$ is the active power loss of the ith line; M_1 is penalty coefficient of overload; L is the load which exceeds the total load demand of power system; M_2 is a very large penalty value when the network is not radial.

3. Harmony Search Algorithm

Harmony search (HS) algorithm is a relatively new metaheuristic algorithm, which was proposed by Geem et al. [9]. Like other heuristic algorithms imitating natural phenomena or artificial ones, HS algorithm is also a heuristic algorithm mimicking the improvisation process of music players, where musicians improvise the pitches of their instruments to search for a perfect state of a harmony.

In HS algorithm, musical performances seek a perfect state of harmony determined by aesthetic estimation, as the optimization algorithms seek a global optimum determined by objective function value. Specifically, musical instrument i $(i = 1, 2, \ldots, n)$ is analogous to the ith decision vector of the optimization problems. Each tone of the instrument is analogous to each value of the decision variable. The harmony H_j $(j = 1, 2, \ldots, n)$ produced by musical instruments is analogous to the jth solution of the optimization problems.

Aesthetic evaluation is analogous to the objective function. The main control parameters of HS algorithm are harmony memory (HM), Harmony Memory Size (HMS), Harmony Memory Considering Rate (HMCR), Pitch Adjusting Rate (PAR), and Band Width (BW). Here, HM is a memory location where all the solution vectors are stored; HMCR and PAR are parameters that are used to improve the solution vector [11].

In the process of iteration, each new harmony vector $x^{\text{new}} = (x_1^{\text{new}}, x_2^{\text{new}}, \ldots, x_n^{\text{new}})$ is generated based on three rules: (i) memory consideration, (ii) pitch adjustment, and (iii) random selection. Generating a new harmony is called "improvisation" [11]. In the memory consideration, the value of each component is updated as follows:

$$x_i^{\text{new}} = \begin{cases} x_i^j, & j \in (1, 2, \ldots, \text{HMS}), \ \text{rand}_1 < \text{HMCR} \\ x_i \in X_i, & \text{else,} \end{cases} \tag{2}$$

where rand_1 is a random number uniformly distributed in the range of $[0, 1]$ and X_i is the value space of the ith variable.

Each component obtained by the memory consideration is examined to determine whether it should be pitch-adjusted. The PAR parameter is the rate of pitch-adjustment. The equation of pitch-adjustment can be described as follows:

$$x_i^{\text{new}} = \begin{cases} x_i^j \pm \text{rand}_2 * \text{BW}, \\ \qquad \text{rand}_2 < \text{PAR (when } x_i \text{ is continuous)} \\ x_i (k + m), \\ \qquad \text{rand}_2 < \text{PAR (when } x_i \text{ is discrete)} \\ x_i^{\text{new}}, \quad \text{else,} \end{cases} \tag{3}$$

where rand_2 is a random number uniformly distributed in the range of $[0, 1]$ and m is a constant, which belongs to the $(-1, 1)$.

4. Improved Harmony Search Algorithm

4.1. HMCR. HMCR $\in [0, 1]$ determines whether the value of a decision variable is to be chosen from HM. In order to ensure that the algorithm can quickly find local optima in the early operation and the solutions obtained in the later are diverse, this paper adopts the following linear decreasing strategy to update HMCR [12]:

$$\text{HMCR}(t) = \text{HMCR}_{\max} - \frac{(\text{HMCR}_{\max} - \text{HMCR}_{\min}) * t}{T_{\max}}, \tag{4}$$

where t denotes iteration number; $T_{\max}$ is the maximum total number of iterations; $\text{HMCR}_{\max}$ and $\text{HMCR}_{\min}$ represent maximum and minimum harmony memory considering rate, respectively.

4.2. PAR. In HS algorithm, PAR plays a role in controlling local search. The appropriate PAR can avoid the search being trapped in local optimum effectively. Normally, the smaller

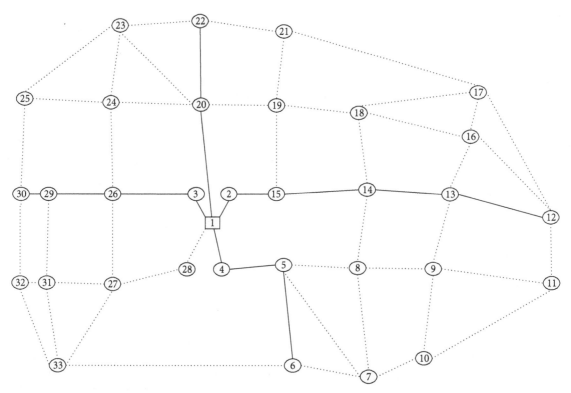

FIGURE 1: The existing network.

PAR is beneficial to quickly find the local optimal solution in early search stage, while the larger PAR is propitious to jump out the local optimal in the later stage. Therefore, dynamic change strategy for PAR is incorporated into the algorithm in this paper; the mathematical expression for PAR is

$$PAR(t) = \frac{PAR_{max} - PAR_{min}}{\pi/2} * \arctan t + PAR_{min}, \quad (5)$$

where $PAR(t)$ denotes pitch adjusting rate for the tth generation; PAR_{max} and PAR_{min} represent maximum and minimum harmony memory considering rate, respectively.

4.3. BW. The appropriate BW can be potentially useful in adjusting convergence rate of algorithm to optimal solution. In this paper, BW changes from large to small. BW changes dynamically with generation number as expressed as follows:

$$BW(t) = BW_{max} - \frac{BW_{max} - BW_{min}}{T_{max}} * t, \quad (6)$$

where $PAR(t)$ denotes pitch band width for the tth generation; BW_{max} and BW_{min} represent maximum and minimum harmony memory considering rate, respectively.

4.4. The Optimization Steps after Algorithm Improved. The optimization steps are summarized in the following.

Step 1. Initialize the HS algorithm parameters. Initialize the maximum number of iterations T_{max}; the harmony memory

size (HMS), the maximum and minimum harmony memory considering rate, $HMCR_{max}$ and $HMCR_{min}$; the maximum and minimum pitch adjusting rate, PAR_{max} and PAR_{min}; the maximum and minimum band width, BW_{max} and BW_{min}.

Step 2. Initialize the harmony memory (HM).

Step 3. Improvise a new harmony from the HM. Use (2), (3), (4), (5), and (6) to improvise a new harmony.

Step 4. Update the HM. Use (1) to evaluate fitness of the new harmony. If the new harmony is better than the worst harmony in the HM, the worst harmony is excluded from the HM and the new harmony is included in the HM.

Step 5. Inspect termination condition. The IHS will be terminated if the number of iterations meets the maximum number of iterations T_{max}. Else go to Step 3.

5. Example Analysis

In this paper, the proposed method for optimal distribution network planning is applied to a 10 kV distribution system in a northern Chinese city using MATLAB 2011b. The network consists of a power supply point (110 KV substation), 32 load points, and 12 existing lines. 18 new load points are added to the existing network. The existing network is shown in Figure 1, in which the solid lines denote the existing lines and the dotted line denotes the expansible line. The coordinates and power of each load point are shown in Table 1.

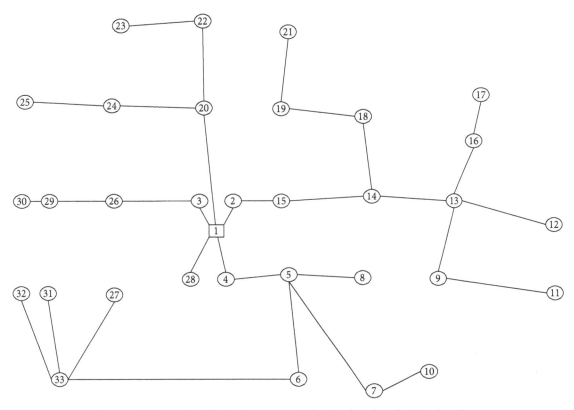

FIGURE 2: The optimal distribution network planning based on the HIS algorithm.

Using the improved algorithm to optimize the distribution network planning mentioned above, the input parameters are set as follows: C_{1i} = 0.155, C_{2i} = 0.05 yuan/KWh, $\tau_{\max i}$ = 3000 h, HMS = 30, HMCR$_{\max}$ = 0.95, HMCR$_{\min}$ = 0.6, PAR$_{\max}$ = 0.99, PAR$_{\min}$ = 0.01, BW$_{\max}$ = 1.0, BW$_{\min}$ = 0.0001, and $T_{\max}$ = 1000. The optimal distribution network planning based on the HIS algorithm is shown in Figure 2.

For further analysis, the IHS algorithm proposed in this paper, HS from [13], PSO from [14], Artificial Fish Swarm Algorithm (AFSA) from [15], Improved Ant Colony algorithm (IAC) from [16], Cross-Entropy Method (CE) [17–19], and two typical evolutionary multiobjective optimization algorithms, Nondominated Sorting Genetic Algorithm version II (NSGA-II) [20–22] and Multiobjective Particle Swarm Optimization Algorithm (MOPSO) [23–25], are compared in optimizing the power network planning. In the case study, 50 independent runs were made for each of the optimization methods involving 50 different initial trial solutions for each optimization method. The parameters of each optimization method are shown in Table 2. The comparison results are shown in Table 3.

Comparing the results of Table 3, it can be found that the best solution (minimum cost) obtained by IHS algorithm is better than that of any other method. In terms of best solution and average optimal solution, it is very evident that the IHS algorithm proposed in this paper is superior to HS, PSO, AFSA, IAC, CE, NSGA-II, and MOPSO. This suggests that IHS algorithm has very strong stability and robustness. When to solve the multiobjective distribution network planning

problem, the two typical evolutionary multiobjective optimization algorithms: NSGA-II and MOPSO are significantly superior to the HS, PSO, AFSA, IAC, and CE in terms of stability and robustness. But long execution times for these algorithms suggest that they reach the solution at a very slow speed. Though IHS algorithm obtained slightly better minimum cost and average cost than MOPSO, the average execution time used by IHS algorithm is less than that of MOPSO obviously. From the point of execution time, the average execution time of IHS algorithm is the minimum except CE. Although the execution time of CE is less than that of IHS algorithm, the best solution and average optimal solution obtained by the IHS algorithm are significantly better than that of CE. The reasonable average execution time of IHS algorithm suggests that IHS algorithm is capable of reaching the solution at a very high speed. Therefore, it can be concluded that IHS not only has found the highest quality results among all the algorithms compared, but also possesses greater stability and better robustness to solve such kinds of distribution network planning problem. IHS algorithm is an effective method to solve the distribution network planning problem.

6. Conclusion

Distribution network planning is a multiobjective, discrete, nonlinear, and large-scale optimization problem. This paper proposes an improved harmony search (IHS) algorithm to solve the distribution network planning problem. The

TABLE 1: The coordinates and state of load points.

Number	Abscissa (m)	Ordinate (m)	Load (KVA)
1	2463.4	801.7	substation
2	2462.5	808.4	500
3	2457.1	807.9	400
4	2460.6	773.3	200
5	2481.4	775.3	600
6	2477.5	728.8	800
7	2503.2	724.5	400
8	2503.7	772.8	200
9	2530.8	773.4	500
10	2528.5	730.3	800
11	2572.3	778	400
12	2573.6	799.9	600
13	2533.6	807.7	500
14	2508.3	809.4	400
15	2478.7	808.2	200
16	2535.4	837.5	500
17	2537.7	854.4	1000
18	2507	844.7	400
19	2478.5	849	500
20	2455.2	849.4	800
21	2481.4	871.9	600
22	2455.9	873.5	600
23	2434	873	200
24	2433.5	850	200
25	2404.2	851.1	1000
26	2433.9	807.8	500
27	2434.3	775.2	800
28	2456.5	776.3	400
29	2417.6	808.3	200
30	2403.5	808	200
31	2416.4	774.6	600
32	2403.5	773.7	1000
33	2421.3	729.7	200

TABLE 2: The parameters of each optimization method.

Algorithms	Parameters
HS	HMS = 30, HMCR = 0.95, PAR = 0.05, BW = 0.06
PSO	$c_1 = 2, c_2 = 2, w_{max} = 0.9, w_{min} = 0.4$, population = 40
AFSA	Step = 0.3, visual = 1.8, $\delta = 0.618$, $A_q = 0.9$, $c = 0.85$, $t_0 = 50$, population = 50
IAC	$C = 0.5$, $a = 1.003$, $\rho = 0.7$, population = 300
CE	P = 0.01, tol = 0.15, $p_0 = 0.5$, N = 50
NSGA-II	$p_c = 0.8$, $p_m = 0.33$, $\eta_c = 2$, $\eta_m = 20$, $QUOTE$ $T_{max} = 500$, population = 200
MOPSO	$w_0 = 0.35$, $w_1 = 1.0$, $\beta = 0.1$, $\gamma = 0.6$, N = 100, $T_{max} = 250$, population = 100

TABLE 3: The comparison results of distribution network planning for some optimization algorithm.

Algorithms	Best solution/10^8\$	Average optimal solution/10^8\$	Average execution time/s
HS	1.1005	1.2061	70.83
PSO	1.1090	1.2162	71.25
AFSA	1.0746	1.1860	80.61
IAC	1.0772	1.1560	65.34
CE	1.1108	1.2307	53.05
NSGA-II	1.0487	1.1452	108.32
MOPSO	1.0441	1.1367	104.19
IHS	1.0432	1.1358	54.58

parameters of basic HS algorithm are specifically improved for distribution network planning problem. The improved method can improve the global search ability and prevent basic HS algorithm into a local optimum. And the improved algorithm has a fast calculation and a good convergence. The numerical example shows that HIS algorithm not only can obtain the highest quality results but also possesses greater stability and better robustness. It is obvious that IHS can acquire satisfactory solution for distribution network planning.

Conflict of Interests

The authors declare that there is no conflict of interests regarding the publication of this paper.

References

[1] J. Salehi and M.-R. Haghifam, "Long term distribution network planning considering urbanity uncertainties," *International Journal of Electrical Power and Energy Systems*, vol. 42, no. 1, pp. 321–333, 2012.

[2] M. Sedghi, M. Aliakbar-Golkar, and M.-R. Haghifam, "Distribution network expansion considering distributed generation and storage units using modified PSO algorithm," *International Journal of Electrical Power and Energy Systems*, vol. 52, no. 1, pp. 221–230, 2013.

[3] M. Sedghi and M. Aliakbar-Golkar, "Distribution network expansion using hybrid SA/TS algorithm," *Iranian Journal of Electrical and Electronic Engineering*, vol. 5, no. 2, pp. 122–130, 2009.

[4] Y. Yang, G. Wei, B. Zhou, and X. Zhang, "Distribution network planning based on fuzzy expected value model," *Transactions of China Electrotechnical Society*, vol. 26, no. 4, pp. 200–206, 2011.

[5] H. Xu, L. Xin, H. Wang, and N. Yang, "Distribution network planning based on improved genetic algorithm," *Guangdong Electric Power*, vol. 23, no. 6, pp. 6–9, 2010.

[6] X. Zhenxia and J. Gu, "Application of particle swarm optimization algorithm to distribution network planning," *Relay*, vol. 34, no. 6, pp. 29–33, 2006.

[7] Y. Liang and H. Guan, "Medium-voltage distribution network planning based on improved ant colony optimization integrated with spanning tree," *Transactions of the Chinese Society of Agricultural Engineering*, vol. 29, no. 1, pp. 143–148, 2013.

[8] W. Sun and T. Ma, "The power distribution network structure optimization based on improved ant colony algorithm," *Journal of Intelligent and Fuzzy Systems*, vol. 26, no. 6, pp. 2799–2804, 2014.

[9] Z. W. Geem, J. H. Kim, and G. V. Loganathan, "A new heuristic optimization algorithm: harmony search," *Simulation*, vol. 76, no. 2, pp. 60–68, 2001.

[10] Z.-G. Lu, J. Liu, J. Wu, and Y.-B. He, "Application of artificial fish swarm algorithm in power distribution network planning," *High Voltage Engineering*, vol. 34, no. 3, pp. 565–602, 2008.

[11] L. D. S. Coelho and V. C. Mariani, "An improved harmony search algorithm for power economic load dispatch," *Energy Conversion and Management*, vol. 50, no. 10, pp. 2522–2526, 2009.

[12] Y. Chen and Y. Gao, "Multi-objective self-adaptive harmony search algorithm," *Computer Engineering and Applications*, vol. 47, no. 31, pp. 108–111, 2011.

[13] W.-L. Xiang, M.-Q. An, Y.-Z. Li, R.-C. He, and J.-F. Zhang, "An improved global-best harmony search algorithm for faster optimization," *Expert Systems with Applications*, vol. 41, no. 13, pp. 5788–5803, 2014.

[14] D. Tang, Y. Cai, J. Zhao, and Y. Xue, "A quantum-behaved particle swarm optimization with memetic algorithm and memory for continuous non-linear large scale problems," *Information Sciences*, vol. 289, no. 24, pp. 162–189, 2014.

[15] X. Cheng, Q. Zhang, Z. Wang, and H. Zhao, "Distribution network structure planning based on AFSA," *Relay*, vol. 35, no. 21, pp. 34–38, 2007.

[16] W. Sun, W. Shang, and D. Niu, "Application of improved ant colony optimization algorithm in distribution network planning," *Power System Technology*, vol. 30, no. 15, pp. 85–89, 2006.

[17] C. Lu, Y. Lu, and J. Zha, "A cross-entropy method for solving 0-1 knapsack problem," *Computer Simulation*, vol. 24, no. 7, pp. 183–187, 2007.

[18] K. Chepuri and T. Homem-de-Mello, "Solving the vehicle routing problem with stochastic demands using the cross-entropy method," *Annals of Operations Research*, vol. 134, pp. 153–181, 2005.

[19] I. Giagkiozis, R. C. Purshouse, and P. J. Fleming, "Generalized decomposition and cross entropy methods for many-objective optimization," *Information Sciences*, vol. 282, pp. 363–387, 2014.

[20] S. Kannan, S. Baskar, J. D. McCalley, and P. Murugan, "Application of NSGA-II algorithm to generation expansion planning," *IEEE Transactions on Power Systems*, vol. 24, no. 1, pp. 454–461, 2009.

[21] K. Deb, A. Pratap, S. Agarwal, and T. Meyanvan, "A fast and e litist multi-objective genetic algorithm: NSGA-11," *IEEE Transactions on Evolutionary Computation*, vol. 6, no. 2, pp. 182–197, 2002.

[22] S. H. Yang and U. Natarajan, "Multi objective optimization of cutting parameters in turning process using differential evolution and non-dominated sorting genetic algorithm-II approaches," *International Journal of Advanced Manufacturing Technology*, vol. 49, no. 5–8, pp. 773–784, 2010.

[23] C.-Y. Zhang, M.-Y. Chen, C.-Y. Luo, J.-Q. Zhai, and Y. Jiang, "Power system reactive power optimization based on multi-objective particle swarm algorithm," *Power System Protection and Control*, vol. 38, no. 20, pp. 153–158, 2010.

[24] C. A. Coello Coello, G. T. Pulido, and M. S. Lechuga, "Handling multiple objectives with particle swarm optimization," *IEEE Transactions on Evolutionary Computation*, vol. 8, no. 3, pp. 256–279, 2004.

[25] M. A. Abido, "Multiobjective particle swarm optimization for optimal power flow problem," in *Proceedings of the Optimization Power System Conference*, vol. 8, pp. 241–268, Aswan, Egypt, 2010.

7

Iterative Forward-Backward Pursuit Algorithm for Compressed Sensing

Feng Wang,[1] **Jianping Zhang,**[2] **Guiling Sun,**[1] **and Tianyu Geng**[1]

[1]*College of Electronic Information and Optical Engineering, Nankai University, Tianjin 300350, China*
[2]*School of Electronic Information and Electrical Engineering, Shanghai Jiaotong University, Shanghai 200030, China*

Correspondence should be addressed to Guiling Sun; sungl@nankai.edu.cn

Academic Editor: Jar Ferr Yang

It has been shown that iterative reweighted strategies will often improve the performance of many sparse reconstruction algorithms. Iterative Framework for Sparse Reconstruction Algorithms (IFSRA) is a recently proposed method which iteratively enhances the performance of any given arbitrary sparse reconstruction algorithm. However, IFSRA assumes that the sparsity level is known. Forward-Backward Pursuit (FBP) algorithm is an iterative approach where each iteration consists of consecutive forward and backward stages. Based on the IFSRA, this paper proposes the Iterative Forward-Backward Pursuit (IFBP) algorithm, which applies the iterative reweighted strategies to FBP without the need for the sparsity level. By using an approximate iteration strategy, IFBP gradually iterates to approach the unknown signal. Finally, this paper demonstrates that IFBP significantly improves the reconstruction capability of the FBP algorithm, via simulations including recovery of random sparse signals with different nonzero coefficient distributions in addition to the recovery of a sparse image.

1. Introduction

Compressed Sensing (CS) is a new paradigm in signal processing which was put forward by [1, 2]. Many algorithms have been proposed to solve this problem, which seems to be intractable. They can be roughly divided into three categories: Greedy Pursuit, Convex Relaxation, and Bayesian Framework. Greedy methods iteratively identify elements of the estimated support set. At last, these methods use a simple least-square to recover the original signal. They mainly include Matching Pursuit (MP) algorithm [3], Orthogonal Matching Pursuit (OMP) [4], Subspace Pursuit (SP) [5], Compressive Sampling MP (CoSaMP) [6], Look Ahead OMP (LAOMP) [7], and Forward-Backward Pursuit (FBP) [8]. CS has been widely used in many fields, such as wireless sensor network [9, 10] and magnetic resonance imaging (MRI) [11–14].

In [15], the author proposes a general iterative framework to improve the performance of any arbitrary sparse reconstruction algorithm, called Iterative Framework for Sparse Reconstruction Algorithms (IFSRA). After applying the framework to MP, OMP, CoSaMP, BPDN [16], and Smoothed L0 (SL0) [17], the performance of those algorithms has been raised. However, IFSRA requires the sparsity level to be known.

FBP, a novel two-stage greedy approach, uses a forward step to enlarge the support estimate by α atoms, while the backward step eliminates $\beta < \alpha$ atoms from it. In [8], the author demonstrates that the exact recovery of FBP can be significantly better than OMP, while the run times of FBP and OMP are almost the same. However, this paper shows that the performance of FBP can be further enhanced.

By inheriting the iterative idea of IFSRA, this paper proposes the Iterative Forward-Backward Pursuit (IFBP) algorithm. Different from the IFSRA, the IFBP does not need to know the sparsity level in advance. By setting appropriate initial atoms and iterative step, IFBP gradually iterates to approach the spare signal. The simulations demonstrate that the exact recovery rate of IFBP is significantly better than FBP.

2. Compressed Sensing and Reconstruction Algorithm

2.1. Compressed Sensing Theory. Consider a standard CS measurement, where a sparse signal is collected through linear measurements via

$$\mathbf{b} = \mathbf{A}\mathbf{x}, \tag{1}$$

where $\mathbf{x}$ is a K sparse signal of length N, K denotes the number of nonzero elements in $\mathbf{x}$, $\mathbf{A}$ is an $M \times N$ random matrix, and $\mathbf{b}$ is the observation vector of length M with $K < M < N$. However, it is analytically ill-posed to recover $\mathbf{x}$ from the observation vector $\mathbf{b}$. Because $\mathbf{x}$ is a sparse signal, CS reformulates (1) as a sparsity-promoting optimization problem:

$$\mathbf{x} = \arg\min \quad \|\mathbf{x}\|_0$$
$$\text{subject to} \quad \mathbf{A}\mathbf{x} = \mathbf{b}, \tag{2}$$

where $\|\mathbf{x}\|_0$ indicates the number of nonzero elements in $\mathbf{x}$.

2.2. Iterative Framework for Sparse Signal Reconstruction. The seminal work by Candès et al. [18] shows that the reconstruction performance of Convex Relaxation Methods can be improved by a reweighted strategy. In [15], the author extends the iterative framework to an arbitrary sparse reconstruction algorithm.

Each iteration of IFSRA mainly includes three major tasks: estimation, fusion, and regularization.

  (i) Estimation: Use original algorithm to get the result of the regularized sparse problem.

  (ii) Fusion: Keep only K potential atoms from the intersection of the estimate of this regularized sparse reconstruction problem and the estimate in the previous iteration.

  (iii) Regularization: Regularize the measurement matrix $\mathbf{A}$ and the measurement vector $\mathbf{b}$ which is prepared for the next iteration.

The termination condition of IFSRA is that the l_2 norm of the regularized measurement vector increases.

2.3. The Forward-Backward Pursuit Algorithm. FBP, as an iterative two-stage algorithm, needs two factors: α and β ($\beta < \alpha$). The former is called the forward step size, while the latter is called the backward step size. At the first stage, FBP expands the estimated support set by $\alpha > 1$ atoms. Subsequently, the algorithm computes the orthogonal projection of the observed vector onto the subspace defined by the estimated support set. At the second stage, FBP eliminates β atoms with the smallest contributions to the projection to reduce the size of the estimated support set. The termination condition, which controls whether to stop these forward and backward

---

Input: Φ, $\mathbf{y}$
Define: α, β, $K_{\max}$, ε
Initialization: $T^0 = \varnothing$, $\mathbf{r}^0 = \mathbf{y}$, $k = 0$, $flag = 1$
while $\|\mathbf{r}^k\|_2 \ge \varepsilon\|\mathbf{y}\|_2$ **do**
  $k = k + 1$
  forward step:
  $$T_f = \arg\max_{J:|J|=\alpha} \left\|\Phi_J^* \mathbf{r}^{k-1}\right\|_1$$
  $$\tilde{T}^k = T^{k-1} \cup T_f$$
  $$\mathbf{w} = \arg\min_{\mathbf{w}} \left\|\mathbf{y} - \Phi_{\tilde{T}^k}\mathbf{w}\right\|_2$$
  backward step:
  $$T_b = \arg\min_{J:|J|=\beta} \|\mathbf{w}_J\|_1$$
  $$T^k = \tilde{T}^k - T_b$$
  projection:
  $$\mathbf{w} = \arg\min_{\mathbf{w}} \left\|\mathbf{y} - \Phi_{T^k}\mathbf{w}\right\|_2$$
  $$\mathbf{r}^k = \mathbf{y} - \Phi_{T^k}\mathbf{w}$$
  termination rule:
  if $|T^k| \ge K_{\max}$ **then**
    $flag = 0$;
    break
  end if
end while
$\tilde{\mathbf{x}} = 0$
$\tilde{\mathbf{x}}_{T^k} = \mathbf{w}$
return $\tilde{\mathbf{x}}$, T^k, $flag$

ALGORITHM 1: FBP algorithm [8].

---

steps, is related to the energy of the residue. If the energy of the residue either vanishes or is less than a threshold, which is proportional to the energy of the observed vector, the algorithm has to return a result. Algorithm 1 gives the pseudocode of the FBP algorithm.

Compared with OMP, SP, and BP, FBP has obvious advantages, when the magnitudes of the nonzero elements start spanning a wider range, as for the Gaussian distribution or the uniform distribution. When increasing α and keeping $\alpha - \beta$ fixed, we can improve the recovery performance, while the run time also increases. From the simulations in [8], we observe that choosing $\alpha \in [0.2M, 0.3M]$ and keeping $\beta = \alpha - 1$ result in the optimal recovery performance. Moreover, the parameter $K_{\max}$, which is useful in case of a fail, also decides the number of the iterations. In order to adapt to the IFBP algorithm, this paper make a little change to the pseudocode of the FBP algorithm in Algorithm 1. Note that, by ignoring the variable $flag$ in Algorithm 1, we get the standard FBP.

3. Iterative Forward-Backward Pursuit

3.1. The Iterative Framework. By exploiting the information available in the estimate of the current iteration, the IFSRA algorithm improves the sparse reconstruction performance in the subsequent iteration(s). Assuming that the estimated support set $\hat{T}_k$, which is obtained in the kth iteration, contains S_k true atoms, we need to identify only $K - S_k$ true atoms from $N - K$ atoms listed in $\widehat{T}_k^c$. Based on this idea, the new problem in the $(k + 1)$th iteration can be interpreted as a reduced dimensional problem. Thus, we only need to recover a sparser signal than $\mathbf{x}$, while the number of measurements is also M. Thus, when retaining S_k true atoms in $\widehat{T}_k$, we are likely to obtain a better signal estimate in the $(k+1)$th iteration [15].

Because the sparsity level K is known, IFSRA can easily determine the number of the reserved atoms. However, if we do not know the sparsity level K, the iteration will not perform well. For example, FBP would return $K_{\max}$ atoms, when FBP does not accurately reconstruct the original signal. If we retain all $K_{\max}$ atoms without any further processing, the simulation shows that the iterative framework has no effect on improving the performance of FBP. This paper solves the problem by adding two parameters: I and S. The parameter I denotes the number of the reserved atoms after the first iteration. The parameter S denotes the number of the added atoms in the subsequent iteration(s). Experimental simulation results show that this iterative framework can effectively improve the performance of FBP, without the need for the sparsity level K.

3.2. The Iterative Forward-Backward Pursuit Algorithm. In [8], the author points out that we can get the optimal recovery performance in practice, when choosing $\alpha \in [0.2M, 0.3M]$ and $\beta = \alpha - 1$. In other words, for $M = 100$ and $\alpha = 20$, when $\beta = 19$, the result of the algorithm is the best for both exact recovery rate and reconstruction error. The performance of $\beta = 18$ is just lower than $\beta = 19$. This paper proposes the IFBP algorithm to further enhance the performance of FBP by using the iterative framework.

First, IFBP runs FBP. If FBP exits the iteration in the way that the energy of the residue is less than the default threshold, IFBP uses the result of the FBP as the final result. Different from IFSRA, IFBP algorithms are able to get the estimated signal after the first iteration. Note that IFSRA needs at least two iterations due to the iterative termination condition. If FBP exits the iteration in the way that the maximum size of the estimated support set is more than $K_{\max}$, IFBP retains I potential atoms in the estimated support set. In the subsequent iterations, IFBP adds only S potential atoms to the estimated support set after fusing the estimate of this regularized sparse reconstruction problem and the estimate in the previous iteration. IFBP is iterated as long as the energy of the regularized measurement vector decreases.

3.3. The Acceleration Strategy. Both IFSRA and IFBP improve the performance of the algorithms through the iterations. IFSRA only offers a general iterative framework. However, this paper would exploit the character of FBP to reduce the run time of IFBP.

In the kth ($k > 1$) iteration, the FBP algorithm, which is the parent algorithm of IFBP in this paper, could exit the iteration in the way that the energy of the residue is less than the default threshold. Once this happens, the algorithm is likely to have found all the remaining real atoms. If we add all of those atoms to the estimated support set at once, the number of iterations will be greatly reduced. Meanwhile, the

---

Input: $\mathbf{A}_{M \times N}$, $\mathbf{b}_{M \times 1}$.
Define: I, S
Initialization: $k = 0$, $\mathbf{A}_0 = \mathbf{A}$, $\mathbf{r}_0 = \mathbf{b}$, $\widehat{T}_0 = \phi$, $\gamma = I - S$;
(1)　　**repeat**
(2)　　　　$k = k + 1$;
(3)　　　　$\gamma = \gamma + S$;
Estimation Steps:
(4)　　　　$[\widetilde{\mathbf{x}}_k^*, \widetilde{T}_k^*, flag] = \text{FBP}(\mathbf{A}_{k-1}, \mathbf{r}_{k-1})$;
(5)　　　　$\widetilde{T}_k$ = set of indices of atoms of $\mathbf{A}$ listed in $\widetilde{T}_k^*$;
(6)　　　　If $flag = 1$, then $\widehat{T} = \widehat{T}_{k-1} \cup \widetilde{T}_k$, go to (15).
Fusion Steps:
(7)　　　　$\Gamma_k = \widetilde{T}_k \cup \widehat{T}_{k-1}$;
(8)　　　　$\mathbf{v}_{\Gamma_k} = \mathbf{A}_{\Gamma_k}^\dagger \mathbf{b}$, $\mathbf{v}_{\Gamma_k^c} = \mathbf{0}$; $\triangleright \mathbf{v} \in R^{N \times 1}$
(9)　　　　$\widehat{T}_k = \text{supp}(\mathbf{v}^\gamma)$;
Regularization Steps:
(10)　　　$\mathbf{U}_k = \mathbf{I} - \mathbf{A}_{\widehat{T}_k} \mathbf{A}_{\widehat{T}_k}^\dagger$;
(11)　　　$\mathbf{r}_k = \mathbf{U}_k \mathbf{b}$; $\triangleright$ regularize $\mathbf{b}$ using $\widehat{T}_k$
(12)　　　$\mathbf{A}_k = \mathbf{U}_k \mathbf{A}_{\widehat{T}_k^c}$; $\triangleright$ regularize $\mathbf{A}$ using $\widehat{T}_k$
(13)　　**until** ($\|\mathbf{r}_k\|_2 \geq \|\mathbf{r}_{k-1}\|_2$);
(14)　　$\widehat{T} = \widehat{T}_{k-1}$;
(15)　　$\widehat{\mathbf{x}}_{\widehat{T}} = \mathbf{A}_{\widehat{T}}^\dagger \mathbf{b}$, $\widehat{\mathbf{x}}_{\widehat{T}^c} = \mathbf{0}$; $\triangleright \widehat{\mathbf{x}} \in R^{N \times 1}$
Outputs: $\widehat{\mathbf{x}}$ and $\widehat{T}$.

ALGORITHM 2: IFBP algorithm.

exact recovery rate of IFBP would not decline. Algorithm 2 gives the pseudocode of the IFBP algorithm.

The main idea of the proposed algorithm is using two parameters to reconstruct the signal step by step. The proposed algorithm overcomes the problem that iterations need the sparsity level K in [15]. By preserving the useful atoms in each iteration, the proposed algorithm expands the estimated support set step by step. Meanwhile, the proposed algorithm exploits the character of FBP to reduce the number of iterations. Thus, the proposed algorithm applies the reweighting scheme into the FBP algorithm without the sparsity level.

4. Experimental Evaluation

4.1. The Recovery of the Sparse Signals. In order to demonstrate the superiority of the algorithm, we compare the exact recovery rates, average recovery error, and run times of IFBP with those of FBP for signals with nonzero elements drawn from the Gaussian and uniform distributions. The nonzero entries of the Gaussian sparse signals are drawn from the standard Gaussian distribution. Meanwhile, nonzero elements of the uniform sparse signals are distributed uniformly in $[-1, 1]$. The observation matrix, which is different for each test signal, is drawn from the Gaussian distribution with mean 0 and standard deviation $1/N$. Then, we normalize each column norm to unity. During the experiments, we use MATLAB to perform these algorithms.

In these simulations, we choose $N = 256$ and $M = 100$ while K varies from 15 to 48. For each K, recovery simulations are repeated over 500 times, where the randomly generated Gaussian and uniform sparse signals are different for each

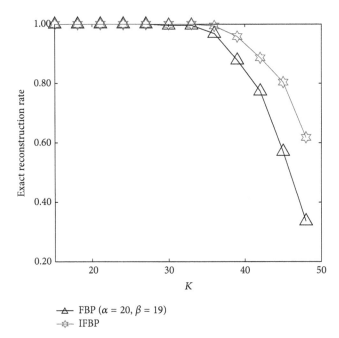

FIGURE 1: Exact recovery rates for the Gaussian sparse vectors ($\alpha = 20$, $\beta = 19$).

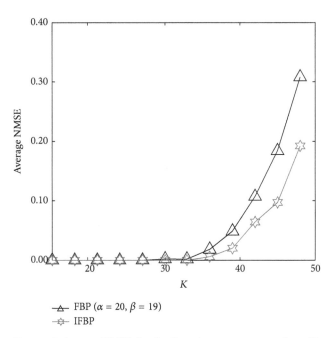

FIGURE 2: Average NMSE for the Gaussian sparse vectors ($\alpha = 20$, $\beta = 19$).

test. We use the Average Normalized Mean-Squared-Error (ANMSE) to scale the recovery error, which is defined as

$$\text{ANMSE} = \frac{1}{500} \sum_{i=1}^{500} \frac{\left\| \mathbf{x}_i - \widehat{\mathbf{x}}_i \right\|_2^2}{\left\| \mathbf{x}_i \right\|_2^2}, \tag{3}$$

where $\widehat{\mathbf{x}}_i$ denotes the recovery of the ith test vector $\mathbf{x}_i$. In addition, another evaluation criterion, called the exact recovery rate, is also used in these tests. It represents the ratio of perfectly recovered test samples to the whole test data. The exact recovery condition is selected as $\| \mathbf{x} - \widehat{\mathbf{x}} \|_2 \leq 10^{-2} \| \mathbf{x} \|_2$ [8].

In these tests, we select $K_{\max} = 50$ and the termination parameter $\varepsilon = 10^{-6}$, which are the same for FBP and IFBP. Meanwhile, this paper selects $I = 0.1M$ and $S = 0.5I$ for IFBP.

Reference [8] points out that choosing $\alpha \in [0.2M, 0.3M]$ and $\beta = \alpha - 1$ leads to the optimal recovery performance in practice. This paper chooses FBP ($\alpha = 20$, $\beta = 19$) and FBP ($\alpha = 30$, $\beta = 29$) as the parent algorithm of IFBP, respectively.

First, we test the performance of IFBP with FBP ($\alpha = 20$, $\beta = 19$) as the parent algorithm. Figures 1 and 2 depict the reconstruction performance of IFBP for the Gaussian sparse signals in comparison to FBP ($\alpha = 20$, $\beta = 19$). Analogous results are provided in Figures 3 and 4 for the uniform ensemble as well.

In Figure 1, we observe that the exact recovery rates of IFBP are significantly better than FBP. When K is small, both FBP and IFBP can guarantee 100% to reconstruct the original signal. With K increasing, the exact recovery rates of two algorithms decrease. At $K = 30$, FBP starts to fail. However, IFBP failures begin when $K = 36$. The exact recovery rate of FBP drops to 33.6% at $K = 48$, where IFBP is 61.8%. By

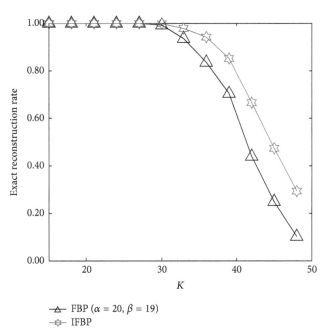

FIGURE 3: Exact recovery rates for the uniform sparse vectors ($\alpha = 20$, $\beta = 19$).

the proposed method of this paper, the exact recovery rate of FBP at $K = 48$ increases by 80%. As for ANMSE, IFBP is also the better performer from Figure 2. At $K = 48$, the ANMSE of FBP grows to 0.31, while IFBP reduces the ANMSE down to 0.19. Note that the performance of both IFBP and FBP declines when the coefficient distribution changes from the Gaussian distribution to the uniform distribution. This is related to the involved correlation-maximization step, that is,

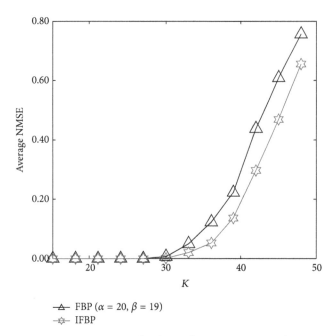

FIGURE 4: Average NMSE for the uniform sparse vectors ($\alpha = 20$, $\beta = 19$).

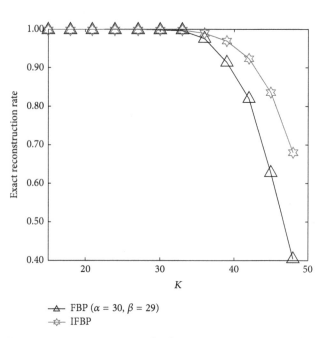

FIGURE 5: Exact recovery rates for the Gaussian sparse vectors ($\alpha = 30$, $\beta = 29$).

choosing the largest magnitude elements of $\mathbf{\Phi} \times \mathbf{r}^{k-1}$, which becomes more prone to errors when the nonzero elements of the underlying sparse signals span a narrower range [8].

Investigating Figures 3 and 4, which depict recovery results for the uniform sparse signals, we observe a similar behavior as well. IFBP results in significant improvement over FBP in both exact recovery rates and ANMSE. The exact recovery rate of IFBP is 29.4% at $K = 48$, which is nearly three times FBP. Meanwhile, IFBP provides 0.1 ANMSE improvement over FBP.

Then, we take FBP ($\alpha = 30$, $\beta = 29$) as the parent algorithm of IFBP in Figures 5, 6, 7, and 8. Similar to the previous test case, IFBP yields better recovery rates and ANMSE than FBP for both the Gaussian sparse signals and the uniform sparse signals.

It is noted that IFBP is computationally more demanding than the parent FBP as it runs the parent FBP multiple times to enhance the sparse signal reconstruction. In addition, it may be observed that IFBP with FBP ($\alpha = 30$, $\beta = 29$) as the parent algorithm results in a better performance, compared to IFBP with FBP ($\alpha = 20$, $\beta = 19$) as the parent algorithm. This is due to the parent algorithm, which has severe effect on IFBP.

4.2. The Recovery of the Sparse Image. In this section, we evaluate the performance of the proposed IFBP using real-world signal. We use a similar simulation setup used in [8]. The recovery is performed on the 256×256 image "lena," which should be divided into 8×8 blocks in advance. The pretreatment is to ensure that each 8×8 block is K sparse in the 2D Haar Wavelet basis, $\mathbf{\Psi}$, where $K = 12$. Namely, each block only keeps the $K = 12$ largest magnitude wavelet coefficients. Thus, the recovery problem is broken into a

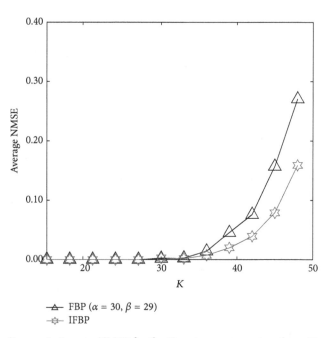

FIGURE 6: Average NMSE for the Gaussian sparse vectors ($\alpha = 30$, $\beta = 29$).

number of smaller and simpler problems. In order to adapt to the small size, we take the observation size $M = 32$, which is the same for each block. The observation matrix $\mathbf{\Phi}$ is randomly drawn from the Gaussian distribution with mean 0 and standard deviation $1/N$. Then, we normalize each column norm to unity. The parameters are selected as $K_{\max} = 16$ and $\varepsilon = 10^{-6}$. We take FBP ($\alpha = 10$, $\beta = 9$) as the parent algorithm of IFBP in this example. Meanwhile, this example selects $I = 4$ and $S = 0.5I$ for IFBP.

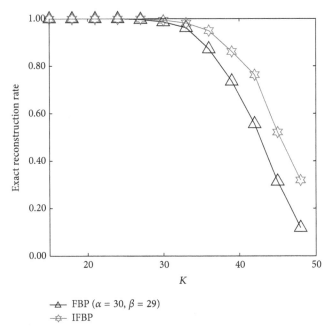

FIGURE 9: Test image "lena."

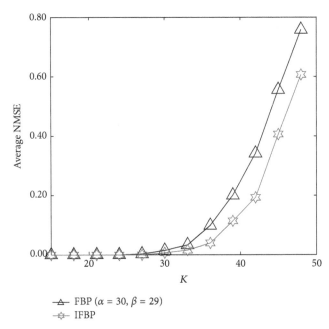

FIGURE 7: Exact recovery rates for the uniform sparse vectors ($\alpha = 30$, $\beta = 29$).

FIGURE 10: FBP ($\alpha = 10$, $\beta = 9$), PSNR = 28.6 dB.

FIGURE 11: IFBP, PSNR = 29.9 dB.

FIGURE 8: Average NMSE for the uniform sparse vectors ($\alpha = 30$, $\beta = 29$).

5. Conclusions

Combining FBP with IFSRA, this paper proposes IFBP algorithm. Unlike the IFSRA, IFBP iterates the FBP without prior information of the sparsity. IFBP can significantly improve the performance of FBP by adjusting the number of atoms which are added to the estimated support set in the first iteration and the subsequent iteration(s). Meanwhile, IFBP judges the result of the parent algorithm in the first iteration and overcomes the problem that IFSRA has to iterate at least twice due to the iterative termination condition. In addition, this paper uses the acceleration strategy to reduce the number of the iterations. The efficacy of IFBP in applications is shown using numerical simulations on both spare signals and the spare image. More important, the IFBP algorithm provides

Figure 9 is the test image "lena." The results of FBP and IFBP are shown in Figures 10 and 11. In this example, the Peak Signal-to-Noise Ratio (PSNR) value of FBP is 28.6 dB, while IFBP promotes the PSNR up to 29.9 dB. This example shows that IFBP has the ability to generate more accurate recovery than FBP for a signal with realistic nonzero coefficient distribution.

a useful idea for algorithm improvement, where the sparsity level is unknown.

Competing Interests

The authors declare that there is no conflict of interests regarding the publication of this paper.

Acknowledgments

This work was supported by the Specialized Research Fund for the Doctoral Program of Higher Education (no. 20130031110032), the National Natural Science Foundation of China (no. 61171140), and Tianjin Key Technology Program of the Ministry of Science and Technology (no. 14ZCZDNC00014).

References

[1] E. J. Candes and T. Tao, "Near-optimal signal recovery from random projections: universal encoding strategies?" *IEEE Transactions on Information Theory*, vol. 52, no. 12, pp. 5406–5425, 2006.

[2] D. L. Donoho, "Compressed sensing," *IEEE Transactions on Information Theory*, vol. 52, no. 4, pp. 1289–1306, 2006.

[3] S. G. Mallat and Z. Zhang, "Matching pursuits with time-frequency dictionaries," *IEEE Transactions on Signal Processing*, vol. 41, no. 12, pp. 3397–3415, 1993.

[4] J. A. Tropp and A. C. Gilbert, "Signal recovery from random measurements via orthogonal matching pursuit," *IEEE Transactions on Information Theory*, vol. 53, no. 12, pp. 4655–4666, 2007.

[5] W. Dai and O. Milenkovic, "Subspace pursuit for compressive sensing signal reconstruction," *IEEE Transactions on Information Theory*, vol. 55, no. 5, pp. 2230–2249, 2009.

[6] D. Needell and J. A. Tropp, "CoSaMP: iterative signal recovery from incomplete and inaccurate samples," *Applied & Computational Harmonic Analysis*, vol. 26, no. 3, pp. 301–321, 2009.

[7] S. Chatterjee, D. Sundman, and M. Skoglund, "Look ahead orthogonal matching pursuit," in *Proceedings of the 36th IEEE International Conference on Acoustics, Speech, and Signal Processing (ICASSP '11)*, pp. 4024–4027, Prague, Czech Republic, May 2011.

[8] N. B. Karahanoglu and H. Erdogan, "Compressed sensing signal recovery via forward-backward pursuit," *Digital Signal Processing*, vol. 23, no. 5, pp. 1539–1548, 2013.

[9] C. Li, J. Wang, and M. Li, "Efficient cross-layer optimization algorithm for data transmission in wireless sensor networks," *Journal of Electrical and Computer Engineering*, vol. 2015, Article ID 545798, 6 pages, 2015.

[10] X.-Y. Liu, Y. Zhu, L. Kong et al., "CDC: compressive data collection for wireless sensor networks," *IEEE Transactions on Parallel & Distributed Systems*, vol. 26, no. 8, pp. 2188–2197, 2015.

[11] R. Otazo, E. Candès, and D. K. Sodickson, "Low-rank plus sparse matrix decomposition for accelerated dynamic MRI with separation of background and dynamic components," *Magnetic Resonance in Medicine*, vol. 73, no. 3, pp. 1125–1136, 2015.

[12] Y. Zhang, S. Wang, G. Ji, and Z. Dong, "Exponential wavelet iterative shrinkage thresholding algorithm with random shift for compressed sensing magnetic resonance imaging," *IEEJ Transactions on Electrical and Electronic Engineering*, vol. 10, no. 1, pp. 116–117, 2015.

[13] Y. Zhang, J. Yang, J. Yang, A. Liu, and P. Sun, "A novel compressed sensing method for magnetic resonance imaging: exponential wavelet iterative shrinkage-thresholding algorithm with random shift," *International Journal of Biomedical Imaging*, vol. 2016, Article ID 9416435, 10 pages, 2016.

[14] Y. Zhang, Z. Dong, P. Phillips, S. Wang, G. Ji, and J. Yang, "Exponential wavelet iterative shrinkage thresholding algorithm for compressed sensing magnetic resonance imaging," *Information Sciences*, vol. 322, Article ID 11611, pp. 115–132, 2015.

[15] S. K. Ambat and K. V. S. Hari, "An iterative framework for sparse signal reconstruction algorithms," *Signal Processing*, vol. 108, pp. 351–364, 2015.

[16] S. S. Chen, D. L. Donoho, and M. A. Saunders, "Atomic decomposition by basis pursuit," *SIAM Journal on Scientific Computing*, vol. 20, no. 1, pp. 33–61, 1998.

[17] H. Mohimani, M. Babaie-Zadeh, and C. Jutten, "A fast approach for overcomplete sparse decomposition based on smoothed norm," *IEEE Transactions on Signal Processing*, vol. 57, no. 1, pp. 289–301, 2009.

[18] E. J. Candès, M. B. Wakin, and S. P. Boyd, "Enhancing sparsity by reweighted ℓ_1 minimization," *Journal of Fourier Analysis and Applications*, vol. 14, no. 5-6, pp. 877–905, 2008.

8

Multialgorithmic Frameworks for Human Face Recognition

Radhey Shyam and Yogendra Narain Singh

Department of Computer Science & Engineering, Institute of Engineering and Technology, Lucknow 226 021, India

Correspondence should be addressed to Radhey Shyam; shyam0058@gmail.com

Academic Editor: Igor Djurović

This paper presents a critical evaluation of multialgorithmic face recognition systems for human authentication in unconstrained environment. We propose different frameworks of multialgorithmic face recognition system combining holistic and texture methods. Our aim is to combine the uncorrelated methods of the face recognition that supplement each other and to produce a comprehensive representation of the biometric cue to achieve optimum recognition performance. The multialgorithmic frameworks are designed to combine different face recognition methods such as (i) Eigenfaces and local binary pattern (LBP), (ii) Fisherfaces and LBP, (iii) Eigenfaces and augmented local binary pattern (A-LBP), and (iv) Fisherfaces and A-LBP. The matching scores of these multialgorithmic frameworks are processed using different normalization techniques whereas their performance is evaluated using different fusion strategies. The robustness of proposed multialgorithmic frameworks of face recognition system is tested on publicly available databases, for example, AT & T (ORL) and Labeled Faces in the Wild (LFW). The experimental results show a significant improvement in recognition accuracies of the proposed frameworks of face recognition system in comparison to their individual methods. In particular, the performance of the multialgorithmic frameworks combining face recognition methods with the devised face recognition method such as A-LBP improves significantly.

1. Introduction

Biometrics is a technology that examines unique physiological or behavioral characteristics of an individual for his/her authentication. It provides a mechanism of automatic recognition of individuals based on their one or more biometric cues. The recognition system which is typically based on a single biometric cue has not always yielded the desired results, because of the problems of noisy data, lack of uniqueness, and spoofing attacks. In the critical applications such as border crossing and emigrant check points, biometric systems of a single cue are not able to provide the desired level of performance. Therefore, multibiometric systems are used, but major challenges of these systems are to gather the information from multiple biometric cues of an individual and their fusion, for example, unobtrusive biometrics (face and fingerprint) with obtrusive biometrics (iris and ECG) fulfilling the objective that they supplement each other [1, 2]. These systems are computationally expensive and raise the response time too. One possible solution of these issues is to work on a single biometric cue with different representation so as to analyze it comprehensively for better recognition of individuals.

In order to make a viable biometric system that works more effectively in various applications under different conditions the multialgorithmic biometric approach could be a possible solution; in particular, unobtrusive biometrics such as face could be chosen as a suitable biometric identifier. Marcialis and Roli have proposed the fusion of two well-known face recognition algorithms, namely, principal component analysis (PCA) and linear discriminant analysis (LDA) that conformed benefits of fused algorithms in video-based surveillance applications [3]. Mian et al. have presented 2D and 3D multimodal hybrid face recognition algorithm and tested its performance on the FRGC v1.0 dataset [4]. Zakariya et al. have presented a multialgorithmic based approach using PCA and discrete cosine transformation (DCT) for personal identification and proved its usefulness [5]. Kar et al. have developed a multialgorithmic based face recognition system, harnessing the combination of gray level statistical correlation method with PCA or DCT methods, in order to intensify the performance of the systems [6]. Lone et al. have developed a face recognition system based on the consolidation of scores obtained from different techniques, such as PCA, DCT, template matching using correlation, and partitioned iterative function system [7]. Imran et al. have proposed fusion using popular subspace methods including PCA, LDA, locality preserving projection, and independent component analysis [8]. It is computed by considering different combinations of set of two, three, and four subspace methods. Their results have shown an improved performance of multialgorithmic face recognition technique.

The aim of this work is to combine the uncorrelated face recognition approaches such as holistic and texture based representations to achieve the multialgorithmic frameworks. The fusion of multiple information of a biometric cue shows an improvement in the recognition performance of the biometric system. This paper presents different frameworks of face recognition system utilizing multialgorithmic techniques for achieving the optimum recognition performance. The concern is to combine the normalized scores of the uncorrelated face recognition methods, to achieve the multialgorithmic characteristics, for the individual judgment. The proposed frameworks of multialgorithmic face recognition system are devised from the following face recognition techniques: (i) Eigenfaces [10] and local binary pattern (LBP) [11, 12], (ii) Fisherfaces [13] and LBP, (iii) Eigenfaces and augmented local binary pattern (A-LBP) [14–16], and (iv) Fisherfaces and A-LBP. The performance of these frameworks is evaluated using different fusion strategies.

The remainder of the paper is structured as follows: Section 2 presents a review of existing face recognition techniques. The frameworks of proposed multialgorithmic face recognition system are given in Section 3. Section 4 shows the experimental results obtained from the proposed frameworks that are tested on the public domain databases, such as AT & T (ORL) [17] and Labeled Faces in the Wild (LFW) [18]. Finally, the discussion and conclusion are outlined in Section 5.

2. Face Recognition Methods

Recognizing individuals from their faces is natural phenomena and this task is effortlessly performed by us in our daily life. An automatic face recognition system is typically designed to compute the similarity of the facial images. Over thousands of research papers are published every year on face recognition. Most of the published methods are performed well in controlled environments, for example, Eigenfaces and Fisherfaces [19, 20]. The other methods that are claimed to be performed better in uncontrolled environment mainly include LBP and A-LBP [11, 12, 14–16]. These approaches may be broadly categorized on the basis of their representations, that is, (i) holistic methods, for example, Eigenfaces and Fisherfaces, and (ii) texture based methods, for example, LBP and A-LBP.

In the last two decades, different face recognition methods based on holistic approach of facial representation are proposed [21]. It includes some of the well-known face recognition algorithms: principal component analysis (Eigenfaces) [10], linear discriminant analysis [22], Fisherfaces [13], independent component analysis [23], and elastic bunch graph matching [24]. A texture based technique uses a type of texture representation of facial images to be recognized. It includes the well-known texture representation methods, LBP [11, 12], SIFT [25], and SURF [26] whereas LBP is more popular among them. LBP is a feature based approach which is being used for classification purposes in computer vision. A LBP operator labels the pixels of an image with decimal numbers and also encodes the local structure around each pixel. Each pixel is compared with its eight neighbors in 3×3 neighborhood by subtracting the central pixels value as a threshold. The resulting nonnegative values are encoded with 1 and others with 0. A binary number is obtained by concatenating all these binary codes in a clockwise direction starting from top-left corner and placed left to right. Its decimal value is then computed and used for the labeling perspective. The derived binary numbers are called LBP [11, 12].

We have worked on the modified approach of LBP called augmented local binary pattern (A-LBP) that makes use of nonuniform patterns in the representation process [16]. In the prior work of LBP, the nonuniform patterns are either treated as noise and discarded during the texture representations or used in combination with the uniform patterns. Our developed method considers the nonuniform patterns and extracts the discriminatory information available to them, so as to prove their usefulness. They are used in combination with the neighboring uniform patterns and extract the useful information from the local descriptors [14, 15].

3. Proposed Framework of Multialgorithmic Face Recognition System

The framework of the multialgorithmic face recognition systems is shown in Figure 1. The framework first preprocesses the input which is a set of images to make them acceptable for further processing. Next, the images are passed to different face recognition systems that employ holistic and texture based approaches that compute the scores that are to be used in matching process. The scores are normalized to make them homogeneous. The scores are now fused depending upon the choice of algorithms. Thus, we obtain total scores of fused algorithms. These scores are finally used in matching process and thus genuine and impostor scores are generated after comparing with the test images.

In this experiment, concern of the proposed frameworks is to fuse distinct face recognition algorithms with our A-LBP face recognition algorithm that is claimed to be better in uncontrolled environment and to achieve the robust face recognition systems. The following pair of strategies is used to fuse. It includes (i) Eigenfaces and LBP, (ii) Fisherfaces and LBP, (iii) Eigenfaces and A-LBP, and (iv) Fisherfaces and A-LBP.

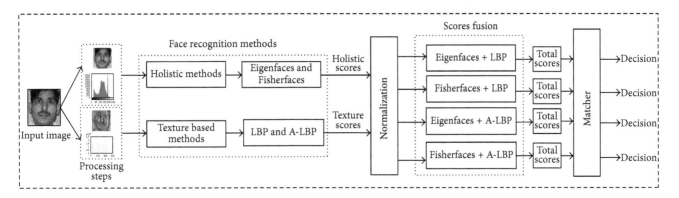

FIGURE 1: The framework of multialgorithmic face recognition systems [9].

The Eigenfaces technique is typically based on linearly projecting the image space to a lower dimension. The Fisherfaces technique which employs the principal component analysis for dimensionality reduction results in projection direction that maximizes the total scatter across all the classes. Principal component analysis retains unfavorable changes due to illumination and facial expression [10]. Fisherfaces is used to find out the basis vectors that minimizes within-class matrix differences and maximizes between-class matrix distances [27]. Thus, ratio of the between-class scatter and the within-class scatter is maximized [13].

Contrary to Eigenfaces and Fisherfaces, the local binary pattern is robust to the changes of illumination and facial expressions. It is a simple and efficient operator, consolidating statistical and structural approaches, both in the texture analysis. It is a powerful grayscale invariant metric derived from a general definition of texture in a local neighborhood. Due to its discriminating power and computational simplicity, it becomes a popular approach [11, 12]. Contrasting to LBP, our proposed A-LBP technique also considered the nonuniform patterns and transformed them into uniform patterns for texture representation and classification, thus preserving the discriminatory information of the chosen cues [14–16].

3.1. Score Normalization Techniques. Normalization is a process of transformation and mapping of heterogeneous scores (i.e., different scales) of distinct biometrics and makes them homogeneous (i.e., common scales) [28]. We obtain the multialgorithmic biometric frameworks where the matching scores of different biometrics or algorithms are transformed and mapped to a common scale before fusion.

Different score normalization techniques are found in literature, the most common among are min–max (MM) and tanh [29]. Let us assume that $O_k^T = \{r_{k_1}^T, r_{k_2}^T, \ldots, r_{k_N}^T\}$ be the set of true scores of N individuals and $O_k^I = \{r_{k_1}^I, r_{k_2}^I, \ldots, r_{k_n}^I\}$ be the set of impostor scores of those individuals, where $n = N \times (N-1)$ for the biometric method k. The composite set

of matching scores is denoted as O_k (i.e., $O_k = O_k^T \cup O_k^I$ and $|O_k^T \cup O_k^I| = N + n = N^2$).

The distance scores (r_{k_i}') of user i for method k can be converted into similarity scores in the common range. Suppose it should be in $[0, 1]$ using the following formula:

$$r_{k_i} = \frac{\max\left(O_k^T, O_k^I\right) - r_{k_i}'}{\max\left(O_k^T, O_k^I\right) - \min\left(O_k^T, O_k^I\right)}, \tag{1}$$

where r_{k_i} is the similarity scores of method k. Otherwise, if the distance scores lie in the range $[\min(O_k), \max(O_k)]$ then they are simply converted into similarity scores by subtracting them, from the value of $\max(O_k)$, that is, $\max(O_k - r_{k_i}')$. The summary of these score normalization techniques is as follows:

MM: it transforms the raw scores into the common range of $[0, 1]$ using

$$n_{k_i} = \frac{r_{k_i} - \min\left(O_k\right)}{\max\left(O_k\right) - \min\left(O_k\right)}. \tag{2}$$

Tanh: it corresponds to the raw scores of O_k in the common range of $[0, 1]$ as

$$n_{k_i} = \frac{1}{2} * \left[\tanh\left\{ 0.01 * \left(\frac{r_{k_i} - \mu_{O_k^T}}{\sigma_{O_k^T}} \right) \right\} + 1 \right], \tag{3}$$

where $\mu_{O_k^T}$ and $\sigma_{O_k^T}$ are the mean and the standard deviation of the true matching scores of method k, respectively, and n_{k_i} is the normalized scores of that method k.

3.2. Fusion Techniques. Kittler et al. have evolved a theoretical framework for reconciling the evidence achieved from different schemes, such as sum rule, max rule, and min rule [30]. In order to use these schemes, the matching scores are converted into a posteriori probabilities conforming to a true user and an impostor. They consider the problem of classifying an input pattern Z into one of the m possible classes based on the evidence presented by R different classifiers. Let $\vec{x_i}$ be the feature vector provided to the ith classifier and let outputs of the respective classifiers be $p(w_j \mid \vec{x_i})$, that is, the a posteriori probability of the pattern Z belonging to class w_j given the feature vector $\vec{x_i}$. Let $c \in \{1, 2, \ldots, m\}$ be the class to which the input pattern Z is finally assigned. The following fusion rules have been generalized by Jain et al. for computing the value of class c [31]:

Sum rule: it assumes that the a posteriori probabilities computed by the respective classifiers do not deviate from the prior probabilities. This rule is preferred when there is a high level of noise leading to vagueness in the classification problem. It assigns the input pattern to class c such that

$$c = \underset{j}{\operatorname{argmax}} \sum_{i=1}^{R} p\left(w_j \mid \vec{x_i}\right). \tag{4}$$

Max rule: it approximates the mean of the a posteriori probabilities by the maximum value. The input pattern is assigned to class c such that

$$c = \underset{j}{\operatorname{argmax}} \max_{i} p\left(w_j \mid \vec{x_i}\right). \tag{5}$$

Min rule: it is derived by bounding the product of a posteriori probabilities. Here, the input pattern is assigned to class c such that

$$c = \underset{j}{\operatorname{argmax}} \min_{i} p\left(w_j \mid \vec{x_i}\right), \tag{6}$$

where argmax is simply an operator and $p(w_j \mid \vec{x_i})$ is the measurement process model of ith representation.

4. Experimental Results

4.1. Face Databases. The proposed frameworks of multialgorithmic face recognition system are tested on different public domain face databases, for example, AT & T (ORL) [17] and Labeled Faces in the Wild [18]. The first database AT & T (ORL) consists of 40 subjects whereas each subject has 10 samples, and each image is downsized towards the size of 49 × 60. Next, Labeled Faces in the Wild database consists of 40 subjects, and there are 10 samples per subject and each image is downsized to the size of 64 × 64. These databases are different in the degree of variation, for instance, pose, illumination, expression, and the eye glasses that are presented in their facial images. A total of 800 face images are used to recognize 80 distinct individuals. The proposed frameworks of multialgorithmic face recognition system are trained for each face database independently, whereas the test face images are selected arbitrarily from the available training faces for each individual and their performance is computed.

4.2. Performance Metrics. The performance of the proposed frameworks of multialgorithmic face recognition system is computed using equal error rate (EER), which is an error, where the probability of acceptance is assumed to be the same as the probability of rejection of the people who should be correctly verified. The performance is also verified using the receiver operating characteristic (ROC) curves. The ROC curve is a two-dimensional measure of classification performance that plots the probability of the true acceptance rate (TAR) against the probability of the false acceptance rate (FAR), where TAR = 100 − FAR. Accuracy of the system can be computed using FAR and false rejection rates (FRR):

$$\text{Accuracy (\%)} = 100 - \left(\frac{\text{FAR} + \text{FRR}}{2}\right). \tag{7}$$

The acceptance threshold is selected from the receiver operating characteristic curve so as to produce EER; that is, FAR = FRR (the cross point where the false acceptance rate and the false rejection rates are the same). The values of FAR and FRR depend on the chosen threshold. As the threshold increases the FAR decreases and the FRR increases and vice versa. There is trade-off between the choice of FAR and FRR values that depend on the security and throughput requirements of the system to be used.

4.3. Recognition Performance Using MM Normalization Technique. Recognition performance of the proposed frameworks of multialgorithmic face recognition system is tested on publicly available databases using a Bray Curtis dissimilarity metric [32]. The recognition accuracy results obtained from the fusion of face recognition techniques using different normalization techniques are shown in Table 1. The improvement in recognition performance of different frameworks of face recognition system is clearly visible. For example, recognition performance is found better for tanh normalization technique using sum rule of fusion for AT & T (ORL) database. Further, a significant improvement in the recognition performance is also found for LFW database for same normalization and fusion techniques. The matching scores are distributed normally and thus the sum rule of fusion reduces the variance present in the scores; therefore performance improves. It results in the better recognition rate as compared to other fusion strategies.

The ROC curves for AT & T (ORL) database are plotted for different frameworks of multialgorithmic face recognition system using MM normalization technique that are shown in Figure 2. The recognition accuracy results of the fused uncorrelated algorithms such as Eigenfaces and LBP, Fisherfaces and LBP, Eigenfaces and A-LBP, and Fisherfaces and A-LBP using sum, max, and min rule are shown, respectively, in Figures 2(a), 2(b), and 2(c). Among the four multialgorithmic approaches, the last three approaches report better TAR value of 97.79%, 97.05%, and 97.95% (Table 1), respectively, using sum rule of fusion, whereas the first multialgorithmic approach reports a better value of 95.38% using the max

TABLE 1: Recognition accuracies of uncorrelated face recognition methods and their fusion using different normalization and fusion techniques.

Algorithms	Database	Normalization techniques	Accuracies (%)			
			Unibiometric	Multialgorithmic fusion		
				Sum rule	Max rule	Min rule
Eigenfaces (E) Fisherfaces (F) LBP (L) A-LBP (A)	AT & T (ORL) [17]	MM	(E): 95.45 (F): 97.50 (L): 94.52 (A): 95.00	(E + L): 95.32 (F + L): **97.79** (E + A): **97.05** (F + A): **97.95**	(E + L): **95.38** (F + L): 97.50 (E + A): 95.42 (F + A): 97.50	(E + L): 94.97 (F + L): 97.28 (E + A): 96.86 (F + A): 97.50
Eigenfaces (E) Fisherfaces (F) LBP (L) A-LBP (A)	AT & T (ORL) [17]	Tanh	(E): 96.54 (F): 97.50 (L): 94.49 (A): 94.87	(E + L): 95.64 (F + L): **97.79** (E + A): **97.31** (F + A): **97.95**	(E + L): 93.24 (F + L): 97.50 (E + A): 94.97 (F + A): 97.44	(E + L): 95.38 (F + L): 97.44 (E + A): 95.13 (F + A): 97.60
Eigenfaces (E) Fisherfaces (F) LBP (L) A-LBP (A)	LFW [18]	MM	(E): 65.00 (F): 70.00 (L): 65.29 (A): 67.37	(E + L): **72.24** (F + L): **72.50** (E + A): **72.50** (F + A): **72.14**	(E + L): 72.18 (F + L): 72.14 (E + A): 72.46 (F + A): 70.25	(E + L): 60.32 (F + L): 70.00 (E + A): 62.11 (F + A): 69.29
Eigenfaces (E) Fisherfaces (F) LBP (L) A-LBP (A)	LFW [18]	Tanh	(E): 65.03 (F): 69.84 (L): 65.42 (A): 67.12	(E + L): 69.93 (F + L): **72.50** (E + A): **72.62** (F + A): 72.24	(E + L): **71.73** (F + L): 70.19 (E + A): 69.93 (F + A): **72.30**	(E + L): 65.19 (F + L): 67.91 (E + A): 65.03 (F + A): 67.91

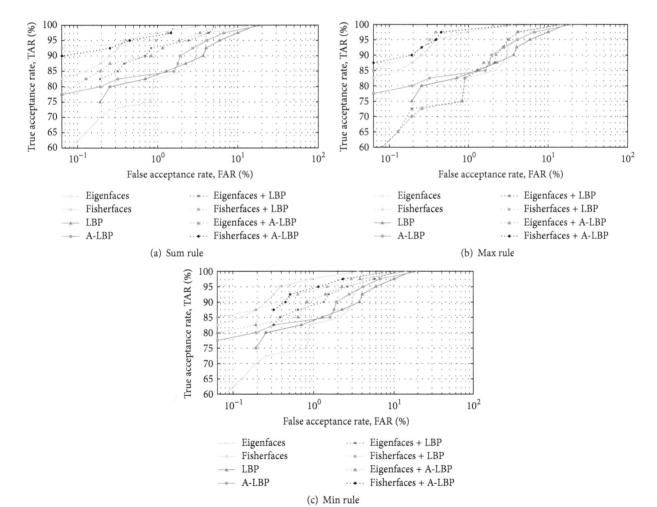

(a) Sum rule

(b) Max rule

(c) Min rule

FIGURE 2: Performance of multialgorithmic frameworks of face recognition system using MM normalization on AT & T (ORL) database under different fusion strategies.

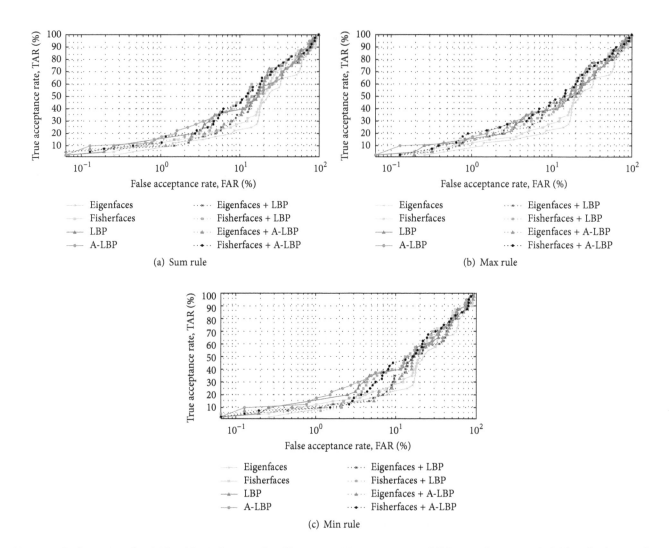

FIGURE 3: Performance of multialgorithmic frameworks of face recognition system using MM normalization on LFW face database under different fusion strategies.

rule of fusion. On these multialgorithmic frameworks, the recognition results reach 100% of TAR at 3% of FAR, 4% of FAR, and 8% of the FAR, respectively. A similar trend is also observed for the proposed frameworks on LFW face database.

The ROC curves plotted for the reported results of different frameworks and fusion strategies are shown in Figure 3.

4.4. Recognition Performance Using Tanh Normalization Technique. The ROC curves for AT & T (ORL) database are plotted for different frameworks of multialgorithmic face recognition system using tanh normalization technique that are shown in Figure 4. The recognition results of the fused techniques, for example, Eigenfaces and LBP, Fisherfaces and LBP, Eigenfaces and A-LBP, and Fisherfaces and A-LBP techniques on distinct fusion methods, are shown, respectively, in Figures 4(a), 4(b), and 4(c). The multialgorithmic

frameworks report better TAR value of 95.64%, 97.79%, 97.31%, and 97.95% (Table 1), respectively, using sum rule. On these multialgorithmic frameworks, the recognition results reach 100% of TAR at 1.5% of FAR, 6% of FAR, and 10% of the FAR, respectively. A similar trend in the recognition results is also reported for the proposed frameworks of multialgorithmic face recognition system on LFW face database. The ROC curves of LFW database are shown in Figure 5. As compared to MM, tanh normalization technique performs better, because of its sensitiveness to the outliers.

5. Conclusion

This paper has presented the novel frameworks of multialgorithmic face recognition system and evaluated their performance in noncooperative environment. These frameworks are developed by combining evidences presented by the

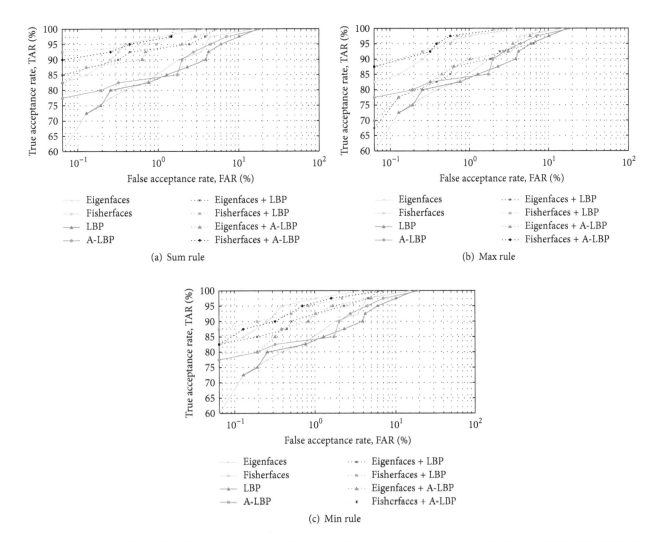

FIGURE 4: Performance of multialgorithmic frameworks of face recognition system using tanh normalization on AT & T (ORL) database under different fusion strategies.

uncorrelated face recognition methods. We have evaluated the performance of different unibiometric face recognition methods such as Eigenfaces, Fisherfaces, LBP, and A-LBP on publicly available face databases such as AT & T (ORL) and LFW. The performance of the proposed frameworks of multialgorithmic face recognition system obtained from the fusion of Eigenfaces and LBP, Fisherfaces and LBP, Eigenfaces and A-LBP, and Fisherfaces and A-LBP on the stated databases is computed. The recognition results of the proposed frameworks are evaluated using different normalization and fusion techniques.

The strength of the proposed frameworks of multialgorithmic face recognition system is that they are prepared from unibiometric methods and provide a robust solution rather than creating a complex method. Thus, the proposed frameworks have reduced the complexities of multibiometric systems to a considerable extent. In most cases, the fused techniques have shown significant improvement in recognition performance in comparison to their unibiometric

systems. It has also observed that the sum rule plays an important role in comparison to other chosen fusion methods, such as the max and min rules because it reduces the variance present in the matching scores of different methods and thus improves the recognition accuracy. The evaluated frameworks of multialgorithmic face recognition system may contribute an important role in identification of individual faces in the noncooperative environment.

Competing Interests

The authors declare that there are no competing interests regarding the publication of this paper.

Acknowledgments

The authors acknowledge the Institute of Engineering and Technology (IET), Lucknow, Dr. A. P. J. Abdul Kalam Technical University, Uttar Pradesh, Lucknow, for their partial

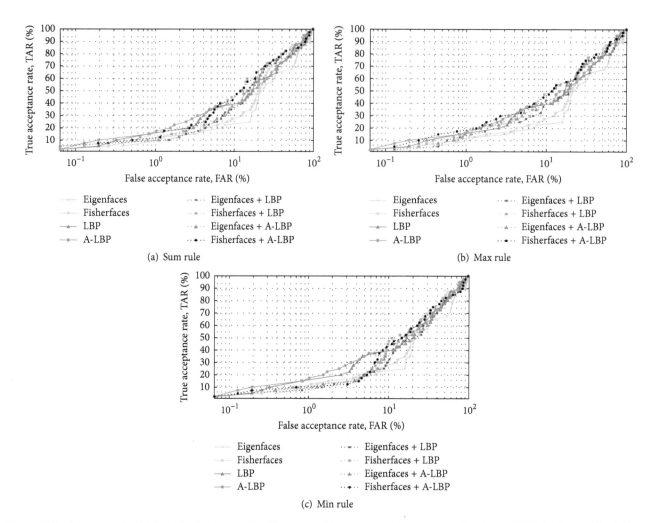

FIGURE 5: Performance of multialgorithmic frameworks of face recognition system using tanh normalization on LFW database under different fusion strategies.

financial support to carry out this research under the Technical Education Quality Improvement Programme (TEQIP-II) grant.

References

[1] Y. N. Singh, S. K. Singh, and P. Gupta, "Fusion of electrocardiogram with unobtrusive biometrics: an efficient individual authentication system," *Pattern Recognition Letters*, vol. 33, no. 14, pp. 1932–1941, 2012.

[2] Y. N. Singh, "Human recognition using Fisher's discriminant analysis of heartbeat interval features and ECG morphology," *Neurocomputing*, vol. 167, pp. 322–335, 2015.

[3] G. L. Marcialis and F. Roli, "Fusion of face recognition algorithms for video-based surveillance systems," in *Multisensor Surveillance Systems: The Fusion Perspective*, pp. 235–249, Springer US, Boston, Mass, USA, 2003.

[4] A. Mian, M. Bennamoun, and R. Owens, "2D and 3D multimodal hybrid face recognition," in *Computer Vision—ECCV 2006*, vol. 3953 of *Lecture Notes in Computer Science*, pp. 344–355, Springer, Berlin, Germany, 2006.

[5] S. M. Zakariya, R. Ali, and M. A. Lone, "Automatic face recognition using multi-algorithmic approaches," in *Contemporary Computing*, S. Aluru, S. Bandyopadhyay, and U. V. Catalyurek, Eds., vol. 168 of *Communications in Computer and Information Science*, pp. 501–512, Springer, 2011.

[6] S. Kar, S. Hiremath, D. G. Joshi, V. K. Chadda, and A. Bajpai, "A multi-algorithmic face recognition system," in *Proceedings of the 14th International Conference on Advanced Computing and Communications (ADCOM '06)*, pp. 321–326, Surathkal, India, December 2006.

[7] M. A. Lone, S. M. Zakariya, and R. Ali, "Automatic face recognition system by combining four individual algorithms," in *Proceedings of the International Conference on Computational Intelligence and Communication Systems (CICN '11)*, pp. 222–226, October 2011.

[8] M. Imran, S. Noushath, A. Abdesselam, K. Jetly, and Karthikeyan, "Efficient multi-algorithmic approaches for face recognition using subspace methods," in *Proceedings of the 1st International Conference on Communications, Signal Processing and Their Applications (ICCSPA '13)*, pp. 1–6, IEEE, Sharjah, United Arab Emirates, February 2013.

[9] R. Shyam and Y. N. Singh, "Identifying individuals using multi-modal face recognition techniques," *Procedia Computer Science*, vol. 48, pp. 666–672, 2015.

[10] M. A. Turk and A. P. Pentland, "Eigenfaces for recognition," *Journal of Cognitive Neuroscience*, vol. 3, no. 1, pp. 71–86, 1991.

[11] T. Ojala, M. Pietikäinen, and D. Harwood, "A comparative study of texture measures with classification based on feature distributions," *Pattern Recognition*, vol. 29, no. 1, pp. 51–59, 1996.

[12] T. Ojala, M. Pietikäinen, and T. Mäenpää, "Multiresolution gray-scale and rotation invariant texture classification with local binary patterns," *IEEE Transactions on Pattern Analysis and Machine Intelligence*, vol. 24, no. 7, pp. 971–987, 2002.

[13] P. N. Belhumeur, J. P. Hespanha, and D. J. Kriegman, "Eigenfaces vs. fisherfaces: recognition using class specific linear projection," *IEEE Transactions on Pattern Analysis and Machine Intelligence*, vol. 19, no. 7, pp. 711–720, 1997.

[14] R. Shyam and Y. N. Singh, "Face recognition using augmented local binary pattern and Bray Curtis dissimilarity metric," in *Proceedings of the 2nd International Conference on Signal Processing and Integrated Networks (SPIN '15)*, pp. 779–784, Noida, India, February 2015.

[15] R. Shyam and Y. N. Singh, "Analysis of local descriptors for human face recognition," in *Proceedings of 3rd International Conference on Advanced Computing, Networking and Informatics: ICACNI 2015, Volume 1*, vol. 43 of *Smart Innovation, Systems and Technologies*, pp. 263–269, Springer, Berlin, Germany, 2015.

[16] R. Shyam and Y. N. Singh, "Recognizing individuals from unconstrained facial images," in *Intelligent Systems Technologies and Applications*, S. Berretti, S. M. Thampi, and P. R. Srivastava, Eds., vol. 384 of *Advances in Intelligent Systems and Computing*, pp. 383–392, Springer, 2016.

[17] F. S. Samaria and A. C. Harter, "Parameterisation of a stochastic model for human face identification," in *Proceedings of the 2nd IEEE Workshop on Applications of Computer Vision*, pp. 138–142, Sarasota, Fla, USA, December 1994.

[18] G. B. Huang, M. Ramesh, T. Berg, and E. Learned-Miller, "Labeled faces in the wild: a database for studying face recognition in unconstrained environments," Tech. Rep. 07-49, University of Massachusetts, Amherst, Mass, USA, 2007.

[19] R. Shyam and Y. N. Singh, "A taxonomy of 2D and 3D face recognition methods," in *Proceedings of the 1st International Conference on Signal Processing and Integrated Networks (SPIN '14)*, pp. 749–754, IEEE, Noida, India, February 2014.

[20] R. Shyam and Y. N. Singh, "Automatic face recognition in digital world," *International Journal of Advances in Computing and Information Technology*, vol. 2, no. 1, pp. 64–70, 2015.

[21] A. S. Nicole, "Facial comparisons by subject matter experts: their role in biometrics and their training," in *Advances in Biometrics: Third International Conference on Biometrics (ICB '09), Alghero, Italy, June 2009*, Lecture Notes in Computer Science, pp. 161–168, Springer, 2009.

[22] J. Lu, K. N. Plataniotis, and A. N. Venetsanopoulos, "Face recognition using LDA-based algorithms," *IEEE Transactions on Neural Networks*, vol. 14, no. 1, pp. 195–200, 2003.

[23] M. S. Bartlett, J. R. Movellan, and T. J. Sejnowski, "Face recognition by independent component analysis," *IEEE Transactions on Neural Networks*, vol. 13, no. 6, pp. 1450–1464, 2002.

[24] L. Wiskott, J.-M. Fellous, N. Krüger, and C. D. Von Malsburg, "Face recognition by elastic bunch graph matching," *IEEE Transactions on Pattern Analysis and Machine Intelligence*, vol. 19, no. 7, pp. 775–779, 1997.

[25] D. G. Lowe, "Distinctive image features from scale-invariant keypoints," *International Journal of Computer Vision*, vol. 60, no. 2, pp. 91–110, 2004.

[26] H. Bay, A. Ess, T. Tuytelaars, and L. Van Gool, "Speeded-Up Robust Features (SURF)," *Computer Vision and Image Understanding*, vol. 110, no. 3, pp. 346–359, 2008.

[27] R. A. Fisher, "The use of multiple measurements in taxonomic problems," *Annals of Eugenics*, vol. 7, no. 2, pp. 179–188, 1936.

[28] R. Shyam and Y. N. Singh, "Robustness of score normalization in multibiometric systems," in *Information Systems Security*, vol. 9478 of *Lecture Notes in Computer Science*, pp. 542–550, Springer, Berlin, Germany, 2015.

[29] Y. N. Singh and P. Gupta, "Quantitative evaluation of normalization techniques of matching scores in multimodal biometric systems," in *Advances in Biometrics: International Conference, ICB 2007, Seoul, Korea, August 27–29, 2007. Proceedings*, vol. 4642 of *Lecture Notes in Computer Science*, pp. 574–583, Springer, Berlin, Germany, 2007.

[30] J. Kittler, M. Hatef, R. P. W. Duin, and J. Matas, "On combining classifiers," *IEEE Transactions on Pattern Analysis and Machine Intelligence*, vol. 20, no. 3, pp. 226–239, 1998.

[31] A. Jain, K. Nandakumar, and A. Ross, "Score normalization in multimodal biometric systems," *Pattern Recognition*, vol. 38, no. 12, pp. 2270–2285, 2005.

[32] R. Shyam and Y. N. Singh, "Evaluation of eigenfaces and fisherfaces using bray curtis dissimilarity metric," in *Proceedings of the 9th IEEE International Conference on Industrial and Information Systems (ICIIS '14)*, pp. 1–6, Gwalior, India, December 2014.

9

Parallel Nonnegative Matrix Factorization with Manifold Regularization

Fudong Liu ⓘ**, Zheng Shan, and Yihang Chen**

State Key Laboratory of Mathematical Engineering and Advanced Computing, Zhengzhou, Henan 450001, China

Correspondence should be addressed to Fudong Liu; lwfydy@126.com

Academic Editor: Tongliang Liu

Nonnegative matrix factorization (NMF) decomposes a high-dimensional nonnegative matrix into the product of two reduced dimensional nonnegative matrices. However, conventional NMF neither qualifies large-scale datasets as it maintains all data in memory nor preserves the geometrical structure of data which is needed in some practical tasks. In this paper, we propose a parallel NMF with manifold regularization method (PNMF-M) to overcome the aforementioned deficiencies by parallelizing the manifold regularized NMF on distributed computing system. In particular, PNMF-M distributes both data samples and factor matrices to multiple computing nodes instead of loading the whole dataset in a single node and updates both factor matrices locally on each node. In this way, PNMF-M succeeds to resolve the pressure of memory consumption for large-scale datasets and to speed up the computation by parallelization. For constructing the adjacency matrix in manifold regularization, we propose a two-step distributed graph construction method, which is proved to be equivalent to the batch construction method. Experimental results on popular text corpora and image datasets demonstrate that PNMF-M significantly improves both scalability and time efficiency of conventional NMF thanks to the parallelization on distributed computing system; meanwhile it significantly enhances the representation ability of conventional NMF thanks to the incorporated manifold regularization.

1. Introduction

Data representation is a fundamental problem in data analysis. A good representation typically uncovers the latent structure of a dataset by reducing the dimensionality of data. Several methods including principal component analysis (PCA), linear discriminant analysis (LDA), and vector quantization (VQ) have addressed this issue. Recently, nonnegative matrix factorization (NMF) [1] incorporates nonnegativity constraint to obtain parts-based representation of data, and thus it has been widely applied in many applications, such as document clustering [2, 3], image recognition [4, 5], audio processing [6], and video processing [7].

However, conventional NMF suffers from a few deficiencies: (1) conventional NMF usually works in batch mode and requires all data to reside in memory, and this leads to tremendous storage overhead as the increase of the data samples and (2) conventional NMF ignores the geometrical structure embedded in data and causes unsatisfactory representation ability. To overcome the first deficiency, either

parallel or distributed algorithms have been proposed for NMF to fit for large-scale datasets. Kanjani [8] utilized multithreading to develop a parallel NMF (PNMF) based on multicore machine. Robila and Maciak [9] introduced two thread-level parallel versions for traditional multiplicative solution and adaptive projected gradient method. However, their methods are prohibited for large-scale datasets due to the memory limitation of a single computer. Liu et al. [10] proposed a distributed NMF (DNMF) to analyze large-scale web dyadic data and verified its effectiveness on distributed computing systems. Dong et al. [11] also attempted to design a PNMF based on the distributed memory platform with the message passing interface library. Although all the above parallel NMF algorithms achieve a considerable speedup in terms of scalability, they cannot consider the geometric structure in dataset. To overcome the second deficiency, Cai et al. [12] proposed graph-regularized NMF (GNMF) which extended conventional NMF by constructing an affinity graph [13] to encode the geometrical information of data and enhanced representation ability. Gu et al. [14] further extended GNMF to avoid trivial solution and scale transfer problems by imposing a normalized cut-like constraint on the cluster assignment matrix. Lu et al. [15] incorporated manifold regularization into NMF for hyperspectral unmixing and obtained desirable unmixing performance. These improved algorithms get better representation ability but work inefficiently for large-scale datasets. Liu et al. [16] introduced the geometric structure of data into incremental NMF [17, 18] and utilized two efficient sparse approximations, buffering and random projected tree, to process large-scale datasets. Yu et al. [19] also presented an incremental GNMF algorithm to improve scalability. But these algorithms only performed well for incremental or streaming datasets and could not deal with large-scale batch datasets. In addition, Guan et al. [20] and Liu et al. [21], respectively, introduce Manhattan distance and large-cone penalty for NMF to improve representation and generalization ability.

In conclusion, none of the above works can simultaneously overcome both deficiencies due to the great computation for calculating the decomposition and the storage requirement of the adjacency matrix. In this paper, we take the best of advantages of parallel NMF and manifold regularized NMF and design a parallel NMF with manifold regularization method (PNMF-M) by parallelizing manifold regularized NMF on distributed computing systems. In particular, PNMF-M distributes both data samples and factor matrices to multiple computing nodes in a balanced way and parallelizes the update for both factor matrices locally on each node. Since the graph construction is the bottleneck of the computation of PNMF-M, we adopt a two-step distributed graph construction method to compute the adjacency matrix and obtain an adjacent graph equivalent to that constructed in batch mode. Experimental results on popular text corpora and image datasets show that PNMF-M not only outperforms conventional NMF in terms of both scalability and time efficiency by parallelization, but also significantly enhances the representation ability of conventional NMF by incorporating manifold regularization.

2. Related Work

This section gives a brief review of PNMF, GNMF, and their corresponding popular algorithms. Details are as follows.

2.1. PNMF. Due to working in batch mode, conventional NMF requires to process masses of large matrix operations, which is inevitably confronted with high time overhead. Parallel processing is often an efficient method to speed up computing intensive algorithms. In general, the parallelism of the algorithms is embodied in two aspects. The first aspect is computation flow, but unfortunately conventional NMF is highly correlated among the computing steps and could not be decomposed into uncorrelated tasks. So the second aspect, data structure, is taken into account. A feasible plan is to divide the data into small blocks and assign them to different processing units.

Robila and Maciak [9] implement a common example of parallel NMF. Let the input data matrix $X = [x_1, \ldots, x_n] \in \mathbb{R}^{m \times n}$, the basis matrix $U \in \mathbb{R}^{m \times k}$, and the coefficient matrix

$V \in \mathbb{R}^{k \times n}$. Given that there are p processing units, both k and n are exactly divisible by p. They divide the above three matrices into p equally sized submatrices by column; that is, $X = [X_1, \ldots, X_p]$, $U = [U_1, \ldots, U_p]$, and $V = [V_1, \ldots, V_p]$. They still minimize the cost function of conventional NMF and obtain the update rules for V and U as follows:

$$\left(V_s^{t+1}\right)_{rj} = \left(V_s^t\right)_{rj} \frac{\left(U^{t^{\mathrm{T}}} X_s\right)_{rj}}{\left(U^{t^{\mathrm{T}}} U^t V_s^t\right)_{rj}}$$

$$\left(U_s^{t+1}\right)_{ir} = \left(U_s^t\right)_{ir} \frac{\left(X V_s^{t+1^{\mathrm{T}}}\right)_{ir}}{\left(U^t V_s^{t+1} V_s^{t+1^{\mathrm{T}}}\right)_{ir}}, \tag{1}$$

where t denotes the iteration number, $s = 1, \ldots, p$, $i = (s-1) * (k/p) + 1, \ldots, s * (k/p)$, $j = (s-1) * (n/p) + 1, \ldots, s * (n/p)$, and $r = 1, \ldots, k$.

By parallelizing conventional NMF, PNMF can achieve the same representation ability, while reducing the time complexity.

2.2. GNMF. In common, conventional NMF performs the factorization in the Euclidean space, which cannot get satisfactory solution. Based on manifold assumption [22], GNMF embeds the intrinsic geometric structure of the data space in conventional NMF to overcome the above defect.

One of the representative algorithms for GNMF is proposed by Cai et al. [12]. They define the graph weight matrix $W \in \mathbb{R}^{n \times n}$, which is obtained by computing the weight relationship between any two data samples in input data matrix X. Furthermore, another two matrices are derived from W. One is the diagonal matrix D whose entries are row or column sum of W, that is, $D_{ii} = \sum_{j=1}^n W_{ij} = \sum_{i=1}^n W_{ij}$, and the other is $L = D - W$, which is called graph Laplacian. They utilize Lagrangian multiplier method to solve the above problem and derive the following update rules:

$$\left(V^{t+1}\right)_{rj} = \left(V^t\right)_{rj} \frac{\left(U^{t^{\mathrm{T}}} X + \lambda V^t W\right)_{rj}}{\left(U^{t^{\mathrm{T}}} U^t V^t + \lambda V^t D\right)_{rj}} \tag{2}$$

$$\left(U^{t+1}\right)_{ir} = \left(U^t\right)_{ir} \frac{\left(X V^{t+1^{\mathrm{T}}}\right)_{ir}}{\left(U^t V^{t+1} V^{t+1^{\mathrm{T}}}\right)_{ir}}, \tag{3}$$

where $\lambda \geq 0$ is the regularization parameter, t denotes the iteration number, $i = 1, \ldots, m$, $j = 1, \ldots, n$, and $r = 1, \ldots, k$.

By incorporating the geometric structure, GNMF can significantly improve representation ability in comparison to conventional NMF.

3. Parallel Manifold Regularized Nonnegative Matrix Factorization

In conventional GNMF, the intrinsic low dimensional manifold structure embedded in the dataset is expressed by n by n graph weight matrix W. From the update rule (2), we can

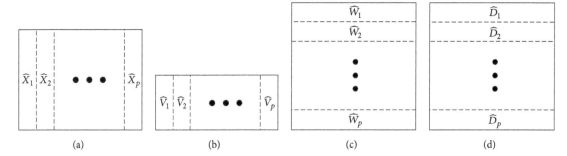

FIGURE 1: Data partitioning strategy for updating V in PNMF-M.

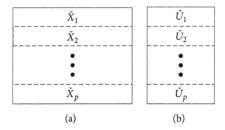

FIGURE 2: Data partitioning strategy for updating U in PNMF-M.

easily see that the manifold terms in conventional GNMF give rise to a lot of additional computations compared with NMF. Therefore, we describe the proposed PNMF-M in this section, which improves this issue by distributing both data samples and factor matrices to multiple computing nodes while parallelizing the update for both factor matrices and manifold construction.

3.1. Data Partition and Distributed Computing.
We still assume $X \in \mathbb{R}^{m \times n}$, $U \in \mathbb{R}^{m \times k}$, $V \in \mathbb{R}^{k \times n}$, $W \in \mathbb{R}^{n \times n}$, and p as the input data matrix, basis matrix, coefficient matrix, graph weight matrix, and number of processors, respectively.

PNMF-M divides X and V into p blocks in the column direction, namely, $X = [\widehat{X}_1, \widehat{X}_2, \ldots, \widehat{X}_p]$, $V = [\widehat{V}_1, \widehat{V}_2, \ldots, \widehat{V}_p]$, as shown in Figures 1(a) and 1(b); thus each of the first $p-1$ blocks consists of $\lceil n/p \rceil$ columns and the last one consists of $n - \lceil n/p \rceil \times (p-1)$ columns. Similarly, PNMF-M divides X and U into p blocks in the row direction as shown in Figures 2(a) and 2(b); that is, $X = [\check{X}_1^T, \check{X}_2^T, \ldots, \check{X}_p^T]^T$, $U = [\check{U}_1^T, \check{U}_2^T, \ldots, \check{U}_p^T]^T$, so each of the first $p-1$ blocks consists of $\lceil m/p \rceil$ rows and the last one consists of $m - \lceil m/p \rceil \times (p-1)$ rows.

As the scale of W is much larger than those of X, U, and V, the weight matrix W should be distributed across p processors. The same is true for D. To this end, PNMF-M divides W and D into p blocks in the row direction, namely, $W = [\widehat{W}_1^T, \widehat{W}_2^T, \ldots, \widehat{W}_p^T]^T$, $D = [\widehat{D}_1^T, \widehat{D}_2^T, \ldots, \widehat{D}_p^T]^T$. In this way, each of the first $p-1$ blocks is a $\lceil n/p \rceil \times n$-dimensional matrix and the last one is a $(n - \lceil n/p \rceil \times (p-1)) \times n$-dimensional matrix, as described in Figures 1(c) and 1(d).

According to [12], to take the advantage of manifold regularization, PNMF-M optimizes the following objective:

$$F = \|X - UV\|_F^2 + \lambda Tr\left(VLV^T\right), \quad (4)$$

where λ denotes the regularization parameter and $L = D - W$.

Since each update for U (or V) needs the latest value of V (or U), it is difficult to distribute the updates for them on p processors. According to the aforementioned data partitioning strategy, PNMF-M reformulates the multiplicative update rules in [12], at the tth iteration, as follows:

$$\left(\widehat{V}_s^{t+1}\right)_{rj} = \left(\widehat{V}_s^t\right)_{rj} \frac{\left(U^{t^T}\widehat{X}_s\right)_{rj} + \lambda \sum_{f=1}^p \left(\widehat{V}_f^t \widehat{W}_f\right)_{rj}}{\left(U^{t^T}U^t\widehat{V}_s^t\right)_{rj} + \lambda \sum_{f=1}^p \left(\widehat{V}_f^t \widehat{D}_f\right)_{rj}} \quad (5)$$

$$\left(\check{U}_s^{t+1}\right)_{ir} = \left(\check{U}_s^t\right)_{ir} \frac{\left(\check{X}_s V^{t+1^T}\right)_{ir}}{\left(\check{U}_s^t V^{t+1} V^{t+1^T}\right)_{ir}} \quad (6)$$

where t denotes the iteration number, $s = 1, \ldots, p$, $i = (s-1) \times \lceil m/p \rceil + 1, \ldots, s \times \lceil m/p \rceil$, $j = (s-1) \times \lceil n/p \rceil + 1, \ldots, s \times \lceil n/p \rceil$ (note that when $s = p$, $i = (p-1) \times \lceil m/p \rceil + 1, \ldots, m$, $j = (p-1) \times \lceil n/p \rceil + 1, \ldots, n$), with $r = 1, \ldots, k$.

In each iteration round, PNMF-M updates each block of V and U locally by (5) and (6), respectively, and inserts the reduction for the whole factors among processors between (5) and (6). Since our algorithm is developed on a distributed computing system with 40 Gb/s Infiniband interconnection network whose communication overloads among processors are relatively low, this updating strategy significantly speeds up the calculation of manifold regularized NMF by the distributed computing.

3.2. Manifold Construction.
Besides data partition and distributed computing, manifold construction is another key factor in PNMF-M. In the update rule (5), updating $\widehat{V}_s$ in the

> **Input**: data matrix $X \in \mathbb{R}^{m \times n}$, reduced dimensionality $k \in \mathbb{N}$, regularization parameter $\lambda \in \mathbb{R}$, tolerance $\tau \in \mathbb{R}$, parallelism $p \in \mathbb{N}$
> **Output**: basis matrix $U \in \mathbb{R}^{m \times k}$, coefficient matrix $V \in \mathbb{R}^{k \times n}$
> (1) Assign $\widehat{X}_i$, $\breve{X}_i$, $\breve{U}_i$, and $\widehat{V}_i$ to P_i as described in Figures 1 and 2
> (2) Compute $\text{idx}(i)$ from $\widehat{X}_i$
> (3) Send $\widehat{X}_i$ to the other $p - 1$ processes P_j
> (4) Receive $\widehat{X}_j$ from the other $p - 1$ processes P_j to obtain $\text{idx}(j)$
> (5) Merge all p index sets to construct $\widehat{W}_i$
> (6) **repeat**
> (7)   Apply (5) to update $\widehat{V}_i^{t+1}$
> (8)   Send $\widehat{V}_i^{t+1}$ to the other $p - 1$ processes P_j
> (9)   Receive $\widehat{V}_j^{t+1}$ from the other $p - 1$ processes P_j to constitute V^{t+1}
> (10)   Apply (6) to update $\breve{U}_i^{t+1}$
> (11)   Send $\breve{U}_i^{t+1}$ to the other $p - 1$ processes P_j
> (12)   Receive $\breve{U}_j^{t+1}$ from the other $p - 1$ processes P_j to constitute U^{t+1}
> (13) **until** convergence
> (14) **return** $\breve{U}_i$ and $\widehat{V}_i$

ALGORITHM 1: PNMF-M procedure.

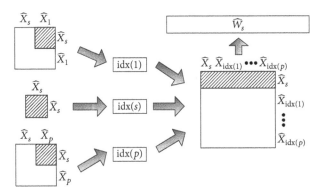

FIGURE 3: Manifold construction in PNMF-M.

sth processing unit requires the products of $\widehat{V}_f$ and $\widehat{W}_f$ in all p processing units. However, directly constructing the global adjacency graph from the input data matrix X costs $\Theta(n^2)$ time in manifold learning and heavily prohibits manifold regularized NMF for large-scale datasets. In this subsection, we design an efficient construction method by means of the communications between different processing units.

In Figure 1(c), we can see that the sth processor simply holds $\widehat{W}_s$ which is a part of the global manifold W and represents the weight relationship between data samples in $\widehat{X}_s$ and all the data samples in X. Originally, it needs the entire data matrix X to construct $\widehat{W}_s$, and the tremendous storage requirement becomes the bottleneck which restricts the scalability of the algorithm. It is therefore critical to construct the manifold in an efficient way. To overcome this drawback, in this paper, we design a two-step manifold construction method by means of high-throughput interconnection network.

Figure 3 depicts the details of the construction method. Without loss of generality, we take the sth processor P_s as an example to demonstrate both steps. In the first step, PNMF-M

first constructs locally an adjacency subgraph from $\widehat{X}_s$ in P_s relative to the adjacency graph constructed from X and thus obtains an index set $\text{idx}(s)$ which contains local neighbor indices of each data sample in $\widehat{X}_s$. Then, P_s utilizes high-throughput interconnection network to take turns to receive data samples from the other $s - 1$ remote processors. When $\widehat{X}_f$ comes, where $f = 1, 2, \ldots, p$ except s, PNMF-M reconstructs an adjacency subgraph from $\widehat{X}_s$ and $\widehat{X}_f$ and obtains an index set $\text{idx}(f)$ which contains remote neighbor indices of each data sample in $\widehat{X}_s$. In the second step, PNMF-M computes the weight relationship between $\widehat{X}_s$ and data sample matrix $\widehat{X}_{\text{idx}(f)}$ indicated by each index set $\text{idx}(f)$ and picks out the final neighbor indices of each data sample in $\widehat{X}_s$ to construct a manifold $\widehat{W}_s$ in P_s.

In our method, we select k-nearest neighbors (k-NN) mode in [22] to construct the graph, and thus the proposed construction method can be proved to get a manifold equivalent to the batch construction method. Since each processor can discard data sample matrix received from remote processors after constructing adjacency subgraph, PNMF-M greatly reduces the storage overhead and improves the scalability.

3.3. PNMF-M Algorithm. We are now ready to alternatively apply the update rules (5) and (6) to solve PNMF-M. Algorithm 1 shows the pseudocode on distributed computing systems. Given that p processes exist in PNMF-M, Algorithm 1 first partitions data samples and factor matrices according to Figures 1 and 2 and assigns the associated submatrices to each process P_i (Statement (1)). Then, P_i begins to locally construct its private weight matrix in parallel. It first computes $\text{idx}(i)$ from $\widehat{X}_i$ in the local process (Statement (2)) and then receives $\widehat{X}_j$ from the other $p - 1$ processes P_j to obtain $\text{idx}(j)$ (Statement (4)). Next, it merges all p index sets to construct $\widehat{W}_i$ (Statement (5)). Then, P_i alternatively employs the update

TABLE 1: Statistics of benchmark datasets.

	Reuters	TDT2	MNIST	COIL
Number of samples	21578	64527	70000	7200
Number of samples used	8067	9394	10000	7200
Number of attributes	18933	36771	784	1024
Number of clusters	135	100	10	100
Number of clusters used	30	30	10	100
Max. cluster size	3713	1844	1135	72
Min. cluster size	18	52	892	72
Med. cluster size	45	131	1009	72
Avg. cluster size	269	313	1000	72

rules (5) and (6) to obtain its private coefficient submatrix $\widehat{V}_i$ (Statement (7)) and basis submatrix $\breve{U}_i$ (Statement (10)) until the termination condition for the iteration is satisfied.

Notice that updating $\widehat{V}_i$ requires the basis matrix U which consists of p submatrices $\breve{U}_j$ distributed across each process P_j, where $j = 1, 2, \ldots, p$, as shown in (5). Hence, Algorithm 1 has to insert the interprocess communication to implement the reduction for U before updating $\widehat{V}_i$ (Statement (11)-(12)). Similarly, Algorithm 1 also requires increasing the interprocess communication to achieve the reduction for V before updating $\widehat{U}_i$ (Statements (8) and (9)).

4. Experimental Evaluation

In this section, we verify the proposed PNMF-M by comparing it with PNMF in [11] and GNMF in [12], which incorporate parallel computing and manifold regularization into NMF, respectively.

4.1. Datasets and Evaluation Metrics. We choose Reuters and TDT2 text corpora widely used for document clustering and MNIST and COIL100 image databases used for pattern recognition and machine learning as our benchmark datasets. Table 1 lists their detailed statistics.

In this experiment, we utilize canonical k-means clustering method to transform the coefficient matrix obtained by our algorithm into the labels of data samples, then compare them with the labels provided by the benchmark datasets, and finally use the accuracy (AC) and the normalized mutual information (NMI) to evaluate the clustering performance of each tested algorithm. For the way to compute AC and NMI, Xu et al. [2] and Cai et al. [12] have given detailed description, so we need not explain them here.

To evaluate the scalability of our proposed algorithm, we record the execution time of each tested algorithm and utilize the speedup (SP) and time cost (TC) as metrics, where SP denotes the speedup obtained by PNMF-M relative to GNMF and TC denotes the time cost introduced by PNMF-M relative to PNMF; that is,

$$
\begin{aligned}
\text{SP} &= \frac{\text{Time}_{\text{GNMF}}}{\text{Time}_{\text{PNMF-M}}} \\
\text{TC} &= \frac{\text{Time}_{\text{PNMF-M}}}{\text{Time}_{\text{PNMF}}}.
\end{aligned}
\tag{7}
$$

TABLE 2: Experimental parameters for clustering performance evaluation.

Experimental parameter	Value
Regularization parameter (λ)	100
Tolerance (τ)	10^{-4}
Neighbor mode	k-NN ($k = 5$)
Parallelism (p)	ceil($n/1000$)

4.2. Clustering Performance Comparisons. We collect data samples in multiple clusters randomly selected from the benchmark datasets and provide them and the corresponding cluster number to each tested algorithm. All the tested algorithms are run 50 times on different data subsets each of which consists of some part of clusters randomly selected from the whole clusters. We compute the mean of them for each given cluster number as the final clustering performance. At the same time, we also compute the mean of SP and TC to verify the effectiveness of PNMF-M.

Table 2 lists the values of main experimental parameters for clustering performance evaluation. In our experiment, we set regularization parameter to 100 and the tolerance to 10^{-4} as the termination condition of each iteration. In addition, we employ k-NN definition to construct the graph weight matrix and set k to 5. For parallel algorithms, we adaptively select the parallelism p according to the number of samples n and set $p = \text{ceil}(n)$, where ceil(x) means rounding up x to an integer.

Figures 4–7 report AC and NMI versus the cluster number on four benchmark datasets, respectively. Figure 8 reports SP and TC of our algorithm versus the cluster number on four benchmark datasets.

Through comparative analysis, we can obtain the following observations:

(1) Since the manifold constructed in PNMF-M is equivalent to that constructed in GNMF, both obtain the same clustering performance on all four benchmark datasets.

(2) PNMF-M gets better clustering performance than PNMF in terms of both AC and NMI, because PNMF-M incorporates the intrinsic geometric structure of data and obtains the same clustering performance as GNMF, while PNMF ignores the manifold structure of the dataset.

(3) GNMF directly constructs the manifold from the entire data matrix in a single processing node, which incurs

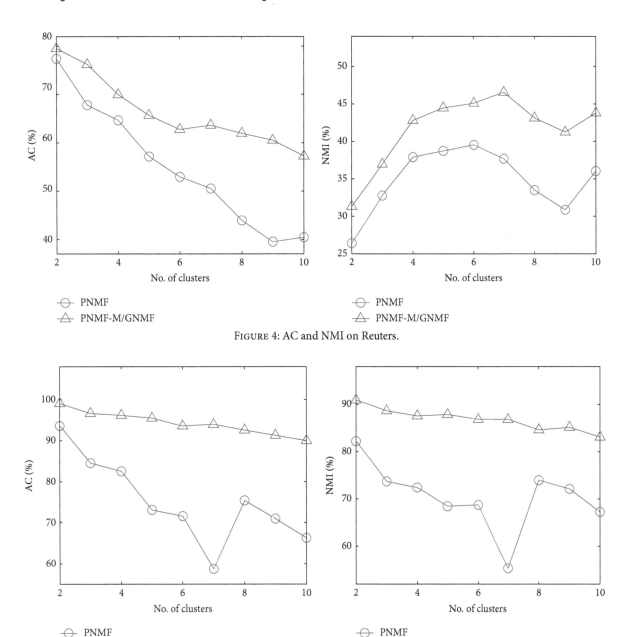

FIGURE 4: AC and NMI on Reuters.

FIGURE 5: AC and NMI on TDT2.

tremendous computation and storage overhead. In contrast, PNMF-M designs a two-step distributed method to accelerate the manifold construction. In addition, PNMF-M parallelizes the update procedure to eliminate large size matrix operations in the update rules and further reduces the computation and storage overhead. According to Figure 8, PNMF-M acquires about 4–10 times speedup on four benchmark datasets relative to GNMF.

(4) Compared with PNMF, PNMF-M requires to construct the manifold in parallel and introduce the manifold term into the update rule for the coefficient matrix, which inevitably increases the computation overhead of the algorithm to some extent. PNMF-M pays about 2–4 times cost on four benchmark datasets relative to PNMF, as shown in Figure 8.

4.3. Scalability Comparisons. We collect increasing scale data subsets in all the clusters randomly selected from the benchmark datasets as the input datasets of each tested algorithm, run them in the same hardware configuration and software environment as listed in Table 3, and verify the scalability by comparing their execution time and evaluating SP achieved by PNMF-M. In our experiments, we set parallelism to 2 (PNMF-M2), 4 (PNMF-M4), 8 (PNMF-M8), and 16 (PNMF-M16) for PNMF-M, respectively.

Figure 9 reports SP achieved by PNMF-M with different parallelism on four benchmark datasets relative to GNMF. We can draw the conclusions from it as follows:

(1) When the number of input data samples is small (below about $5 * 10^3$), SP obtained by PNMF-M is less than the corresponding parallelism. This is because all processing

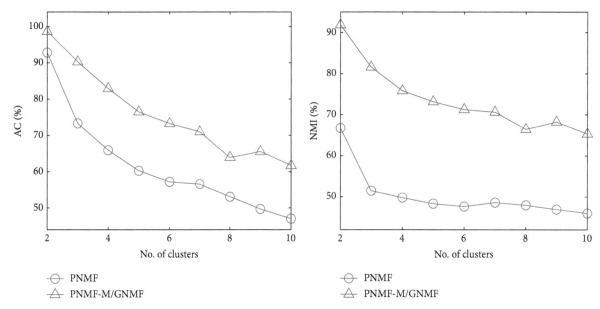

FIGURE 6: AC and NMI on MNIST.

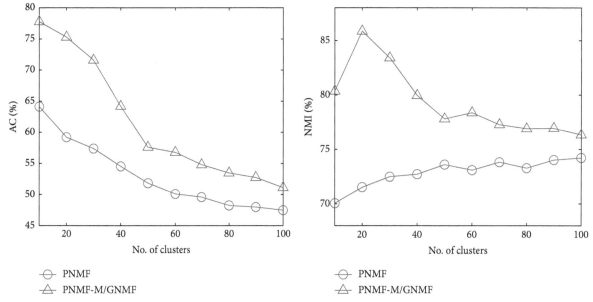

FIGURE 7: AC and NMI on COIL100.

TABLE 3: Experimental environment for scalability evaluation.

Number of nodes	16
Memory capacity on a single node	16 TB
Maximum number of threads	24
Operating system	Ubuntu
Interconnection network	Infiniband
Peak bandwidth of network	40 Gb/s

nodes need to communicate with each other to construct the manifold during the execution of PNMF-M, which introduces communication latency into parallel computation.

(2) When the number of input data samples is large (above about $5 * 10^3$), SP achieved by PNMF-M is more than the corresponding parallelism. The reason is that all the input data samples reside in external storage before the execution of each tested algorithm. But GNMF requires all data to be loaded into memory during its execution, which goes beyond the memory capacity in a single processing node and has to load large amounts of data samples by virtual memory. To address the problem, PNMF-M divides the input data into multiple subsets and stores them in different processing node, which reduces memory access overhead caused by loading data.

(3) In the case of small input data samples, PNMF-M achieves better SP on MNIST and COIL100 than on Reuters

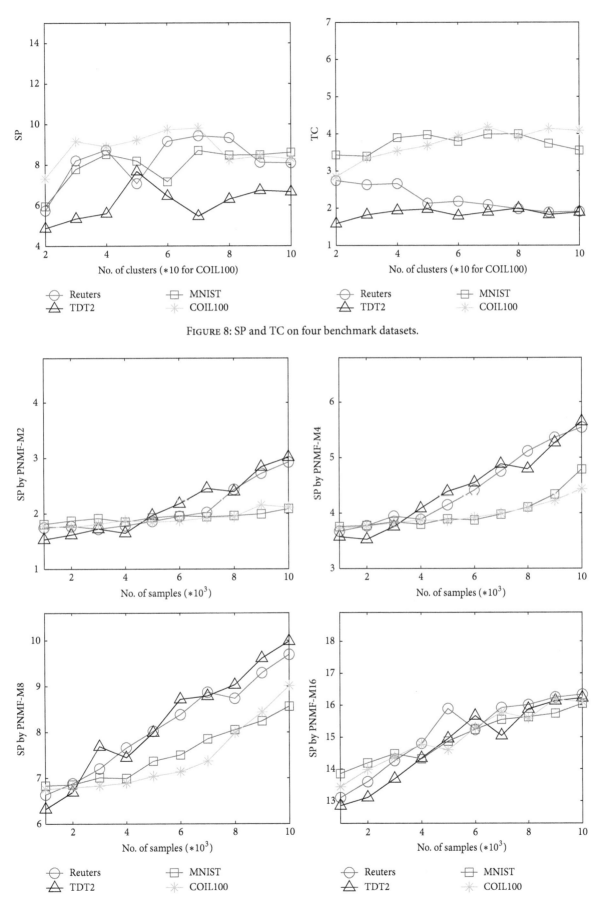

FIGURE 8: SP and TC on four benchmark datasets.

FIGURE 9: Speedup by PNMF-M on four benchmark datasets.

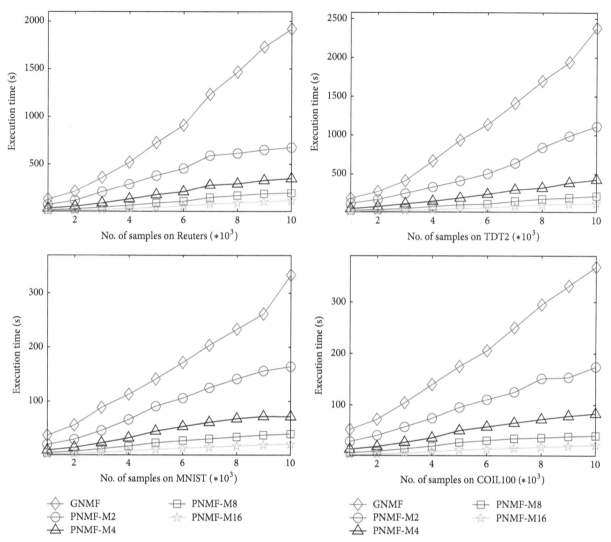

FIGURE 10: Execution time on four benchmark datasets.

and TDT2 when parallelism for PNMF-M is equal to 2, 4, and 8. But the result is the opposite with the increase of the number of input data samples. The main reason for this result is twofold: one is based on the two analyses mentioned in (1) and (2) and the other is that memory and communication overhead for a single data sample in Reuters and TDT2 are larger because the dimensionality of data in them is higher than that in MNIST and COIL100. But when parallelism for PNMF-M increases to 16, the overhead caused by high dimensionality is spread over each processing node. Hence, SP obtained by PNMF-M16 has little difference among four benchmark datasets.

In addition, we also compare the execution time of all the tested algorithms on four benchmark datasets, as shown in Figure 10. It is obvious that the increasingly widening gap of the execution time exists between serial algorithm (GNMF) and parallel algorithms (PNMF-M2, PNMF-M4, PNMF-M8, and PNMF-M16). It is because GNMF involves lots of large size matrix operations during the manifold construction and updating procedure, and the time consumed by them grows nonlinearly as the number of data samples and attributes

increase, while PNMF-M transforms them into relatively small size matrix operations and utilizes multiple processing nodes to perform them in parallel. Hence, PNMF-M achieves better scalability than GNMF.

5. Conclusion

In this paper, we proposed a parallel nonnegative matrix factorization with regularization method (PNMF-M) which introduced manifold regularization into conventional NMF and parallelized it on distributed computing systems. In PNMF-M, besides the balanced data partition strategy, we conducted the update procedure in parallel. In particular, we presented a two-step distributed graph construction method and obtained a manifold equivalent to that constructed in batch mode. Experimental results showed that PNMF-M not only outperforms conventional NMF in terms of both scalability and time efficiency thanks to the parallelization, but also significantly enhances the representation ability of conventional NMF thanks to the manifold regularization.

Conflicts of Interest

The authors declare that there are no conflicts of interest regarding the publication of this paper.

References

[1] D. D. Lee and H. S. Seung, "Learning the parts of objects by non-negative matrix factorization," *Nature*, vol. 401, no. 6755, pp. 788–791, 1999.

[2] W. Xu, X. Liu, and Y. Gong, *Document clustering based on non-negative matrix factorization*, 2003, SIGIR, 2003.

[3] F. Shahnaz, M. W. Berry, V. P. Pauca, and R. J. Plemmons, "Document clustering using nonnegative matrix factorization," *Information Processing & Management*, vol. 42, no. 2, pp. 373–386, 2006.

[4] L. Miao and H. Qi, "Endmember extraction from highly mixed data using minimum volume constrained nonnegative matrix factorization," *IEEE Transactions on Geoscience and Remote Sensing*, vol. 45, no. 3, pp. 765–777, 2007.

[5] B. Shen and L. Si, "Non-negative matrix factorization clustering on multiple manifolds," in *Proceedings of the Twenty-Fourth AAAI Conference on Artificial Intelligence*, p. 575, 2010.

[6] R. Rui and C.-C. Bao, "Projective non-negative matrix factorization with Bregman divergence for musical instrument classification," in *Proceedings of the 2012 2nd IEEE International Conference on Signal Processing, Communications and Computing, ICSPCC 2012*, pp. 415–418, China, August 2012.

[7] O. Jenkins and M. Mataric, "Deriving action and behavior primitives from human motion data," in *Proceedings of the IROS 2002: IEEE/RSJ International Conference on Intelligent Robots and Systems*, pp. 2551–2556, Lausanne, Switzerland.

[8] K. Kanjani, "Parallel non-negative matrix factorization for document clustering," Tech. Rep., Texas AM University, 2007.

[9] S. A. Robila and L. G. Maciak, "Considerations on parallelizing nonnegative matrix factorization for hyperspectral data unmixing," *IEEE Geoscience and Remote Sensing Letters*, vol. 6, no. 1, pp. 57–61, 2009.

[10] C. Liu, H. Yang, J. Fan, L. He, and Y. Wang, "Distributed nonnegative matrix factorization for web-scale dyadic data analysis on MapReduce," in *WWW 2010*, pp. 681–690, USA.

[11] C. Dong, H. Zhao, and W. Wang, "Parallel nonnegative matrix factorization algorithm on the distributed memory platform," *International Journal of Parallel Programming*, vol. 38, no. 2, pp. 117–137, 2010.

[12] D. Cai, X. He, J. Han, and T. S. Huang, "Graph regularized nonnegative matrix factorization for data representation," *IEEE Transactions on Pattern Analysis and Machine Intelligence*, vol. 33, no. 8, pp. 1548–1560, 2011.

[13] M. Belkin, V. Sindhwani, and P. Niyogi, "Manifold regularization: a geometric framework for learning from labeled and unlabeled examples," *Journal of Machine Learning Research*, vol. 7, pp. 2399–2434, 2006.

[14] Q. Gu, C. Ding, and J. Han, "On trivial solution and scale transfer problems in graph regularized NMF," in *Proceedings of the 22nd International Joint Conference on Artificial Intelligence (IJCAI '11)*, pp. 1288–1293, Barcelona, Spain, July 2011.

[15] X. Lu, H. Wu, Y. Yuan, P. Yan, and X. Li, "Manifold regularized sparse NMF for hyperspectral unmixing," *IEEE Transactions on Geoscience and Remote Sensing*, vol. 51, no. 5, pp. 2815–2826, 2013.

[16] F. Liu, X. Yang, N. Guan, and X. Yi, "Online graph regularized non-negative matrix factorization for large-scale datasets," *Neurocomputing*, vol. 204, pp. 162–171, 2016.

[17] S. S. Bucak and B. Gunsel, "Video content representation by incremental non-negative matrix factorization," in *Proceedings of the 14th IEEE International Conference on Image Processing (ICIP '07)*, pp. 113–116, San Antonio, Tex, USA, September 2007.

[18] S. S. Bucak and B. Gunsel, "Incremental subspace learning via non-negative matrix factorization," *Pattern Recognition*, vol. 42, no. 5, pp. 788–797, 2009.

[19] Z.-Z. Yu, Y.-H. Liu, B. Li, S.-C. Pang, and C.-C. Jia, "Incremental graph regulated nonnegative matrix factorization for face recognition," *Journal of Applied Mathematics*, vol. 2014, Article ID 928051, 2014.

[20] N. Guan, D. Tao, Z. Luo, and J. Shawe-Taylor, "MahNMF: Manhattan non-negative matrix factorization," https://arxiv.org/abs/1207.3438.

[21] T. Liu, M. Gong, and D. Tao, "Large-cone nonnegative matrix factorization," *IEEE Transactions on Neural Networks and Learning Systems*, vol. 28, no. 9, pp. 2129–2142, 2017.

[22] M. Belkin and P. Niyogi, "Laplacian eigenmaps and spectral techniques for embedding and clustering," in *Advances in Neural Information Processing Systems*, vol. 14, pp. 585–591, 2001.

10

A Russian Keyword Spotting System based on Large Vocabulary Continuous Speech Recognition and Linguistic Knowledge

Valentin Smirnov,[1] **Dmitry Ignatov,**[1] **Michael Gusev,**[1] **Mais Farkhadov,**[2]
Natalia Rumyantseva,[3] **and Mukhabbat Farkhadova**[3]

[1]*Speech Drive LLC, Saint Petersburg, Russia*
[2]*V.A. Trapeznikov Institute of Control Sciences of RAS, Moscow, Russia*
[3]*RUDN University, Moscow, Russia*

Correspondence should be addressed to Mais Farkhadov; mais.farhadov@gmail.com

Academic Editor: Alexey Karpov

The paper describes the key concepts of a word spotting system for Russian based on large vocabulary continuous speech recognition. Key algorithms and system settings are described, including the pronunciation variation algorithm, and the experimental results on the real-life telecom data are provided. The description of system architecture and the user interface is provided. The system is based on CMU Sphinx open-source speech recognition platform and on the linguistic models and algorithms developed by Speech Drive LLC. The effective combination of baseline statistic methods, real-world training data, and the intensive use of linguistic knowledge led to a quality result applicable to industrial use.

1. Introduction

The need to understand business trends, ensure public security, and improve the quality of customer service has caused a sustainable development of speech analytics systems which transform speech data into a measurable and searchable index of words, phrases, and paralinguistic markers. Keyword spotting technology makes a substantial part of such systems. Modern keyword spotting engines usually rely on either of three approaches, namely, phonetic lattice search [1, 2], word-based models [3, 4], and large vocabulary speech recognition [5]. While each of the approaches has got its pros and cons [6] the latter starts to be prominent due to public availability of baseline algorithms, cheaper hardware to run intensive calculations required in LVCSR and, most importantly, high-quality results.

Most recently a number of innovative approaches to spoken term detection were offered such as various recognition system combination and score normalization, reporting 20% increase in spoken term detection quality (measured as ATWV) [7, 8]. Deep neural networks application in

LVCSR is starting to achieve wide adoption [9]. Thanks to the IARPA Babel program aimed at building systems that can be rapidly applied to any human language in order to provide effective search capability for analysts to efficiently process massive amounts of real-world recorded speech [10] in recent years wide research has been held to develop technologies for spoken term detection systems for low-resource languages. For example, [11] describes an approach for keyword spotting in Cantonese based on large vocabulary speech recognition and shows positive results of applying neural networks to recognition lattice rescoring. Reference [12] provides an extensive description of modern methods used to build a keyword spotting system for 10 low-resource languages with primary focus on Assamese, Bengali, Haitian Creole, Lao, and Zulu. Deep neural network acoustic models are used both as feature extractor for a GMM-based HMM system and to compute state posteriors and convert them into scaled likelihoods by normalizing by the state priors. Data augmentation via using multilingual bottleneck features is offered (the topic is also covered in [13]). Finally language independent and unsupervised acoustic models are trained for languages with no training data. An average MTWV reported for these languages ranges from 0.22 for Zulu to 0.67 for Haitian Creole. In [14] the use of recurrent neural networks for example-based word spotting in real time for English is described. Compared to more widespread text-based systems, this approach makes use of spoken examples of a keyword to build up a word-based model and then do the search within speech data. As an alternative to hybrid ANN-HMM approaches authors in [15] offer a pure NN based keyword search system for conversational telephone speech in Vietnamese and Lao. For Vietnamese the "pure" NN system provides ATWV comparable with that reported for a baseline hybrid system while working significantly faster (real-time factor 3.4 opposed to 5.3 for a hybrid system).

As high-quality language modeling is an indispensable part of any modern keyword spotting system, a lot of effort is now aimed at improving LMs. One of the most recent trends is to use web data in training. The advent of the Internet has provided rich amount of data to be easily available for speech recognition community [16]. This is of particular interest for low-resource languages and among most recent improvements [17] suggests an approach to effectively deal with the challenge of normalizing and filtering the web data for keyword spotting. Two methods are offered, one using perplexity ranking and the other using out-of-vocabulary words detection. This resulted in more than 2% absolute improvement in ATWV across 5 low-resourced languages. Reference [18] covers the aspect of augmenting baseline LMs with carefully chosen web data, showing that blogs and movie subtitles are more relevant for language modeling of conversational telephone speech and help to obtain large reductions in out-of-vocabulary keywords.

Russian research in the domain of speech recognition falls in line with global scientific trends. It is noteworthy however that most frequently the research is conducted to meet a more general target of creating LVCSR systems per se with no specific focus on spoken term detection. The most well-known systems include Yandex SpeechKit [19] used to recognize spoken search queries via web and mobile applications, real-time speech recognition system by Speech Technology Center [20] used for transcribing speech in the broadcasting news, LVCSR system developed by SPIIRAS [21, 22] used for recognizing speech in multimodal environments, and speech recognition system by scientific institute Specvuzavtomatika [23] based on deep neural networks.

Current paper presents the results of the ongoing research underlying the commercial software for speech analytics. The software design follows the concept of a minimum viable product, which motivates incremental complication of the technology while the product evolves. Such approach motivated us to rely on generally available open-source toolkits and a number of readily available knowledge-based methods developed under our previous studies.

Sections 2 and 3 outline the overall setup of applying LVCSR technology to keyword spotting for Russian telephone conversational speech, including the key system parameters and the description of experiments run to assess the quality and performance of the system. Special focus is given to linguistic components used at the training and spotting stage. Section 4 describes the off-the-shelf speech analytics system developed using the ideas and results discussed in this paper.

2. Key System Parameters

The system described in the paper is intended to be used to perform keyword search in telephone conversational speech. The system is provided both as SDK to be integrated with speech recording systems and as a stand-alone MS Windows application. The system is created on top of CMU Sphinx [24]; this framework has been chosen due to its simplicity and licensing model which allows for freely using the code in commercial applications. Following the idea of minimum viable product we mostly use the standard settings across all system modules. 13 MFCCs with their derivatives and acceleration are used in the acoustic front-end; triphone continuous density acoustic models are trained on around 200 hours of telephone-quality Russian speech (8 kHz, 8 bit, Mono) recorded by 200 native speakers. 5-state HMMs are used with diagonal covariation matrix, and CART (classification and regression trees) algorithm is used to cluster acoustic models into 9000 senones, each senone being described by 10 to 30 Gaussians. Texts in the training database for language models are transcribed automatically with a morphological and contextual linguistic processor [25]. A set of transcription variation rules are applied. Unigram and bigram language models are trained on hundreds of thousands of modern Russian e-books generally available on the Internet. Decoder makes use of a standard CMU Sphinx token-passing algorithm with pruning methods widely employed in the system setup including maximum beam width, word insertion penalty, and acoustic likelihood penalty.

The core novelty of the system is granted by extensive use of linguistic knowledge on both the training and spoken term detection steps. The system uses a linguistic processor with built-in information on Russian morphology which helps to generate high-quality transcriptions for any word form and thus train more viable acoustic models. The same processor is used to generate various forms of words which ensures better spoken term detection on the spotting step. A rule-based transcription variation algorithm is applied to generate alternative phoneme sequences. Ultimately on the language modeling step the texts are automatically prefiltered by the type of text to let only dialogues stay in the training corpus.

3. Algorithms, Associated Problems, and Solution

3.1. Acoustic Front-End. While throughout the system standard MFCCs are used, an additional effort was required to make the front-end work for keyword spotting in a real-world application. First, audio files to be analyzed are chunked into 10-second long chunks in order to split the decoding process over multiple CPUs. An overlap of 1 second is used to guarantee that a keyword is not truncated between two subsequent speech segments. Further on, a parsing algorithm

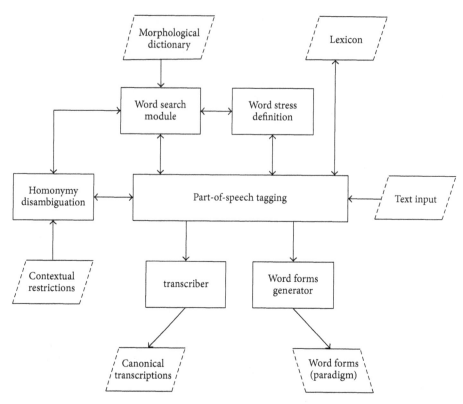

FIGURE 1: Linguistic processor.

is applied to combine partial decoding results into a single file in order to avoid redundant false alarms. The future plan is to use VAD to divide the audio stream into phrases which would better suit the LVCSR-based approach used in this paper; however, our current VAD implementation has shown worse results, hence the use of chunks of equal length.

3.2. Acoustic Modeling, Grapheme-to-Phoneme Conversion, and a Transcription Variation Algorithm. The system discussed in the paper is intended to be used in real-world telephone environment under low sound quality conditions. To cover this requirement the acoustic model is trained on real-world data encountering the telephone channel quality speech in Russian telephone networks. Continuous density HMMs are used, resulting in a representative set of 9000 senones each described with a GMM with 10–30 components.

Under our previous research [25] a linguistic processor has been developed which makes use of information on morphological characteristics of around 600 000 Russian words (see the structure on Figure 1) to transcribe words and generate forms of words. Processor parses the text and defines the part of speech for every word in the sentence; then the word stress is defined, and a set of preprogrammed contextual grapheme-to-phoneme rules is applied to derive a canonical ("ideal") word transcription.

The current state of the art for transcribing words in speech recognition systems is to use statistical grapheme-to-phoneme converters [26, 27]. The research has been held on combining various techniques, for example, in [28] Conditional Random Fields and Joint-Multigram Model

are used to bring an additional improvement in quality. Studies have been done [29, 30] to introduce weighted finite state transducers to grasp the probabilities of in-word phonetic sequences. Altogether these studies outline the key advantages of probabilistic approach compared to knowledge-based methods, namely, language independency (easily ported to a new language), ability to generalize and provide transcriptions to new (out-of-vocabulary) words, and the need of a smaller footprint of linguistic data (and hence effort) to train a grapheme-to-phoneme converter.

On the other hand, the majority of the results shared in cited studies relate to languages characterized with low number of word forms (e.g., English and French). Meanwhile Russian is a highly inflectional language with a word stress depending on the exact word form in the paradigm and a high frequency of homonymy also affecting word stress and thus being a source for potential transcription errors [31]. This means that one needs a much bigger hand-crafted lexicon to train a high-quality probabilistic grapheme-to-phoneme converter for Russian. This obstacle together with the concept of minimum viable product described above motivated us to set probabilistic grapheme-to-phoneme conversion as a target for our future research and to use a readily available high-quality knowledge-based linguistic processor instead. Another important factor which guided this choice is the ability to disambiguate homonymy and to generate word forms (to be discussed later on).

The key element of the acoustic model training process is transcription variation. Every phrase used to train the models receives several alternative transcriptions by applying

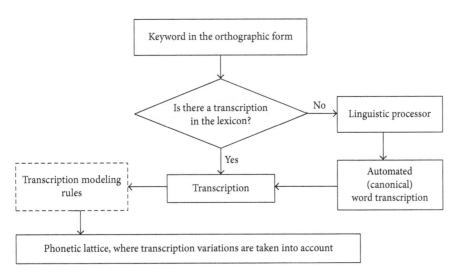

FIGURE 2: Transcription variation algorithm.

a set of predefined linguistic rules. Then on the training step CMU Sphinx train module chooses the best alternative which maximizes expectation. The experiments showed a 4% absolute increase in keyword detection rate achieved thanks to such implementation (please refer to Section 4 for more details on experiments). At the moment the rules are derived manually based on linguistic knowledge. The list of rules is then embedded in the recognizer which is run on a training dataset to define which rules provide for quality improvement and should be kept in the production system. As the next step of our research we plan to develop a sufficient corpus to train these rules automatically.

The ultimate list of transcription variation rules chosen on the training set contains 30 contextual phoneme-to-phoneme and grapheme-to-phoneme mappings based on both from the modern research on Russian spontaneous speech [32] and from the authors' proper experiments with real-life data audio analysis. The main steps of the transcription variation algorithm are outlined below (please also refer to Figure 2):

(1) A textual annotation of the trained database is loaded.

(2) If the word is not in the lexicon (used mainly for foreign words and named entities), automatic transcriber is launched which makes use of the digitized dictionary of the Russian language, containing 600 thousand words with morphological information and a part-of-speech (POS) tagger. As a result of this stage the word stress is assigned to the right syllable of every word.

(3) Automated, or canonical, transcription is generated by applying context-dependent letter-to-phone rules.

(4) Pronunciation variation is executed by iteratively applying a separate set of phoneme-to-phoneme and grapheme-to-phoneme transcription modeling rules to the canonical transcriptions.

It is well known that knowledge-based rules, being "laboratory" in origin, may happen to be inadequate when confronted with real-world data. However this was our intent to check this critical assumption on our test material. Moreover, during the past decades, Russian phonetics has undergone a general shift from laboratory speech to fully spontaneous [32, 33], and the rules we use are based on vast research on spontaneous speech traits.

The rules are divided into two main groups. The first contains substitution, deletion, and insertion rules, which apply to initial phonetic transcriptions. Here are some examples of such rules:

(i) [@] ("schwa"), followed by a consonant, is deleted in the unstressed position after stressed syllable.

(ii) [f] is deleted from consonant sequence [fs] + (any) unvoiced consonant.

(iii) Affricates [c] and [tʃ'] are substituted by fricatives [s] and [ʃʲ], respectively (sign j denotes that a consonant is palatalized).

(iv) Sonorant [j] is deleted before unstressed vowel at the beginning of words.

(v) Noise stops (e.g., [p], [t], [pʲ], and [tʲ]) are deleted in the final position after vowels due to implosive pronunciation (i.e., without burst following articulators closure).

The second group of rules makes use of both morphological and orthographical level of linguistic representation. Hence, this is not correction to initial transcriptions (phoneme-to-phoneme rules) but a separate set of grapheme-to-phoneme rules. Here are some examples:

(i) [@j@] and [uju] in unstressed inflections of adjectives "–ая" and "–ую" are changed to [@e] and [u], respectively.

(ii) [@v@], [iv@], and [iv@] in unstressed noun inflections "–ого" and "–его" are changed to [@@], [i@], and [i@].

(iii) [@t] in verb inflections "–ат" is changed to [it].

For frequent words we also added another set of rules, which generate simplified pronunciation, which is common to informal spontaneous speech. These include [d^j] and [v] deletion in intervocalic position, [s^{j}t^j] changing to [s^j], and so forth.

3.3. Language Models and the Choice of Relevant Content to Train Them. Initially language models have been trained with a few gBs of user-generated content to be found on the Internet, including public forums, social networks, and chats. The idea behind this was that such content would better represent spontaneous speech and thus ensuring more sustainable keyword spotting results. However the experiments have shown that such linguistic material occurred to bear an intrinsic drawback, because it contains enormous number of spelling errors which led to a statistic bias and wrong lemmas to appear in the lexicon. Hence a decision was taken to rely on standard and error-free texts derived from a wide range of books of different genres available on the Internet. Only books by modern authors (1990s and later) were chosen to reflect current traits of Russian speech. However only the dialogues have been extracted from such books to guarantee the "live" style of communication, which is characteristic of real-world telephone speech. 2 gB of raw text data was used as a result to train a unigram and bigram language models containing 600 000 Russian lemmas. The LMs were trained using SRILM toolkit [34] with Good-Turing discounting algorithm applied.

Current research in the domain of language modeling is focused on applying deep neural networks and high-level LM rescoring [35]. In our case there is insufficient data to train such models, which motivated us to shift to much simpler models. As outlined in Section 3.4 we do not rely on the most probable word sequence in the recognition result to detect keywords; rather we want to generate as diverse and "rough" lattice on the indexing step to guarantee high probability for the spoken term detection. Simple bigram/unigram language modeling fits this aim quite well.

3.4. Decoding, Word Spotting, and Automated Word Form Generation. The main idea behind using LVCSR to find keywords is to transform speech signal into a plain text and then search for the word in this text. However due to diverse types of communication context in the telephone conversational speech it is not viable to use the top decoding result per se. Rather, it makes sense to parse the resulting recognition lattice to find every possible node with the keyword. Hence speech is first indexed into recognition lattices; the keyword search is performed on-demand at a later stage.

To improve spotting results we make intensive use of the linguistic processor described above. When a word is entered as a search query its forms are automatically generated by addressing the morphological dictionary (see Figure 1) and a set of variants are derived for the word which are then searched in the lattice and appear in the recognition results list. For example, when the word "кусок" is to be searched

TABLE 1: Experimental results.

Parameter	Value
MTWV	0.37
RTF	2.0

(Russian word for "a piece") all the words containing this sequence will be searched within a recognition lattice; hence the user will be able to spot the words "куска" and "куском" and so forth. Since Russian is an inflectional language numerous forms are available for one word. Consequently low-order (unigram and bigram) language models used in our system cause the recognizer to make errors in the word endings. The simple idea described above helps to avoid errors and achieve much better results.

4. Experimental Results

The system described hereby is intended to be used in real-world applications to analyze telephone-quality speech. To test it a 10-hour database including the recordings of dialogues of around 50 speakers has been recorded using the hardware and software of SpRecord LLC (http://www.spre-cord.ru/). 1183 different keywords are searched within the database. The signal-to-noise ratio falls between 5 and 15 dB, reflecting an adverse real telephone channel environment.

Maximum Term-Weighted Value (MTWV) is a predicted metric corresponding to the best TWV for all values of the decision threshold; θ (see formula (1)) and real-time factor (RTF) metrics (formula (2)) are used to evaluate system performance; the former metric reflects the quality of word spotting, and the latter reflects its speed. RTF parameter is calculated on 1 CPU unit of 3 gHz. The results are shown in Table 1.

$$\text{TWV}(\theta) = 1 - \left[P_{\text{Miss}}(\theta) + \beta \cdot P_{\text{FA}}(\theta)\right]. \tag{1}$$

θ is the threshold used to determine a hit or a miss, and β is the weight that accounts for the presumed prior probability of a term and the relative costs of misses and false alarms are equal to 0.999 in our study.

$$\text{RTF} = \frac{T_{\text{proc}}}{T_{\text{set}}}. \tag{2}$$

T_{proc} is the time spent on processing the file, and T_{set} is the duration of the test set.

In order to understand whether these results correspond to the current state of the art we compared them to the result of another scientific group for spoken term detection in telephone conversational of another underresourced language (Cantonese) [11]. What we saw is that our results in terms of keyword search quality fall in between those reported for Cantonese when GMMs are used in the acoustic model and are slightly worse when deep neural networks are used (MTWV 0.335 and 0.441, resp.). As for the real-time factor our results outperform those reported in [14], which may be attributed to a relatively small number of Gaussians we use per senone.

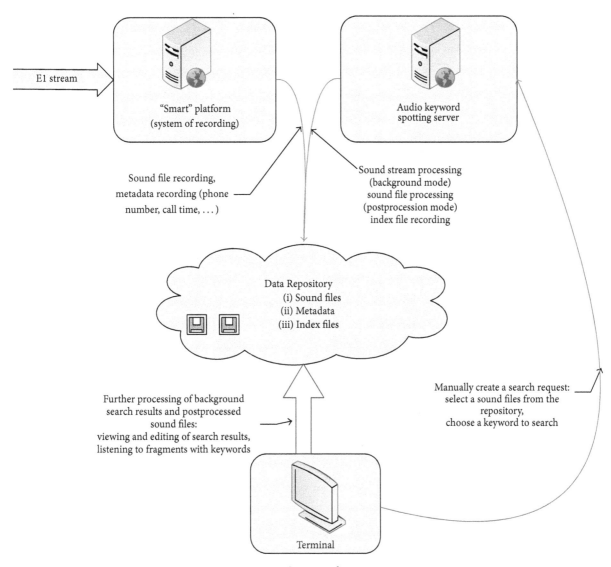

FIGURE 3: System architecture.

5. System Architecture and User Interface

5.1. Principal Components. The algorithms described in Section 2 were used in creating "ANALYZE" software—an industrial speech analytics system. Figure 3 outlines the key system components: word spotting server, terminal, and data repository. Word spotting server processes speech data and saves index with positions of searched keywords into the database. The terminal is used to schedule or launch immediate search queries and to view the search results. The search is performed in two steps: first, the lattice with speech recognition results is generated for each wave file; second, the keyword is found via a substring search within this lattice. The data repository contains both speech files and corresponding indices.

5.2. User Interface. The key problems of human-machine interaction within speech analytics systems, including accurate treatment of the keyword spotting results, and the role

of in the optimization of workflows in modern organizations are reflected in [36–39]. Figure 4 outlines the user interface of the ANALYZE software which has been developed based on use-cases validated with the end-users. Usability and use-case integrity were tested in the real-world environment. All settings are available in 1-2 clicks; real-time reporting is shown on the screen; navigation panel provides access to all needed functions. Table 1 with search results provides easy filtering and listening modes. Figure 3 presents the main board of the system's user interface.

An essential benefit of the software is the ability to work in real-time mode on the workstations with limited resources, which makes it worthy for small organizations with a fraction of telephone lines in use.

6. Conclusion and Further Plans

A keyword spotting system for Russian based on LVCSR has been described in this paper. General availability of

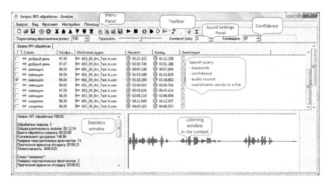

FIGURE 4: The user interface of the "ANALYZE" software.

open-source software made it easy to be implemented and linguistic modules helped to improve the system quality, while representative training and test data ensured the applicability of the system to real-world problems.

The ongoing research is aimed at further tuning the acoustic and language models, trying probabilistic frameworks for grapheme-to-phoneme conversion, data-driven transcription variation, introducing noise compensation and pause detection into the front-end and at creating specific confidence measures to minimize false alarms which are caused by frequent words in the language model.

In building our automated keyword spotting system based on large vocabulary continuous speech recognition we relied on the results of the scientific community, namely, the open-source software CMU Sphinx for acoustic modeling and decoding and SRILM for language modeling. At the same time the system has several technological advantages: the use of linguistic knowledge in training and decoding, namely, a morphological parser of texts and transcription variation to generate word transcriptions, transcription variation rules, and automated generation of word forms on the spotting step; real-world industrial data used to train acoustic models; accurate language modeling achieved via cautious choice of training data; real-time operation mode on limited computer resources.

We believe that high-quality automated keyword spotting system based on large vocabulary continuous speech recognition for online speech data analysis can be used both as a technological platform to create effective integrated systems for monitoring and as a ready-to-use solution to monitor global information space.

Competing Interests

The authors declare that they have no competing interests.

Acknowledgments

The authors would like to thank SpRecord LLC authorities for providing real-world telephone-quality data used in training and testing of the keyword spotting system described in this paper.

References

[1] T. J. Hazen, F. Richardson, and A. Margolis, "Topic identification from audio recordings using word and phone recognition lattices," in *Proceedings of the IEEE Workshop on Automatic Speech Recognition and Understanding (ASRU '07)*, pp. 659–664, Kyoto, Japan, December 2007.

[2] D. A. James and S. J. Young, "A fast lattice-based approach to vocabulary independent wordspotting," in *Proceedings of the IEEE International Conference on Acoustics, Speech and Signal Processing*, vol. 1, pp. 377–380, Adelaide, Australia, 1994.

[3] I. Szöke, P. Schwarz, P. Matějka, L. Burget, M. Karafiát, and J. Černocký, "Phoneme based acoustics keyword spotting in informal continuous speech," in *Text, Speech and Dialogue: 8th International Conference, TSD 2005, Karlovy Vary, Czech Republic, September 12–15, 2005. Proceedings*, vol. 3658 of *Lecture Notes in Computer Science*, pp. 302–309, Springer, Berlin, Germany, 2005.

[4] M. Yamada, M. Naito, T. Kato, and H. Kawai, "Improvement of rejection performance of keyword spotting using anti-keywords derived from large vocabulary considering acoustical similarity to keywords," in *Proceedings of the 9th European Conference on Speech Communication and Technology*, Lisbon, Portugal, September 2005.

[5] M. Matsushita, H. Nishizaki, H. Nishizaki, S. Nakagawa et al., "Evaluating multiple LVCSR model combination in NTCIR-3 speech-driven web retrieval task," in *Proceedings of the 8th European Conference on Speech Communication and Technology (EUROSPEECH '03)*, pp. 1205–1208, Geneva, Switzerland, September 2003.

[6] I. Szoke et al., "Comparison of keyword spotting approaches for informal continuous speech," in *Proceedings of the 2nd Joint Workshop on Multimodal Interaction and Related Machine Learning Algorithms (INTERSPEECH '05)*, pp. 633–636, Edinburgh, UK, 2005.

[7] D. Karakos, R. Schwartz, S. Tsakalidis et al., "Score normalization and system combination for improved keyword spotting," in *Proceedings of the IEEE Workshop on Automatic Speech Recognition and Understanding (ASRU '13)*, pp. 210–215, Olomouc, Czech Republic, December 2013.

[8] J. Mamou, J. Cui, X. Cui et al., "System combination and score normalization for spoken term detection," in *Proceedings of the 38th IEEE International Conference on Acoustics, Speech, and Signal Processing (ICASSP '13)*, pp. 8272–8276, Vancouver, Canada, May 2013.

[9] G. Hinton, L. Deng, D. Yu et al., "Deep neural networks for acoustic modeling in speech recognition," *IEEE Signal Processing Magazine*, vol. 29, no. 6, pp. 82–97, 2012.

[10] M. Harper, "IARPA Babel Program," https://www.iarpa.gov/index.php/research-programs/babel?highlight=WyJiYWJlbCJd.

[11] J. Cui, X. Cui, B. Ramabhadran et al., "Developing speech recognition systems for corpus indexing under the IARPA Babel program," in *Proceedings of the 38th IEEE International Conference on Acoustics, Speech and Signal Processing (ICASSP '13)*, pp. 6753–6757, IEEE, Vancouver, Canada, May 2013.

[12] M. J. F. Gales, K. M. Knill, A. Ragni, and S. P. Rath, "Speech recognition and keyword spotting for low resource languages: babel project research at CUED," in *Proceedings of the 4th International Workshop on Spoken Language Technologies for Under-Resourced Languages*, pp. 16–23, Petersburg, Russia, 2014.

[13] F. Grézl, M. Karafiát, and M. Janda, "Study of probabilistic and Bottle-Neck features in multilingual environment," in *Proceedings of the IEEE Workshop on Automatic Speech Recognition and Understanding (ASRU '11)*, pp. 359–364, December 2011.

[14] P. Baljekar, J. F. Lehman, and R. Singh, "Online word-spotting in continuous speech with recurrent neural networks," in *Proceedings of the IEEE Workshop on Spoken Language Technology (SLT '14)*, pp. 536–541, South Lake Tahoe, Nev, USA, December 2014.

[15] K. Kilgour and A. Waibel, "A neural network keyword search system for telephone speech," in *Speech and Computer: 16th International Conference, SPECOM 2014, Novi Sad, Serbia, October 5–9, 2014. Proceedings*, A. Ronzhin, R. Potapova, and V. Delic, Eds., pp. 58–65, Springer, Berlin, Germany, 2014.

[16] I. Bulyko, M. Ostendorf, M. Siu, T. Ng, A. Stolcke, and Ö. Çetin, "Web resources for language modeling in conversational speech recognition," *ACM Transactions on Speech and Language Processing*, vol. 5, no. 1, article 1, 2007.

[17] A. Gandhe, L. Qin, F. Metze, A. Rudnicky, I. Lane, and M. Eck, "Using web text to improve keyword spotting in speech," in *Proceedings of the IEEE Workshop on Automatic Speech Recognition and Understanding (ASRU '13)*, pp. 428–433, Olomouc, Czech Republic, December 2013.

[18] G. Mendels, E. Cooper, V. Soto et al., "Improving speech recognition and keyword search for low resource languages using web data," in *Proceedings of the 16th Annual Conference of the International Speech Communication Association (Interspeech '15)*, pp. 829–833, Dresden, Germany, September 2015.

[19] SpeechKit API, http://api.yandex.ru/speechkit/.

[20] K. Levin, I. Ponomareva, A. Bulusheva et al., "Automated closed captioning for Russian live broadcasting," in *Proceedings of the 15th Annual Conference of the International Speech Communication Association (INTERSPEECH '14)*, pp. 1438–1442, Singapore, September 2014.

[21] A. Karpov, I. Kipyatkova, and A. Ronzhin, "Speech recognition for east slavic languages: the case of russian," in *Proceedings of the 3rd International Workshop on Spoken Languages Technologies for Under-resourced Languages (SLTU '12)*, pp. 84–89, Cape Town, South Africa, 2012.

[22] A. Karpov, K. Markov, I. Kipyatkova, D. Vazhenina, and A. Ronzhin, "Large vocabulary Russian speech recognition using syntactico-statistical language modeling," *Speech Communication*, vol. 56, no. 1, pp. 213–228, 2014.

[23] M. Zulkarneev, R. Grigoryan, and N. Shamraev, "Acoustic modeling with deep belief networks for Russian Speech," in

Speech and Computer: 15th International Conference, SPECOM 2013, Pilsen, Czech Republic, September 1–5, 2013. Proceedings, vol. 8113 of *Lecture Notes in Computer Science*, pp. 17–23, Springer, Berlin, Germany, 2013.

[24] K.-F. Lee, H.-W. Hon, and R. Reddy, "An overview of the SPHINX speech recognition system," *IEEE Transactions on Acoustics, Speech, and Signal Processing*, vol. 38, no. 1, pp. 35–45, 1990.

[25] V. A. Smirnov, M. N. Gusev, and M. P. Farkhadov, "The function of linguistic processor in the system for automated analysis of unstructured speech data," *Automation and Modern Technologies*, no. 8, pp. 22–28, 2013.

[26] M. Bisani and H. Ney, "Joint-sequence models for grapheme-to-phoneme conversion," *Speech Communication*, vol. 50, no. 5, pp. 434–451, 2008.

[27] T. Hain, "Implicit modelling of pronunciation variation in automatic speech recognition," *Speech Communication*, vol. 46, no. 2, pp. 171–188, 2005.

[28] D. Jouvet, D. Fohr, and I. Illina, "Evaluating grapheme-to-phoneme converters in automatic speech recognition context," in *Proceedings of the IEEE International Conference on Acoustics, Speech and Signal Processing (ICASSP '12)*, pp. 4821–4824, IEEE, Kyoto, Japan, March 2012.

[29] L. Lu, A. Ghoshal, and St. Renals, "Acoustic data-driven pronunciation lexicon for large vocabulary speech recognition," in *Proceedings of the IEEE Workshop on Automatic Speech Recognition and Understanding (ASRU '13)*, pp. 374–379, Olomouc, Czech Republic, December 2013.

[30] S. G. Paulo and L. C. Oliveira, "Generation of word alternative pronunciations using weighted finite state transducers," in *Proceedings of the Interspeech 2005*, pp. 1157–1160, Lisbon, Portugal, September 2005.

[31] I. Kipyatkova, A. Karpov, V. Verkhodanova, and M. Železný, "Modeling of pronunciation, language and nonverbal units at conversational Russian speech recognition," *International Journal of Computer Science and Applications*, vol. 10, no. 1, pp. 11–30, 2013.

[32] L. V. Bondarko, A. Iivonen, L. C. W. Pols, and V. de Silva, "Common and language dependent phonetic differences between read and spontaneous speech in russian, finnish and dutch," in *Proceedings of the 15th International Congress of Phonetic Sciences (ICPhS '03)*, pp. 2977–2980, Barcelona, Spain, 2003.

[33] L. V. Bondarko, N. B. Volskaya, S. O. Tananaiko, and L. A. Vasilieva, "Phonetic properties of russian spontaneous speech," in *Proceedings of the 15th International Congress of Phonetic Sciences (ICPhS '03)*, p. 2973, Barcelona, Spain, 2003.

[34] A. Stolcke, "SRILM-an extensible language modeling toolkit," in *Proceedings of the International Conference on Spoken Language Processing*, Denver, Colo, USA, September 2002.

[35] T. Mikolov, M. Karafiát, L. Burget, J. Cernocký, and S. Khudanpur, "Recurrent neural network based language model," *Interspeech*, vol. 2, no. 3, 2010.

[36] R. V. Bilik, V. A. Zhozhikashvili, N. V. Petukhova, and M. P. Farkhadov, "Analysis of the oral interface in the interactive servicing systems. II," *Automation and Remote Control*, vol. 70, no. 3, pp. 434–448, 2009.

[37] V. A. Zhozhikashvili, N. V. Petukhova, and M. P. Farkhadov, "Computerized queuing systems and speech technologies," *Control Sciences*, no. 2, pp. 3–7, 2006.

11

Robust Recursive Algorithm under Uncertainties via Worst-Case SINR Maximization

Xin Song,[1] **Feng Wang,**[2] **Jinkuan Wang,**[1] **and Jingguo Ren**[1]

[1]*Engineering Optimization and Smart Antenna Institute, Northeastern University at Qinhuangdao,*
Qinhuangdao 066004, China
[2]*State Grid Ningxia Information & Communication Company, Great Wall East Road, No. 277, Xingqing District,*
Ningxia 750000, China

Correspondence should be addressed to Xin Song; sxin78916@mail.neuq.edu.cn

Academic Editor: Peter Jung

The performance of traditional constrained-LMS (CLMS) algorithm is known to degrade seriously in the presence of small training data size and mismatches between the assumed array response and the true array response. In this paper, we develop a robust constrained-LMS (RCLMS) algorithm based on worst-case SINR maximization. Our algorithm belongs to the class of diagonal loading techniques, in which the diagonal loading factor is obtained in a simple form and it decreases the computation cost. The updated weight vector is derived by the descent gradient method and Lagrange multiplier method. It demonstrates that our proposed recursive algorithm provides excellent robustness against signal steering vector mismatches and the small training data size and, has fast convergence rate, and makes the mean output array signal-to-interference-plus-noise ratio (SINR) consistently close to the optimal one. Some simulation results are presented to compare the performance of our robust algorithm with the traditional CLMS algorithm.

1. Introduction

Adaptive beamforming is used for enhancing a desired signal while suppressing interference and noise at the output of an array of sensors. It has a long and rich history of practical applications to numerous areas such as sonar, radar, radio astronomy, medical imaging, and more recently wireless communications [1–5].

In the practical applications, the adaptive beamforming methods become very sensitive to any violation of underlying assumptions on the environment, sources, or sensor array. The performance of the existing adaptive array algorithms is known to degrade substantially in the presence of even slight mismatches between the actual and presumed array responses to the desired signal. Similar types of degradation can take place when the signal array response is known precisely, but the training sample size is small. Therefore, robust approaches to adaptive beamforming appear to be one of the important issues. There are several efficient approaches to

design robust adaptive beamformers, such as the linearly constrained minimum variance beamformer [6], the eigenspace-based beamformer [7], and the projection beamforming techniques [8]. For instance, additional linear constraints on the array beam pattern have been proposed to better attenuate the interference and broaden the response around the nominal look direction [9]. There is another popular class of robust beamforming techniques called diagonal loading (DL) [10]. In these methods the array correlation matrix is loaded with an appropriate multiple, called the loading level, of the identity matrix in order to satisfy the imposed quadratic constraint. However, it is somewhat difficult to calculate the loading level with uncertain bounds of the array steering vector, which may not be available in practical situations. Based on a spherical or ellipsoidal uncertainty set of the array steering vectors, robust Capon beamforming maximizes the output power, which belongs to the extended class of diagonal loading methods, but the corresponding value of diagonal loading can be calculated precisely [11, 12].

From the above analysis, we note that these methods cannot be expected to provide sufficient robustness improvements.

In more recent years, some new robust adaptive beamforming approaches have been proposed [13–17]. The problem of finding a weight vector maximizes the worst-case SINR over the uncertainty model. With a general convex uncertainty model, the worst-case SINR maximization problem can be solved by using convex optimization [13]. In [14], a robust downlink beamforming optimization algorithm is proposed for secondary multicast transmission in a multiple-input multiple-output (MIMO) spectrum sharing cognitive radio (CR) network. Recognizing that all channel covariance matrices form a Riemannian manifold, Ciochina et al. propose worst-case robust downlink beamforming on the Riemannian manifold in order to model the set of mismatched channel covariance matrices for which robustness shall be guaranteed [15]. In [16], a robust beamforming scheme is proposed for the multiantenna nonregenerative cognitive relay network where the multiantenna relay with imperfect channel state information (CSI) helps the communication of single-antenna secondary users (SUs). Exploiting imperfect channel state information (CSI), with its error modeled by added Gaussian noise, robust beamforming in cognitive radio is developed, which optimizes the beamforming weights at the secondary transmitter [17].

Apart from the LMS-type algorithm, another well-known iterative adaptive algorithm is the recursive least square (RLS) algorithm or the complex-valued widely linear RLS algorithm, which updates the weight vector with small steady-state misadjustment and fast convergence speed. However, the RLS-type algorithms have much higher computation cost than the LMS-type algorithms [18, 19]. In order to reduce the complexity, RLS algorithm based on orthonormal polynomial basis function is proposed, which is as simple as LMS algorithm [20]. To yield low complexity cost and keep fast convergence speed, the LMS algorithms based on variable step size have been presented in [21–23]. These LMS algorithms can have faster convergence speed and require less computational cost per iteration than the RLS-type algorithms. However, they cannot enjoy both fast tracking and small misadjustment with simple implementation. It is known that the performance of traditional CLMS algorithm degrades seriously due to the small training sample size and signal steering vector mismatches. In this paper, in order to overcome the drawbacks of CLMS algorithm, we propose a robust CLMS algorithm based on worst-case SINR maximization, which provides sufficient robustness against some types of mismatches. The parameters in our paper can derive in a simple form, which decreases computation cost. The improved performance of the proposed algorithm is demonstrated by comparing with traditional linearly CLMS algorithm via several examples.

2. Background

2.1. Mathematical Formulation.
We consider a uniform linear array (ULA) with M omnidirectional sensors spaced by the distance d. We assume D narrowband incoherent plane waves that impinge from directions of arrival $\{\theta_0, \theta_1, \ldots, \theta_{D-1}\}$. The output of a designed beamformer is expressed as follows:

$$y(k) = \mathbf{w}^H \mathbf{x}(k), \tag{1}$$

where $\mathbf{x}(k) = [x_1(k), \ldots, x_M(k)]^T$ is the complex vector of array observation, M is the array number, and $\mathbf{w} = [w_1, \ldots, w_M]^T$ is the complex vector of weights; here $(\cdot)^H$ and $(\cdot)^T$ are the Hermitian transpose and transpose, respectively. The array observation at time k can be written as

$$\mathbf{x}(k) = \mathbf{s}(k) + \mathbf{n}(k) + \mathbf{i}(k) = s_0(k)\mathbf{a} + \mathbf{n}(k) + \mathbf{i}(k), \tag{2}$$

where $\mathbf{s}(k)$, $\mathbf{n}(k)$, and $\mathbf{i}(k)$ are the desired signal, noise, and interference components, respectively. Here $s_0(k)$ is the desired signal waveform, and $\mathbf{a}$ is the signal steering vector.

The weights can be optimized from the following maximum of the signal-to-interference-plus-noise ratio (SINR):

$$\text{SINR} = \frac{\sigma_s^2 \left| \mathbf{w}^H \mathbf{a} \right|^2}{\mathbf{w}^H \mathbf{R}_{i+n} \mathbf{w}}, \tag{3}$$

where σ_s^2 is the signal power and $M \times M$ interference-plus-noise correlation matrix $\mathbf{R}_{i+n}$:

$$\mathbf{R}_{i+n} = E\left\{ (\mathbf{n}(k) + \mathbf{i}(k))(\mathbf{n}(k) + \mathbf{i}(k))^H \right\}. \tag{4}$$

2.2. Linearly Constrained-LMS (CLMS) Algorithm.
Linear constrained-LMS algorithm is a real-time constrained algorithm for determining the optimal weight vector. The problem of finding optimum beamformer weights is as follows:

$$\min_{\mathbf{w}} \quad \mathbf{w}^H \mathbf{R}_{i+n} \mathbf{w}$$
$$\text{subject to} \quad \mathbf{w}^H \mathbf{a} = 1. \tag{5}$$

Using Lagrange multiplier method to solve problem (5), the optimal weight vector can be derived:

$$\mathbf{w}_{\text{opt}} = \frac{\mathbf{R}_{i+n}^{-1} \mathbf{a}}{\mathbf{a}^H \mathbf{R}_{i+n}^{-1} \mathbf{a}}. \tag{6}$$

In practical situations, we cannot know completely the signal characteristics and it is also time-varying circumstance. So, we need to update the weights in an iterative manner. The Lagrange function of (5) is written as

$$H(\mathbf{w}, \lambda) = \mathbf{w}^H \mathbf{R}_{i+n} \mathbf{w} + \lambda \left(\mathbf{w}^H \mathbf{a} - 1 \right). \tag{7}$$

Computing the gradient of (7), we can update the weight vector of CLMS algorithm:

$$\mathbf{w}(k+1) = \mathbf{w}(k) - \mu_1 \nabla$$
$$= \mathbf{w}(k) - \mu_1 \left[2\mathbf{R}_{i+n} \mathbf{w}(k) + \lambda \mathbf{a} \right], \tag{8}$$

where μ_1 is the step size and ∇ is the gradient vector of $H(\mathbf{w}, \lambda)$. Inserting (8) into linear constraint $\mathbf{w}^H \mathbf{a} = 1$, we can obtain the Lagrange multiplier:

$$\lambda = \frac{1}{\mu_1} \frac{\mathbf{a}^H \mathbf{w}(k) - 1}{\mathbf{a}^H \mathbf{a}} - 2\frac{\mathbf{a}^H}{\mathbf{a}^H \mathbf{a}} \mathbf{R}_{i+n} \mathbf{w}(k). \tag{9}$$

According to (8) and (9), the weight vector of traditional CLMS algorithm can be rewritten as [24]

$$\mathbf{w}(k+1) = \mathbf{P}\left[\mathbf{w}(k) - \mu_1 \mathbf{R}_{i+n}\mathbf{w}(k)\right] + \mathbf{\Psi}, \qquad (10)$$

where $\mathbf{\Psi} = \mathbf{a}[\mathbf{a}^H\mathbf{a}]^{-1}$ and $\mathbf{P} = \mathbf{I} - \mathbf{a}[\mathbf{a}^H\mathbf{a}]^{-1}\mathbf{a}^H$.

From (10), we note that the performance of the traditional CLMS algorithm is dependent on exact signal steering vector and it is sensitive to some types of mismatches. In addition, the interference-plus-noise correlation matrix $\mathbf{R}_{i+n}$ is unknown. Hereby, the sample covariance matrix

$$\widehat{\mathbf{R}}_N = \frac{1}{N}\sum_{k=1}^{N}\mathbf{x}(k)\mathbf{x}^H(k) \qquad (11)$$

is used to substitute $\mathbf{R}_{i+n}$ in (10), where N is the training sample size. Therefore, the performance degradation of CLMS algorithm can occur due to the signal steering vector mismatches and small training sample size.

3. Robust CLMS Algorithm Based on Worst-Case SINR Maximization

In order to solve the above-mentioned problems of the linearly constrained-LMS algorithm, we propose a robust recursive algorithm based on worst-case SINR maximization, which provides robustness against mismatches.

We assume that, in practical situations, the mismatch vector $\mathbf{e}$ is norm-bounded by some known constant $\varepsilon > 0$; that is,

$$\|\mathbf{e}\| \le \varepsilon. \qquad (12)$$

Then, the actual signal steering vector belongs to a ball set:

$$\boldsymbol{\varphi}(\varepsilon) = \{\mathbf{c} \mid \mathbf{c} = \mathbf{a} + \mathbf{e}, \ \|\mathbf{e}\| \le \varepsilon\}. \qquad (13)$$

The weight vector is selected by minimizing the mean output power while maintaining a distortionless response for the mismatched steering vector. So, the cost function of robust constrained-LMS (RCLMS) algorithm is formulated as

$$\min_{\mathbf{w}} \quad \mathbf{w}^H\widehat{\mathbf{R}}_N\mathbf{w}$$
$$\text{subject to} \quad \min_{\mathbf{c}\in\boldsymbol{\varphi}(\varepsilon)}\left|\mathbf{w}^H\mathbf{c}\right| \ge 1. \qquad (14)$$

According to [25], the constraint in (14) is equivalent to the following form:

$$\min_{\mathbf{c}\in\boldsymbol{\varphi}(\varepsilon)}\left|\mathbf{w}^H\mathbf{c}\right| = 1. \qquad (15)$$

Using (15), problem (14) can be rewritten in the following way:

$$\min_{\mathbf{w}} \quad \mathbf{w}^H\widehat{\mathbf{R}}_N\mathbf{w}$$
$$\text{subject to} \quad \left|\mathbf{w}^H\mathbf{a} - 1\right|^2 = \varepsilon^2\mathbf{w}^H\mathbf{w}. \qquad (16)$$

In order to improve the robustness against the mismatch that may be caused by the small training sample size, we can get a further extension of the optimization problem (16). The actual covariance matrix is

$$\widehat{\mathbf{R}}_d = \widehat{\mathbf{R}}_N + \mathbf{\Delta}, \qquad (17)$$

where $\mathbf{\Delta}$ is the norm of the error matrix and it is bounded by a certain constant r, $\|\mathbf{\Delta}\| \le r$.

Applying the worst-case performance optimization, we can rewrite

$$\min_{\mathbf{w}}\max_{\|\mathbf{\Delta}\|\le r} \quad \mathbf{w}^H\left(\widehat{\mathbf{R}}_N + \mathbf{\Delta}\right)\mathbf{w}$$
$$\text{subject to} \quad \left|\mathbf{w}^H\mathbf{a} - 1\right|^2 = \varepsilon^2\mathbf{w}^H\mathbf{w}. \qquad (18)$$

To obtain the optimal weight vector, we can first solve the following simpler problem [26]:

$$\min_{\mathbf{\Delta}} \quad -\mathbf{w}^H\left(\widehat{\mathbf{R}}_N + \mathbf{\Delta}\right)\mathbf{w}$$
$$\text{subject to} \quad \|\mathbf{\Delta}\| \le r. \qquad (19)$$

Using Lagrange multiplier method to yield the matrix error,

$$\mathbf{\Delta} = r\frac{\mathbf{w}\mathbf{w}^H}{\|\mathbf{w}\|}. \qquad (20)$$

Consequently, the minimization problem (18) is converted to the following form:

$$\min_{\mathbf{w}}\max_{\|\mathbf{\Delta}\|\le r} \quad \mathbf{w}^H\left(\widehat{\mathbf{R}}_N + r\mathbf{I}\right)\mathbf{w}$$
$$\text{subject to} \quad \left|\mathbf{w}^H\mathbf{a} - 1\right|^2 = \varepsilon^2\mathbf{w}^H\mathbf{w}. \qquad (21)$$

The solution to (21) can be derived by minimizing the Lagrange function:

$$f(\mathbf{w}, \lambda)$$
$$= \mathbf{w}^H\widehat{\mathbf{R}}_l\mathbf{w} \qquad (22)$$
$$+ \lambda\left(\varepsilon^2\mathbf{w}^H\mathbf{w} - \mathbf{w}^H\mathbf{a}\mathbf{a}^H\mathbf{w} + \mathbf{w}^H\mathbf{a} + \mathbf{a}^H\mathbf{w} - 1\right),$$

where $\widehat{\mathbf{R}}_l = \widehat{\mathbf{R}}_N + r\mathbf{I}$ and λ is Lagrange multiplier. Computing the gradient vector of $H(\mathbf{w}, \lambda)$, we can get the gradient ∇:

$$\nabla = \left(\widehat{\mathbf{R}}_l + \lambda\varepsilon^2\mathbf{I} - \lambda\mathbf{a}\mathbf{a}^H\right)\mathbf{w} + \lambda\mathbf{a}. \qquad (23)$$

The gradient of $H(\mathbf{w}, \lambda)$ is equal to zero and we can obtain the optimum weight vector:

$$\mathbf{w}_{\text{opt}} = \vartheta(\lambda)\left(\widehat{\mathbf{R}}_l + \lambda\varepsilon^2\mathbf{I}\right)^{-1}\mathbf{a}, \qquad (24)$$

where $\vartheta(\lambda) = \lambda/(\lambda\mathbf{a}^H(\widehat{\mathbf{R}}_l + \lambda\varepsilon^2\mathbf{I})^{-1}\mathbf{a} - 1)$.

From (24), we note that the proposed algorithm belongs to the class of diagonal loading techniques, but the loading factor is calculated in a complicated way.

Using (23), the updated weight vector is obtained by

$$\mathbf{w}(k+1) = \mathbf{w}(k) - \mu[\mathbf{Bw}(k) + \lambda \mathbf{a}], \quad (25)$$

where $\mathbf{B} = \widehat{\mathbf{R}}_l + \lambda \varepsilon^2 \mathbf{I} - \lambda \mathbf{a}\mathbf{a}^H$ and μ is step size.

Next, we need to compute the Lagrange multiplier λ. The quadratic constraint of the optimization problem (21) is

$$h(\mathbf{w}) = 1, \quad (26)$$

where

$$h(\mathbf{w}) = \mathbf{w}^H(k)\left(\varepsilon^2 \mathbf{I} - \mathbf{a}\mathbf{a}^H\right)\mathbf{w}(k) + \mathbf{a}^H\mathbf{w}(k)$$
$$+ \mathbf{w}^H(k)\mathbf{a}. \quad (27)$$

Inserting (25) into (26), we can obtain the Lagrange multiplier λ:

$$\lambda = \frac{1}{2\mu^2\left[\mathbf{F}^H(k)\left(\varepsilon^2 \mathbf{I} - \mathbf{a}\mathbf{a}^H\right)\mathbf{F}(k)\right]}\left(\zeta(k) + \chi(k)\right), \quad (28)$$

where

$$\mathbf{F}(k) = \left(\varepsilon^2 \mathbf{I} - \mathbf{a}\mathbf{a}^H\right)\mathbf{w}(k) + \mathbf{a},$$

$$\mathbf{q}(k) = \left[\mathbf{I} - \mu\left(\widehat{\mathbf{R}}_l + r\mathbf{I}\right)\right]\mathbf{w}(k),$$

$$\zeta(k) = \mu\left[\mathbf{q}^H(k)\left(\varepsilon^2 \mathbf{I} - \mathbf{a}\mathbf{a}^H\right)\mathbf{F}(k)\right.$$
$$\left. + \mathbf{F}^H(k)\left(\varepsilon^2 \mathbf{I} - \mathbf{a}\mathbf{a}^H\right)\mathbf{P}(k) + \mathbf{F}^H(k)\mathbf{a} + \mathbf{a}^H\mathbf{F}(k)\right],$$

$$\chi(k) = \mathbf{P}^H(k)\left(\varepsilon^2 \mathbf{I} - \mathbf{a}\mathbf{a}^H\right)\mathbf{q}(k) + \mathbf{q}^H(k)\mathbf{a}$$
$$+ \mathbf{a}^H\mathbf{q}(k),$$

$$\rho^H(k)\rho(k) = \zeta^H(k)\zeta(k) - 4\mu^2\mathbf{F}^H(k)\left(\varepsilon^2 \mathbf{I} - \mathbf{a}\mathbf{a}^H\right)$$
$$\cdot \mathbf{F}(k)\left(\chi(k) - 1\right). \quad (29)$$

3.1. The Choice of Step Size. The weight vector (25) is rewritten as

$$\mathbf{w}(k+1) = \left[\mathbf{I} - \mu\mathbf{B}\right]\mathbf{w}(k) - \mu\lambda\mathbf{a}. \quad (30)$$

Let

$$\mathbf{B} = \mathbf{\Sigma}\mathbf{\Lambda}\mathbf{\Sigma}^H, \quad (31)$$

where $\mathbf{\Lambda}$ is a diagonal matrix in which the diagonal elements of matrix $\tau_1 \geq \tau_2 \geq \cdots \geq \tau_M$ are equal to the eigenvalues of $\mathbf{B}$, and the columns of $\mathbf{\Sigma}$ contain the corresponding eigenvectors.

We can get the following equation via multiplying (30) by $\mathbf{\Sigma}^H$:

$$\mathbf{\Sigma}^H\mathbf{w}(k+1) = \left[\mathbf{I} - \mu\mathbf{\Lambda}\right]\mathbf{\Sigma}^H\mathbf{w}(k) - \mu\lambda\mathbf{\Sigma}^H\mathbf{a}. \quad (32)$$

As demonstrated in (32), if the proposed algorithm converges, it is required to satisfy the constrained condition:

$$\left|1 - \mu\tau_i\right| < 1. \quad (33)$$

It follows from (33) that

$$0 < \mu < \frac{2}{\tau_{\max}}, \quad (34)$$

where $\tau_{\max}$ is the maximum eigenvalue:

$$\tau_{\max} < \sum_{i=1}^{M} \tau_i = \text{trace}[\mathbf{B}]. \quad (35)$$

In recursive algorithm, the choice of the step size μ is very important and it is varied with each new training snapshot [27, 28].

Therefore, we can obtain the optimal parameter μ:

$$\mu = \frac{1}{5\,\text{trace}[\mathbf{B}]}. \quad (36)$$

3.2. The Approximation of Lagrange Multiplier. From (28) and (29), we note that the computation cost of weight vector is very high. Next, we obtain the Lagrange multiplier by linear combination to decrease the computation cost.

From (24), the proposed beamformer belongs to the class of diagonal loading techniques. According to [29], we consider a linear combination of $\mathbf{R}_{i+n}$ and $\widehat{\mathbf{R}}_l$:

$$\mathbf{R}_c = \rho\mathbf{R}_{i+n} + \upsilon\widehat{\mathbf{R}}_l, \quad (37)$$

where the parameters $\rho > 0$ and $\upsilon > 0$. The initial value of $\mathbf{R}_{i+n}$ is assumed to identify matrix $\mathbf{I}$ [30]. We can rewrite (37) as

$$\widehat{\mathbf{R}}_c = \widehat{\mathbf{R}}_l + \frac{\rho}{\upsilon}\mathbf{I}. \quad (38)$$

Contrasting the diagonal loading covariance matrices $\widehat{\mathbf{R}}_l + \lambda\varepsilon^2\mathbf{I}$ in (24) and $\widehat{\mathbf{R}}_l + (\rho/\upsilon)\mathbf{I}$ in (38), we note that the parameter $\lambda\varepsilon^2$ is replaced by ρ/υ. In this way, we can compute the Lagrange multiplier λ as follows:

$$\lambda = \frac{\rho}{\upsilon} \cdot \frac{1}{\varepsilon^2}. \quad (39)$$

From (39), the Lagrange multiplier is calculated simply, which decreases the complexity cost of the proposed algorithm. We need first to obtain the parameters ρ and υ. Minimize the following function:

$$g = \min E\left\{\left\|\mathbf{R}_c - \mathbf{R}_x\right\|^2\right\}, \quad (40)$$

where $\mathbf{R}_x = E[\mathbf{x}(k)\mathbf{x}^H(k)]$ is the theoretical covariance matrix. By inserting (37) into (40), we have [31]

$$g = E\left\{\left\|\upsilon\left(\widehat{\mathbf{R}}_l - \mathbf{R}_x\right) + \rho\mathbf{I} - (1-\upsilon)\mathbf{R}_x\right\|^2\right\}$$
$$= \upsilon^2 E\left\{\left\|\widehat{\mathbf{R}}_l - \mathbf{R}_x\right\|^2\right\} - 2\rho(1-\upsilon)\,\text{tr}(\mathbf{R}_x)$$
$$+ (1-\upsilon)^2\left\|\mathbf{R}_x\right\|^2 + \rho^2 M. \quad (41)$$

Computing the gradient of (41) with respect to ρ, for fixed v, we can give the optimal value:

$$\rho_0 = \frac{(1 - v_0) \operatorname{tr}(\mathbf{R}_x)}{M}. \tag{42}$$

Inserting ρ_0 into (41) and replacing v_0 by v, minimization problem is written as

$$\min_v v^2 E\left\{\left\|\widehat{\mathbf{R}}_l - \mathbf{R}_x\right\|^2\right\} \\ + \frac{(1 - v)^2 \left\{\left\|\mathbf{R}_x\right\|^2 M - \operatorname{tr}^2(\mathbf{R}_x)\right\}}{M}. \tag{43}$$

By minimizing (43), the optimal solution for v is derived as

$$v_0 = \frac{\alpha}{\alpha + \sigma}, \tag{44}$$

where $\sigma = E\{\|\widehat{\mathbf{R}}_l - \mathbf{R}_x\|^2\}$ and $\alpha = \|\mathbf{R}_x\|^2 - \operatorname{tr}^2(\mathbf{R}_x)/M$.

In practical situations, $\mathbf{R}_x$ is replaced by $\widehat{\mathbf{R}}_l$ to obtain estimation value:

$$\widehat{\alpha} = \left\|\widehat{\mathbf{R}}_l\right\|^2 - \frac{\operatorname{tr}^2\left(\widehat{\mathbf{R}}_l\right)}{M}. \tag{45}$$

We can estimate the parameter σ:

$$\widehat{\sigma} = \sum_{m=1}^{M} \left[\frac{1}{N^2} \sum_{n=1}^{N} \left\|\widehat{r}_m - \mathbf{x}(n) x_m^*(n)\right\|^2 \right] \\ = \frac{1}{N^2} \sum_{n=1}^{N} \|\mathbf{x}(n)\|^4 - \frac{1}{N} \left\|\widehat{\mathbf{R}}_l\right\|^2, \tag{46}$$

where $x_m(n)$ is the mth element of $\mathbf{x}(n)$.

Substituting (45) and (46) into (44), the estimation value of v_0 is written as

$$\widehat{v}_0 = \frac{\widehat{\alpha}}{\widehat{\alpha} + \widehat{\sigma}}. \tag{47}$$

Inserting (45) and (46) into (42), we can obtain estimation value of ρ_0:

$$\widehat{\rho}_0 = \frac{(1 - \widehat{v}_0) \operatorname{tr}\left(\widehat{\mathbf{R}}_l\right)}{M}. \tag{48}$$

Consequently, we can obtain the expression of Lagrange multiplier:

$$\widehat{\lambda} = \frac{\widehat{\rho}_0}{\widehat{v}_0} \cdot \frac{1}{\varepsilon^2}. \tag{49}$$

Our proposed RCLMS algorithm belongs to the class of diagonal loadings, but the diagonal loading factor is derived fully automatically from the observation vectors without the need of specifying any user knowledge. The parameter ε is determined easily and we can conclude that the proposed RCLMS algorithm is not sensitive to the choice of

TABLE 1: The complexity cost of the conventional constrained-LMS.

	Complexity cost
$\mathbf{R}_{i+n}$	$O(M^2 \times N + 1)$
$\boldsymbol{\Psi}$	$O(2M + 1)$
$\mathbf{P}$	$O(2M^2 + 1)$
$\mathbf{P}\mathbf{w}(k)$	$O(M^2)$
$\mu_1 \mathbf{P}\mathbf{R}_{i+n}\mathbf{w}(k)$	$O(M^3 + M^2 + M)$
Total complexity cost	$O(M^3 + (N + 4)M^2 + 3M + 3)$

TABLE 2: The complexity cost of the proposed robust CLMS.

	Complexity cost
$\widehat{\lambda}$	$O(M^2 + M \times N + N + 12)$
$\mu\widehat{\lambda}\mathbf{a}$	$O(M + 1)$
$\widehat{\mathbf{R}}_l$	$O(M^2 \times N + 1)$
$\lambda\varepsilon^2\mathbf{I}$	$O(M^2 + 2)$
$\lambda\mathbf{a}\mathbf{a}^H$	$O(2M^2)$
$\mu\mathbf{B}\mathbf{w}(k)$	$O(M^2 + M)$
Total complexity cost	$O((N + 5)M^2 + (N + 2)M + N + 16)$

parameter ε in [28]. From the literature [11], it is clear that the major computational demand of the algorithm comes from the eigendecomposition, which requires $O(M^3)$ flops. This leads to a high computational cost. However, the proposed algorithm, which does not need eigendecomposition, can reduce the complexity to $O(M^2)$ flops. In addition, robust Capon algorithm and our proposed algorithm belong to the class of the diagonal loadings, in which the loading factors can be calculated precisely.

3.3. The Analysis of Complexity Cost. The complexity cost of two algorithms can be shown as in Tables 1 and 2.

4. Simulation Results

In this section, we present some simulations to justify the performance of the proposed robust recursive algorithm based on worst-case SINR maximization. We assume a uniform linear array with $M = 10$ omnidirectional sensors spaced half a wavelength apart. For each scenario, 200 simulation runs are used to obtain each simulation point. Assume that both directions of arrival (DOAs) of the presumed and actual signal are $0°$ and $3°$, respectively. This corresponds to a $3°$ mismatch in the direction of arrival. Suppose that two interfering sources are plane waves impinging from the DOAs $-50°$ and $50°$, respectively. We choose the parameter $r = 9$.

Example 1 (output SINR versus the number of snapshots). We assume that signal-to-noise ratio SNR = 10 dB and the parameter $\varepsilon = 3$. Figure 1 shows the performance of the methods tested in no mismatch case. From Figure 1, we see that the output SINR of traditional CLMS is about 14 dB. Note that it is sensitive to the small training sample size. However, our proposed algorithm can provide improved robustness.

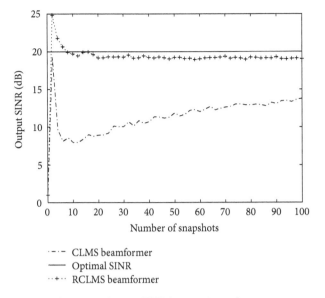

FIGURE 1: Output SINR in no-mismatch case.

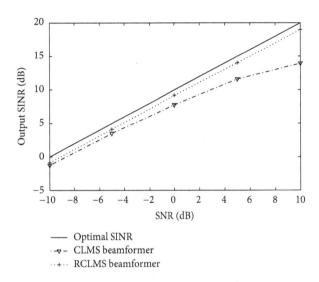

FIGURE 3: Output SINR in no-mismatch case.

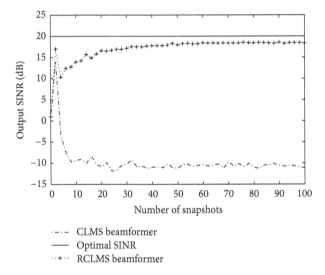

FIGURE 2: Output SINR in a 3° mismatch case.

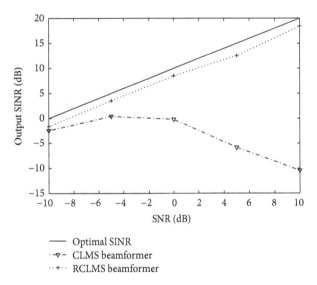

FIGURE 4: Output SINR in a 3° mismatch case.

Figure 2 shows the array output SINR of the methods tested in a 3° mismatch.

In Figure 2, we note that the output SINR of CLMS algorithm is about −10 dB, which is sensitive to the signal steering vector mismatches. However, that of the proposed robust CLMS (RCLMS) algorithm is about 18 dB, which is close to the optimal one. In this scenario, the proposed recursive algorithm outperforms the traditional linear constrained-LMS algorithm. Moreover, robust constrained-LMS algorithm has faster convergence rate.

Example 2 (output SINR versus SNR). In this example, there is a 3° mismatch in the signal look direction. We assume that the fixed training data size N is equal to 100. Figure 3 displays

the performance of these algorithms versus the SNR in no-mismatch case. The performance of these algorithms versus the SNR in a 3° mismatch case is shown in Figure 4.

In this example, the traditional algorithm is very sensitive even to slight mismatches which can easily occur in practical applications. It is observed from Figure 4 that, with the increase of SNR, CLMS algorithm has poor performance at all values of the SNR. However, our proposed recursive robust algorithm provides improved robustness against signal steering vector mismatches and small training sample size, has faster convergence rate, and yields better output performance than the CLMS algorithm.

5. Conclusions

In this paper, we propose a robust constrained-LMS algorithm based on the worst-case SINR maximization. The RCLMS algorithm provides robustness against some types of mismatches and offers faster convergence rate. The updated weight vector is derived by the gradient descent method and Lagrange multiplier method, in which the diagonal loading factor is obtained in a simple form. This decreases the computation cost. Some simulation results demonstrate that the proposed robust recursive algorithm enjoys better performance as compared with the traditional CLMS algorithm.

Conflict of Interests

The authors declare that there is no conflict of interests regarding the publication of this paper.

Acknowledgments

The authors would like to thank the anonymous reviewers for their insightful comments that helped improve the quality of this paper. This work is supported by Program for New Century Excellent Talents in University (no. NCET-12-0103), by the National Natural Science Foundation of China under Grant no. 61473066, by the Fundamental Research Funds for the Central Universities under Grant no. N130423005, and by the Natural Science Foundation of Hebei Province under Grant no. F2012501044.

References

[1] T. S. Rapapport, Ed., *Smart Antennas: Adaptive Arrays, Algorithms, and Wireless Position Location*, IEEE, Piscataway, NJ, USA, 1998.

[2] R. T. Compton Jr., R. J. Huff, W. G. Swarner, and A. Ksienski, "Adaptive arrays for communication system: an overview of the research at the Ohio State University," *IEEE Transactions on Antennas and Propagation*, vol. AP-24, no. 5, pp. 599–607, 1976.

[3] A. B. Gershman, E. Németh, and J. F. Böhme, "Experimental performance of adaptive beamforming in a sonar environment with a towed array and moving interfering sources," *IEEE Transactions on Signal Processing*, vol. 48, no. 1, pp. 246–250, 2000.

[4] Y. Kaneda and J. Ohga, "Adaptive microphone-array system for noise reduction," *IEEE Transactions on Acoustics, Speech, and Signal Processing*, vol. 34, no. 6, pp. 1391–1400, 1986.

[5] J. Li and P. Stoica, *Robust Adaptive Beamforming*, John Wiley & Sons, New York, NY, USA, 2005.

[6] R. A. Monzingo and T. W. Miller, *Introduction to Adaptive Arrays*, Wiley, New York, NY, USA, 1980.

[7] L. Chang and C.-C. Yeh, "Performance of DMI and eigenspace-based beamformers," *IEEE Transactions on Antennas and Propagation*, vol. 40, no. 11, pp. 1336–1348, 1992.

[8] D. D. Feldman and L. J. Griffiths, "Projection approach for robust adaptive beamforming," *IEEE Transactions on Signal Processing*, vol. 42, no. 4, pp. 867–876, 1994.

[9] Q. Zou, Z. L. Yu, and Z. Lin, "A robust algorithm for linearly constrained adaptive beamforming," *IEEE Signal Processing Letters*, vol. 11, no. 1, pp. 26–29, 2004.

[10] B. D. Carlson, "Covariance matrix estimation errors and diagonal loading in adaptive arrays," *IEEE Transactions on Aerospace and Electronic Systems*, vol. 24, no. 4, pp. 397–401, 1988.

[11] J. Li, P. Stoica, and Z. Wang, "On robust Capon beamforming and diagonal loading," *IEEE Transactions on Signal Processing*, vol. 51, no. 7, pp. 1702–1715, 2003.

[12] J. Li, P. Stoica, and Z. Wang, "Doubly constrained robust Capon beamformer," *IEEE Transactions on Signal Processing*, vol. 52, no. 9, pp. 2407–2423, 2004.

[13] S.-J. Kim, A. Magnani, A. Mutapcic, S. P. Boyd, and Z.-Q. Luo, "Robust beamforming via worst-case SINR maximization," *IEEE Transactions on Signal Processing*, vol. 56, no. 4, pp. 1539–1547, 2008.

[14] Y. W. Huang, Q. Li, W.-K. Ma, and S. Z. Zhang, "Robust multicast beamforming for spectrum sharing-based cognitive radios," *IEEE Transactions on Signal Processing*, vol. 60, no. 1, pp. 527–533, 2012.

[15] D. Ciochina, M. Pesavento, and K. M. Wong, "Worst case robust downlink beamforming on the Riemannian manifold," in *Proceedings of the 38th IEEE International Conference on Acoustics, Speech, and Signal Processing (ICASSP '13)*, pp. 3801–3805, May 2013.

[16] Q. Li, Q. Zhang, and J. Qin, "Robust beamforming for cognitive multi-antenna relay networks with bounded channel uncertainties," *IEEE Transactions on Communications*, vol. 62, no. 2, pp. 478–487, 2014.

[17] G. Zheng, S. Ma, K.-K. Wong, and T.-S. Ng, "Robust beamforming in cognitive radio," *IEEE Transactions on Wireless Communications*, vol. 9, no. 2, pp. 570–576, 2010.

[18] S. C. Douglas, "Widely-linear recursive least-squares algorithm for adaptive beamforming," in *Proceedings of the IEEE International Conference on Acoustics, Speech, and Signal Processing (ICASSP '09)*, pp. 2041–2044, IEEE, Taipei, Taiwan, April 2009.

[19] E. Eweda, "Comparison of RLS, LMS, and sign algorithms for tracking randomly time-varying channels," *IEEE Transactions on Signal Processing*, vol. 42, no. 11, pp. 2937–2944, 1994.

[20] S. J. Yao, H. Qian, K. Kang, and M. Y. Shen, "A recursive least squares algorithm with reduced complexity for digital predistortion linearization," in *Proceedings of the 38th IEEE International Conference on Acoustics, Speech, and Signal Processing (ICASSP '13)*, pp. 4736–4739, May 2013.

[21] J. Apolinario Jr., M. L. R. Campos, and P. S. R. Diniz, "Convergence analysis of the binormalized data-reusing LMS algorithm," *IEEE Transactions on Signal Processing*, vol. 48, no. 11, pp. 3235–3242, 2000.

[22] Y.-M. Shi, L. Huang, C. Qian, and H. C. So, "Shrinkage linear and widely linear complex-valued least mean squares algorithms for adaptive beamforming," *IEEE Transactions on Signal Processing*, vol. 63, no. 1, pp. 119–131, 2015.

[23] T. Aboulnasr and K. Mayyas, "A robust variable step-size LMS-type algorithm: analysis and simulations," *IEEE Transactions on Signal Processing*, vol. 45, no. 3, pp. 631–639, 1997.

[24] L. C. Godara, "Application of antenna arrays to mobile communications, part II: beam-forming and direction-of-arrival considerations," *Proceedings of the IEEE*, vol. 85, no. 8, pp. 1195–1245, 1997.

[25] S. A. Vorobyov, A. B. Gershman, and Z.-Q. Luo, "Robust adaptive beamforming using worst-case performance optimization: a solution to the signal mismatch problem," *IEEE Transactions on Signal Processing*, vol. 51, no. 2, pp. 313–324, 2003.

[26] S. Shahbazpanahi, A. B. Gershman, Z.-Q. Lou, and K. M. Wong, "Robust adaptive beamforming for general-rank signal models," *IEEE Transactions on Signal Processing*, vol. 51, no. 9, pp. 2257–2269, 2003.

[27] A. Elnashar, "Efficient implementation of robust adaptive beamforming based on worst-case performance optimisation," *IET Signal Processing*, vol. 2, no. 4, pp. 381–393, 2008.

[28] A. Elnashar, S. M. Elnoubi, and H. A. El-Mikati, "Further study on robust adaptive beamforming with optimum diagonal loading," *IEEE Transactions on Antennas and Propagation*, vol. 54, no. 12, pp. 3647–3658, 2006.

[29] P. Stoica, J. Li, X. Zhu, and J. R. Guerci, "On using a priori knowledge in space-time adaptive processing," *IEEE Transactions on Signal Processing*, vol. 56, no. 6, pp. 2598–2602, 2008.

[30] O. Ledoit and M. Wolf, "A well-conditioned estimator for large-dimensional covariance matrices," *Journal of Multivariate Analysis*, vol. 88, no. 2, pp. 365–411, 2004.

[31] J. Li, L. Du, and P. Stoica, "Fully automatic computation of diagonal loading levels for robust adaptive beamforming," in *Proceedings of the IEEE International Conference on Acoustics, Speech and Signal Processing (ICASSP 08)*, pp. 2325–2328, IEEE, Las Vegas, Nev, USA, April 2008.

12

Effective Inertial Hand Gesture Recognition using Particle Filtering based Trajectory Matching

Zuocai Wang,[1] **Bin Chen** (iD),[1,2] **and Jin Wu** (iD)[3]

[1]*Chengdu Institute of Computer Applications, Chinese Academy of Science, University of Chinese Academy of Sciences, Chengdu 610041, China*
[2]*Guangzhou Electronic Science Inc. of Chinese Academy of Science, Guangzhou, China*
[3]*School of Aeronautics and Astronautics and School of Automation, University of Electronic Science and Technology of China (UESTC), Chengdu, China*

Correspondence should be addressed to Bin Chen; chenbin306@sohu.com and Jin Wu; jin_wu_uestc@hotmail.com

Academic Editor: Tiancheng Li

Hand gesture recognition has become more and more popular in applications like intelligent sensing, robot control, smart guidance, and so on. In this paper, an inertial sensor based hand gesture recognition method is proposed. The proposed method obtains the trajectory of the hand by using a position estimator. The proposed method utilizes the attitude estimation to produce velocity and position estimation. A particle filter (PF) is employed to estimate the attitude quaternion from gyroscope, accelerometer, and magnetometer sensors. The improvement is based on the resampling method making the original filter much faster to converge. After smoothing, the trajectory is then converted to low-definition images which are further sent to a backpropagation neural network (BP-NN) based recognizer for matching. Experiments on real-world hardware are carried out to show the effectiveness and uniqueness of the proposed method. Compared with representative methods using accelerometer or vision sensors, the proposed method is proved to be fast, reliable, and accurate.

1. Introduction

With the development of mobile platforms, applications on hand gesture recognition have become more and more popular. For instance, Google Inc. released its Google Project Glass in 2012 which utilizes a very simple hand gesture recognition system. Basically, the hand gesture recognition systems can be classified into two groups: the vision-based and the inertia sensor based [1].

As has been proposed in [2, 3], the vision-based hand gesture recognition system tracks user's hand's feature, analyzes user's motion, and outputs the final interpreted command. The most widely used recognition methods are artificial-intelligence-based methods [4–6], for example, the neural network, supported vector machine, and hidden Markov model. This kind of recognition system is relatively reliable but it costs too much time consumption on the modeling and matching. According to stereo vision theory [7], at least one camera is needed to accurately estimate the three-dimensional attitude and velocity of a certain object. However, such configuration of the system will enlarge the economic cost of the system significantly, including the core processors and the data acquisition system. Also the time complexity of data processing and computation are high, which limits the development of applications on mobile platforms.

Other recognition methods are inertial sensor based [8]. These methods usually use low cost MEMS accelerometers to detect the motion of human hand [9–13]. Gyroscopes can also be used to measure the attitude of the user's hand in order to analyze the gesture more accurately [14, 15]. Combining the gyroscopes and accelerometers together the real-time velocity can be determined which is helpful for hand gesture recognition [16, 17]. However, the accuracy of the method is to be improved since by using only one sensor output the observability of the gesture may not be satisfactory.

The above methods are developed due to the advances in computer vision and integrated sensor fusion. In vision-based hand gesture recognition, the feature extraction, and learning are always important. There are many related techniques like the Scale-Invariant Feature Transform (SIFT [18]), Gradient Location and Orientation Histogram (GLOH [19]), Convolutional Neural Network (CNN [20]), and so on. Extracting motion from a picture requires the analysis of the correspondence between the current frame and last frame, for example, the RANdom Sample Consensus (RANSAC [21]). However, these techniques are time-costly. In fact, by using inertial sensors, the object's motion can be computed with much simpler frameworks. These years the attitude and position estimation based on MEMS sensors have been extensively studied [22], which provides us with new ways of obtaining hand's motion [23].

The main purpose of this research is to find a way that adopts inertial sensors only to determine the correct human hands gesture. According to existing papers published between 2012 and 2016, many of them use learning techniques to model the gesture via captured sensor data at one certain moment. At this point, it is not so reliable and accurate because a gesture can only be well determined if the history data is also included for analysis. To implement this, the trajectory determination is vital. Therefore, this paper first computes the trajectory of human hand by inertial integration of attitude, velocity, and position. What has to be pointed out is that the attitude estimation significantly influences the results of velocity and position; hence a PF is introduced for accurate and convergent estimates of attitude quaternion. In this paper, we mainly have the following contributions:

(1) We use inertial sensors including gyroscopes and accelerometers to estimate the position of the user's hand. The first step is to fuse these sensor outputs into the attitude quaternion using the PF. The velocity and position update is then performed using the ZUPT-aided equations.

(2) After recording the trajectory of the hand, the trace is saved as a low-definition image which will be further sent into a BP-NN based gesture recognition system proposed in [24].

(3) The proposed method is systematically verified by experiments showing its advantages in estimation accuracy and feasibility of implementation. It is also compared to a representative gesture recognition algorithm based on accelerometer, which gives proof of its superiority on the success rate.

Figure 1 shows the structure of the recognition system of our paper. This papers is briefly structured as follows: Section 2 introduces the trajectory estimation method. Section 3 includes the BP-NN based hand gesture recognition method. Experiment, simulations, and results are given in Section 4. Section 5 contains the concluding remarks.

2. Relative Position Estimation

2.1. Attitude Determination. In this paper, rotation vectors and quaternions are used for attitude determination. Rotation vector is an effective form for rotational representation. In

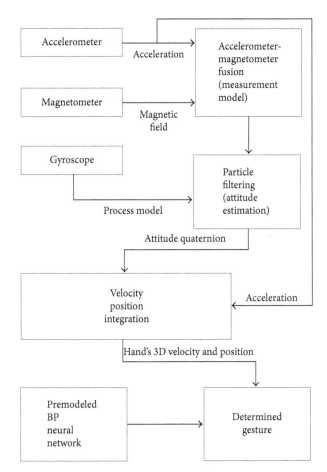

FIGURE 1: Basic structure of the system.

fact rotation vector is the eigenvalue of the direction cosine matrix (DCM) and can be given by [25]

$$(\mathbf{C} - \mathbf{I})\,\Phi = 0, \tag{1}$$

where $\mathbf{C}$ is the DCM, $\mathbf{I}$ is the identity matrix, and Φ is the rotation vector which can be defined by

$$\Phi = \begin{bmatrix} \Phi_x & \Phi_y & \Phi_z \end{bmatrix}^{\mathrm{T}}, \tag{2}$$

where Φ_x is the projection of Φ on x-axis, Φ_y is the projection of Φ on y-axis, and Φ_z is the projection of Φ on z-axis. The differential equation of the rotation vector can be given by [25]

$$\dot{\Phi} = \omega + \frac{1}{2}\Phi \times \omega + \frac{1}{12}\Phi \times (\Phi \times \omega), \tag{3}$$

where ω is the real-time angular velocity which can be given by $\omega = (\omega_x, \omega_y, \omega_z)^T$. Generally speaking, (3) can be simplified as

$$\dot{\Phi} = \omega + \frac{1}{2}\Phi \times \omega \tag{4}$$

By integrating (4), the real-time rotation vector can be calculated. The most important characteristic of the rotation vector is that the rotation vector can compensate for noncommutative error effectively. In 1971, Bortz proposed an attitude estimation method that used rotation vector to avoid coning error [26]. Twelve years later, Miller proposed a discrete-rotation-vector based method with three samples in one integration period [27]. Savage summarized several compensation methods in [28, 29]. According to Savage's theory, the three-sample rotation vector method supposed that the angular velocity can be given by a two-order polynomial within one updating period:

$$\omega(t + \xi) = \mathbf{a} + 2\mathbf{b}\xi + 3\mathbf{c}\xi^2, \tag{5}$$

where $\mathbf{a}, \mathbf{b}, \mathbf{c}$ can be given by [25]

$$\mathbf{a} = \frac{1}{2}\left(11\Delta\theta_1 - 7\Delta\theta_2 + 2\Delta\theta_3\right)$$

$$\mathbf{b} = \frac{9}{2h^2}\left(-2\Delta\theta_1 + 3\Delta\theta_2 - \Delta\theta_3\right) \tag{6}$$

$$\mathbf{c} = \frac{9}{2h^3}\left(\Delta\theta_1 - 2\Delta\theta_2 + \Delta\theta_3\right).$$

Expanding (4) with Taylor Series, we have

$$\mathbf{\Phi}(t + h) = \mathbf{\Phi}(t) + \dot{\mathbf{\Phi}}(t)h + \frac{\ddot{\mathbf{\Phi}}(t)h^2}{2!} + \cdots. \tag{7}$$

Suppose $\mathbf{\Phi}(t) = 0$, multiorder derivatives of the rotation vector can be given by

$$\mathbf{\Phi}(t) = 0,$$

$$\mathbf{\Phi}'(t) = \mathbf{a},$$

$$\mathbf{\Phi}''(t) = 2\mathbf{b},$$

$$\mathbf{\Phi}^{(3)}(t) = 6\mathbf{c} + \mathbf{a} \times \mathbf{b},$$

$$\mathbf{\Phi}^{(4)}(t) = 6\left(\mathbf{a} \times \mathbf{c}\right),$$

$$\mathbf{\Phi}^{(5)}(t) = 6\left(\mathbf{b} \times \mathbf{c}\right),$$

$$\mathbf{\Phi}^{(n)}(t) = 0, \quad n \geq 6. \tag{8}$$

Inserting (8) into (7), the discrete form of (4) can be obtained [28]:

$$\mathbf{\Phi}(t + h) = \mathbf{a}h + \mathbf{b}h^2 + \mathbf{c}h^3 + \frac{h^3}{6}\left(\mathbf{a} \times \mathbf{b}\right) + \frac{h^4}{4}\left(\mathbf{a} \times \mathbf{c}\right)$$

$$+ \frac{h^5}{10}\left(\mathbf{b} \times \mathbf{c}\right) \tag{9}$$

$$= \Delta\theta + \frac{33}{80}\left(\Delta\theta_1 \times \Delta\theta_3\right) + \frac{57}{80}\Delta\theta_2$$

$$\times\left(\Delta\theta_3 - \Delta\theta_1\right),$$

where $\Delta\theta = \Delta\theta_1 + \Delta\theta_2 + \Delta\theta_3$ is the vector sum of angular increments. Equation (9) is called the three-sample rotation vector algorithm. Once the rotation vector is calculated, it can be converted to a quaternion:

$$\mathbf{q}(h) = \left[\cos\frac{\phi}{2} \quad \frac{\Phi_x}{\phi}\sin\frac{\phi}{2} \quad \frac{\Phi_y}{\phi}\sin\frac{\phi}{2} \quad \frac{\Phi_z}{\phi}\sin\frac{\phi}{2}\right]^T, \tag{10}$$

where $\phi = \sqrt{\Phi_x^2 + \Phi_y^2 + \Phi_z^2}$ denotes the length of the rotation vector. Multiplying the quaternions from the initial time, the DCM from hand to geographical coordinate system can be given by [28]

$$\mathbf{C}_b^n = \begin{pmatrix} \left(q_0^2 + q_1^2 - q_2^2 - q_3^2\right) & 2\left(q_1q_2 - q_0q_3\right) & 2\left(q_1q_3 - q_0q_2\right) \\ 2\left(q_1q_2 - q_0q_3\right) & \left(q_0^2 - q_1^2 + q_2^2 - q_3^2\right) & 2\left(q_0q_1 + q_2q_3\right) \\ 2\left(q_1q_3 + q_0q_2\right) & 2\left(q_2q_3 - q_0q_1\right) & \left(q_0^2 - q_1^2 - q_2^2 + q_3^2\right) \end{pmatrix}, \tag{11}$$

where b represents hand while n represents North-East-Down (NED) Coordinate System. The DCM forms the mathematical platform of the Strapdown Inertial Navigation System (SINS).

The MEMS gyroscope usually has bias in the output which leads to the drift of the attitude's integral. In this way, accelerometer is usually used for compensating for the drift. In engineering practice, observers and optimal filtering techniques are usually adopted to improve the accuracy of the attitude estimation [23]. In the next subsection, we would like to introduce one Improved Unscented Particle Filter for such state estimation.

2.2. Particle Filtering for Attitude Estimation. The inertial attitude determination can be acquired from equations in last subsection. However, in real practice, other sensors like accelerometer and magnetometer are integrated with gyroscope for much more accurate and stable results. We now introduce the particle filtering algorithm which was proposed in [30]. Assume that the discrete state space has the following model:

$$\mathbf{X}_k = f\left(\mathbf{X}_{k-1}\right) + \mathbf{W}_k,$$

$$\mathbf{L}_k = h\left(\mathbf{X}_k\right) + \mathbf{V}_k, \tag{12}$$

where $\mathbf{X}_k$, $\mathbf{L}_k$ represent the state vector and observation vector, respectively. $\mathbf{W}_k, \mathbf{V}_k$ are independent zero-mean white Gaussian noises (WGNs). Then the particle filtering has the following calculation procedure:

(1) *Initialization*: at $k = 0$, we extract N sample point $x_0^{(i)}$ and weight $w_0^{(i)} = 1/N$ from the importance function, where $i = 1, 2, \ldots, N$. Using

$$w_{k+1}^{(i)} \propto w_k^i \frac{p\left(\mathbf{L}_{k+1} \mid \mathbf{X}_{k+1}^{(i)}\right) p\left(\mathbf{X}_{k+1}^{(i)} \mid \mathbf{X}_k^{(i)}\right)}{Q\left(\mathbf{X}_{k+1}^{(i)} \mid \mathbf{X}_k^{(i)}, \mathbf{L}_{k+1}\right)}, \quad (13)$$

where Q denotes the importance function and p is the probability density function, we may compute the particle's weight. It is also noted that here the former p denotes the likelihood function while the latter is the state transition one.

(2) *Forecast*: at time epoch k, we forecast N particles using the state model where the process noise is subjected to the probability density function $p(\mathbf{W}_k)$.

(3) *Update*: the importance of N particles is updated using $w_{k+1}^{(i)} = w_k^{(i)} p(\mathbf{L}_{k+1} \mid \mathbf{X}_{k+1}^{(i)})$ and then normalization and then using norm 1.

(4) *Resampling*: given the threshold number of the particles as N_{th}, we can calculate the effective number of particles by

$$N_{\text{eff}} = \frac{1}{\sum_{i=1}^{N} \left[w_k^{(i)}\right]^2}. \quad (14)$$

When we get $N_{\text{eff}} < N_{\text{th}}$, we may resample the N particles and obtain their weights. Then using $\widehat{\mathbf{X}}_k = (1/N) \sum_{i=1}^{N} w_k^{(i)} \mathbf{X}_k^{(i)}$ the final estimated state can be computed. In this paper, the resampling technique is chosen as the residual resampling.

The presented scheme is a sequential Monte Carlo suboptimal method. In attitude estimation, the quaternion can be used as the state vector. The accelerometer-magnetometer combination can be used for measurement model. The measurement equation, that is,

$$\begin{aligned} \mathbf{A}^b &= \mathbf{C}\mathbf{A}^r \\ \mathbf{M}^b &= \mathbf{C}\mathbf{M}^r, \end{aligned} \quad (15)$$

can show that the direction cosine matrix is the quadratic function of the attitude quaternion. Hence there is nonlinearities inside the measurement model and it is very suitable to use particle filtering for state estimation.

With the above algorithm, we may improve the conventional nonlinear estimation results that mainly generated from Extended Kalman Filter (EKF [31]). Here we define the state variable as $\mathbf{X} = (q_0, q_1, q_2, q_3)^T$. The state propagation model is given in the last subsection and the variance information has been systematically derived. Related materials can be found in [32]. Then, with the presented approach, the filtering can be recursively continued.

2.3. Velocity and Position Determination. The differential equation of velocity can be given by [28]

$$\dot{\mathbf{v}}^n = \mathbf{C}_b^n \mathbf{f}^b - (2\omega_{ie}^n + \omega_{en}^n) \times \mathbf{v}^n + \mathbf{g}^n, \quad (16)$$

where $\mathbf{v}$ is the velocity of hand, $\mathbf{f}^b$ is the acceleration measured by the accelerometer, ω_{ie}^n is the rotational angular velocity of the Earth in NED, ω_{en}^n is the angular velocity of NED relative to the Earth-Centered, Earth-Fixed (ECEF) Coordinate system and $\mathbf{g}^n$ is the vector of gravity which can be written as

$$\mathbf{g}^n = \begin{bmatrix} 0 & 0 & g \end{bmatrix}^T, \quad (17)$$

where g is the local gravitational acceleration. Usually, MEMS gyroscopes cannot sense the rotational angular velocity of the Earth, so that ω_{en}^n is much smaller than ω_{ie}^n in most low-speed cases. So (13) can be simplified in this paper as follows:

$$\dot{\mathbf{v}}^n = \mathbf{C}_b^n \mathbf{f}^b + \mathbf{g}^n \quad (18)$$

In accordance with (15), the discrete form of the velocity update equation can be given by [29]

$$\mathbf{v}_k = \mathbf{v}_{k-1} + \mathbf{C}_{k-1} \int_{t_{k-1}}^{t_k} (\mathbf{f} + \Delta\theta \times \mathbf{f}) \, dt + \int_{t_{k-1}}^{t_k} \mathbf{g} \, dt, \quad (19)$$

where $\mathbf{C}_{k-1}$ is the DCM at the moment of k and $\Delta\theta$ is the angular increment which is a function of time. Let

$$\begin{aligned} \Delta\mathbf{v}_{sf(k)} &= \int_{t_{k-1}}^{t_k} (\mathbf{f} + \Delta\theta \times \mathbf{f}) \, dt \\ \Delta\mathbf{v}_{g(k)} &= \int_{t_{k-1}}^{t_k} \mathbf{g} \, dt \end{aligned} \quad (20)$$

and (16) can be written as

$$\mathbf{v}_k = \mathbf{v}_{k-1} + \mathbf{C}_{k-1}\Delta\mathbf{v}_{sf(k)} + \Delta\mathbf{v}_{g(k)} \quad (21)$$

Obviously, the most significant item of (17) is $\mathbf{C}_{k-1}\Delta\mathbf{v}_{sf(k)}$ which can be derived as follows:

$$\begin{aligned} \Delta\mathbf{v}_{sf(k)} &= \Delta\mathbf{v}_k + \frac{1}{2}\Delta\theta_k \times \Delta\mathbf{v}_k \\ &+ \frac{1}{2}\int_{t_{k-1}}^{t_k} [\Delta\theta(t) \times \mathbf{f}(t) + \Delta\mathbf{v}(t) \times \omega(t)] \, dt. \end{aligned} \quad (22)$$

Let $\Delta\mathbf{v}_{\text{scul}(k)} = (1/2)\int_{t_{k-1}}^{t_k} [\Delta\theta(t) \times \mathbf{f}(t) + \Delta\mathbf{v}(t) \times \omega(t)] dt$ be the sculling motion item. According to [29], the three-sample-based sculling motion item can be given by

$$\begin{aligned} \Delta\mathbf{v}_{\text{scul}(k)} &= \frac{33}{80} \left(\Delta\theta_{k,1} \times \Delta\mathbf{v}_{k,3} + \Delta\mathbf{v}_{k,1} \times \Delta\theta_{k,3}\right) \\ &+ \frac{57}{80} \left(\Delta\theta_{k,1} \times \Delta\mathbf{v}_{k,2} + \Delta\theta_{k,2} \times \Delta\mathbf{v}_{k,3} + \Delta\mathbf{v}_{k,1}\right) \\ &\times \Delta\theta_{k,2} + \Delta\mathbf{v}_{k,2} \times \Delta\theta_{k,3}\big). \end{aligned} \quad (23)$$

With (16), (17), (18), (19), and (20), the real-time velocity can be calculated. The position of the hand in NED can be also calculated by integrating the velocity which can be given by

$$\mathbf{p}^n = \int_0^t \mathbf{v}^n d\tau. \quad (24)$$

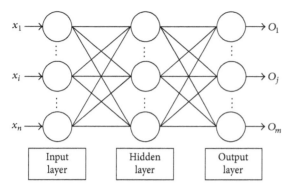

FIGURE 2: The structure of BPNN.

Here, we suppose that the initial position vector is $\mathbf{p}_0{}^n = \mathbf{0}$ and the real-time position of the hand will be calculated and recorded. The recorded trace will be projected to the vertical plane and the projected trace will be saved as a 64×32 image which can be recognized later using BP-NN.

In real applications, the velocity and position estimation may diverge due to the bias of the accelerometer. In this way, the zero-velocity update (ZUPT) is introduced to overcome such disadvantages [33]. That is to say, when the acceleration is measured to be less than a settled threshold (usually the absolute value of the accelerometer's bias), the acceleration would not be integrated, so as to the position.

3. Recognition of Gesture

3.1. The Structure of BP-NN.
The backpropagation neural network is a Multilayer Neural Network (MNN) which owns at least three layers and each layer of the BP-NN consists of several neurons. Each neuron in the hidden layer is connected with all the neurons in both the front layer and the rear layer while there is no connection between neurons within a layer. When training the BP-NN, the activation values of the neurons will spread from the input layer to the output layer. To lower the error between expected output values and the feedback values, the backpropagation algorithm (BPA) will be used to adjust the weights between the neurons from the output layer to the input layer. Just like the feedback control in Modern Control Theory, the error will then be decreased time after time. When the error is less than a predetermined threshold, the training process stops and the trained BP-NN can be used for gesture recognition. In this paper, the three-layer BP-NN is used for recognition. A three-layer BP-NN can be illustrated in Figure 2.

3.2. The Training Algorithm of BP-NN.
According to neural networks theory, the basic training methods can be given as follows.

Let $f(x)$ be the activation function of the input layer, hidden layer, and output layer. In this paper, the Sigmoid Transfer Function (STF) $f(x) = 1/(1 + e^{-x})$, Linear Transfer Function (LTF) $f(x) = x$, and Hyperbolic Tangent Sigmoid Transfer Function (HTSTF) $f(x) = 2/(1 + e^{-x}) - 1$ are used for representing activation functions.

The training process of BP-NN is actually an optimization problem. The training algorithm based on Gradient Descent Method (GDM) can be given by

$$w_{ij}(n+1) = w_{ij}(n) + \Delta w_{ij}$$
$$\Delta w_{ij} = \eta \delta_j O_i, \tag{25}$$

where η is the training efficiency, O_i denotes the real output of the ith neuron, and δ_j is the error of the jth neuron. δ_j can be given by

$$\delta_j$$
$$= \begin{cases} (y_j - O_j) O_j (1 - O_j), & N_j \in OutputLayer \\ O_j (1 - O_j) \sum_k \delta_k w_{jk}, & N_j \in HiddenLayer, \end{cases} \tag{26}$$

where y_j is the ideal output of the jth neuron, O_j is the real output of the jth neuron, and N_j denotes the jth neuron.

3.3. Grid-Based Feature Extraction.
As has been utilized in [34], the grid statistical feature extraction method is very popular. In this paper, the image is divided into $16 \times 8 = 128$ grids. We use digits from 0 to 9 as the ideal hand gesture. The divided numbers 0 and 8 can be given in Figure 3.

4. Experiment

4.1. Platform Setup.
The proposed algorithm fuses the inertial sensor data into attitude quaternion and then computes the velocity and position. Here the position's history can well describe the trajectory of the human hand. In this case, we especially design one experimental platform for such validation. In Figure 4, the tower development platform with NXP Kinetis MK60DN512 microcontroller is presented. The employed platform owns the core processing speed of 100 MHz along with the interfaces of SDIO, SPI, UART, WIFI, and CAN Bus. This allows for the data acquisition and logging of wearable inertial sensors. A miniature inertial sensor module including MPU6000 gyroscope, accelerometer combination, and HMC5983 magnetometer is attached to the designed platform using the RS232 cable free of electromagnetic interference (see Figure 5). The module is in the size of $3 \text{ cm} \times 3 \text{ cm}$, making it much more flexible to be mounted on human's hand. The data polling rate is set to 500 Hz for MPU6000 and 220 Hz for HMC5983. Apart from this, the miniature module can also produce the reference attitude outputs in quaternion. According to the reference manual of this product, the attitude estimation algorithms is effective and accomplished by EKF. In the later comparisons, the results are going to be compared with such reference Euler angles.

4.2. Attitude, Velocity, and Position Estimation.
The initial attitude is set as $\mathbf{X}_0 = \mathbf{q} = (1, 0, 0, 0)^T$. The initial variance of the state vector is defined as $\Sigma_{\mathbf{W}_0} = 0.001 \mathbf{I}_{4 \times 4}$. In the particle filtering design, we set $N = 50$ while the threshold is $N_{th} = N$. The raw sensor data is shown in Figure 6 while

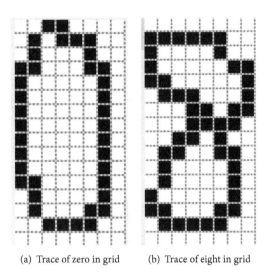

(a) Trace of zero in grid   (b) Trace of eight in grid

FIGURE 3: Illustration of grid-based feature extraction.

FIGURE 4: Designed hardware for data acquisition from hand gesture sensor.

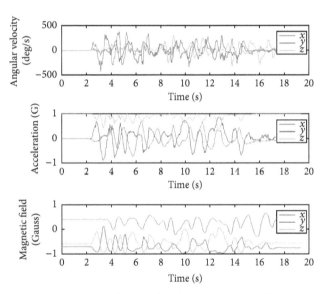

FIGURE 6: Inertial sensor data from miniature module.

the generated attitude outputs are shown in Figure 7. We can see that the proposed attitude estimator has basically the same performance with reference system.

The calculated attitude is then used for velocity and position integral. After the position integral, the trajectory are saved as images. The first 30 trajectories are used as training samples. And the printing character is also added to the set of training samples which can be shown in Line 4 of Figure 8.

4.3. Neural Network. The Neural Network Toolbox of MAT-LAB is utilized for training the BP-NN. In this section, the Levenberg-Marquardt Method (LMM) and GDM are adopted as training algorithm, respectively. The Mean Square Error (MSE) was used as the evaluation standard of the performance of trained BP-NN. The performances of the BP-NNs are compared with different training algorithms and

FIGURE 5: Gesture sensor including 3-axis gyroscope, accelerometer, and magnetometer and reference Euler angles.

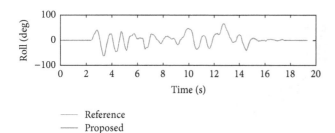

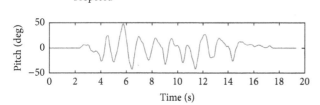

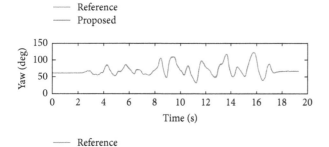

FIGURE 7: Attitude estimation results.

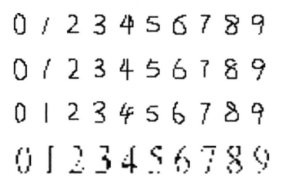

FIGURE 8: Training samples.

TABLE 1: Grouped MSEs.

Trn. func.	Act. func.		
	STF	LTF	HTSTF
LMM	$MSE_{1,1}$	$MSE_{1,2}$	$MSE_{1,3}$
GDM	$MSE_{2,1}$	$MSE_{2,2}$	$MSE_{2,3}$

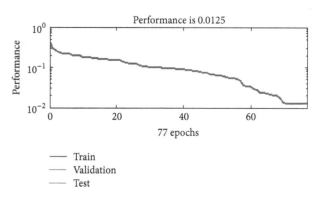

FIGURE 9: Performance of trained BP-NN using LMM.

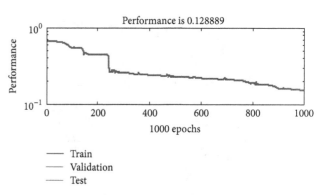

FIGURE 10: Performance of trained BP-NN using GDA.

activation functions, which are shown in Figures 9 and 10 and Tables 1 and 2.

As can be seen in Figures 9 and 10, the performance of LMM is better than GDM in this case. MSEs from different combinations are grouped into Table 1.

MSEs of the test data can be given as in Table 2.

Obviously, GDM is not reliable in this paper at all because its success rate is too low for real applications. The STF-LMM combination shows the best performance among all the combinations. The STF-LMM combination can be used for recognition, which is a component of the proposed system.

4.4. Gesture Recognition Results. With the designed system shown above, we make several comparison experiments with a recent representative method. This method is proposed by Xu et al. in which an accelerometer is adopted for gesture recognition [13]. The advantage of the proposed method is that it logs the history gesture movements so that the hand gesture can be determined more accurately. We first generate several gestures with the designed platform and then use the aforementioned parameters and modeled BP-NN to verify the success rate of both methodologies. The general results are summarized in Table 3.

We can see that, for some instant gestures, the two methods show not much macroscopic differences. However, when the gesture becomes slow, which relies on the history identification of itself, the proposed method shows much more superiority. This verifies the parameters and models described above and also proves the feasibility and efficiency of the proposed algorithm.

5. Conclusion

In this paper, we propose a hand gesture recognition system that combines inertial sensors and BP-NN together. Rotation

TABLE 2: Tested MSEs.

Gesture	0	1	2	3	4	5	6	7	8	9
Trace										
$MSE_{1,1}$	$1.7e-08$	$2.9e-09$	$2.8e-17$	$1.7e-08$	$6.4e-10$	$2.2e-10$	$1.2e-09$	$5.4e-9$	$1.6e-10$	$8.4e-09$
$MSE_{1,2}$	$1.1e-01$	Wrong	$4.8e-02$	Wrong	$8.1e-02$	$7.4e-02$	Wrong	Wrong	$7.0e-02$	Wrong
$MSE_{1,3}$	$6.3e-04$	$1.3e-03$	$1.0e-03$	$4.5e-04$	$1.6e-05$	$5.0e-03$	$3.3e-05$	$1.0e-03$	$1.5e-03$	$6.4e-06$
$MSE_{2,1}$	$7.8e-02$	Wrong	$8.9e-02$	Wrong	$3.7e-02$	Wrong	Wrong	Wrong	$2.2e-02$	Wrong
$MSE_{2,2}$	$9.8e-02$	Wrong	$1.1e-01$	Wrong	Wrong	Wrong	Wrong	Wrong	$9.9e-02$	Wrong
$MSE_{2,3}$	$1.0e-01$	Wrong	Wrong	Wrong	$9.7e-02$	Wrong	Wrong	Wrong	$1.1e-01$	Wrong

TABLE 3: Gesture recognition results.

Algorithm	"One," fast	"One," slow	"Nine," fast	"Nine," slow
Proposed	98.76%	92.43%	89.96%	88.27%
Compared	97.45%	65.22%	90.13%	43.78%

vector method is used to compensate for the noncommutative errors in the determination of attitude, velocity, and position. Particle filtering is introduced to generate accurate attitude outputs from these sensors. Throughout the real-world experiments, the best activation function and training function of the BP-NN are determined successfully. The final tested performance of the BP-NN proved the effectiveness of our method. However, it should be noted that the robustness of our method has not been verified yet. In the future, we will combine different hand gesture recognition methods together in further researches to develop a new robust and more accurate recognition system.

Conflicts of Interest

The authors declare no conflicts of interest regarding this manuscript.

Acknowledgments

This research was supported by National Science Foundation of China (Grant no. 61450010).

References

[1] S. M. Mankar and S. A. Chhabria, "Review on hand gesture based mobile control application," in *Proceedings of the 2015 International Conference on Pervasive Computing (ICPC '15)*, IEEE, Pune, India, January 2015.

[2] V. Bhame, R. Sreemathy, and H. Dhumal, "Vision based hand gesture recognition using eccentric approach for human computer interaction," in *Proceedings of the 3rd International Conference on Advances in Computing, Communications and Informatics (ICACCI '14)*, pp. 949–953, IEEE, New Delhi, India, September 2014.

[3] Z. Xu and H. Zhu, "Vision-based detection of dynamic gesture," in *Proceedings of the 2009 International Conference on Test and Measurement (ICTM '09)*, pp. 223–226, IEEE, Hong Kong, December 2009.

[4] Q. Bai, Y. Zhang, J. Tan, L. Zhao, and Z. Qi, "Recognition of the numbers of numerical civilian instruments based on BP neural network," in *Proceedings of the International Conference on Industrial Machatronics and Automation*, pp. 105–108, IEEE, 2009.

[5] S. Gai, G. Yang, S. Zhang, and M. Wan, "New banknote number recognition algorithm based on support vector machine," in *Proceedings of the 2013 2nd IAPR Asian Conference on Pattern Recognition, ACPR 2013*, pp. 176–180, IEEE, Japan, November 2013.

[6] F. Li and S. Gao, "Character recognition system based on back-propagation neural network," in *Proceedings of the 2010 International Conference on Machine Vision and Human-Machine Interface (MVHI '10)*, pp. 393–396, IEEE, China, April 2010.

[7] R. Szeliski, *Computer Vision*, Springer, 2010.

[8] J. Wu, Z. Zhou, B. Gao, R. Li, Y. Cheng, and H. Fourati, "Fast linear quaternion attitude estimator using vector observations," *IEEE Transactions on Automation Science and Engineering*, 2017.

[9] A. Akl, C. Feng, and S. Valaee, "A novel accelerometer-based gesture recognition system," *IEEE Transactions on Signal Processing*, vol. 59, no. 12, pp. 6197–6205, 2011.

[10] E.-S. Choi, W.-C. Bang, S.-J. Cho, J. Yang, D.-Y. Kim, and S.-R. Kim, "Beatbox music phone: gesture-based interactive mobile phone using a tri-axis accelerometer," in *Proceedings of the IEEE International Conference on Industrial Technology (ICIT '05)*, pp. 97–102, IEEE, Hong Kong, December 2005.

[11] J. Rao, T. Gao, Z. Gong, and Z. Jiang, "Low cost hand gesture learning and recognition system based on hidden markov model," in *Proceedings of the 2009 2nd International Symposium on Information Science and Engineering (ISISE '09)*, pp. 433–438, IEEE, Shanghai, China, December 2009.

[12] R. Xie, X. Sun, X. Xia, and J. Cao, "Similarity matching-based extensible hand gesture recognition," *IEEE Sensors Journal*, vol. 15, no. 6, pp. 3475–3483, 2015.

[13] R. Xu, S. Zhou, and W. J. Li, "MEMS accelerometer based nonspecific-user hand gesture recognition," *IEEE Sensors Journal*, vol. 12, no. 5, pp. 1166–1173, 2012.

[14] A. I. Bhuyan and T. C. Mallick, "Gyro-accelerometer based control of a robotic arm using AVR microcontroller," in *Proceedings of the 9th International Forum on Strategic Technology (IFOST '14)*, pp. 409–413, IEEE, Cox's Bazar, Bangladesh, October 2014.

[15] Z. Lu, X. Chen, Q. Li, X. Zhang, and P. Zhou, "A hand gesture recognition framework and wearable gesture-based interaction

prototype for mobile devices," *IEEE Transactions on Human-Machine Systems*, vol. 44, no. 2, pp. 293–299, 2014.

[16] Y.-L. Hsu, C.-L. Chu, Y.-J. Tsai, and J.-S. Wang, "An inertial pen with dynamic time warping recognizer for handwriting and gesture recognition," *IEEE Sensors Journal*, vol. 15, no. 1, pp. 154–163, 2015.

[17] S. Zhou, F. Fei, G. Zhang et al., "2D human gesture tracking and recognition by the fusion of MEMS inertial and vision sensors," *IEEE Sensors Journal*, vol. 14, no. 4, pp. 1160–1170, 2014.

[18] D. G. Lowe, "Distinctive image features from scale-invariant keypoints," *International Journal of Computer Vision*, vol. 60, no. 2, pp. 91–110, 2004.

[19] K. Mikolajczyk and C. Schmid, "A performance evaluation of local descriptors," *IEEE Transactions on Pattern Analysis and Machine Intelligence*, vol. 27, no. 10, pp. 1615–1630, 2005.

[20] M. Matsugu, K. Mori, Y. Mitari, and Y. Kaneda, "Subject independent facial expression recognition with robust face detection using a convolutional neural network," *Neural Networks*, vol. 16, no. 5-6, pp. 555–559, 2003.

[21] C. Ye, S. Hong, and A. Tamjidi, "6-DOF Pose Estimation of a Robotic Navigation Aid by Tracking Visual and Geometric Features," *IEEE Transactions on Automation Science and Engineering*, vol. 12, no. 4, pp. 1169–1180, 2015.

[22] Z. Zhou, Y. Li, J. Liu, and G. Li, "Equality constrained robust measurement fusion for adaptive kalman-filter-based heterogeneous multi-sensor navigation," *IEEE Transactions on Aerospace and Electronic Systems*, vol. 49, no. 4, pp. 2146–2157, 2013.

[23] J. Wu, Z. Zhou, J. Chen, H. Fourati, and R. Li, "Fast complementary filter for attitude estimation using low-cost MARG sensors," *IEEE Sensors Journal*, vol. 16, no. 18, pp. 6997–7007, 2016, http://ieeexplore.ieee.org/lpdocs/epic03/wrapper.htm?arnumber=7508437=0pt.

[24] Y. Shi, W. Fan, and G. Shi, "The research of printed character recognition based on neural network," in *Proceedings of the 2011 4th International Symposium on Parallel Architectures, Algorithms and Programming (PAAP '11)*, pp. 119–122, China, December 2011.

[25] P. G. Savage, *Strapdown Analytics*, Strapdown Associates Inc., 1997.

[26] J. E. Bortz, "A new mathematical formulation for strapdown inertial navigation," *IEEE Transactions on Aerospace and Electronic Systems*, vol. AES-7, no. 1, pp. 61–66, 1971.

[27] R. B. Miller, "A new strapdown attitude algorithm," *Journal of Guidance, Control, and Dynamics*, vol. 6, no. 4, pp. 287–291, 1983.

[28] P. G. Savage, "Strapdown inertial navigation integration algorithm design. Part 1. Attitude algorithms," *Journal of Guidance, Control, and Dynamics*, vol. 21, no. 1, pp. 19–28, 1998.

[29] P. G. Savage, "Strapdown inertial navigation integration algorithm design part 2: velocity and position algorithms," *Journal of Guidance, Control, and Dynamics*, vol. 21, no. 2, pp. 208–221, 1998.

[30] J. S. Liu and R. Chen, "Sequential Monte Carlo methods for dynamic systems," *Journal of the American Statistical Association*, vol. 93, no. 443, pp. 1032–1044, 1998.

[31] A. M. Sabatini, "Quaternion-based extended Kalman filter for determining orientation by inertial and magnetic sensing," *IEEE Transactions on Biomedical Engineering*, vol. 53, no. 7, pp. 1346–1356, 2006.

[32] R. G. Valenti, I. Dryanovski, and J. Xiao, "A linear Kalman filter for MARG orientation estimation using the algebraic quaternion algorithm," *IEEE Transactions on Instrumentation and Measurement*, vol. 65, no. 2, pp. 467–481, 2016.

[33] Z. Wang, H. Zhao, S. Qiu, and Q. Gao, "Stance-Phase Detection for ZUPT-Aided Foot-Mounted Pedestrian Navigation System," *IEEE/ASME Transactions on Mechatronics*, vol. 20, no. 6, pp. 3170–3181, 2015.

[34] Y. Zhang, S. Xie, and S. Wei, "Industrial character recognition based on grid feature and wavelet moment," in *Proceedings of the 2013 IEEE International Conference on Imaging Systems and Techniques (IST '13)*, pp. 56–59, IEEE, Beijing, China, October 2013.

13

Image Blocking Encryption Algorithm based on Laser Chaos Synchronization

Shu-Ying Wang,[1] Jian-Feng Zhao,[2] Xian-Feng Li,[3] and Li-Tao Zhang[4]

[1]*Department of Nationalities, Huanghe Science and Technology College, Zhengzhou 450053, China*
[2]*Department of Information Engineering, Henan Polytechnic, Zhengzhou 450046, China*
[3]*College of Mathematics and Science, Lanzhou Jiaotong University, Lanzhou 730070, China*
[4]*Department of Mathematics and Physics, Zhengzhou Institute of Aeronautical Industry Management, Zhengzhou 450015, China*

Correspondence should be addressed to Jian-Feng Zhao; zjfzwf@126.com

Academic Editor: Wen Chen

In view of the digital image transmission security, based on laser chaos synchronization and Arnold cat map, a novel image encryption scheme is proposed. Based on pixel values of plain image a parameter is generated to influence the secret key. Sequences of the drive system and response system are pretreated by the same method and make image blocking encryption scheme for plain image. Finally, pixels position are scrambled by general Arnold transformation. In decryption process, the chaotic synchronization accuracy is fully considered and the relationship between the effect of synchronization and decryption is analyzed, which has characteristics of high precision, higher efficiency, simplicity, flexibility, and better controllability. The experimental results show that the encryption algorithm image has high security and good antijamming performance.

1. Introduction

With the rapid development of information transmission technology, electronic data interchange is an important way to communicate and exchange information. Multimedia information with secure communication problems urgently needs to be solved. Characteristics of chaotic sequence have natural advantages in cryptography. During the late 1980s, the British mathematician Matthews put forward the chaos into cryptography firstly [1]. As the traditional encryption technique DES cannot be directly used for image encryption, recently many special properties of chaotic maps are suitable to encrypt digital image and provide a new idea to select data security problem of multimedia information [2–7].

The laser chaos not only has complex phenomena of all dissipative systems, but also has excellent characteristics such as built-in self-test ability (BIST), pulse generation, closeness to the ideal model, and easiness of design compared with theory. Chaotic laser signal with inherent broad band, noise, and unpredictable characteristics greatly increased the difficulty of optoelectronic reconnaissance and is an important technology of optical information security. The laser-based digital communication was put forward by Colet and Roy in 1994 [8] and became increasingly popular in recent years [9–11].

Synchronization is a basic characteristic of complex system and the phenomenon generally exists in natural ecosystem and artificial system such as biology, engineering, and machinery [12, 13]. Synchronization of chaotic systems and secure communication have become research hotspots of nonlinear system [14, 15]. With simple structure the linear feedback controller is easily implemented physically and has high practical value, but chaos synchronization is rarely applied in digital image encryption [16, 17].

This paper is organized as follows. In Section 2, linear feedback synchronization of Lorenz-Haken is introduced. In Section 3, based on chaos synchronization, a novel image encryption algorithm is proposed. In Section 4, numerical simulation is given to illustrate the effectiveness of the proposed algorithm. Finally, the paper concludes in Section 5.

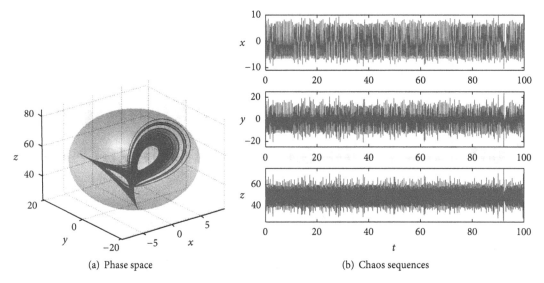

(a) Phase space   (b) Chaos sequences

FIGURE 1: Laser chaos.

2. Linear Feedback Synchronization of Lorenz-Haken Laser Chaos

The mathematical description of the Lorenz-Haken laser chaos [20] is

$$\dot{x} = a\left(y - x\right),$$
$$\dot{y} = bx - y - xz,   \qquad (1)$$
$$\dot{z} = xy - cz,$$

where $X = (x, y, z)^T$ is state vector of system (1) and a, b, c are system parameters assigned to $(a, b, c) = (1.4253, 50, 0.2775)$. Initial conditions are $(x_0, y_0, z_0) = (1, 0, 50)$ and time is $t \in [0, 100s]$.

In view of the boundary of chaotic attractor, there are positive numbers M_x, M_y, and M_z, and $|x| \le M_x$, $|y| \le M_y$, and $|z| \le M_z$. Figure 1 shows the phase diagram of chaotic system and state variables which meet the range $-9 < x < 9$, $-21 < y < 21$, and $21 < z < 81$.

System (1) is used as the drive system, and the response system is defined as follows:

$$\dot{x}_1 = a\left(y_1 - x_1\right) + u_1,$$
$$\dot{y}_1 = bx_1 - y_1 - x_1 z_1 + u_2,   \qquad (2)$$
$$\dot{z}_1 = x_1 y_1 - cz_1 + u_3.$$

Suppose that error variables of the system are $e_1 = x - x_1$, $e_2 = y - y_1$, and $e_3 = z - z_1$. A linear feedback controller is selected as $u_i = -k_i e_i$, $(i = 1, 2, 3)$.

Then we get the error system:

$$\dot{e}_1 = \left(k_1 - a\right)e_1 + ae_2,$$
$$\dot{e}_2 = be_1 + \left(k_2 - 1\right)e_2 + xz - x_1 z_1,   \qquad (3)$$
$$\dot{e}_3 = \left(k_3 - c\right)e_3 - xy + x_1 y_1.$$

The Lyapunov function is designed as $V = (1/2)(e_1^2 + e_2^2 + e_3^2)$; then tracking along system (3), we obtain its time derivative:

$$\begin{aligned}
\dot{V} &= e_1 \dot{e}_1 + e_2 \dot{e}_2 + e_3 \dot{e}_3 \\
&= (k_1 - a)e_1^2 + ae_1 e_2 + be_1 e_2 + (k_2 - 1)e_2^2 \\
&\quad + (k_3 + b)e_3^2 + (xz - x_1 z_1)e_2 + (k_3 - c)e_3^2 \\
&\quad + (x_1 y_1 - xy)e_3 \\
&= \left(k_1 - a + \frac{(a + b - z)^2 + y^2}{4}\right)e_1^2 + k_2 e_2^2 \\
&\quad + (k_3 - c + 1)e_3^2 - \left(e_2 - \frac{a + b - z}{2}e_1\right)^2 \\
&\quad - \left(e_3 - \frac{y}{2}e_1\right)^2.
\end{aligned} \qquad (4)$$

To obtain the asymptotic stability of error system, that is to say, $\dot{V} \le 0$, the following conditions need to be satisfied:

$$k_1 - a + \frac{(a + b - z)^2 + y^2}{4} < 0,$$
$$k_2 < 0,   \qquad (5)$$
$$k_3 - c + 1 < 0.$$

Sufficient conditions of the feedback gains k_1, k_2, and k_3 are

$$k_1 < a - \frac{(a + b)^2 + M_z^2 + M_y^2}{4},$$
$$k_2 < 0,   \qquad (6)$$
$$k_3 < c - 1.$$

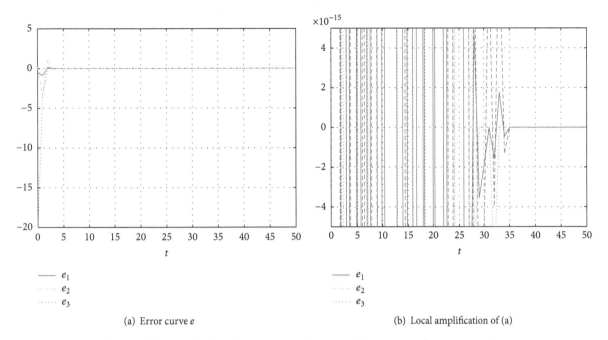

(a) Error curve e

(b) Local amplification of (a)

FIGURE 2: The synchronization error curves between drive system and response system.

TABLE 1: Components of matrix B.

$m = 0$	$m = 1$	$m = 2$	$m = 3$
$B = \{B, x, y, z\}$	$B = \{B, z, x, y\}$	$B = \{B, y, z, x\}$	$B = \{B, x, z, y\}$

In numerical simulation experiment, the slave system is considered with the same parameters as the master system. Initial state variables of them are $(x(0), y(0), z(0)) = (1, 0, 30)$ and $(x(0), y(0), z(0)) = (1, 0, 30)$, respectively. Figure 2 presents the synchronization error curves between drive system and response system which approaches to zero gradually. Completely synchronization is achieved in five seconds by using macroscopic observation, but in fact there is a synchronization error. The enlargement of partial positions of error curve is shown in Figure 2(b).

3. Description of the Algorithm

The original image of size $L = M \times N$, where M and N denote numbers of row and column, respectively. By scanning line by line, the original image is rearranged into matrix P:

(1) Parametric perturbation is defined by adopting formula $T = \mathrm{mod}(\sum_{i=1}^{L} P(i), L)/(L - 1)$. Parameters x_0, y_0, z_0, a, b, c, and r are selected as secret key; $\{x, y, z\}$ are obtained by every chaos iteration. Then $n_0 = 1000$ data points are abandoned and state variables are recombined. Let $m = \mathrm{mod}(\mathrm{abs}(x(n_0 : n_0 + L - 1) + y(n_0 : n_0 + L - 1) + z(n_0 : n_0 + L - 1)), 3)$, and extend zero matrix B in Table 1.

(2) The sequence B is processed as follows:

$$K(i) = \mathrm{mod}\left(\mathrm{floor}\left(\left(|B(i)| - \mathrm{floor}(|B(i)|)\right) \times 10^{m_2}\right), 256\right), \tag{7}$$

where $m_2 \in Z^+$, $1 \le m_2 \le 15$, and $i = 1, 2, \ldots, L$. $|x|$ is absolute of x, and floor(x) indicates down integral function. Obviously, $K(i) \in [0, 255]$ after modular arithmetic. In the paper positive integral $m_2 = 10$. Chaotic sequence B shown in Figure 3(a) is treated as K; self-correlation of K is approximate to zero presented in Figure 3(b). Figure 3(c) displays the local amplification at longitudinal amplification, and most of data are concentrated in interval $[-0.002, 0.002]$. After preprocessing the randomness of chaotic sequence is improved distinctly, and sequence after treatment is more suitable in cryptography.

(3) Exclusive OR operation and modular arithmetic are imposed to the plain image by using sequence K. The first pixel point is encrypted individually, and its encryption exerts effect on encryption of the second pixel. The pixels are encrypted alternately as follows:

$$C(2) = [P(2) + K(2)] \bmod 256$$
$$\oplus [C(1) + K(L)] \bmod 256$$

for $i = 3 : 2 : L$

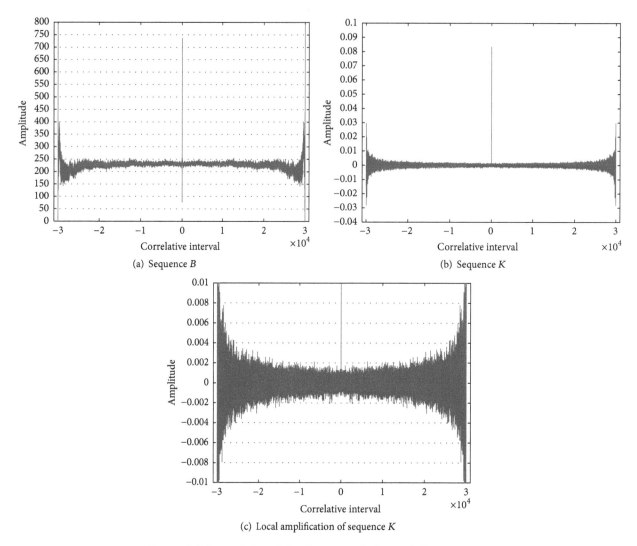

FIGURE 3: Self-correlation of chaotic sequence before and after treatment.

$C(i)$

$= [P(i) + K(i)] \bmod 256$

$\oplus [C(i-2) + K(i+L)] \bmod 256$

end

for $i = 4:2:L$

$C(i)$

$= [P(i) + K(i)] \bmod 256$

$\oplus [C(i-2) + K(L-i)] \bmod 256$

end

$$(8)$$

The encrypted pixel sequence $\{C(i)\}$ is transformed into matrix C of size $M \times N$ with reshape command.

(4) In the process of scrambling, general Arnold transform is used to scramble image C and get scrambled image D. RGB segments of color digital image are scrambled by general Arnold transform with different parameters.

For the given symmetric algorithm, decryption is the inverse operation of encryption, described as follows:

(1) The final encrypted image D is inversely scrambled to get image C.

(2) Chaotic sequences of response system are used to perform antisubstitution decryption operation; the calculation formula is as follows:

for $i = L: -2:3$

$P(i)$

$= \bmod (C(i) \oplus \bmod (C(i-2) \oplus K(i+L), 256), 256)$

$\oplus K(i)$

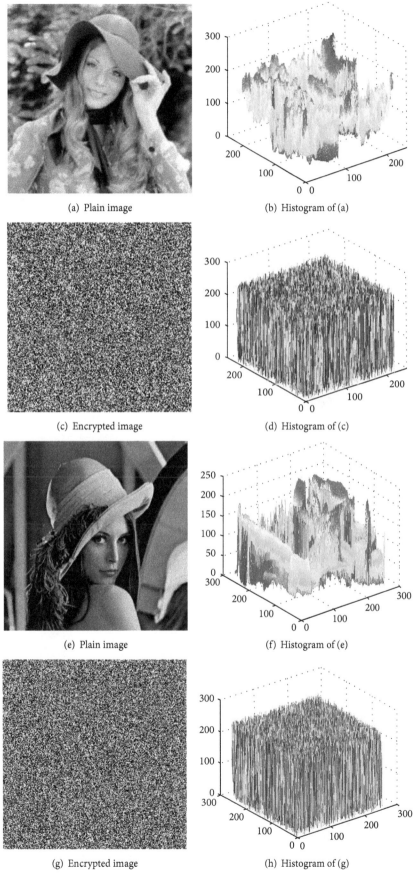

(a) Plain image

(b) Histogram of (a)

(c) Encrypted image

(d) Histogram of (c)

(e) Plain image

(f) Histogram of (e)

(g) Encrypted image

(h) Histogram of (g)

FIGURE 4: Continued.

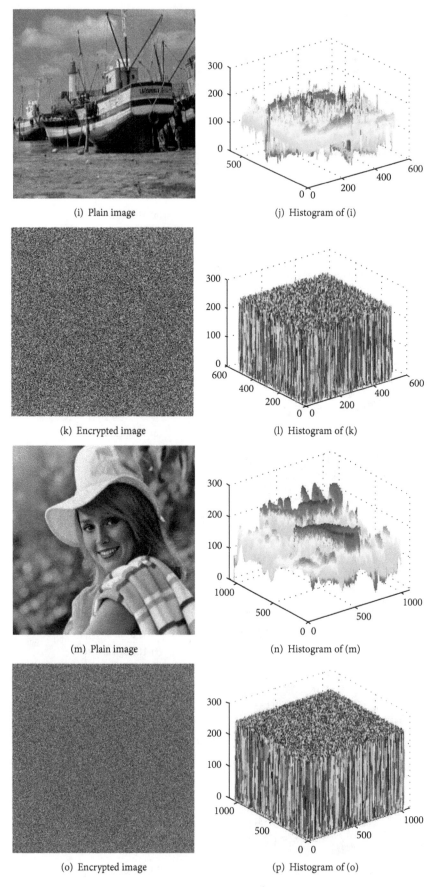

(i) Plain image

(j) Histogram of (i)

(k) Encrypted image

(l) Histogram of (k)

(m) Plain image

(n) Histogram of (m)

(o) Encrypted image

(p) Histogram of (o)

FIGURE 4: Continued.

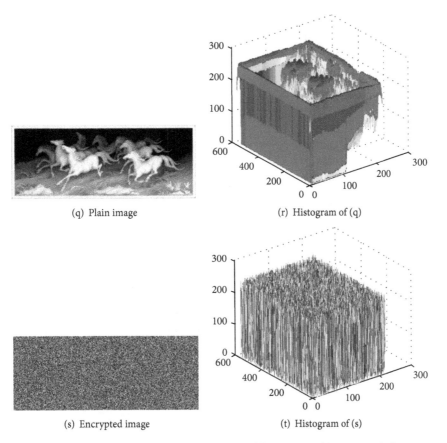

(q) Plain image

(r) Histogram of (q)

(s) Encrypted image

(t) Histogram of (s)

FIGURE 4: The histograms of gray images with different sizes: (a) 220 × 220; (e) 256 × 256; (i) 512 × 512; (m) 1024 × 1024; and (q) 220 × 565.

end

for $i = L : -2 : 4$

$P(i)$

$= \mathrm{mod}\,(C(i) \oplus \mathrm{mod}\,(C(i-2) \oplus K(L-i), 256), 256)$

$\oplus K(i)$

end

$P(2)$

$= \mathrm{mod}\,(C(2) \oplus \mathrm{mod}\,(C(1) \oplus K(L), 256), 256)$

$\oplus K(2)$

$P(1)$

$= \mathrm{mod}\,(C(1) \oplus \mathrm{mod}\,(C(L) \oplus K(L), 256), 256)$

$\oplus K(1)$

$$(9)$$

In encryption algorithm, the digital image is stored as two-dimensional array, including pixel position scrambling and pixel value substitution. For an image of size $L = M \times N$, the total time complexity is $O(L)$ analyzed from the viewpoint of the "big-O notation." Therefore, the efficiency of execution of the algorithm is ideal.

4. Numerical Simulation Results

To verify the effectiveness of the above algorithm, different types of images are carried out in experimentation by using MATLAB platform. Statistical histogram describes the distribution of image pixel. Under the ideal condition, histogram of encrypted image should be approximate to distribute evenly. Histograms of gray image, binary image, and color image and their encrypted images are proposed in Figures 4, 5, and 6, respectively. The eight fine horses gray image is a high resolution image with 370 dpi shown in Figure 4(q). We can see that the gray pixel values of the original image are concentrated in some values, but the histograms of different encrypted images are highly uniform.

4.1. Correlation Coefficients of Adjacent Pixels. Encryption algorithm is designed to reduce the correlation coefficients of adjacent pixels between plain image and encrypted image for resisting statistical attacks. Correlation coefficients of entire randomly selected 3000 pairs of horizontally, vertically, diagonally, and counterdiagonally adjacent pixels are determined. The correlation coefficients between two adjacent pixels of image are calculated by the following formula:

$$R_{xy} = \frac{\mathrm{Conv}\,(x, y)}{\sqrt{D(x)}\sqrt{D(y)}}, \tag{10}$$

TABLE 2: Correlation coefficient of different plain images and cipher images.

Plain image	Horizontal	Vertical	Diagonal	Counterdiagonal
Gray girl (220 × 220)				
Plain image	0.972389	0.973428	0.946752	0.949101
Encrypted image	-2.342213×10^{-4}	1.178432×10^{-4}	4.210485×10^{-5}	-1.094222×10^{-4}
Gray Lena (256 × 256)				
Plain image	0.972953	0.970462	0.916925	0.938441
Encrypted image	-4.156125×10^{-4}	-2.552108×10^{-4}	-2.788174×10^{-5}	-4.829102×10^{-7}
Encrypted image [18]	0.000848277	0.00370914	−0.000189	
Encrypted image [19]	−0.0025	−0.0006	−0.0050	
Gray boat (512 × 512)				
Plain image	0.833645	0.941003	0.850811	0.833801
Encrypted image	-1.234977×10^{-4}	-2.219543×10^{-5}	3.325240×10^{-5}	7.915527×10^{-5}
Binary image (256 × 256)				
Plain image	0.986849	0.984293	0.965644	0.995392
Encrypted image	0.001569	1.869499×10^{-4}	-1.574389×10^{-4}	-1.099277×10^{-4}
Gray Elaine (1024 × 1024)				
Plain image	0.978254	0.966275	0.956931	0.955351
Encrypted image	8.903521×10^{-4}	1.018005×10^{-4}	6.933169×10^{-5}	7.263636×10^{-4}
Eight fine horses (220 × 565)				
Plain image	0.989809	0.983595	0.972294	0.972537
Encrypted image	5.485211×10^{-4}	1.546712×10^{-4}	-7.799651×10^{-5}	-8.218992×10^{-4}
Color baboon (512 × 512 × 3)				
Red				
Plain image	0.772788	0.583314	0.573087	0.509744
Encrypted image	3.495943×10^{-4}	8.087366×10^{-6}	2.572029×10^{-4}	-4.644542×10^{-5}
Green				
Plain image	0.807396	0.654726	0.650771	0.597617
Encrypted image	-5.508956×10^{-4}	-4.001587×10^{-4}	7.277112×10^{-5}	4.782903×10^{-4}
Blue				
Plain image	0.877479	0.790278	0.786803	0.761251
Encrypted image	-7.206039×10^{-5}	4.348691×10^{-4}	-8.564954×10^{-5}	-4.391072×10^{-4}

where

$$E(x) = \frac{1}{N} \sum_{i=1}^{N} x_i,$$

$$D(x) = \frac{1}{N} \sum_{i=1}^{N} [x_i - E(x)]^2, \quad (11)$$

$$\text{Conv}(x, y) = \frac{1}{N} \sum_{i=1}^{N} [x_i - E(x)][y_i - E(y)],$$

where x and y are pixel values of two adjacent pixels in the image.

Figure 7 and Table 2 display distribution of the randomly selected pairs of adjacent pixels in four directions of the original and encrypted image. If the correlation of the encrypted images is close to zero, then it informs good encryption quality. It is clear that the correlation coefficient of the proposed algorithm is smaller than that of other methods proposed in [18, 19].

4.2. Information Entropy.

The concept information entropy was put forward by Shannon [21], which lays the foundation for information theory and digital communication. Information entropy is commonly used to express image texture features and measure the randomness. The entropy $H(x)$ is measured by the formula $H(x) = -\sum_{i=1}^{n} p(x_i)\log_2 p(x_i)$, where $p(x_i)$ denotes the probability of symbol x_i. In theory, the maximum entropy is $H_{\max} = -(1/256)\log_2(1/256) \times 256 = 8$ for a gray image.

From Table 3, it is clear that our approach can encrypt a low entropy image to get higher entropy image which has random information content. The entropy of the encrypted image is actually closer to the maximum entropy than the plain image. The gray distribution of the encrypted image is more uniform, and its security is improved greatly. Obviously the encryption algorithm has better ability to resist statistical attack.

4.3. Decryption Effect.

In numerical simulation, encrypted gray Lena image is decrypted by abandoning 0 points, 1000 points, 3000 points, 5000 points, and 7000 points, and

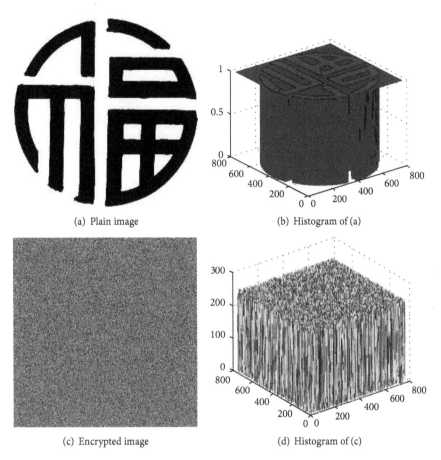

(a) Plain image

(b) Histogram of (a)

(c) Encrypted image

(d) Histogram of (c)

FIGURE 5: The binary image with size of 256×256.

TABLE 3: The entropy of plain image and its corresponding encrypted image.

	Gray images						Color baboon		
	Girl	Lena	Boat	Binary	Elaine	Eight fine horses	Red	Green	Blue
Plain image	7.7256	7.5769	7.1951	1.0060	7.5030	6.9958	7.7532	7.4642	7.7722
Encrypted image	7.9887	7.9898	7.9910	7.9916	7.9915	7.9905	7.9916	7.9917	7.9915

their effects are represented in Figure 8. When the complete synchronization has not yet been achieved, the decryption effect is better with more abandoned points unsynchronized. Subtle difference between plain image and decrypted image cannot be observed subjectively. To avoid uncertainty of subjective evaluation, subjective evaluation is necessary for recovery performance. Common objective indexes are Mean Square Error (MSE) and Peak Signal to Noise Ratio (PSNR) defined as follows:

$$\text{MSE} = \frac{1}{M \cdot N} \sum_{i=1}^{M} \sum_{j=1}^{N} \| P(i,j) - I(i,j) \|^2,$$

$$\text{PSNR} = 10 \cdot \log_{10} \left(\frac{\text{MAX}_I^2}{\text{MSE}} \right). \tag{12}$$

MSE is Mean Square Error between plain image P and processed image I; MAX_I indicates that the maximum number of image colors is 255 with 8 bits per sample. PSNR is essentially identical to MSE, which is the logarithmic representation of MSE. However, MSE has poor correlation with subjective evaluation, so PSNR is usually used as evaluation index. PSNR is inversely proportional to effect of image encryption. When PSNR is more than 28 dB, the decrypted image has better quality. In fact it cannot even distinguish difference with the naked eye when PSNR is up to [35 dB, 40 dB]. After abandoning 0 points, 1000 points, 3000 points, 5000 points, and 7000 points, MSE and PSNR of decrypted gray are listed in Table 4. Comparing with the encrypted Lena, abandoning 7000 points has minimal distortion.

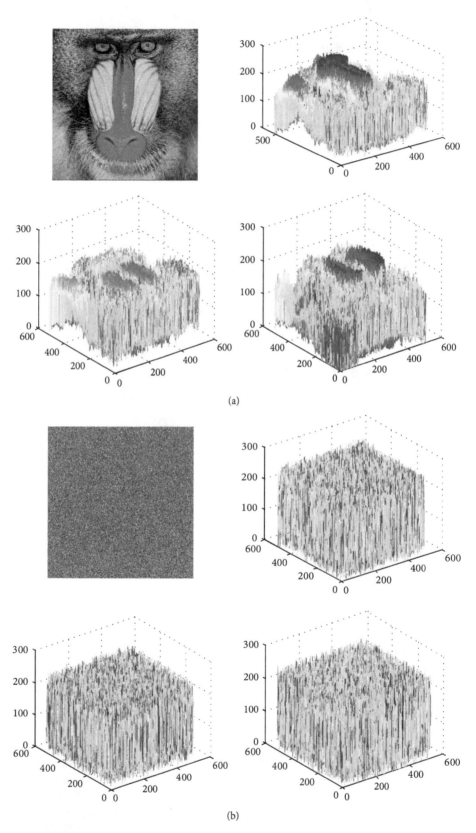

FIGURE 6: The color parrot image: (a) the plain image and histograms of its RGB segments and (b) the encrypted image and histograms of its RGB segments.

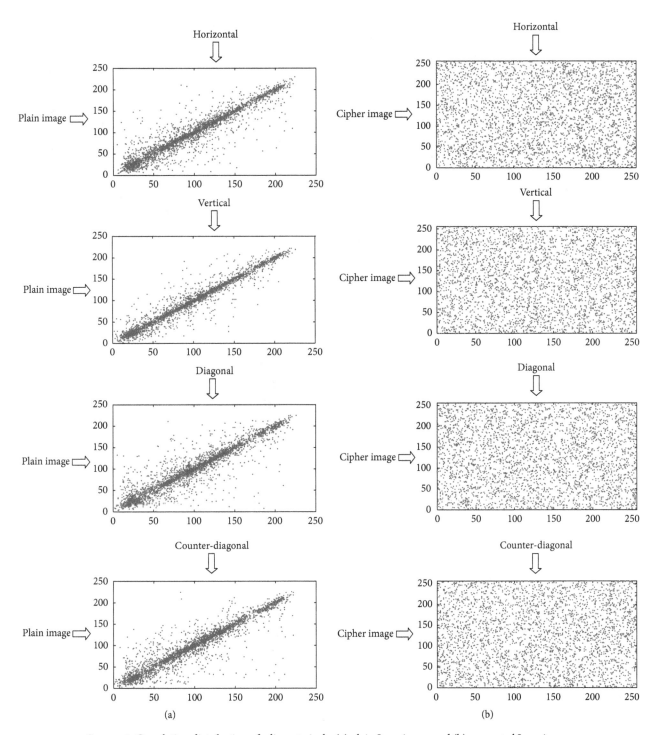

FIGURE 7: Correlation distribution of adjacent pixels: (a) plain Lena image and (b) encrypted Lena image.

4.4. Anti-Interference Attack. During transmission and other treatments, it is subjected to interferences and attacks. The anti-interference attack is an important indicator of testing the quality of the decryption algorithm. Encrypted images with 25% occlusion and 50% occlusion are represented in Figures 9(a) and 9(b); their decrypted images are shown in Figures 9(d) and 9(e), respectively. It is clear that the occlusion parts are diffused uniformly to the whole image;

therefore algorithm of the paper has strong capability against cropping operation.

If the encrypted image is added, salt-and-pepper noise is seen with noise density 0.002, when using the same key to restore the attacked image; the decrypted images are shown in Figure 9(f). It is clear that the encryption algorithm for salt-and-pepper noise attack has good ability to resist interference attack.

(a) Reject 0 points   (b) Reject 1000 points   (c) Reject 3000 points

(d) Reject 5000 points   (e) Reject 7000 points

FIGURE 8: Decryption images of Lena with different dispose points.

TABLE 4: MSE and PSNR of different encrypted images under different reject points.

Value	Reject points					
	0	1000	3000	5000	7000	Encrypted Lena
MSE	733.9676	648.8245	372.7224	62.9877	0.1208	9009.3366
PSNR	19.4740	20.0094	22.4169	30.1382	57.3078	8.5838

5. Conclusion

Linear feedback controller is designed to synchronize the laser chaos and has higher precision. Steady-state error of synchronization reached 10^{-14}. Based on synchronization a novel encryption algorithm is designed. Numerical simulation results show that the given algorithm has sufficiently large key space, highly sensitive keys, better pixel distribution characteristics, and good performance against ciphertext-only attack, differential attack, chosen plaintext attack, and statistical attack. The algorithm can be widely used in secure communication of multimedia data. Linear feedback controller has convenient operation and strong applicability and is suitable for industrial application. The synchronization of chaotic laser systems is applied in image encryption

transmission and achieved good results. The algorithm can realize complete encryption in sender and lossless decryption in the receiver, so as to achieve digital image encryption transmission function.

Competing Interests

The authors declare that they have no competing interests.

Acknowledgments

This research is supported by the National Natural Science Foundation of China (no. 11501525) and the Aeronautical Science Foundation of China (no. 2013ZD55006).

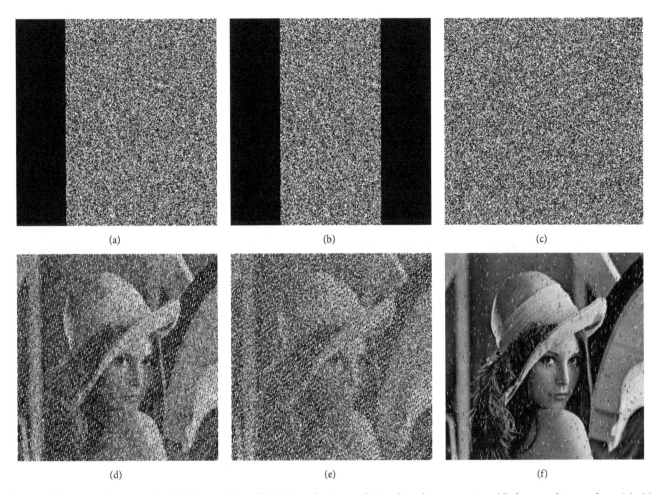

FIGURE 9: Encrypted image with (a) 25% occlusion, (b) 50% occlusion, and (c) salt-and-pepper noise; (d) decrypted image from (a), (e) decrypted image from (b), and (f) decrypted image from (c).

References

[1] R. Matthews, "On the derivation of a 'chaotic' encryption algorithm," *Cryptologia*, vol. 13, no. 1, pp. 29–42, 1989.

[2] G. R. Chen, Y. B. Mao, and C. K. Chui, "A symmetric image encryption scheme based on 3D chaotic cat maps," *Chaos, Solitons and Fractals*, vol. 21, no. 3, pp. 749–761, 2004.

[3] S. Behnia, A. Akhshani, H. Mahmodi, and A. Akhavan, "A novel algorithm for image encryption based on mixture of chaotic maps," *Chaos, Solitons and Fractals*, vol. 35, no. 2, pp. 408–419, 2008.

[4] C. X. Zhang, S. M. Yu, and G. R. Chen, "Design and implementation of compound chaotic attractors," *International Journal of Bifurcation and Chaos*, vol. 22, no. 5, Article ID 1250120, 13 pages, 2012.

[5] G. D. Ye and K.-W. Wong, "An efficient chaotic image encryption algorithm based on a generalized Arnold map," *Nonlinear Dynamics*, vol. 69, no. 4, pp. 2079–2087, 2012.

[6] X. J. Wu, C. X. Bai, and H. B. Kan, "A new color image cryptosystem via hyperchaos synchronization," *Communications in Nonlinear Science and Numerical Simulation*, vol. 19, no. 6, pp. 1884–1897, 2014.

[7] J. F. Zhao, S. Y. Wang, Y. X. Chang, and X. F. Li, "A novel image encryption scheme based on an improper fractional-order chaotic system," *Nonlinear Dynamics*, vol. 80, no. 4, pp. 1721–1729, 2015.

[8] P. Colet and R. Roy, "Digital communication with synchronized chaotic lasers," *Optics Letters*, vol. 19, no. 24, pp. 2056–2058, 1994.

[9] L. Wu and S. Q. Zhu, "Multi-channel communication using chaotic synchronization of multi-mode lasers," *Physics Letters A: General, Atomic and Solid State Physics*, vol. 308, no. 2-3, pp. 157–161, 2003.

[10] J. M. Buldú, J. García-Ojalvo, and M. C. Torrent, "Multimode synchronization and communication using unidirectionally coupled semiconductor lasers," *IEEE Journal of Quantum Electronics*, vol. 40, no. 6, pp. 640–650, 2004.

[11] Y.-D. Chu, X.-F. Li, J.-G. Zhang, and Y.-X. Chang, "Nonlinear dynamics analysis of a modified optically injected semiconductor lasers model," *Chaos, Solitons and Fractals*, vol. 41, no. 1, pp. 14–27, 2009.

[12] L. Glass and M. C. Mackey, *From Clocks to cHaos: The Rhythms of Life*, Princeton University Press, Princeton, NJ, USA, 1988.

[13] A. T. Winfree, *The Geometry of Biological Time*, vol. 12, Springer, New York, NY, USA, 1990.

[14] A. Y. Leung, X.-F. Li, Y.-D. Chu, and X.-B. Rao, "A simple adaptive-feedback scheme for identical synchronizing chaotic systems with uncertain parameters," *Applied Mathematics and Computation*, vol. 253, pp. 172–183, 2015.

[15] M. Mamat, W. S. Mada Sanjaya, and D. S. Maulana, "Numerical simulation chaotic synchronization of Chua circuit and its application for secure communication," *Applied Mathematical Sciences*, vol. 7, no. 1–4, pp. 1–10, 2013.

[16] S. Banerjee, L. Rondoni, S. Mukhopadhyay, and A. P. Misra, "Synchronization of spatiotemporal semiconductor lasers and its application in color image encryption," *Optics Communications*, vol. 284, no. 9, pp. 2278–2291, 2011.

[17] C. K. Volos, I. M. Kyprianidis, and I. N. Stouboulos, "Image encryption process based on chaotic synchronization phenomena," *Signal Processing*, vol. 93, no. 5, pp. 1328–1340, 2013.

[18] A. Kumar and M. K. Ghose, "Extended substitution-diffusion based image cipher using chaotic standard map," *Communications in Nonlinear Science and Numerical Simulation*, vol. 16, no. 1, pp. 372–382, 2011.

[19] C. K. Huang, C. W. Liao, S. L. Hsu, and Y. C. Jeng, "Implementation of gray image encryption with pixel shuffling and gray-level encryption by single chaotic system," *Telecommunication Systems*, vol. 52, no. 2, pp. 563–571, 2013.

[20] X. S. Luo, *Theory and Methods of Chaos Control Synchronization and Its Applications*, Guangxi Normal University Press, Guilin, China, 1st edition, 2007 (Chinese).

[21] C. E. Shannon, "Communication theory of secrecy systems," *The Bell System Technical Journal*, vol. 28, no. 4, pp. 656–715, 1949.

14

Fast Image Segmentation using Two-Dimensional Otsu based on Estimation of Distribution Algorithm

Wuli Wang,[1,2,3] Liming Duan,[1,2] and Yong Wang[4]

[1]*Engineering Research Center of Industrial Computed Tomography Nondestructive Testing of the Education Ministry of China, Chongqing University, Chongqing, China*

[2]*College of Mechanical Engineering, Chongqing University, Chongqing, China*

[3]*College of Information and Control Engineering, China University of Petroleum (East China), Qingdao, China*

[4]*Chongqing Huayu Heavy Machinery & Electrical Co., Ltd., Chongqing, China*

Correspondence should be addressed to Liming Duan; duanliming163@163.com

Academic Editor: Tongliang Liu

Traditional two-dimensional Otsu algorithm has several drawbacks; that is, the sum of probabilities of target and background is approximate to 1 inaccurately, the details of neighborhood image are not obvious, and the computational cost is high. In order to address these problems, a method of fast image segmentation using two-dimensional Otsu based on estimation of distribution algorithm is proposed. Firstly, in order to enhance the performance of image segmentation, the guided filtering is employed to improve neighborhood image template instead of mean filtering. Additionally, the probabilities of target and background in two-dimensional histogram are exactly calculated to get more accurate threshold. Finally, the trace of the interclass dispersion matrix is taken as the fitness function of estimation of distributed algorithm, and the optimal threshold is obtained by constructing and sampling the probability model. Extensive experimental results demonstrate that our method can effectively preserve details of the target, improve the segmentation precision, and reduce the running time of algorithms.

1. Introduction

Image segmentation is the technology and process of segmenting an image into multiple segments with characteristics and extracting regions of interest, and it is the basis of image analysis. The quality of image segmentation directly affects the results of the subsequent image processing [1].

Image segmentation methods mainly include threshold method [2, 3], edge detection method [4], region method [5], graph cut method [6], clustering method [7–12], and machine learning based method [13–15]. In recent years, machine learning, especially the deep learning represented by convolution neural networks (CNN), has captured more attention in image segmentation [15–19]. However, such methods require a multitude of annotated images as samples for training, which is a very time-consuming. In addition, in practice, a small amount of real images as training sample, such as dozens of computed tomography (CT) scanning images, is unable to achieve the desired results.

Threshold technique is simple and effective for image segmentation, which has been widely used in computer vision and pattern recognition. There are several popular threshold methods including Otsu, maximum entropy, minimum cross entropy, and histogram [20, 21]. Compared to other threshold segmentation methods, Otsu is the most popular for grayscale image segmentation [22]. In order to enhance the performance of the classical Otsu, a series of improvements have been proposed [23–26]. However, those improved Otsu methods still only use the one-dimensional gray histogram of image without considering the spatial information of image, which is similar to the classical Otsu method. When the image is affected by noneven brightness, noise, and other factors, the result of image segmentation is not ideal, even incorrect. For this reason, Liu and Li [27] extended the Otsu from one dimension to two dimensions and proposed an Otsu method based on two-dimensional gray histogram. By combining the pixel information with the spatial correlation information between the pixel and its neighborhood, the proposed method is able to provide better segmentation results than one-dimensional Otsu. Nevertheless, the two-dimensional Otsu enlarges the search space into two dimensions, which increases the complexity of the algorithm and expands the computational cost with exponential growth. Consequently, some fast algorithms have been proposed, one of which is the introduction of artificial intelligence algorithm. The intelligent search strategy is employed to speed up solving the global optimal threshold instead of exhaustion method. Sun [28] and Deng et al. [29] applied the genetic algorithm to image segmentation based two-dimensional Otsu, which improves the efficiency of algorithm to some extent but fails to address the premature convergence problem of genetic algorithm. The two-dimensional Otsu based artificial fish swarm algorithm [30] is not sensitive to the selection of initial value and parameter, robust, simple, and easy to implement, but easy to fall into local optimum and low convergence accuracy. Tang et al. [31] and Guo et al. [32] introduced the particle swarm algorithm into the method of image segmentation based on the two-dimensional Otsu. Although the algorithm manifests simple, easy to operate, and general characteristics, the diversity of particles disappears rapidly when the selection of the parameter or the population size is not appropriate. And the above defects of the algorithm can lead to precocious and fall into local optimum. Sun et al. [33] adopted a method of image segmentation using two-dimensional Otsu based on simulated annealing algorithm, which shows its superiority in searching the global minimal solution but also has the disadvantage of slow convergence speed. The above-mentioned two-dimensional Otsu methods based on intelligent algorithm enhance the calculation efficiency of two-dimensional Otsu to a certain extent. However, the sum of probabilities of target and background on the main diagonal of two-dimensional histogram is still approximately 1, which is similar to the traditional two-dimensional Otsu. This approximation has been proved to be incompatible with the real image by Fan and Zhao [34] and Wu et al. [35]. And the curve and oblique methods based on two-dimensional Otsu were, respectively, proposed to get a satisfying effect of image segmentation, but the applicability of these two methods is poor [36]. Furthermore, the existing two-dimensional Otsu methods employ the mean filtering template to construct two-dimensional histogram, which loses the edges and detailed features of the neighborhood image and influences the effect of image segmentation.

In this paper, in order to improve the effect of segmentation and reduce computational cost of two-dimensional Otsu algorithm, a novel fast image segmentation method using two-dimensional Otsu based on estimation of distributed algorithm is proposed. Firstly, to obtain the approving performance of image segmentation, the guided filtering is employed to improve neighborhood image template instead of the mean filtering. Moreover, the probabilities of the target and background in two-dimensional histogram are exactly calculated to get more accurate threshold. Finally, in order to segment the image quickly and accurately, the estimation of distribution algorithm [37] with outstanding searching ability and fast convergence speed is applied to find the optimal segmentation threshold.

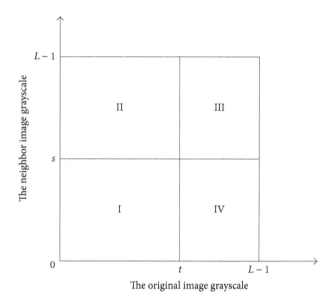

FIGURE 1: Two-dimensional histogram.

2. Improvements to Method of Two-Dimensional Otsu

The method of two-dimensional Otsu applies the two-dimensional histogram comprising the image gray and its neighborhood image average gray to find the optimal threshold and then divides the image into the target and background. The main diagonal regions I and III of the two-dimensional histogram denote, respectively, the target and background; the subdiagonal regions II and IV present severally the edge and noise, as shown in Figure 1.

Under the method of traditional two-dimensional Otsu, the sum of probabilities of the target and background is approximate to 1, and the sum of probabilities of the edge and noise is approximate to 0. This approximation is only satisfied under certain conditions, which has been confirmed in theory and experiment by the literatures [34–36]. The accuracy of image segmentation is low when the approximation is not true. In addition, the neighborhood image is obtained by a mean filtering template under the method of traditional two-dimensional Otsu, which can effectively eliminate the Gaussian noise of image but also obscure the edge and detailed features of image and affect the performances of image segmentation. Therefore, in order to enhance the performances of image segmentation, the traditional two-dimensional Otsu is improved from two aspects: using the guided filtering to build a new neighborhood template and accurately calculating the probabilities of the target and background.

2.1. Construction of Neighborhood Template Based on Guided Filtering. In order to enhance the effect of image segmentation under two-dimensional Otsu method, we introduce the guided filtering to improve the neighborhood template, which can preferably preserve features of the edge and details [38]. The guided filtering is a filtering method that restrains the details of image and is similar to the bilateral filtering. However, compared with the bilateral filtering, the performance of guided filtering is better and the algorithm is faster. It can be regarded as a local linear model, defined as

$$q_i = \sum_j W_{ij}(I)\, p_j, \tag{1}$$

where I represents the guided image, p denotes the input image, q stands for the output image, i, j is the index of the pixel, and $W_{ij}(I)$ is the filter kernel function, and defined as

$$W_{ij}(I) = \frac{1}{|\omega|^2} \sum_{k:(i,j)\in\omega_k} \left(1 + \frac{(I_i - \mu_k)(I_j - \mu_k)}{\sigma_k^2 + \varepsilon}\right), \tag{2}$$

where ω_k is the kth window of kernel function, $|\omega|$ is the number of pixels in the window, μ_k and σ_k^2 denote the mean value and the variance of a window in I, and ε is the smoothing factor. Here, the local window radius is set to 2, the value of ε is set to 0.04, and then the number of pixels in the window is $|\omega| = (2 \times r + 1)^2 = 25$.

A new neighborhood template can be constructed by using the guided filtering with preserving the edge and details of image instead of the mean filtering, which can preferably construct the image two-dimensional histogram and advance the performance of image segmentation.

2.2. Exact Calculation of the Two-Dimensional Otsu

Step 1. Construct two tuples according to the gray values of original image and the filtered neighbor image by the guided filtering, denoted as the gray value of original image and the gray value of neighbor image. If the frequency of two tuples (i, j) is expressed as f_{ij}, then the corresponding joint probability density can be defined as

$$p_{ij} = \frac{f_{ij}}{N}, \quad i, j = 1, 2, \ldots, L, \tag{3}$$

where N is the number of pixels and L is the gray level of image, and there is

$$\sum_{i=1}^{L} \sum_{j=1}^{L} p_{ij} = 1. \tag{4}$$

Step 2. Calculate accurately the probabilities P_{I} and P_{III} of the target and background regions in the two-dimensional histogram:

$$P_{\mathrm{I}} = \sum_{i=1}^{t} \sum_{j=1}^{s} p_{ij},$$

$$P_{\mathrm{III}} = \sum_{i=t+1}^{L} \sum_{j=s+1}^{L} p_{ij}, \tag{5}$$

where t and s represent the threshold values of original image and neighbor image, respectively.

Step 3. Calculate, respectively, the corresponding mean vectors $\boldsymbol{\mu}_0^*$ and $\boldsymbol{\mu}_1^*$ of the target and background:

$$\boldsymbol{\mu}_0^* = \left(\mu_{0i}^*, \mu_{0j}^*\right)^T = \left[\sum_{i=1}^{t}\sum_{j=1}^{s}\frac{i \cdot p_{ij}}{P_{\mathrm{I}}}, \sum_{i=1}^{t}\sum_{j=1}^{s}\frac{j \cdot p_{ij}}{P_{\mathrm{I}}}\right]^T,$$

$$\boldsymbol{\mu}_1^* = \left(\mu_{1i}^*, \mu_{1j}^*\right)^T \tag{6}$$

$$= \left[\sum_{i=t+1}^{L}\sum_{j=s+1}^{L}\frac{i \cdot p_{ij}}{P_{\mathrm{III}}}, \sum_{i=t+1}^{L}\sum_{j=s+1}^{L}\frac{j \cdot p_{ij}}{P_{\mathrm{III}}}\right]^T.$$

Step 4. Calculate the total mean vector $\boldsymbol{\mu}_T^*$ on the two-dimensional histogram:

$$\boldsymbol{\mu}_T^* = \left(\mu_{Ti}^*, \mu_{Tj}^*\right)^T = \left(\sum_{i=1}^{L}\sum_{j=1}^{L}i \cdot p_{ij}, \sum_{i=1}^{L}\sum_{j=1}^{L}j \cdot p_{ij}\right)^T. \tag{7}$$

Step 5. Calculate the trace of interclass dispersion matrix $t_r S_B^*(t, s)$:

$$t_r S_B^*(t, s) = P_{\mathrm{I}}(t, s) \cdot \left[\left(\mu_{0i}^* - \mu_{Ti}^*\right)^2 + \left(\mu_{0j}^* - \mu_{Tj}^*\right)^2\right]$$

$$+ P_{\mathrm{III}}(t, s) \cdot \left[\left(\mu_{1i}^* - \mu_{Ti}^*\right)^2 + \left(\mu_{1j}^* - \mu_{Tj}^*\right)^2\right] = P_{\mathrm{I}}(t, s)$$

$$\cdot \left[\left(\sum_{i=1}^{t}\sum_{j=1}^{s}\frac{i \cdot p_{ij}}{P_{\mathrm{I}}(t, s)} - \sum_{i=1}^{L}\sum_{j=1}^{L}i \cdot p_{ij}\right)^2\right.$$

$$\left.+ \left(\sum_{i=1}^{t}\sum_{j=1}^{s}\frac{j \cdot p_{ij}}{P_{\mathrm{I}}(t, s)} - \sum_{i=1}^{L}\sum_{j=1}^{L}j \cdot p_{ij}\right)^2\right] + P_{\mathrm{III}}(t, s) \tag{8}$$

$$\cdot \left[\left(\sum_{i=t+1}^{L}\sum_{j=s+1}^{L}\frac{i \cdot p_{ij}}{P_{\mathrm{III}}(t, s)} - \sum_{i=1}^{L}\sum_{j=1}^{L}i \cdot p_{ij}\right)^2\right.$$

$$\left.+ \left(\sum_{i=t+1}^{L}\sum_{j=s+1}^{L}\frac{j \cdot p_{ij}}{P_{\mathrm{III}}(t, s)} - \sum_{i=1}^{L}\sum_{j=1}^{L}j \cdot p_{ij}\right)^2\right].$$

Step 6. Calculate the optimal threshold (T^*, S^*):

$$(T^*, S^*) = \arg \max_{1 \le t, s \le L} \left\{t_r S_B^*(t, s)\right\}. \tag{9}$$

The improved two-dimensional Otsu algorithm suffers from a high computational cost. Consequently, we introduce the estimation of distribution algorithm with favorable global convergence ability and high computation efficiency to find the optimal segmentation threshold (T^*, S^*).

3. Fast Image Segmentation Using Two-Dimensional Otsu Method Based on Estimation of Distribution Algorithm

As a new type of optimization algorithm in the field of evolutionary computation, the estimation of distribution algorithm proposes a new evolutionary model [39]. There are no genetic operations such as crossover and mutation in the estimation of distribution algorithm, which is different from the traditional evolutionary algorithm. The estimation of distribution algorithm predicts the best searching region according to sampling and statistical learning for searching space and generates the optimal new individual. The algorithm using the macrolevel evolution method based on search space has superior global search ability and positive convergence rate [38]. The two-dimensional Otsu method searches the optimal combination of image threshold and neighborhood image threshold in the global range, and the two variables are independent of each other. Accordingly, the variable independent estimation of distribution algorithm is employed to solve the optimal segmentation threshold in the two-dimensional Otsu.

The gray value of a pixel in the image and a pixel in its neighborhood image is represented by the individual $X = (x_1, x_2)$, where the ranges of x_1 and x_2 are 0 to 255. The ith individual in the gth generation is denoted as $X_i^g = (x_{i1}^g, x_{i2}^g)$, the population size is indicated by the PopSize, and the largest generation of evolution is expressed by the MaxGen. The flowchart of image segmentation using two-dimensional Otsu based on estimation of distribution algorithm is shown in Figure 2, and the concrete steps are as follows.

Step 1 (initialize the population). The current evolutionary generation g is initialized to 1, and the initial population is obtained by random sampling referring to the literature [40]:

$$\text{Popul}^1 = \left\{ X_i^1 \mid i = 1, 2, \ldots, \text{PopSize} \right\}. \tag{10}$$

Step 2 (calculate the individual fitness). The trace of interclass dispersion matrix is regarded as the fitness function, as seen in (8). Firstly, let $t = x_{i1}^g$, $s = x_{i2}^g$ in (8), and calculate fitness value $\text{fitness}_{X_i^g}$ of individual X_i^g in the gth generation. Then similar method is applied to calculate the fitness values of other individuals in the gth generation. Finally, the fitness values of all individuals are obtained:

$$\text{Fitn}_g = \left\{ \text{fitness}_{X_i^g} \mid i = 1, 2, \ldots, \text{PopSize} \right\}. \tag{11}$$

Step 3 (obtain the optimal fitness and the best individual). Calculate the optimal fitness $\text{BestFitn}_g = \text{Max}(\text{Fitn}_g)$, and the corresponding individual is the best individual $X_{\text{best}}^g = (x_{\text{best}1}^g, x_{\text{best}2}^g)$ in the population.

Step 4 (determine whether the termination condition is satisfied). If the evolutionary generation g is not greater than MaxGen, then Step 5 is performed; otherwise, the optimization process is terminated, and the optimal fitness $\text{BestFitn}_{\text{MaxGen}}$ and the best individual $X_{\text{best}}^{\text{MaxGen}}$ are obtained; Step 9 is performed.

Step 5 (select the individual for establishing probability model). In order to ensure that the probability model is sensitive to the search process, the individual who is used to construct the probability model must be able to accurately track the information of probability model. For the sake of preventing the algorithm into local optimal, the individual selection

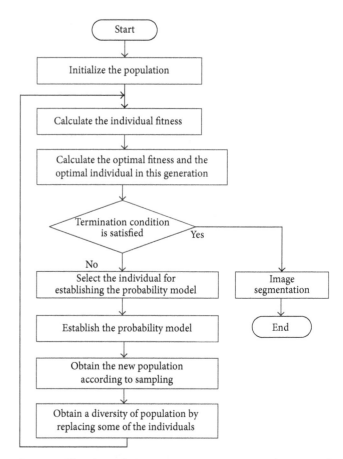

FIGURE 2: Flowchart of image segmentation using two-dimensional Otsu based on estimation of distribution.

should have a certain randomness. Roulette is a proportion of random selection method. On the one hand, in order to ensure the tracking accuracy of probability model, the individual is selected according to the probability of alleles per gene bit. On the other hand, this method does not guarantee that the allele of large probability must be selected and has a certain randomness. In this paper, when the fitness value is the largest, the optimal segmentation threshold is obtained. Therefore, the roulette selection method based on fitness is adopted; that is, the probability that each individual is selected is proportional to its fitness. The specific steps are as follows:

(1) Calculate the relative fitness of each individual $\text{fitness}_{X_i^g} / \sum \text{fitness}_{X_i^g}$, denoted as p_k, where $k = 1, 2, \ldots, \text{PopSize}$ and $\sum p_k = 1$.

(2) According to relative fitness p_k, the disc is divided into PopSize copies, where the central angle of the kth fan is $2\pi p_k$.

(3) Simulate the roulette operation, that is, to generate a random number between 0 and 1. If $p_1 + p_2 + \cdots + p_{k-1} < r$ and $r < p_1 + p_2 + \cdots + p_k$, then individual X_k^g is selected, denoted as $X_1^{g'}$.

(4) Repeat step (3) until the PopSize excellent individuals $\{X_i^{g'} \mid i = 1, 2, \ldots, \text{PopSize}\}$ have been obtained.

Step 6 (establish the probability model). Firstly, construct the Gaussian distribution function according to the excellent individual selected by Step 5. Then, calculate the mean and standard deviation of the first variable for all individuals:

$$\overline{X_1^g} = \sum \frac{X_{i1}^{g'}}{\text{PopSize}},$$

$$\sigma_1^g = \sum \frac{\left(X_{i1}^{g'} - \overline{X_1^g}\right)^2}{\text{PopSize}}, \tag{12}$$

where $i = 1, 2, \ldots, \text{PopSize}$. Mean $\overline{X_2^g}$ and standard deviation σ_2^g of the second variable of all individuals are calculated in a similar manner. The probability distribution function can be expressed as follows:

$$x_1 \sim N\left(\overline{X_1^g}, \sigma_1^g\right),$$

$$x_2 \sim N\left(\overline{X_2^g}, \sigma_2^g\right). \tag{13}$$

Step 7 (obtain the new population by sampling). The sampling method depends on the probability model used by the algorithm. Therefore, the next generation population is generated on the basis of the constructed Gaussian distribution function:

$$\text{Popul}^{g+1} = \left\{X_i^{g+1} \mid i = 1, 2, \ldots, \text{PopSize}\right\}. \tag{14}$$

The individual of the population is denoted as $\mathbf{X}_i^{g+1} = (x_{i1}^{g+1}, x_{i2}^{g+1})$, where $x_{i1}^{g+1} \sim N(\overline{X_1^g}, \sigma_1^g)$, $x_{i2}^{g+1} \sim N(\overline{X_2^g}, \sigma_2^g)$.

Step 8 (establish the diverse population). In order to enhance the diversity of population and avoid the excessive effect on the population, in the first place, p individuals are randomly removed from the current population, where $p = \text{round}(\text{PopSize}/10)$ and $\text{round}(x)$ represents an integer that is closest to x. Then, the optimal p individuals in the previous population are appended to the current population to establish a diverse population. Finally, return to Step 2 and recalculate the fitness of each individual.

Step 9 (image segmentation). On the basis of the optimal threshold $T^* = x_{\text{best1}}^{\text{MaxGen}}$, $S^* = x_{\text{best2}}^{\text{MaxGen}}$ obtained by Step 4, the two-dimensional Otsu method is employed to segment the image.

4. Experimental Results and Analyses

In order to evaluate the performance of image segmentation and the efficiency of the proposed method, a large number of industrial computed tomography (CT) images of different mechanical parts and many images from popular image segmentation dataset are used to test. Extensive experimental results are compared with the results of the following approaches, that is, Otsu, 2D Otsu [27], 2D Otsu-GA [29], 2D Otsu-FSA [30], LCK [10], LSD [11], and ME + PPD [3], quantitatively and qualitatively.

4.1. Comparisons of Segmentation on Real Image. Figure 3 shows the results of image segmentation regarding five real industrial CT images with Gaussian noise under different methods. The cylinder head, carburetor, nuts, aluminum part, and bearing are arranged from left to right; the original image, the results of the traditional two-dimensional Otsu, the results of the 2D Otsu-FSA, the results of the 2D Otsu-GA, and the results of our method are distributed from top to bottom. In order to compare objectively the performances of the above methods, the population size of genetic algorithm, fish swarm algorithm, and estimation of distribution algorithm are set to 20, and evolutionary generations (or optimization times) are set to 50.

The experimental results are shown in Figure 3. For industrial CT images of the nuts and bearing with clear boundary and large target and background discrimination, the above methods can preferably segment the target and background, and the effect is preferable. However, for industrial CT images of the cylinder head, carburetor, and aluminum part with relative blurred boundary, there is a certain gap in the segmentation effects of each method. For the cylinder head image, the traditional two-dimensional Otsu is poor for the detail at the upper right corner of image, and the 2D Otsu-FSA and the 2D Otsu-GA lose the details at the upper right corner and the upper left corner of image, which is inconsistent with the original image. For the carburetor image, we can intuitively see that the detailed features at the bottom of image are lost after the traditional two-dimensional Otsu, the 2D Otsu-FSA, and the 2D Otsu-GA. For the aluminum part image, the traditional two-dimensional Otsu and the 2D Otsu-GA process incorrectly a noise at the upper right of image as a target. Though the noise is well processed by the 2D Otsu-FSA, the detailed feature (i.e., hole) above the left image is lost. The segmentation result of the 2D Otsu-GA also lost the detail, that is, the hole. It can be seen the proposed method can preferably preserve the details of original images with blurred boundary from the last line in Figure 3.

4.2. Comparisons of Computational Cost on Real Image. The computational cost of two-dimensional Otsu based on intelligent algorithm is mainly reflected in calculation of the fitness of individual. In the case of the same population size, the computational cost of different algorithms are qualitatively evaluated by comparing the evolutionary generation of population when the algorithms reach convergence state.

The maximum fitness convergence curves of the aluminum part are obtained by using two-dimensional Otsu methods based on intelligent algorithm, as shown in Figures 4–6. The 2D Otsu-FSA: if the population size n is equal to 10, the fitness is convergent until the number of iterations is about 40. If the population size n is equal to 20, the fitness is convergent when the number of iterations is about 22. If the population size n is equal to 30, the fitness has converged when the number of iterations is close to 12. The 2D Otsu-GA: if the population size n is equal to 10, the fitness is convergent when the number of iterations is about 45. However, the fitness of the algorithm is obviously fluctuant in the process of convergence, which reflects the evolutionary disorder affected by variant randomness under the genetic algorithm.

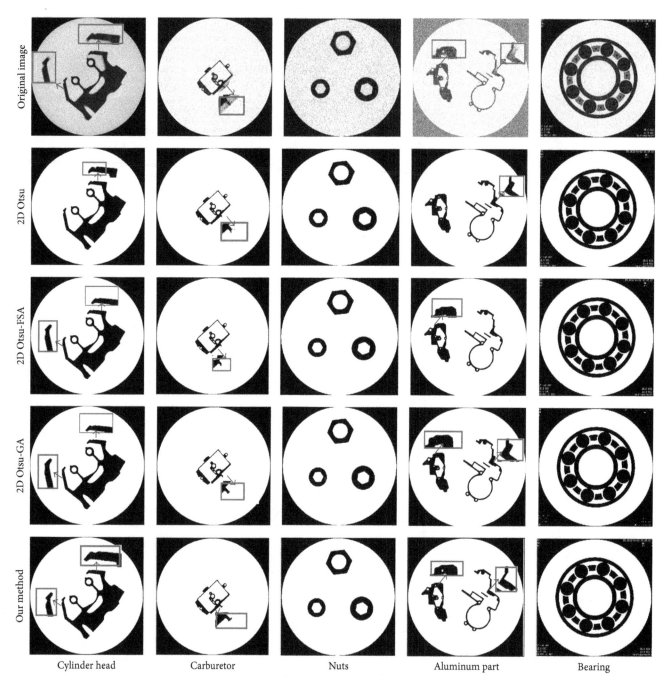

FIGURE 3: Segmentation effect of various methods for different images.

If the population size n is equal to 20, the fitness is convergent when the number of iterations is about 35. If the population size n equals 30, the fitness is convergent when the number of iterations is about 25. Our method: if the population size n equals 10, 20, or 30, the fitness has converged when the number of iterations is only about 25, 10, or 3. In addition, the results of the proposed method are stable after convergence.

According to the above experimental results and analyses, for solving the optimal threshold of two-dimensional Otsu, the estimation of distribution algorithm requires fewer population size and few number of iterations than the genetic algorithm and the fish swarm algorithm. In other words, the estimation of distribution algorithm can effectively reduce the computational cost.

Moreover, in order to compare the efficiencies of the proposed method and the existing methods, objectively and precisely, the mean time of image segmentation under different methods is counted. Table 1 illustrates the mean time of 10 segmentations for 5 industrial CT images. According to the data in Table 1, the speed of the proposed method is about 10, 5, and 3 times faster than the traditional two-dimensional Otsu, 2D Otsu-FSA, and 2D Otsu-GA, respectively.

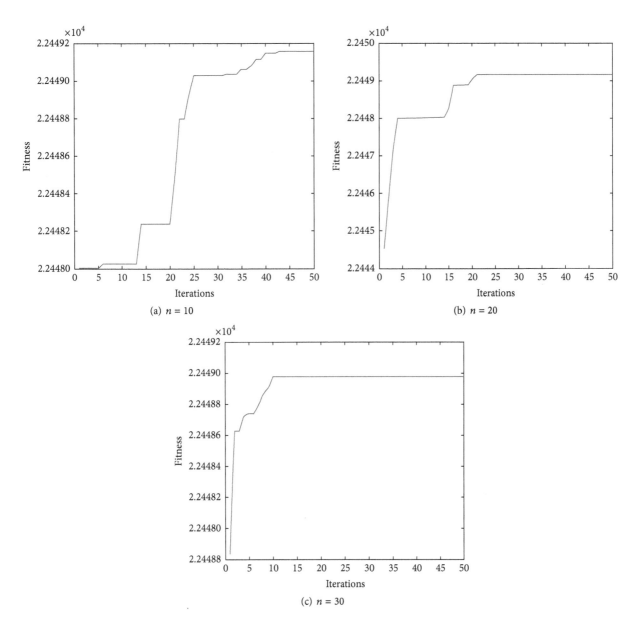

FIGURE 4: The highest fitness convergence curve based on 2D Otsu-FSA.

TABLE 1: Comparison of segmentation time under different methods (s).

Image	Our method	Traditional 2D Otsu	2D Otsu-FSA	2D Otsu-GA
Cylinder head	0.23	2.53	1.25	0.92
Carburetor	0.28	2.66	1.31	0.97
Nuts	0.24	2.58	1.27	0.94
Aluminum part	0.30	2.71	1.39	1.02
Bearing	0.29	2.68	1.37	0.99

4.3. Comparisons of Segmentation on Image Dataset. In this section, we compare our method with Otsu, 2D Otsu, 2D Otsu-FSA, 2D Otsu-GA, ME + PPD, LCK, and LSD on a host of images that come from popular image datasets. As an example, we select a grain image and a tire image from the general image library, a duck image and a bird image from the BSD500 image dataset, and a motorcycle image from the VOC image dataset to demonstrate the comparative results, as illustrated in Figure 7. For rice grains image, our method can preferably retain the completeness of rice grains.

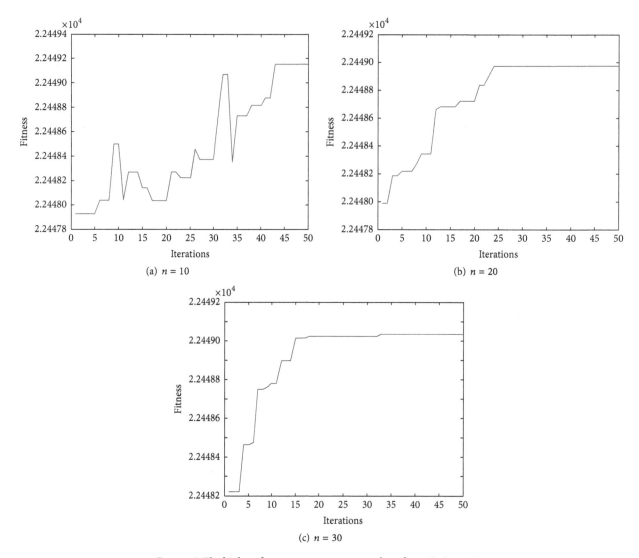

FIGURE 5: The highest fitness convergence curve based on 2D Otsu-GA.

Especially at the bottom of the image, it can better preserve the structural characteristics of rice grains and segment the target from the background. Fortunately, LCK and LSD can also detect the target efficiently. However, these two methods require a high computational cost. With regard to the tire image segmented by the proposed method, the contour details of eight axis are clear; the edges between the inner and outer rings of the tire are favorable. Moreover, the middle four screws are very easy to identify and have only a small black background. For the duck image with simple background, each of above-mentioned methods can obtain a promising result. However, the proposed method can preferably preserve the details, such as the mouth and tail. Compared with 2D Otsu, 2D Otsu-FSA, ME + PPD, and LSD, our method can preferably extract the edges of target on the bird image. Furthermore, our method can more accurately segment out the claw comparing with Otsu, 2D Otsu-GA, ME + PPD, LCK, and LSD. For the motorcycle image with complex contour and scene, the proposed method is favorable on the

details, such as the rearview mirror and support and rear seat. ME + PPD and LCK obtain a preferable performance of the global segmentation. Nevertheless, LCK is time-consuming.

The computational costs of the above methods on the five images in Table 2 are also measured. From this table, we can see that the computational cost of our method is lower than the other methods except Otsu. However, Otsu's segmentation results are not very good.

5. Conclusion

In this paper, we present a fast image segmentation method using two-dimensional Otsu based on estimation of distribution algorithm. The proposed method can preferably preserve the edges and details of the object because the guided filtering template is replaced with the mean filtering template. Furthermore, compared with other existing image segmentation methods, our method has desirable

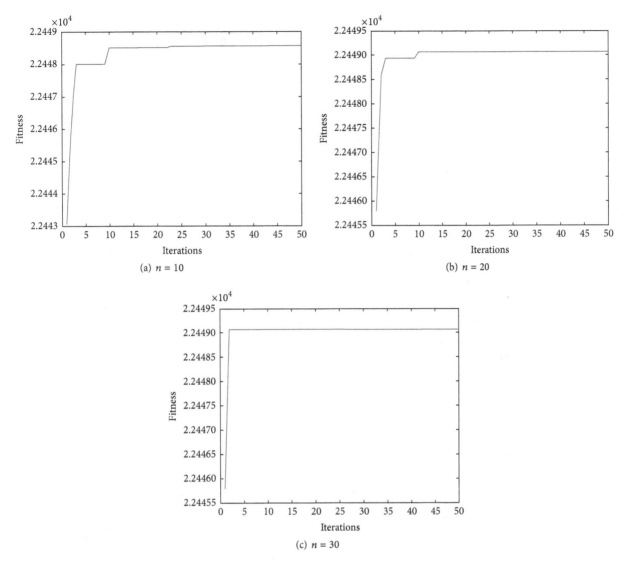

FIGURE 6: The highest fitness convergence curve of our method.

TABLE 2: Comparisons of computational costs (s).

Method	Image				
	Rice	Tire	Duck	Bird	Motorcycle
Otsu	0.011	0.012	0.013	0.015	0.018
2D Otsu	1.46	1.41	2.01	1.71	1.52
2D Otsu-FSA	0.62	0.64	1.16	1.05	0.68
2D Otsu-GA	0.46	0.51	0.86	0.79	0.53
ME + PPD	0.32	0.38	0.28	0.22	0.27
LCK	5.63	13.25	22.36	23.50	19.72
LSD	4.52	9.64	19.45	16.37	15.21
Our	0.14	0.18	0.12	0.09	0.13

segmentation performance and computational cost for image with simple scene. However, similar to other threshold-based image segmentation methods, our method is preferable for the images with the same gray scale range; it has a limitation to the object with large gray scale distribution. In addition, the actual segmentation effect of our method is not perfect in complex scene.

In the future, we plan to preprocess the object so that our segmentation method can perform well for special objects as well as handle more complex images.

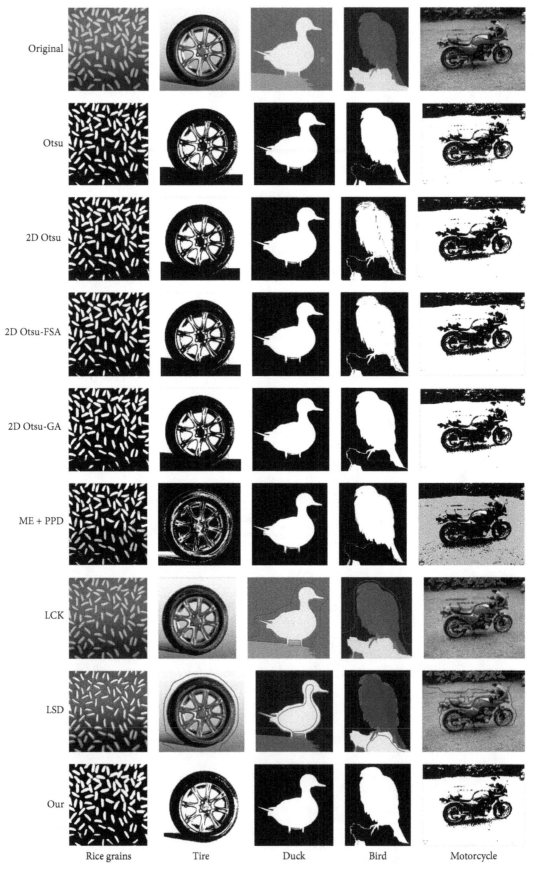

FIGURE 7: Comparisons of image segmentation under various methods.

Conflicts of Interest

The authors declare that they have no conflicts of interest.

Acknowledgments

This paper is supported partly by Chongqing Natural Science Foundation of China (Grant no. cstc2016jcyjA0353) and National Key Scientific Instrument and Equipment Development Projects of China (Grant no. 2013YQ030629).

References

[1] Y. J. Zhang, *Image Engineering*, CN: Tinghua University Press, Beijing, China, 3rd edition, 2013.

[2] W. Khan, "A survey: image segmentation techniques," *International Journal of Future Computer and Communication*, vol. 3, no. 2, pp. 89–93, 2014.

[3] D. Pandey, X. Yin, H. Wang, and Y. Zhang, "Accurate vessel segmentation using maximum entropy incorporating line detection and phase-preserving denoising," *Computer Vision and Image Understanding*, vol. 155, pp. 162–172, 2017.

[4] D. Zhou and S. Tabbone, "A study of edge detection techniques for segmentation computing approaches," *International Journal of Computer Applications*, vol. 1, pp. 35–41, 2010.

[5] T. Zuva, O. Olugbara, S. O. Ojo et al., "Image segmentation, available techniques, developments and open issues," *Canadian Journal on Image Processing and Computer Vision*, vol. 2, no. 3, pp. 20–29, 2011.

[6] B. Peng, L. Zhang, and D. Zhang, "A survey of graph theoretical approaches to image segmentation," *Pattern Recognition*, vol. 46, no. 3, pp. 1020–1038, 2013.

[7] D. Gómez, J. Yáñez, C. Guada, J. Tinguaro Rodríguez, J. Montero, and E. Zarrazola, "Fuzzy image segmentation based upon hierarchical clustering," *Knowledge-Based Systems*, vol. 87, pp. 26–37, 2015.

[8] D. Tao, X. Li, X. Wu, and S. J. Maybank, "General tensor discriminant analysis and Gabor features for gait recognition," *IEEE Transactions on Pattern Analysis and Machine Intelligence*, vol. 29, no. 10, pp. 1700–1715, 2007.

[9] D. Tao, X. Tang, X. Li, and X. Wu, "Asymmetric bagging and random subspace for support vector machines-based relevance feedback in image retrieval," *IEEE Transactions on Pattern Analysis and Machine Intelligence*, vol. 28, no. 7, pp. 1088–1099, 2006.

[10] L. Wang and C. Pan, "Robust level set image segmentation via a local correntropy-based K-means clustering," *Pattern Recognition*, vol. 47, no. 5, pp. 1917–1925, 2014.

[11] L. Wang, H. Wu, and C. Pan, "Region-based image segmentation with local signed difference energy," *Pattern Recognition Letters*, vol. 34, no. 6, pp. 637–645, 2013.

[12] T. Liu, D. Tao, and D. Xu, "Dimensionality-dependent generalization bounds for k-dimensional coding schemes," *Neural Computation*, vol. 28, no. 10, pp. 2213–2249, 2016.

[13] T. L. Liu, Q. Yang, and D. C. Tao, "Understanding how feature structure transfers in transfer learning," in *Proceedings of the Twenty-Sixth International Joint Conference on Artificial Intelligence*, pp. 2365–2371, Melbourne, Australia, 2016.

[14] D. C. Tao, X. Li, X. D. Wu, and S. J. Maybank, "Maybank: geometric mean for subspace selection," *IEEE Transactions on Pattern Analysis and Machine Intelligence*, vol. 31, no. 2, pp. 260–274, 2009.

[15] R. Wang, T. Liu, and D. Tao, "Multiclass learning with partially corrupted labels," *IEEE Transactions on Neural Networks and Learning Systems*, vol. 99, pp. 1–13, 2017.

[16] T. Liu, D. Tao, M. Song, and S. J. Maybank, "Algorithm-dependent generalization bounds for multi-task learning," *IEEE Transactions on Pattern Analysis and Machine Intelligence*, vol. 39, no. 2, article A4, pp. 227–241, 2017.

[17] Y.-T. Chen, X. Liu, and M.-H. Yang, "Multi-instance object segmentation with occlusion handling," in *Proceedings of the IEEE Conference on Computer Vision and Pattern Recognition, CVPR 2015*, pp. 3470–3478, usa, June 2015.

[18] T. Liu and D. Tao, "Classification with Noisy Labels by Importance Reweighting," *IEEE Transactions on Pattern Analysis and Machine Intelligence*, vol. 38, no. 3, pp. 447–461, 2016.

[19] J. Dai, K. He, and J. Sun, "Instance-aware semantic segmentation via multi-task network cascades," in *Proceedings of the IEEE Conference on Computer Vision and Pattern Recognition (CVPR '16)*, pp. 3150–3158, Las Vegas, Nev, USA, 2016.

[20] K. Chen, F. Chen, M. Dai, Z.-S. Zhang, and J.-F. Shi, "Fast image segmentation with multilevel threshold of two-dimensional entropy based on firefly algorithm," *Optics and Precision Engineering*, vol. 22, no. 2, pp. 517–523, 2014.

[21] X.-C. Yuan, L.-S. Wu, and H.-W. Chen, "Rail image segmentation based on Otsu threshold method," *Guangxue Jingmi Gongcheng/Optics and Precision Engineering*, vol. 24, no. 7, pp. 1772–1781, 2016.

[22] M. Sezgin and B. Sankur, "Survey over image thresholding techniques and quantitative performance evaluation," *Journal of Electronic Imaging*, vol. 13, no. 1, pp. 146–168, 2004.

[23] P. J. Herrera, G. Pajares, and M. Guijarro, "A segmentation method using Otsu and fuzzy k-Means for stereovision matching in hemispherical images from forest environments," *Applied Soft Computing Journal*, vol. 11, no. 8, pp. 4738–4747, 2011.

[24] B. F. Buxton, H. Abdallahi, D. Fernandez-Reyes, and W. Jarra, "Development of an extension of the otsu algorithm for multidimensional image segmentation of thin-film blood slides," in *Proceedings of the International Conference on Computing: Theory and Applications, ICCTA '07*, pp. 552–561, Kolkata, India, 2007.

[25] Q. B. Truong and B. R. Lee, "Automatic multi-thresholds selection for image segmentation based on evolutionary approach," *International Journal of Control, Automation and Systems*, vol. 11, no. 4, pp. 834–844, 2013.

[26] X. Y. Xu, E. M. Song, and L. H. Jin, "Characteristic analysis of threshold based on otsu criterion," *Acta Electronica Sinica*, vol. 37, no. 12, pp. 2716–2719, 2009.

[27] J. Z. H. Liu and W. Q. Li, "The automatic thresholding of gray-level pictures via two-dimensional OTSU method," *Acta Automatica Sinica*, vol. 19, no. 1, pp. 101–105, 1993.

[28] J. Sun, "Improved 2D maximum between-cluster variance algorithm and its application to cucumber target segmentation," *Transactions of the Chinese Society of Agricultural Engineering*, vol. 25, no. 10, pp. 176–181, 2009.

[29] H.-G. Deng, R.-L. Wu, and Z.-R. Lai, "Image segmentation of drosophila's compound eyes via two-dimensional OTSU thresholding on the basis of AGA," in *Proceedings of the 2nd International Congress on Image and Signal Processing, CISP '09*, pp. 1–5, Tianjin, China, 2009.

[30] Z. Pan and Y. Q. Wu, "The two-dimensional otsu thresholding based on fish swarm algorithm," *Acta Optica Sinica*, vol. 29, no. 8, pp. 2115–2121, 2009.

[31] Y. G. Tang, D. Liu, and X. P. Guan, "Fast image segmentation based on particle swarm optimization and two-dimension Otsu method," *Control and Decision*, vol. 22, no. 2, pp. 202–205, 2007.

[32] W. Y. Guo, X. F. Wang, and X. Z. Xia, "Two-dimensional Otsu's thresholding segmentation method based on grid box filter," *Optik*, vol. 125, no. 18, pp. 5234–5240, 2014.

[33] F. Sun, H. Wang, and J. Fan, "2D otsu segmentation algorithm based on simulated annealing genetic algorithm for iced-cable images," in *Proceedings of the 2009 International Forum on Information Technology and Applications, IFITA '09*, pp. 600–602, Chengdu, China, 2009.

[34] J. L. Fan and F. Zhao, "Two-dimensional Otsus curve thresholding segmentation method for gray-Level images," *Acta Electronica Sinica*, vol. 40, no. 4, pp. 751–755, 2012.

[35] Y. Q. Wu, Z. H. Pan, and W. Y. Wu, "Image thresholding based on two-dimensional histogram oblique segmentation and its fast recurring algorithm," *Journal on Communications*, vol. 29, no. 4, pp. 77–84, 2013.

[36] X. M. Zhang, Y. J. Sun, and Y. B. Zheng, "Precise two-dimensional otsu's image segmentation and its fast recursive realization," *Acta Electronica Sinica*, vol. 39, no. 8, pp. 1778–1784, 2011.

[37] S. Cao, F. CH. Sun, and L. H. Hu, "Departure airctaft sequence optimization using EDA," *Journal of Tsinghua University (Science & Technology)*, vol. 52, no. 1, pp. 66–71, 2012.

[38] K. He, J. Sun, and X. Tang, "Guided image filtering," *IEEE Transactions on Pattern Analysis and Machine Intelligence*, vol. 35, no. 6, pp. 1397–1409, 2013.

[39] S. Y. Wang, L. Wang, and C. Fang, "Advances in estimation of distribution algorithms," *Control and Decision*, vol. 27, no. 7, pp. 961–966, 2012.

[40] S. D. Zhou and Z. Q. Sun, "A survey on estimation of distribution algorithms," *Acta Automatica Sinica. Zidonghua Xuebao*, vol. 33, no. 2, pp. 113–124, 2007.

15

Modeling PM$_{2.5}$ Urban Pollution using Machine Learning and Selected Meteorological Parameters

Jan Kleine Deters,[1] **Rasa Zalakeviciute,**[2] **Mario Gonzalez,**[2] **and Yves Rybarczyk**[2,3]

[1]*University of Twente, Enschede, Netherlands*
[2]*Intelligent & Interactive Systems Lab (SI^2 Lab), FICA, Universidad de Las Américas, Quito, Ecuador*
[3]*DEE, Nova University of Lisbon and CTS, UNINOVA, Monte de Caparica, Portugal*

Correspondence should be addressed to Yves Rybarczyk; y.rybarczyk@fct.unl.pt

Academic Editor: Lei Zhang

Outdoor air pollution costs millions of premature deaths annually, mostly due to anthropogenic fine particulate matter (or PM$_{2.5}$). Quito, the capital city of Ecuador, is no exception in exceeding the healthy levels of pollution. In addition to the impact of urbanization, motorization, and rapid population growth, particulate pollution is modulated by meteorological factors and geophysical characteristics, which complicate the implementation of the most advanced models of weather forecast. Thus, this paper proposes a machine learning approach based on six years of meteorological and pollution data analyses to predict the concentrations of PM$_{2.5}$ from wind (speed and direction) and precipitation levels. The results of the classification model show a high reliability in the classification of low (<10 μg/m^3) versus high (>25 μg/m^3) and low (<10 μg/m^3) versus moderate (10–25 μg/m^3) concentrations of PM$_{2.5}$. A regression analysis suggests a better prediction of PM$_{2.5}$ when the climatic conditions are getting more extreme (strong winds or high levels of precipitation). The high correlation between estimated and real data for a time series analysis during the wet season confirms this finding. The study demonstrates that the use of statistical models based on machine learning is relevant to predict PM$_{2.5}$ concentrations from meteorological data.

1. Introduction

The effects of rapid growth of the world's population are reflected in the overuse and scarcity of natural resources, deforestation, climate change, and especially environmental pollution. Currently, more than half of the global population lives in urban areas, and this number is expected to grow to about 66% by 2050, mostly due to the urbanization trends in developing countries [1]. According to the latest urban air quality database, 98% of cities in low and middle income countries with more than 100,000 inhabitants do not meet the World Health Organization (WHO) air quality guidelines [2].

A recent study using a global atmospheric chemistry model estimated that 3.3 million annual premature deaths worldwide are linked to outdoor air pollution, which is expected to double by 2050, mostly due to anthropogenic fine particulate matter (aerodynamic diameter < 2.5 μm; PM$_{2.5}$) [3]. Over the last decade, evidence has been growing that exposure to fine particulate air pollution has adverse effects on cardiopulmonary health [4].

A recent air quality study in Quito, the capital of Ecuador, concurs that long-term levels of fine particulate pollution are not only exceeding the WHO's recommended levels of 10 μg/m^3 but also are higher than the national standards of 15 μg/m^3 [5]. And even though the overall levels of fine particulate pollution have been decreasing due to active efforts of the local and national governments in the last decade, in some locations of the city the air quality has continued to deteriorate. The latter reflects the global trends of urbanization and motorization.

In addition to the impact of urbanization and rapid population growth, the pollution levels in the cities are modulated by meteorological factors [6]. Most importantly, the depth of mixing layer (the lower layer of troposphere mixing surface emissions) often depends on solar radiation and thus temperature in the area. The shallower the mixing depth is, the less diluted the daily emissions get. Therefore, temperature shows a reducing impact on fine particulate matter levels, through convection [7]. In addition, the formation and evolution of photochemical smog are dependent on solar radiation and temperature; meanwhile, wind speed tends to help ventilate air pollutants and/or transport them to other areas, even if the emission sources are not present in that region [8, 9]. This can result in increased levels of air pollution downwind from the original source, which directly depends on the wind direction [8]. Increased relative humidity has been shown to make even fine particles heavier, helping the dry deposition process of removal, while precipitation has a direct effect of scavenging by wet deposition [7, 8]. In addition, some studies differentiate between the seasons, as different parameters have different effects during the year, due to the combination of conditions [8, 9]. Thus, it is clearly impossible to rely on a single parameter to fully understand the urban pollution, especially if the study area is in a nonhomogeneous and complex terrain. This fact justifies the elaboration of models that take into account heterogeneous data to predict air quality.

Currently, three major approaches are used to forecast $PM_{2.5}$ concentrations: statistical models, chemical transport, and machine learning. Statistical models, which are mainly based on single variable linear regression, have shown a negative correlation between different meteorological parameters (wind, precipitation, and temperature) and PM concentrations (PM_{10}, $PM_{2.5}$, and $PM_{1.0}$) [7]. Chemical transport and Atmospheric Dispersion Modeling are numerical methods, and the most advanced ones are WRF-Chem and CMAQ. These models can be used to predict atmospheric pollution, but their accuracy relies on an updated source list that is very difficult to produce [10]. In addition, complex geophysical characteristics of locations with complex terrain complicate the implementation of these models of weather and pollution forecast mostly due to the complexity of the air flows (wind speed and direction) around the topographic features [11, 12]. Unlike a pure statistical method, a machine learning approach can consider several parameters in a single model. The most popular classifiers to forecast pollution from meteorological data are artificial Neural Networks [13–15]. Other successful studies use hybrid or mixed models that combine several artificial intelligence algorithms, such as fuzzy logic and Neural Network [16], or Principal Component Analysis and Support Vector Machine [17], or numerical methods and machine learning [10].

Recent studies show that the machine learning approach seems to overcome the other two methods for forecasting pollution [9, 10]. This is the reason why it is increasingly used to predict air quality [13, 17–21]. However, the data mining does not only differ from one study to another, in terms of classification algorithms, but also regarding the used features. Some of them consider a quite exhaustive list of meteorological factors [15, 16], whereas others proceed with a careful selection [13, 14, 17, 22] or do not even use climatic parameters at all [18]. Since machine learning is a very promising method to forecast pollution, we propose applying this approach to predict $PM_{2.5}$ concentration in Quito. This prediction is based on a selection of meteorological features for two main

reasons: first because a model using only meteorological data, which can be easily obtained in any urban area, is cheaper than an air quality monitoring system and second because a general model that may work for any city is not realistic [10], which implies that a selection of meteorological parameters must be performed in order to find the best model for the capital city of Ecuador. Quito is located in the Andes cordillera in the tropical climate zone, characterized by two seasons with different accumulation of precipitation. However, the temperature, the pressure, and even the amount of solar radiation do not vary much during the year. Moreover, the wind direction and speed highly depend on the topographic features of complex terrain in which a city is positioned and usually present one of the biggest challenges in forecasting weather and air quality. Therefore, this research aims to study the connectivity between three selected meteorological factors, wind speed, wind direction, and precipitation, and $PM_{2.5}$ pollution in two districts located in northwestern Quito.

In this work, we first present a spatial visualization of the distribution of fine particulate matter trends according to wind (speed and direction) and precipitation parameters in two locations in Quito. This part includes a description of the preparation of the data for classification. Then, various machine learning models are exploited to classify different levels of $PM_{2.5}$, namely, Boosted Trees and Linear Support Vector Machines. Finally, a Neural Network regression and a time series analysis are applied to provide insight about the parametric boundaries, in which the classification models perform adequately. In the final section, we draw up the main conclusions and suggestions for future work.

2. Data Collection

2.1. Site Description. Unlike most of South America, the most urbanized continent on the planet (81%), Ecuador, is one of the few countries in the region with only 64% of total population living in urban areas [23]. However, the rate of urbanization has increased over the past decade. Quito sprawls north to south on a long plateau lying on the east side of the Pichincha volcano (alt. 4,784 m.a.s.l., meters above sea level) in the Andes cordillera at an altitude of 2,850 m.a.s.l. (see Figure 1). According to the 2010 census, Quito's metro area is currently 4,217.95 km^2 with a population over 2,239,191 and is expected to increase to almost 2.8 million by 2020, making the city the most populous city in the country, overgrowing Guayaquil [24]. The city is contained within a number of valleys at 2,300–2,450 m.a.s.l. and terraces varying from 2,700 to 3,000 m.a.s.l. altitude. Due to Quito's location on the Equator, the city receives direct sunlight almost all year round, and, due to its altitude, Quito's climate is mild, spring-like all year round. The region has two seasons, dry (June–August, average precipitation 14 mm/month) and wet (September–May, average precipitation 59 mm/month), with most of the rainfall in the afternoons. Quito's temperature is almost constant, around 14.5°C, with the prevailing winds from the east. However, due to a complex terrain, the winds in the city are highly variable most of the year (dry season is windier), challenging weather prediction in the region.

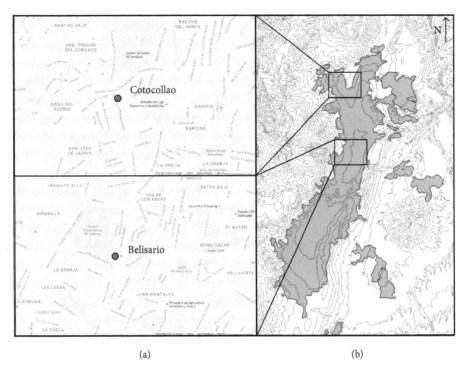

(a)   (b)

FIGURE 1: Topographic map (b) of Quito's urban area (green areas) and Google maps images (a) of the air quality measurement sites (red dots) Cotocollao and Belisario.

For the purpose of this study, the two northwestern air quality monitoring points are presented: Cotocollao and Belisario (see red dots in Figure 1). These districts were chosen to show the variation and complexity of the prediction of fine particulate matter trends even within a relatively small area of Quito with similar topographical characteristics (approximately the same altitude and directly east of the Pichincha volcano).

2.2. Air Quality Measurements Monitoring Network and Instrumentation. The municipal office of environmental quality, *Secretaria de Ambiente*, has been collecting air quality and meteorological data since May 1, 2007, in several sites around the city. The measurement sites run by the *Secretaria de Ambiente* are located in representative areas throughout the city, varying by altitudes depending on municipal districts. We used the real meteorological and PM$_{2.5}$ concentration data from the two most northwestern automatic data collection stations: Belisario (alt. 2,835 m.a.s.l., coord. 78°29′24″W, 0°10′48″S) and Cotocollao (alt. 2,739 m.a.s.l., coord. 78°29′50″W, 0°6′28″S) (see Figure 1). These two sites are approximately 9 km apart from each other. The Belisario measurement site is less than 100 m west of a busy road (Avenida America), 200 m northwest of a busy roundabout, and less than 1,000 m to the east of a major outer highway (Ave. Antonio Jose de Sucre), which runs along the west side of the city, intended to reduce the traffic inside the city (Figure 1). The Cotocollao monitoring site is located in a residential area, with only a few busier streets, and the same outer highway (Ave. Antonio Jose de Sucre) 250 m to the north. Both monitoring sites are inside of the *"Pico y Placa"* zone, implemented in 2010, which, based on the last number of car

license plates, limits rush hour traffic reducing the number of personal vehicles by approximately 20% during the weekdays.

The monitoring stations are positioned on the roofs of relatively tall buildings. Fine particulate matter (PM$_{2.5}$) measurements are conducted using instrumentation validated by the Environmental Protection Agency (EPA) of the United States. For PM$_{2.5}$ Thermo Scientific FH62C14-DHS Continuous, 5014i (EPA Number EQPM-0609-183), was used. The detection limit for this instrument is 5 $\mu g/m^3$ for one-hour averaging. The aerosol data is collected at 10 s intervals, and from this then 10 min, 1-hour, and 24-hour averages are calculated. The latter averaging data is presented in this work. Wind velocity is measured using MetOne/010C and wind direction using MetOne/020C instrumentation. The wind speed sensor and wind direction starting threshold is 0.22 m/s, and the accuracies are 0.07 m/s and 3°, respectively. The precipitation is measured using MetOne/382 and Thies Clima/5.4032.007 equipment. All meteorological parameters have been validated using Vaisala/MAWS100 weather station.

3. Data Preparation

In this section the method for the preparation of the data is presented, in order to proceed with the classification. It includes refining steps to discard useless data, transformations to visually examine and understand the data, and creation of an averaged intensity map of the PM$_{2.5}$ concentrations with respect to the selected meteorological parameters (wind and precipitation).

3.1. Data Refinement. For this study we analyzed the data of six years, starting June 2007 and ending July 2013. The two

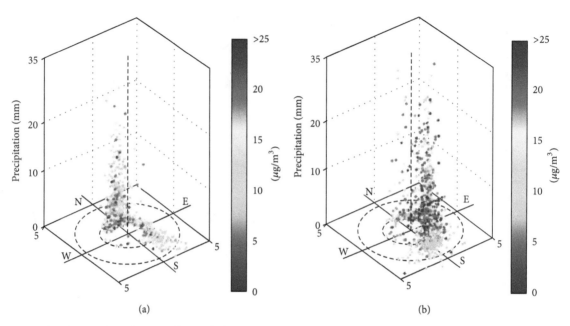

Figure 2: Data distribution for (a) Cotocollao and (b) Belisario, in terms of wind direction, wind speed, precipitation, and PM$_{2.5}$ concentrations (color scale). The inner circle represents wind speeds up to 2 m/s and the outer circle represents wind speeds up to 4 m/s.

datasets (one for each monitoring point) are composed out of 2,223 instances. Each data point consists of 4 parameters indicating daily values of precipitation accumulation (mm), wind direction (0–360°), wind speed (m/s), and observed fine particle concentrations (μg/m^3).

The datasets are cleaned by discarding data points that include any missing values. These data points represent 2.8% and 2.4% of the total data for Belisario and Cotocollao, respectively. It has been demonstrated that missing data of these magnitudes do not influence the classification performance [25]. In addition, considering the very low number of missing values, it is preferable to remove them instead of performing an interpolation, taking into account the following: (i) we proceed with an analysis on discrete variables (day-by-day) and not a time series forecasting and (ii) the PM$_{2.5}$ concentrations are very inconstant from one day to another. Weekend days are also removed from the dataset because the distribution of PM$_{2.5}$ concentrations during the weekdays and weekends is very different for Quito. This could introduce an additional level of complexity in data classification as during the weekdays there are clear rush hour peaks (morning and evening), while on Saturdays PM$_{2.5}$ levels increase between late morning and late afternoon hours. In addition, Sundays can be identified by a drop of PM$_{2.5}$ concentration. These patterns are dictated by human activity changes during the week, therefore, clearly showing PM$_{2.5}$ dependability on traffic. After cleaning, the final datasets are composed of 1,527 instances for Belisario and 1,536 instances for Cotocollao.

3.2. Data Transformation.

To represent the data according to a wind rose plot, the linear scale of wind direction (0–360°) is transformed from polar to Cartesian coordinates where angles increase clockwise and both 0° and 360° are north

(N) (see Figure 2). This mathematical transformation (see (1)) permits a more accurate feature representation of the data for wind direction around the north axis. Otherwise, wind direction angles slightly higher than 0° and slightly lower than 360° would be considered as two opposing directions. This is useful for classification models that are implemented in the next stage. This relates to machine learning models that improve performance if there are continuous relationships between parameters (optimization: smoother clustering task) [26]. This transformation ensures both valid and more informative representation of the original data. In addition, this representation can be completed by the precipitation levels, which are plotted on the z-axis (Figure 2). The color range is mapped from concentrations 0 μg/m^3 to >25 μg/m^3. The threshold of 25 μg/m^3 indicates the values from which the 24-hour concentrations of PM$_{2.5}$ are harmful according to international health standards.

$$x = \sin\left(\frac{\text{Wind Direction}}{360°} \cdot 2\pi\right) \cdot \text{Wind Speed},$$
$$y = \cos\left(\frac{\text{Wind Direction}}{360°} \cdot 2\pi\right) \cdot \text{Wind Speed}. \quad (1)$$

A visual inspection of the transformed data shows that the wind directions corresponding to precipitation are north (N) for Cotocollao (Figure 2(a)) and east (E) for Belisario (Figure 2(b)). The stronger winds tend to take place between south (S) and southeast (SE) for Cotocollao and between southwest (SW) and SE in Belisario. As expected, in both cases these stronger winds seem to account for relatively low levels of PM$_{2.5}$.

3.3. Trend Analyses.

In order to obtain general trends in the distribution of the PM$_{2.5}$ concentrations as a function of wind speed and wind direction, the data are used to generate convolutional based spatial representations. Convolution-based models for spatial data have increased in popularity as a result of their flexibility in modeling spatial dependence and their ability to accommodate large datasets [27]. This generated Convolutional Generalization Model (CGM) [28] is an averaged value of the PM$_{2.5}$ pollution level (PL), in which the regional quantity of influence per data point is modeled as a 2D Gaussian matrix (see (2)). A Gaussian convolution is applied (i) to spatially interpolate data, in order to get a 2D representation from the points' coordinates calculated in (1) and (ii) to smooth the PL concentration values of this representation. A Gaussian kernel is used because it inhibits the quality of monotonic smoothing, and as there is no prior knowledge about the distribution, a kernel density function with high entropy minimizes the information transfer of the convolution step to the processed data [29]. This 2D Gaussian matrix is multiplied by the PL of the given data point and added to the CGM at the coordinates corresponding to the wind speed and direction of this point. Then, the quantity of influence is added to the point. The final step is to divide the total amount of each cell by the quantity of influence, which results in a generalized average value.

$$
\text{CGM (rows, colums)} = \text{PL} \frac{1}{36} \begin{bmatrix} 1 \\ 4 \\ 6 \\ 4 \\ 1 \end{bmatrix} \begin{bmatrix} 1 & 4 & 6 & 4 & 1 \end{bmatrix}. \quad (2)
$$

The general tendencies are as follows: (i) strong winds result in low PM$_{2.5}$ concentrations and (ii) the strongest winds generally come from the similar direction (SE for Cotocollao and S for Belisario). The results of CGMs for both sites are shown in Figure 3 as an overlay on top of the geographic location of their respective monitoring stations. Main highways are indicated in green. The highest concentrations of PM$_{2.5}$ (from yellow to red) tend to be brought by the winds coming from these main highways. It is to note that higher wind speeds for Cotocollao tend to be on the axis of Quito's former airport (grey-green area, center of the map, see Figure 3), currently transformed into a city park. This traffic and structure free corridor seems to accelerate wind speeds, which may explain the reduction of PM$_{2.5}$ concentrations due to better ventilation of this part of the city.

During the study, average PM$_{2.5}$ concentrations in Cotocollao and Belisario are 15.6 μg/m^3 and 17.9 μg/m^3, respectively, both exceeding the national standards. During the studied six years, the area of Belisario was more polluted with more variation in PM$_{2.5}$ concentrations (higher deviation, see Figure 4) and more turbulent (Figure 3) than Cotocollao. These factors could be the result of Belisario being more urbanized.

4. Classification Models

Machine learning models are used to separate the data in different classes of PM$_{2.5}$ concentrations. Supervised learning

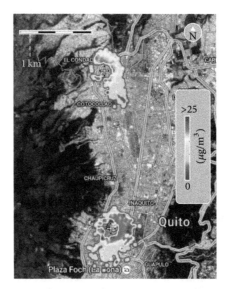

FIGURE 3: CGM visualization, positioned on top of the geographic location of the respective monitoring stations (northwestern part of Quito). The northern CGM visualization is Cotocollao and the southern one is Belisario. Main highways are represented in green.

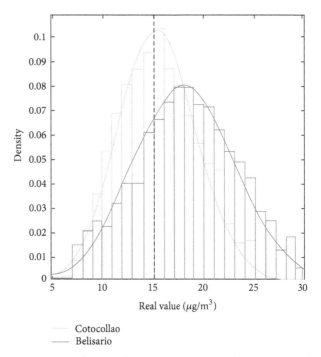

Cotocollao
Belisario

FIGURE 4: Distribution of PM$_{2.5}$ concentrations (June 2007 to July 2013) for Cotocollao and Belisario. Dashed black line represents the national standards and the class seperation boundary (15 μg/m^3).

techniques are applied to create models on this classification task. Here we introduce Boosted Trees (BTs) and Linear Support Vector Machines (L-SVM). A BT combines weak learners (simple rules) to create a classification algorithm, where each misclassified data point per learner gains weight. A following learner optimizes the classification of the highest weighted region. Boosted Trees are known for their

TABLE 1: Binary classification with class separation at 15 μg/m^3.

Model	Location	
	Belisario	Cotocollao
BT	83.2%	67.6%
L-SVM	79.8%	66.3%

TABLE 2: Confusion matrix of binary classification for Cotocollao using a BT. Rows represent the true class and columns represent the predicted class.

Class	<15	>15	TPR/FNR
<15	51.1%	48.9%	**51.1%** **48.9%**
>15	20.3%	79.7%	**79.7%** **20.3%**

TABLE 3: Confusion matrix of Binary classification for Belisario using a BT. Rows represent the true class and columns represent the predicted class.

Class	<15	>15	TPR/FNR
<15	49.0%	51.0%	**49.0%** **51.0%**
>15	5.1%	94.9%	**94.9%** **5.1%**

insensibility to overfitting and for the fact that nonlinear relationships between the parameters do not influence the performance. A L-SVM separates classes with optimal distance. Convex optimization leads the algorithm to not focus on local minima. As these two models are well established and inhibit different qualities, they are used in this section. All computations and visualizations are executed in MathWorks Matlab 2015. Toolboxes for the classifications, the statistics, and machine learning processes are used in all the stages. Furthermore, Matlab's integrated tools for distribution fitting and curve fitting are applied for the different analyses. The initial parameters provided by the Matlab toolbox software are used in this work. ADA boost learning method with a total amount of 30 learners and a maximum number of splits being 20 at a learning rate of 0.1 are the default parameters for the BT. The SVM is initialized with a linear kernel of scale 1.0, a box constrained level of 1.0, and an equal learning rate of 0.1.

Fluctuations in yearly PM$_{2.5}$ concentrations are not taken into account in this classification process as a previous analysis showed a small variation in fine particulate matter pollution levels during the studied period [5]. A binary classification is performed to set a baseline comparison between the different sites. Then, a three-class classification is carried out to assess the separability between three ranges of concentrations of PM$_{2.5}$ (based on WHO guidelines) and provide insight into general classification rules.

4.1. Binary Classification.

In this first classification two classes are used, which represent values above and below 15 μg/m^3. The latter value is selected as it is the National Air Quality Standard of Ecuador for annual PM$_{2.5}$ concentrations (equivalent to WHO's Interim Target-3) [30]. Due to the normal distribution of the datasets, as shown in Figure 4, a higher accuracy for Belisario than Cotocollao is expected, partially because of a priori imbalanced class distribution. A previous study using the same classification shows an accuracy of only 65% for Cotocollao by applying the trees.J48 algorithm, which is a decision tree implementation integrated in the WEKA machine learning workbench [5].

Classification with both BT and L-SVM shows similar results. Table 1 presents the results of this first classification. The implementation of the classification for Belisario outperforms that of Cotocollao. It also suggests that the extreme levels (low and high) of PM$_{2.5}$ could be more straightforward to classify with the current parameters, implying a higher class separability for the Belisario dataset (wider distribution). Tables 2 and 3 show that the concentrations above 15 μg/m^3 for both sites are better classified than those below the 15 μg/m^3 boundary. This is less surprising for Belisario due to

the earlier mentioned class imbalance. For Cotocollao, however, the poor performance for this class can indicate that this class is less distinctive; thus the model optimizes the class above 15 μg/m^3. Note that it is crucial to be able to classify nonattainment (PM$_{2.5}$ > 15 μg/m^3) instances, as wrongly identified nonviolating national standards (PM$_{2.5}$ < 15 μg/m^3) levels would be a less costly error.

In Figure 5(a) Receiver Operating Characteristic (ROC) curves comparison is shown for the binary classifiers presented in Table 1, namely, the BT and L-SVM classifiers. Figure 5(a) depicts the ROC curves for Cotocollao dataset and Figure 5(b) the ROC curves for Belisario dataset. Once the classifiers models are built for every dataset, a validation set is presented to the model, in order to predict the class label. It is also of interest to have the classification scores of the model which indicate the likelihood that the predicted label comes from a particular class. The ROC curves are constructed with this scored classification and the true labels in the validation dataset (Figure 5).

ROC curves are useful to evaluate binary classifiers and to compare their performances in a two-dimensional graph that plots the specificity versus sensitivity. The specificity measures the true negative rate, that is, the proportion of negatives that have been correctly classified: true negatives/negatives = true negatives/(true negatives + false positives). Likewise, the sensitivity measures the true positive rate, that is, the proportion of positives correctly identified: true positives/positives = true positives/(true positives + false negatives). The area under the ROC curve (AUC) can be used as a measure of the expected performance of the classifier, and the AUC of a classifier is equal to the probability that the classifier will rank a randomly chosen positive instance higher than a randomly chosen negative instance [31]. Figure 5(b) shows the performance of the BT and L-SVM classifiers for the Belisario dataset. The BT outperforms the L-SVM classifier in all regions of the ROC space, with [AUC(BT) = 0.72] > [AUC(L-SVM) = 0.66], which means a better performance

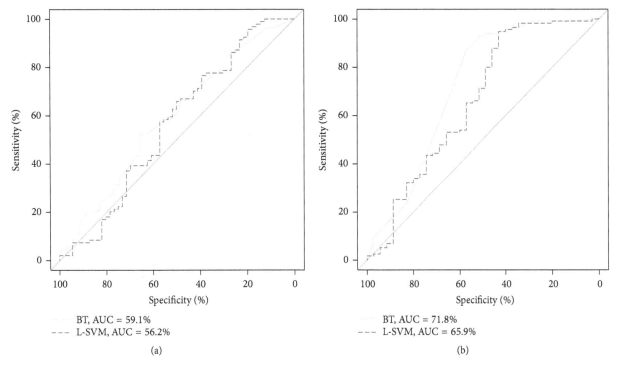

FIGURE 5: ROC curves for Cotocollao (a) and Belisario (b).

for the BT classifier. The BT classifier has a fair performance separating the two classes in the Belisario dataset.

In Figure 5(a) the ROC curves and AUC are presented for the Cotocollao dataset. Again, BT performs better than the L-SVM classifier with [AUC(BT) = 0.59] > [AUC(L-SVM) = 0.56]. This time the classifiers for the Cotocollao dataset have a poor performance separating the two classes, with a performance just slightly better when compared to a random classifier with AUC = 0.5. The classification result is clearly better for Belisario than for Cotocollao. Thus, a three-class classification should identify if for both sites; the extreme concentrations could be better classified than the moderate ones and clarify the low performance for Cotocollao.

4.2. Three-Class Classification. To further analyze the differences of multiple categories of concentration levels, a three-class classification is performed using WHO's guidelines for pollution concentrations as class boundaries. According to these guidelines, health risks are considered low if $PM_{2.5} < 10 \, \mu g/m^3$ (long term, annual WHO's recommended level), moderate if $10 \, \mu g/m^3 > PM_{2.5} < 25 \, \mu g/m^3$, and high if $PM_{2.5} > 25 \, \mu g/m^3$ (short term, 24-hour WHO's recommended level). The objective is to identify if these main pollution thresholds are indeed well separable and thus the weather parameters can account for $PM_{2.5}$ pollution in these three ranges of air quality.

In both studied districts the classes $< 10 \, \mu g/m^3$ and $>25 \, \mu g/m^3$ are relatively small with approximately 10% of the data compared to the class 10–$25 \, \mu g/m^3$. Due to this fact, an alternative BT algorithm is used to take into account these imbalanced classes. This RusBoosted Tree (RBT) approach

TABLE 4: Confusion matrix of three-class classification for Cotocollao using a RBT. Rows represent the true class and columns represent the predicted class.

Class	<10	10–25	>25	TPR/FNR
<10	76.3%	16.3%	7.4%	**76.3%** **23.7%**
10–25	28.3%	28.8%	42.9%	**28.8%** **71.2%**
>25	6.3%	20.3%	73.4%	**73.4%** **26.6%**

endeavors to find an even distribution of performance for all classes instead of finding a global optimum [32]. This leads to a better representation of the separability. The true positive versus false negative rate (TPR/FNR) is shown for each class in the confusion matrices of Cotocollao (Table 4) and Belisario (Table 5).

Tables 4 and 5 show that the correctness in classifying concentrations $< 10 \, \mu g/m^3$ seems to perform adequately. Also, the correct classification for concentrations $> 25 \, \mu g/m^3$ in Cotocollao is fair. However, the false positive rate of this classification is extremely high, because 42.9% of the 10–$25 \, \mu g/m^3$ class gets classified as class $> 25 \, \mu g/m^3$. For Belisario, the separation of classes 10–$25 \, \mu g/m^3$ and $>25 \, \mu g/m^3$ is deficient. In both cases, only the extreme low values can be classified well. Thus, the hypothesis of the extreme concentrations in $PM_{2.5}$ being more straightforward to classify (see Section 4.1) is only partially verified.

Analyzing the wrongly classified samples of class 10–$25 \, \mu g/m^3$ shows that, for samples classified as $<10 \, \mu g/m^3$, the

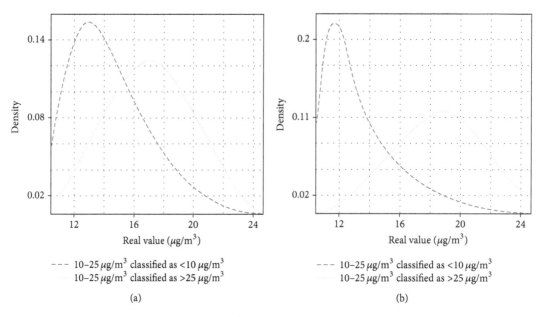

FIGURE 6: Wrongly classified samples of class 10–25 $\mu g/m^3$ with their real value distributions for Cotocollao (a) and Belisario (b).

TABLE 5: Confusion matrix of three-class classification for Belisario using a RBT. Rows represent the true class and columns represent the predicted class.

Class	<10	10–25	25	TPR/FNR
<10	84.8%	9.5%	5.7%	**84.8%** **15.2%**
10–25	12.3%	53.5%	34.2%	**53.5%** **46.5%**
>25	6.5%	45.1%	48.4%	**48.4%** **51.6%**

real values tend to be relatively close to 10 $\mu g/m^3$. This evidence is even stronger for Belisario (Figure 6(b)), than for Cotocollao (Figure 6(a)). This indicates a changeover in values around the decision boundary. The same does not apply to the wrongly classified samples that are grouped as >25 $\mu g/m^3$. As shown in Figure 6 these values are mostly normally distributed around the mean of class 10–25 $\mu g/m^3$. Even though for Belisario the mean is shifted, it is not evident that wrongly classified samples of class 10–25 $\mu g/m^3$ into class 25 $\mu g/m^3$ tend to be closer to values of 25 $\mu g/m^3$, as this shift is mainly caused by the fact that the mean value of the Belisario initial data is higher (see Figure 4). We can conclude that the low performance for Cotocollao in the previous section (Section 4.1) is mainly caused by the fact that the classifier tries to separate values in the range of 10–25 $\mu g/m^3$ and >25 $\mu g/m^3$, which are poorly separable according to the three-class classification.

These results show that values of 10–25 $\mu g/m^3$ and >25 $\mu g/m^3$ are not well separable and thus not largely influenced by the used meteorological parameters. On the contrary, lower

values seem to be largely predictable by wind and precipitation conditions. This statement gains confidence by looking at the wrongly classified data points discussed previously (see Figure 6).

4.3. Classification Rules. Binary classification between all different classes with the use of RBTs provides general rules for classifying the different levels of $PM_{2.5}$ in terms of the parameter space. Here, the well performing rules in classifying $PM_{2.5}$ concentrations < 10 $\mu g/m^3$ are discussed. The rules and their performance can be seen in Table 6. This table shows that rules separating classes < 10 $\mu g/m^3$ versus 10–25 $\mu g/m^3$ and <10 $\mu g/m^3$ versus >25 $\mu g/m^3$ have a high percentage of accuracy. On the contrary, the separation between 10–25 $\mu g/m^3$ and >25 $\mu g/m^3$ is less accurate.

Figure 7 provides a visualization of the data according to the class separation in Table 6 for the example of Cotocollao. The RBT classification of the data as seen in Figures 7(a) and 7(b) creates two clusters for class < 10 $\mu g/m^3$. In the case of Belisario, the RBT classifications result in identifying only one cluster for class < 10 $\mu g/m^3$.

It is to note that, for Cotocollao, the performance increases drastically comparing the binary classifications of <10 $\mu g/m^3$ versus 10–25 $\mu g/m^3$ and <10 $\mu g/m^3$ versus >25 $\mu g/m^3$ (from 73.2% up to 88.9%, see Table 6). In contrast, the performance for Belisario for these two classifications does not differ (from 86.7% to 88.8%). This indicates that the data for Cotocollao are less separable at the 10–25 $\mu g/m^3$ class than for Belisario.

To sum up the outcomes of the classification models, the binary classification utilizing the National and International Air Quality Standards as class labels ($PM_{2.5}$ < 15 $\mu g/m^3$, $PM_{2.5}$ > 15 $\mu g/m^3$) showed a high difference in performance

TABLE 6: Classification rules and pairwise comparisons between the different classes and their respective performance.

Classification	Location	
	Cotocollao	Belisario
	Classification rules	
$<10\,\mu g/m^3$ versus $10–25\,\mu g/m^3$	Wind speed > 2.5 m/s Wind direction = S-SE Wind direction = NW-NE Precipitation > 15 mm	Wind speed > 2.2 m/s Wind direction = SE-SW
	Classification performance	
	73.2% (Figure 7(a))	86.7%
	Classification rules	
$<10\,\mu g/m^3$ versus $>25\,\mu g/m^3$	Wind speed > 2 m/s Wind direction = S-SE Wind direction = NW-NE Precipitation > 1 mm	Wind speed > 2 m/s Wind direction = SE-SW
	Classification performance	
	88.9% (Figure 7(b))	88.8%
$10–25\,\mu g/m^3$ versus $>25\,\mu g/m^3$	60.0%	64.1%

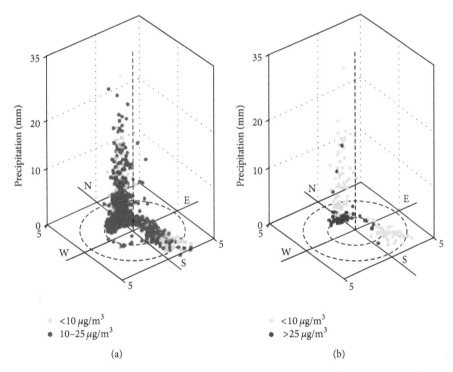

○ $<10\,\mu g/m^3$	○ $<10\,\mu g/m^3$
● $10–25\,\mu g/m^3$	● $>25\,\mu g/m^3$
(a)	(b)

FIGURE 7: Data split for three different classes (see Table 6): (a) $<10\,\mu g/m^3$ versus $10–25\,\mu g/m^3$ and (b) $<10\,\mu g/m^3$ versus $>25\,\mu g/m^3$. Both (a) and (b) are results for Cotocollao mapped in terms of wind direction, wind speed, and precipitation. The inner circle represents wind speeds up to 2 m/s and the outer circle represents wind speeds up to 4 m/s.

between the two sites. In order to explain this difference and the misclassifications, the analysis was refined to a three-class classification based on WHO's guidelines regarding the consequences of $PM_{2.5}$ concentrations on health risks as low ($PM_{2.5} < 10\,\mu g/m^3$), moderate ($PM_{2.5} = 10–25\,\mu g/m^3$), and high ($PM_{2.5} > 25\,\mu g/m^3$). This classification showed high performance in categorizing low concentrations in contrast to high concentrations. Next, we propose a regression analysis to pinpoint the upper boundary of $PM_{2.5}$ values, for which the weather parameters are still able to explain variation in pollution levels that are not described by the classification analysis.

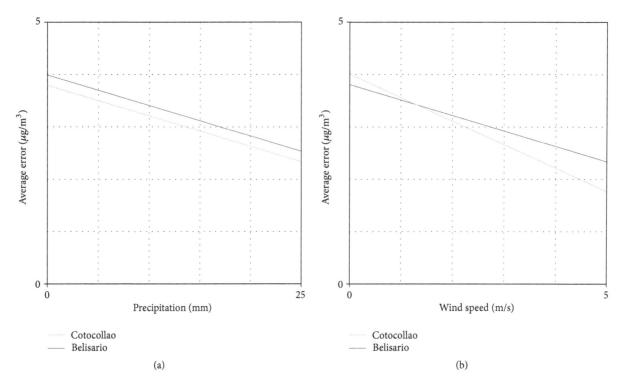

FIGURE 8: Decrease in average prediction error with increasing parameter values (precipitation and wind speed) for Cotocollao (orange) and Belisario (blue).

5. Regression Analyses

In this section an additional machine learning analysis, based on BT, L-SVM, and Neural Networks (NN), is used to perform a regression for both sites. Default parameters provided by the Matlab toolbox software are used to set up the models. NN are appropriate models for highly nonlinear modeling and when no prior knowledge about the relationship between the parameters is assumed. The NN consist of 10 nodes in 1 hidden layer, trained with a Levenberg-Marquardt procedure, in combination with a random data division. Identifying the correlation between the real and predicted values gives us the topological coherence between the input and output parameter values. In addition, the error related to the parameter values provides insight regarding the prediction confidence for determined weather conditions. Also, the analysis of the data trend over time will inform on the applicability of a time series forecasting. Finally, the CGM is used to remark on the possibility of optimizing the regression.

5.1. Regression Models. A regression is performed with three different classifiers. Bin sizes of 0.5 μg/m^3 (0–35 μg/m^3 range) are used for the models that output discrete class values (BT and SVM). This relatively small bin size permits these models to perform regression as their output values closely approach continuous values. The additional parameters of the models are set up as explained in the binary and three-class classification (Sections 4.1 and 4.2). The models are trained with 10-fold cross-validation. The test set is 20% of the

original data. Unlike the NN continuous output values, the discrete output values of the other models can have an effect on the classification error. However, as the bin size is relatively small, we expect the errors related to these types of output to be marginal.

$$\text{MSE} = \frac{1}{n} \cdot \sum_{i=1}^{n} (y_i - \widehat{y}_i)^2. \quad (3)$$

The mean squared error (MSE) is used to measure the classification performance (see (3)). The MSE is the averaged squared error per prediction. The mean absolute percentage error (MAPE) is used to express the average prediction error in terms of percentage of a data point's real value (see (4)). The MAPE function provides a more intuitive understanding of the performance.

$$\text{MAPE} = \frac{\sum_{i=1}^{n} |(y_i - \widehat{y}_i) / y_i|}{n}. \quad (4)$$

An analysis of the confidence levels in relation to the precipitation and wind speed parameters is shown in Figure 8. The prediction confidence rises when the parameter values increase. A level of confidence is explained as the average prediction error (absolute difference between the real and the predicted values, root of MSE) at a certain interval with respect to an input parameter. In Figure 8, fitted lines represent the predicted data in terms of their absolute error with respect to precipitation and wind speed for both sites. The decrease in errors can be seen with respect to increasing

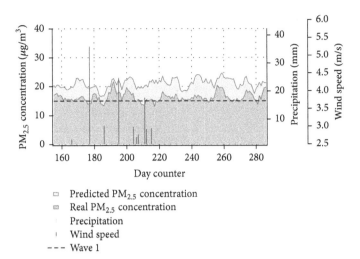

FIGURE 9: Neural Network's regressive prediction of Cotocollao PM$_{2.5}$ concentration (light grey) compared to the real data (dark grey) during the wet season plotted against daily rain accumulation and wind speed thresholds, >1 mm and >2.5 m/s, respectively (see Table 6, thresholds obtained from 3-class classification). The dashed black line represents the national standards for PM$_{2.5}$ annual concentrations.

values of these specified input parameters. It suggests that the prediction of PM$_{2.5}$ concentration is more reliable for extreme than moderate climatic conditions.

Figure 9 shows an example of the comparison of the predictive models of PM$_{2.5}$ concentration and the real PM$_{2.5}$ concentration for Cotocollao during six months of a wet season (first half of 2008). The graph shows the 5-point box-smoothed data to demonstrate the good prediction of the tendency of the PM$_{2.5}$ concentrations. Besides a certain gap, the estimated values seem to fairly correlate with the real data. The correlation analysis shows a significant positive correlation between the real concentrations and the predicted concentrations, $r(130) = 0.5$, $p < 0.000$. Also, the model performance is relatively good throughout the study period. The correlation analysis for all of the data shows a significant positive correlation between the real and predicted PM$_{2.5}$ concentrations, $r(1534) = 0.34$, $p < 0.000$.

This visualization shows that the error of predicted concentration seems to increase when PM$_{2.5}$ concentration increases. The reduction in both real and estimated PM$_{2.5}$ concentrations coincides with rain events and wind speeds above the thresholds defined in Table 6 (>1 mm and >2.5 m/s, resp.).

The results of the MSE for the regression show that in both city sites a NN performs the best (see Table 7). The correlation analysis shows that there is a logarithmic relationship between the real particle concentration values and the prediction (Figure 10). It means that there is an overprediction for low values and an underprediction for high values and an overall decrease in correlation as values get higher. The correlation seems the best for values around 17 μg/m^3 for Cotocollao and 19 μg/m^3 for Belisario.

To sum up, the present input parameters do not well describe an increase in PM$_{2.5}$ concentrations if these levels are transcending values over 20 μg/m^3, as errors increase at this point and prediction values stagnate. Thus, additional parameters must be considered for the prediction of PM$_{2.5}$ levels

TABLE 7: MSE and MAPE of the NN, L-SVM, and BT on regression.

Model	Location	
	Belisario	Cotocollao
NN	22.1 (26%)	40.7 (40%)
L-SVM	26.8 (28%)	41.8 (41%)
BT	28.5 (30%)	44.4 (42%)

TABLE 8: MSE and MAPE of CGM and NN regression.

Model	Location	
	Belisario	Cotocollao
CGM	15.6 (22%)	15.0 (25%)
NN	22.1 (26%)	40.7 (40%)

beyond this concentration threshold, since meteorological factors alone are not able to account for the whole particulate matter concentrations. For instance, considering human activity (e.g., car traffic), which is the main source of pollution, should contribute to the reduction of the overprediction and underprediction observed in our model.

5.2. Optimization. The CGM, as applied in Section 3.3, could be used in classification tasks. In this section a 10-fold cross-validation on regression with this model is applied to compare it with the best performing model (NN).

The results show a substantial reduction in MSE with the CGM regression compared to the NN regression for the two city sites (see Table 8). It is to note that this diminution is particularly high in the case of Cotocollao. It seems that the model is able to better handle the dense (see Figure 4) and noisy (as stated in Section 4.3) data of Cotocollao than the NN. The similar performance in both sites means that this model has the potential to be applied in various situations with similar expected error rates. Further development

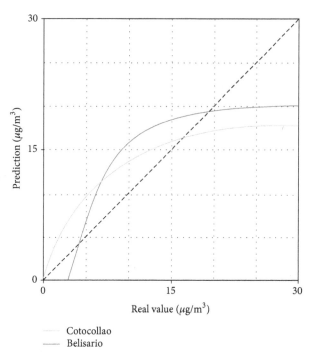

FIGURE 10: Fitted lines representing the correlation between predicted values and real values through a NN algorithm for Cotocollao (orange) and Belisario (blue).

should aid in qualifying the true robustness of this approach by exploiting the possibility of modeling with other spatial dependencies, such as density of measurements and day-by-day shifts, which represent the degree of freedom of parameters related to readings of the previous day(s). The latter dependency could be combined with linear quadratic estimation (LQE) techniques such as Kalman filters to improve the precision.

6. Conclusions and Perspectives

This study proposes a machine learning approach to predict $PM_{2.5}$ concentrations from meteorological data in a high-elevation mid-sized city (Quito, Ecuador). Standard levels of fine particulate matter are classified by using different machine learning models. This classification is performed on six years' records of daily meteorological values of wind speed (m/s), wind direction (0–360°), and precipitation accumulation (mm) for two air quality monitoring sites located in Quito (Cotocollao and Belisario). Although these sites are both in Quito's urbanized area, they exhibit differences in spread and dominance regarding wind features (speed and direction) that account for high $PM_{2.5}$ concentrations and distribution of pollution levels over the years. This could be caused by the fact that Belisario is more urbanized than Cotocollao and more importantly due to the extremely complex terrain of the city.

For these two different districts the results show a high reliability in the classification of low (<10 $\mu g/m^3$) versus high (>25 $\mu g/m^3$) and low (<10 $\mu g/m^3$) versus moderate

(10–25 $\mu g/m^3$) $PM_{2.5}$ concentrations. We found well defined clusters, within the parameter space, for $PM_{2.5}$ concentrations < 10 $\mu g/m^3$. The regression analysis shows that the used parameters can predict $PM_{2.5}$ concentrations up to 20 $\mu g/m^3$ and the accuracy of the predictions is improved in conditions of strong winds and high precipitation for both Cotocollao and Belisario. There is a significant positive correlation between the real concentrations and the predicted concentrations for all the study period. The slightly higher correlation during the rainy season confirms that the model can predict $PM_{2.5}$ concentrations better for more extreme weather conditions.

Using a convolutional based spatial representation (CGM) to perform regression shows improving performance compared to various used machine learning algorithms (NN, L-SVM, and BT). In addition to this model, finding trends over periods of time with the use of time series algorithms could further improve the prediction and would make a long-term forecasting of $PM_{2.5}$ concentrations possible [13].

The main contribution of this study is to propose an alternative approach to chemical transport numerical modeling, such as WRF-Chem or CMAQ, the performance of which depends on several input parameters (emission inventory, orography, etc.) and the accuracy of built-in meteorological models (WRF, MM5). The application of numerical models for complex terrain regions is challenging, since important topographic features are not well represented [11, 33]. This produces imprecisions in not only forecasting air quality, but also relevant meteorology [10, 12, 34, 35]. Here, the proposed model provides a more reliable and more economical alternative to predict $PM_{2.5}$ levels, as it only requires meteorological data acquisition. In addition, accurate meteorological technology is far more affordable compared to air quality sensors that can exceed the price over 100 times. Finally, this model is based on the three basic meteorological parameters (wind speed, wind direction, and precipitation), which have a straightforward effect on pollution. Thus, by considering that our model has a good prediction efficiency for a city of such a complex topography, we argue that it could be successfully applied in other tropical locations (regions of reduced changes in solar angle, temperature, and relative humidity).

Also, this work provides an insight into the main limitations regarding $PM_{2.5}$ prediction from meteorological data and machine learning. The classification and regression show that concentrations > 20 $\mu g/m^3$ seem to be influenced more by additional parameters than the meteorological factors used in this study. For example, although daily temperature, solar radiation, and pressure do not vary much during the year, they might make a difference if analyzed during different times of the day, causing different pollution levels in the city. An interesting approach to tackle this limitation would be to consider a hybrid model that would mix a numerical method (WRF-Chem or CMAQ) with machine learning algorithms [10].

Other climatic conditions and unusual impactful events causing higher pollution levels (festivities, wild fires, accidents, seasonal variability, or natural calamities) could also explain changes in $PM_{2.5}$ concentrations exceeding 20 $\mu g/m^3$.

Future work will consist of identifying the parameters or events causing values above this threshold. Furthermore, we intend to improve our CGM and use it to classify outliers and find their cause. Considering the diverse machine learning models used in air quality prediction, such as Neural Network [13–15], regression [18], decision trees, and Support Vector Machine [17], we applied and tested most of these classifiers in this study. Alternative approaches to improve the accuracy of our model would consist of performing a prediction based on an ensemble of different algorithms of data processing and modeling [16, 17, 22].

Conflicts of Interest

The authors declare that there are no conflicts of interest regarding the publication of this paper.

Acknowledgments

The authors would like to thank David R. Sannino for editing the text.

References

[1] United Nations, Department of Economic and Social Affairs (2015). World Population Prospects, the 2015 Revision, in Population Division edited, UN.

[2] World Health Organization, Media Centre (2016). Air pollution levels rising in many of the world's poorest cities. http://www.who.int/mediacentre/news/releases/2016/air-pollution-rising/.

[3] J. Lelieveld, J. S. Evans, M. Fnais, D. Giannadaki, and A. Pozzer, "The contribution of outdoor air pollution sources to premature mortality on a global scale," Nature, vol. 525, no. 7569, pp. 367–371, 2015.

[4] C. A. Pope and D. W. Dockery, "Health effects of fine particulate air pollution: lines that connect," Journal of the Air and Waste Management Association, vol. 56, no. 6, pp. 709–742, 2006.

[5] Y. Rybarczyk and R. Zalakeviciute, "Machine learning approach to forecasting urban pollution: a case study of Quito," in Proceedings of the IEEE Ecuador Technical Chapters Meeting, (ETCM '16), Guayaquil, Ecuador, 2016.

[6] M. A. Pohjola, A. Kousa, J. Kukkonen et al., "The spatial and temporal variation of measured urban PM_{10} and $PM_{2.5}$ in the Helsinki metropolitan area," Water, Air and Soil Pollution: Focus, vol. 2, no. 5, pp. 189–201, 2002.

[7] Y. Li, Q. Chen, H. Zhao, L. Wang, and R. Tao, "Variations in pm10, pm2.5 and pm1.0 in an urban area of the sichuan basin and their relation to meteorological factors," Atmosphere, vol. 6, no. 1, pp. 150–163, 2015.

[8] J. Wang and S. Ogawa, "Effects of meteorological conditions on PM2.5 concentrations in Nagasaki, Japan," International Journal of Environmental Research and Public Health, vol. 12, no. 8, pp. 9089–9101, 2015.

[9] F. Zhang, H. Cheng, Z. Wang et al., "Fine particles (PM2.5) at a CAWNET background site in central China: chemical compositions, seasonal variations and regional pollution events," Atmospheric Environment, vol. 86, pp. 193–202, 2014.

[10] X. Xi, Z. Wei, R. Xiaoguang et al., "A comprehensive evaluation of air pollution prediction improvement by a machine learning method," in Proceedings of the 10th IEEE International Conference on Service Operations and Logistics, and Informatics, SOLI 2015 - In conjunction with ICT4ALL '15, pp. 176–181, Hammamet, Tunisia, November 2015.

[11] P. A. Jimenez and J. Dudhia, "Improving the representation of resolved and unresolved topographic effects on surface wind in the WRF model," Journal of Applied Meteorology and Climatology, vol. 51, no. 2, pp. 300–316, 2012.

[12] R. Parra and V. Díaz, "Preliminary comparison of ozone concentrations provided by the emission inventory/WRF-Chem model and the air quality monitoring network from the Distrito Metropolitano de Quito (Ecuador)," in Proceedings of the 8th annual WRF User's Workshop, NCAR, Boulder, Colo, USA.

[13] X. Ni, H. Huang, and W. Du, "Relevance analysis and short-term prediction of PM2.5 concentrations in Beijing based on multi-source data," Atmospheric Environment, vol. 150, pp. 146–161, 2017.

[14] J. Chen, H. Chen, Z. Wu, D. Hu, and J. Z. Pan, "Forecasting smog-related health hazard based on social media and physical sensor," Information Systems, vol. 64, pp. 281–291, 2017.

[15] J. Zhang and W. Ding, "Prediction of air pollutants concentration based on an extreme learning machine: the case of Hong Kong," International Journal of Environmental Research and Public Health, vol. 14, no. 2, p. 114, 2017.

[16] P. Jiang, Q. Dong, and P. Li, "A novel hybrid strategy for PM2.5 concentration analysis and prediction," Journal of Environmental Management, vol. 196, pp. 443–457, 2017.

[17] K. P. Singh, S. Gupta, and P. Rai, "Identifying pollution sources and predicting urban air quality using ensemble learning methods," Atmospheric Environment, vol. 80, pp. 426–437, 2013.

[18] C. Brokamp, R. Jandarov, M. B. Rao, G. LeMasters, and P. Ryan, "Exposure assessment models for elemental components of particulate matter in an urban environment: a comparison of regression and random forest approaches," Atmospheric Environment, vol. 151, pp. 1–11, 2017.

[19] M. Arhami, N. Kamali, and M. M. Rajabi, "Predicting hourly air pollutant levels using artificial neural networks coupled with uncertainty analysis by Monte Carlo simulations," Environmental Science and Pollution Research, vol. 20, no. 7, pp. 4777–4789, 2013.

[20] A. Russo, F. Raischel, and P. G. Lind, "Air quality prediction using optimal neural networks with stochastic variables," Atmospheric Environment, vol. 79, pp. 822–830, 2013.

[21] M. Fu, W. Wang, Z. Le, and M. S. Khorram, "Prediction of particular matter concentrations by developed feed-forward neural network with rolling mechanism and gray model," Neural Computing and Applications, vol. 26, no. 8, pp. 1789–1797, 2015.

[22] W. Sun and J. Sun, "Daily $PM_{2.5}$ concentration prediction based on principal component analysis and LSSVM optimized by cuckoo search algorithm," Journal of Environmental Management, vol. 188, pp. 144–152, 2017.

[23] United Nations Development Programme (UNDP), Human development report 2014, Sustaining Human Progress: Reducing Vulnerabilities and Building Resilience.

[24] Instituto Nacional de Estadistica y Censos (INEC), Quito, el cantón más poblado del Ecuador en el 2020, 2013.

[25] E. Acuña and C. Rodriguez, "The treatment of missing values and its effect on classifier accuracy," in Classification, Clustering, and Data Mining Applications, D. Banks, F. R. McMorris, P. Arabie, and W. Gaul, Eds., pp. 639–647, Springer, Berlin, Heidelberg, 2004.

[26] I. Mierswa, M. Wurst, R. Klinkenberg, M. Scholz, and T. Euler, "Yale: rapid prototyping for complex data mining tasks," in *Proceedings of 12th ACM SIGKDD International Conference on Knowledge Discovery and Data Mining*, pp. 935–940, Philadelphia, PA, USA, 2006.

[27] C. A. Calder and N. Cressie, "Some topics in convolution-based spatial modeling," in *Proceedings of the 56th Session of the International Statistics Institute*, International Statistics Institute, Netherlands, 2007.

[28] F. Fouedjio, N. Desassis, and J. Rivoirard, "A generalized convolution model and estimation for non-stationary random functions," *Spatial Statistics*, vol. 16, pp. 35–52, 2016.

[29] J. Babaud, A. P. Witkin, M. Baudin, and R. O. Duda, "Uniqueness of the Gaussian kernel for scale-space filtering," *IEEE Transactions on Pattern Analysis and Machine Intelligence*, vol. 8, no. 1, pp. 26–33, 1986.

[30] MA, "Ministerio Del Ambiente: Norma de Calidad del Aire Ambiente o Nivel de Inmision Libro VI Anexo 4, 2015".

[31] T. Fawcett, "An introduction to ROC analysis," *Pattern Recognition Letters*, vol. 27, no. 8, pp. 861–874, 2006.

[32] C. Seiffert, T. M. Khoshgoftaar, J. Van Hulse, and A. Napolitano, "RUSBoost: A hybrid approach to alleviating class imbalance," *IEEE Transactions on Systems, Man, and Cybernetics Part A:Systems and Humans*, vol. 40, no. 1, pp. 185–197, 2010.

[33] P. A. Jimenez and J. Dudhia, "On the ability of the WRF model to reproduce the surface wind direction over complex terrain," *Journal of Applied Meteorology and Climatology*, vol. 52, no. 7, pp. 1610–1617, 2013.

[34] A. Meij, A. De Gzella, C. Cuvelier et al., "The impact of MM5 and WRF meteorology over complex terrain on CHIMERE model calculations," *Atmospheric Chemistry and Physics*, vol. 9, no. 17, pp. 6611–6632, 2009.

[35] P. Saide, G. Carmichael, S. Spak et al., "Forecasting urban PM10 and PM2.5 pollution episodes in very stable nocturnal conditions and complex terrain using WRF-Chem CO tracer model," *Atmospheric Environment*, vol. 45, no. 16, pp. 2769–2780, 2011.

16

A Searching Method of Candidate Segmentation Point in SPRINT Classification

Zhihao Wang,[1] **Junfang Wang,**[1] **Yonghua Huo,**[1] **Yanjun Tuo,**[1] **and Yang Yang**[2]

[1]*Science and Technology on Information Transmission and Dissemination in Communication Networks Laboratory, Shijiazhuang, China*
[2]*State Key Laboratory of Networking and Switching Technology, Beijing University of Posts and Telecommunications, Beijing, China*

Correspondence should be addressed to Zhihao Wang; cetc540016@sina.com

Academic Editor: Bin-Da Liu

SPRINT algorithm is a classical algorithm for building a decision tree that is a widely used method of data classification. However, the SPRINT algorithm has high computational cost in the calculation of attribute segmentation. In this paper, an improved SPRINT algorithm is proposed, which searches better candidate segmentation point for the discrete and continuous attributes. The experiment results demonstrate that the proposed algorithm can reduce the computation cost and improve the efficiency of the algorithm by improving the segmentation of continuous attributes and discrete attributes.

1. Introduction

In recent years, with the rapid development of economy and the continuous improvement of the level of computer technology, a large number of databases are used in business management, scientific research, and engineering development. In the face of massive storage data, how to find valuable information is a very difficult task. Data mining is to help people to extract valuable information from large, incomplete, random fuzzy data. Classification is a very important section in data mining. The purpose of classification is to construct a function or a model by which data can be classified into one of the given categories. The classification model can achieve the goal of forecasting data [1, 2]. The prediction model is derived from historical data records to represent the trend of the given data, so that it can be used to forecast future data.

The ID3 algorithm is a significant algorithm for building a decision tree [3, 4]. The information gain is used in this algorithm to select node's attributes in a decision tree. But ID3 has the shortcoming of inclining when choosing attributes in the large scale values. The improved method C4.5 is proposed based on the ID3 algorithm [5, 6], and the C4.5 method uses the information gain rate instead of the information gain to select attributes of the decision tree, which improves the efficiency of decision trees. Then many improved algorithms

based on the ID3 algorithm have been proposed, including SLIQ, SPRINT, and other algorithms. The SLIQ [7] algorithm can handle classification of large datasets. The SPRINT algorithm [8–10] based on SLIQ can be unrestricted by memory and its processing speed is considerable.

The SPRINT algorithm has many advantages. This algorithm is unrestricted by memory, and it is a kind of scalable and parallel method of building decision trees. But there are also some shortcomings. For example, finding the best segmentation point of discrete attributes needs a large amount of calculation, and the partition of continuous attributes is unreasonable.

Based on these issues, this paper proposes a new method of searching for the best segmentation point. For the segmentation of discrete attributes, the new method reduces time complexity by avoiding unnecessary computation. For the segmentation of continuous attributes, we can achieve the goal of reducing the depth of decision trees and improving the classification efficiency of decision trees through discretization of continuous attributes.

2. Related Works

Decision tree is one of the most widely used classification models in machine learning applications. Its goal is to extract knowledge from large scale datasets and represent them in a graphically intuitive way.

The paper [1] presents the Importance Aided Decision Tree (IADT), which takes feature importance as an additional domain knowledge for enhancing the performance of learners. Decision tree algorithm finds the most important attributes in each node. Therefore, the mechanism of importance of features in the paper is a relevant domain knowledge for the decision tree algorithm. For automatically designing decision tree, Barros et al. [2] propose a hyperheuristic evolutionary decision tree algorithm tailored to a specific type of classification dataset. The algorithm evolves design components of top-down decision tree induction algorithms.

The key of ID3 algorithm is considering information gain as the reference value for testing attributes, which leads to lower classification accuracy [3]. So the authors in [4] proposed a new scheme for solving the shortcoming of ID3. The paper uses the improved information gain based on dependency degree of condition attributes as a heuristic when it selects the best segmentation attribute.

Ersoy et al. [5] proposed an improved C4.5 classification algorithm with the hypothesis generation process. The algorithm adopts k-best Multi-Hypothesis Tracker (MHT) to reduce the number of generated hypothesis especially in high clutter scenarios.

In order to solve the security problems of intrusion detection system (IDS), attack scenarios and patterns should be analyzed and categorized. The enhanced C4.5 [6] is a combination of tree classifiers for solving security risks in the intrusion detection system. The mechanism uses a multiple level hybrid classifier which relies on labeled training data and mixed data. Thus, the IDS system based on C4.5 mechanism can be trained with unlabeled data and is capable of detecting previous attacks.

SLIQ decision tree solves the problem of sharp decision boundaries which are hardly found in classification. Thus the paper [7] proposes a fuzzy supervised learning in Quest decision tree. The authors construct a fuzzy decision boundary instead of a crisp decision boundary. In order to avoid incomprehensible induction rules in a large and deep decision tree, fuzzy SLIQ constructs a fuzzy binary decision tree, which has significant reduction in tree size.

SPRINT decision tree algorithm can predict the quality level of system modules, which is good for software testing [8]. The paper presents an improved SPRINT algorithm to calibrate classification trees. It provides a unique tree-pruning technique based on the minimum description length (MDL) principle. Based on this, SPRINT tree-based software quality classification mechanisms are used to predict whether a software module is fault-prone or not fault-prone.

3. SPRINT Algorithm

3.1. Description of SPRINT Algorithm. The SPRINT algorithm has no limit to the number of input records and its processing speed is considerable. This algorithm creates a list of attributes and a corresponding statistics table for each attribute of the sample data in the initialization phase. Elements in the list of attributes are known as attribute

records, which consisted of labels, attribute values, and classes. Statistics tables are used to describe the class distribution of a property, and the C above and C below two lines, respectively, describe the class distribution of processed samples and untreated samples.

Steps of the original SPRINT algorithm are as follows:

Maketree (node s) {

If (node s meets the termination conditions) {

Put node s into the queue, labeled as a root node;

Return;

}

For (for each attribute A) {

Update histogram in real time;

Calculate and evaluate the index of segmentation for each candidate segmentation points, and find the best segmentation point;

Find out the best segmentation for node s from the best segmentation for each attribute. Based on it make two part S_1, S_2;

Maketree (S_1);

Maketree (S_2);

}

}

The termination condition of the algorithm has three kinds of cases. (1) No attribute can be used as testing attribute. (2) If all the training samples in the decision tree belong to the same class, the node is used as a leaf node and labeled by this class. (3) The number of training samples is less than the user-defined threshold.

3.2. Segmentation of Attributes. The traditional SPRINT algorithm uses *Gini* index [5] to search for the best segmentation attribute, which provides the minimum *Gini* index representing the largest information gain.

For a dataset D containing N classes, *Gini* is defined as

$$\text{Gini}(D) = 1 - \sum_{j=1}^{N} p_j * p_j. \tag{1}$$

p_j is the frequency of class J in D. If a partition divides the dataset D into two subsets D_1 and D_2, $|D_1|$ and $|D_2|$ represent the number of records in subsets D_1 and D_2, respectively. After the segmentation, the *Gini* value is

$$\text{Gini}(S) = \frac{|D_1|}{|D|} \text{Gini}(D_1) + \frac{|D_2|}{|D|} \text{Gini}(D_2). \tag{2}$$

A segmentation of attribute values providing the least *Gini* value is chosen as the best segmentation [9].

For discrete attributes and continuous attributes, the SPRINT algorithm uses different processing methods.

In order to find discrete attribute segmentation point [7], we assume that the number of a certain attribute's values is n, which should be divided into two parts. All attribute values are considered as possible partition, and then the corresponding *Gini* value is obtained. There are 2^n kinds of possible partitioning ways in total. We need to calculate the *Gini* value for each partitioning way using exhaustive method and then can obtain the best segmentation.

For the solution of finding the continuous attribute's partitioning point, the split can only occur between two values. First the values of the continuous attribute should be sorted and the candidate segmentation points are intermediate points between two values.

After a scan of sorted values, the statistics table should be updated when a record is read. The statistics table contains all the information needed to calculate the *Gini* index. Then we should calculate the *Gini* index to find the segmentation point with the minimum *Gini* value.

Although the traditional method can find the best segmentation point, it is necessary to traverse all of the segmentation in discrete attributes [8], which makes this algorithm have high time complexity. For the segmentation of continuous attributes, dividing them into two consecutive parts in most cases can not reflect the distribution of attribute values.

4. Improved SPRINT

4.1. Segmentation of Discrete Attribute. Taking credit risk of bank as an example, the data record is shown in Table 1.

Values of a discrete attribute with m kinds of classes are divided into two sets, and then there are 2^m types of partitions, which mean that the Gini index values should be calculated for 2^m times. In Table 1, there are four kinds of classes, student, worker, clerk, and retiree, so 2^4 kinds of partitions should be considered. Taking into account commutative law of addition in formula (2), Gini_{sp} value remains unchanged when exchanging attribute values in sets of D_1 and D_2. For example, D_1 = {student, worker} and D_2 = {clerk, retiree}; in this case, Gini_{sp} = 0.375. When attribute values in D_1 and D_2 are exchanged, that is, D_1 = {clerk, retiree} and D_2 = {students, workers}, Gini_{sp} = 0.375.

According to this property, the times of calculating Gini index can be reduced for segmentation of discrete attributes in the SPRINT algorithm. In order to reduce the time complexity of SPRINT algorithm, this paper proposes an improved discrete attribute partition algorithm.

D is a collection of discrete attribute values, and the number of values in D is M. Now the attribute value set D is divided into two sets D_1 and D_2. Select some values from D and put them into D_1. The number of selected values is i. The initial value of i is 1 with one-step growth until $i < M/2$. Values are identical in D_1 and D_2 in the case of $i > M/2$. When M is odd, it is impossible that i is equal to $M/2$. If M is an even number and i is equal to $M/2$, there are $C_M^{M/2}$ kinds of combinations of attribute values in D_1, and 1/2 of attribute combinations are the same as D_2. So after selecting values for D_1, we need search for the same collection in D_2. If there is the same collection in D_2, the collection in D_1 will be deleted. And when the number of D_1 is more than $1/2 * C_M^{M/2}$, the search is stopped.

TABLE 1: Credit risk records of bank.

Number	Profession	Risk
1	Student	High
2	Worker	High
3	Clerk	High
4	Clerk	Low
5	Worker	Low
6	Retiree	High
7	Retiree	High

At the same time when all values in a subset belong to the same class, this subset can be a leaf node that does not need to be partitioned. So we can ignore two cases of {all values} and {empty}. In summary, this paper firstly proposed a new algorithm to reduce calculation of candidate segmentation points for discrete attributes. There are M kinds of different values in a discrete attribute, and the improved algorithm on discrete attributes is as follows.

Step 1. Initialize a class partition table (including four fields: number, first collection, second collection, and *Gini* value), and set the counter $i = 1$, $n = 1$.

Step 2. If $i < M/2$, i values are placed in the first collection of the class partition table and the *Gini* index of this division is calculated and then carry on for the next time.

Step 3. Step 2 ends; $i = i + 1$; compare i with $M/2$. If $i < M/2$, then return to Step 2; if $i = M/2$, execute the next step; if $i > M/2$, skip to Step 6.

Step 4. Put i values in the first collection and the others into the second collection. Search for the values of the first collection in the list of the second collection. Find out if there is a second collection same as the first collection. If there is, this partition will be deleted; otherwise calculate the *Gini* index of this partition.

Step 5. $n = n+1$; compare n with $1/2 * C_M^{M/2}$; if $n \leq 1/2 * C_M^{M/2}$, skip to Step 4. If not, skip to the next step.

Step 6. Find out the minimum *Gini* value based on the optimized class partition table.

It can be seen that the improved algorithm eliminates repeated operations and unnecessary operations, which reduces computation greatly and reduces the time of creating a decision tree.

4.2. Segmentation of Continuous Attribute. Candidate segmentation points are middle points of two continuous values for segmentation of continuous attributes in SPRINT algorithm, and the attribute values are divided into two parts by a middle point. For example, there are two values V_1 and V_2, and their middle point $V = (V_1 + V_2)/2$ is a candidate segmentation point for a continuous attribute. Values (V_i) of this continuous attribute which are less than V belong to a collection, and the values greater than V belong to the other collection. However, in many cases this segmentation method is not conducive to the classification of the target attribute.

This algorithm includes three steps: sorting, classifying, and random combination of continuous attributes. And classifying is a new idea that is not included in the SPRINT algorithm. A continuous attribute A has values $\{a_1, a_2, a_3, \ldots, a_i\}$. The target attribute E has positive and negative examples of $\{P, N\}$. According to the target attribute values continuous attribute values are classified. For target attribute value P, collection 1 is $\{a_{p1}, a_{p2}, \ldots, a_{pi}\}$ and $\{a_{p1}, a_{p2}, \ldots, a_{pi}\} \in \{a_1, a_2, a_3, \ldots, a_i\}$; the corresponding record's target attribute value of a_{pi} is P. Similar to N, collection 2 is $\{a_{n1}, a_{n2}, \ldots, a_{ni}\}$; $\{a_{p1}, a_{p2}, \ldots, a_{pi}\} \cup \{a_{n1}, a_{n2}, \ldots, a_{ni}\} = \{a_1, a_2, a_3, \ldots, a_i\}$. And the values in collection 1 and collection 2 are sorted in ascending or descending order. The following processing is performed on collection 1 and collection 2.

Step 1. Calculate the difference between two neighboring values $c_i = a_{p(i+1)} - a_{pi}$ $(c_i = a_{n(i+1)} - a_{ni})$.

Step 2. Sort the series of c_i in descending order. Find the top x values in series c_i, and the corresponding a_{pi} and $a_{p(i+1)}$ $(a_{ni}$ and $a_{n(i+1)})$ are candidate segmentation points.

Step 3. There are $2 * x$ candidate segmentation points in collection 1 (collection 2). $4 * x$ candidate segmentation points are found in total.

Step 4. Sort $4 * x$ candidate segmentation points in ascending or descending order, $\{v_1, v_2, v_3, v_4, \ldots, v_{(4*x)}\}$.

Step 5. $r_i = v_{(i+1)} - v_i$; find the minimum value in series r_i. The corresponding v_i and $v_{(i+1)}$ are deleted. Add $(v_i + v_{(i+1)})/2$ in series r_i.

Step 6. Repeat Step 5 until the number of series of r_i is x.

Step 7. Divide all values into $x+1$ blocks using x segmentation points. The values of continuous attribute have been divided into $x + 1$ blocks through the above steps, and consider these $x + 1$ blocks as $x + 1$ discrete attribute values; then the segmentation method of discrete attribute values is used to process these blocks.

Step 8. Initialize a class partition table (including four fields: number, first collection, second collection, and *Gini* value), and set the counter $i = 1, m = 1$.

Step 9. If $i < (x + 1)/2$, i blocks are placed randomly in the first collection of the class partition table; the *Gini* index of this division is calculated and then carry on for the next time.

Step 10. If splitting process ended, then set $i = i + 1$ and compare i with $(x + 1)/2$. If $i < (x + 1)/2$, then return to the previous step; if $i = (x + 1)/2$, execute the next step. If $i > (x + 1)/2$, then jump to Step 13.

Step 11. Put i blocks in the first collection and the others into the second collection. Search for the blocks in the list of the

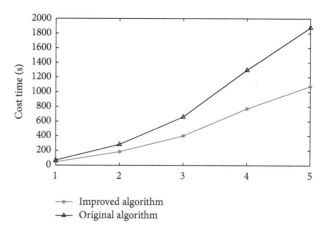

FIGURE 1: Comparison of the SPRINT algorithm and the improved SPRINT algorithm.

second collection and find out the values as same as the first collection. If there is, this partition will be deleted; otherwise calculate the *Gini* index of this partition.

Step 12. $m = m + 1$; compare m with $1/2 * C_{x+1}^{(x+1)/2}$; if $m \leq 1/2 * C_{x+1}^{(x+1)/2}$, return to the previous step. If not, proceed to the next step.

Step 13. Find out the minimum *Gini* value based on the optimized class partition table.

Steps 8–13 are the same as the improved algorithm on discrete attributes.

5. Experiment and Simulation

This experiment uses the dataset of Function [11] as experimental samples. Attributes of the dataset include age, salary, vocation, level, and other attributes. There are discrete attributes, for example, vocation, and continuous attributes, for example, age in the dataset. The VC++ 6.0 is the experiment platform for this experiment. Comparison of the original SPRINT algorithm [9] and the improved SPRINT algorithm is shown in Table 2.

Visualization of data on Table 2 is shown as in Figure 1.

The quantities of data in the five sets are increasing, so the costing time is also growing. As shown in Figure 1, the improved SPRINT algorithm greatly reduces the time to generate decision trees. At the same time, the classified accuracy of the decision tree generated by the improved SPRINT algorithm is also tested.

The comparison results of classification accuracy are shown in Table 3.

As shown in Table 3, the improved SPRINT algorithm almost has the same or slightly better classification accuracy ratios as the original algorithm. With the increasing scale of dataset, the classification accuracy ratios have accordingly decreased. The decision tree becomes larger with the increase of the amount of data, which may result in the decreasing in

TABLE 2: Comparison of the SPRINT algorithm and the improved SPRINT algorithm.

Dataset (10^6)	Costing time of original algorithm (s)	Costing time of improved algorithm (s)	$\dfrac{\text{Costing time of improved algorithm}}{\text{Costing time of original algorithm}} \times 100\%$
1	68	43	63.24%
2	282	182	64.54%
3	661	401	60.67%
4	1298	773	59.55%
5	1879	1076	57.26%

TABLE 3: Classification accuracy of original algorithm and improved algorithm.

Dataset (10^6)	Accuracy of original algorithm (%)	Accuracy of improved algorithm (%)
1	95.8%	98.61%
2	88.7%	89.8%
3	83.8%	83.7%
4	80.2%	80.5%
5	77.4%	77.5%

accuracy. Controlling the size of the decision tree needs to be further researched.

6. Conclusion

In summary, the improved SPRINT algorithm improves the calculation for searching the best segmentation by searching better candidate segmentation point for the discrete and continuous attributes, which reduces the unnecessary operations, increases the speed of generating decision trees, and reduces the time cost greatly.

Competing Interests

The authors declare that there is no conflict of interests regarding the publication of this article.

Acknowledgments

This work was supported by Open Subject Funds of Science and Technology on Information Transmission and Dissemination in Communication Networks Laboratory (ITD-U15002/KX152600011).

References

[1] M. R. A. Iqbal, S. Rahman, S. I. Nabil, and I. U. A. Chowdhury, "Knowledge based decision tree construction with feature importance domain knowledge," in *Proceedings of the 7th International Conference on Electrical and Computer Engineering (ICECE '12)*, pp. 659–662, Dhaka, Bangladesh, December 2012.

[2] R. C. Barros, M. P. Basgalupp, A. A. Freitas, and A. C. P. L. F. De Carvalho, "Evolutionary design of decision-tree algorithms tailored to microarray gene expression data sets," *IEEE Transactions on Evolutionary Computation*, vol. 18, no. 6, pp. 873–892, 2014.

[3] I. Kamwa, S. R. Samantaray, and G. Joós, "On the accuracy versus transparency trade-off of data-mining models for fast-response PMU-based catastrophe predictors," *IEEE Transactions on Smart Grid*, vol. 3, no. 1, pp. 152–161, 2012.

[4] H. He, T. M. McGinnity, S. Coleman, and B. Gardiner, "Linguistic decision making for robot route learning," *IEEE Transactions on Neural Networks and Learning Systems*, vol. 25, no. 1, pp. 203–215, 2014.

[5] Y. Ersoy, M. Efe, and B. Nakiboglu, "Enhancement of multiple hypothesis tracking algorithm with C4.5 algorithm," in *Proceedings of the 20th Signal Processing and Communications Applications Conference (SIU '12)*, pp. 1–4, April 2012.

[6] L. P. Rajeswari and A. Kannan, "An Intrusion Detection System based on multiple level hybrid classifier using enhanced C4.5," in *Proceedings of the International Conference on Signal Processing Communications and Networking (ICSCN '08)*, pp. 75–79, January 2008.

[7] B. Chandra and P. P. Varghese, "Fuzzy SLIQ decision tree algorithm," *IEEE Transactions on Systems, Man, and Cybernetics, Part B: Cybernetics*, vol. 38, no. 5, pp. 1294–1301, 2008.

[8] L. Rutkowski, L. Pietruczuk, P. Duda, and M. Jaworski, "Decision trees for mining data streams based on the McDiarmid's bound," *IEEE Transactions on Knowledge and Data Engineering*, vol. 25, no. 6, pp. 1272–1279, 2013.

[9] M. Guijarro, R. Fuentes-Fernández, P. J. Herrera, Á. Ribeiro, and G. Pajares, "New unsupervised hybrid classifier based on the fuzzy integral: applied to natural textured images," *IET Computer Vision*, vol. 7, no. 4, pp. 272–278, 2013.

[10] M. L. Othman, I. Aris, S. M. Abdullah, M. L. Ali, and M. R. Othman, "Knowledge discovery in distance relay event report: a comparative data-mining strategy of rough set theory with decision tree," *IEEE Transactions on Power Delivery*, vol. 25, no. 4, pp. 2264–2287, 2010.

[11] R. Agrawal, T. Imielinski, and A. Swami, "Database mining: a performance perspective," *IEEE Transactions on Knowledge and Data Engineering*, vol. 5, no. 6, pp. 914–925, 1993.

17

Medical Image Fusion Algorithm based on Nonlinear Approximation of Contourlet Transform and Regional Features

Hui Huang,[1] **Xi'an Feng,**[1] **and Jionghui Jiang**[2]

[1]*School of Marine Science and Technology, Northwestern Polytechnical University, Xi'an 710072, China*
[2]*Zhijiang College of Zhejiang University of Technology, Hangzhou 310024, China*

Correspondence should be addressed to Jionghui Jiang; jiangjionghui@zjc.zjut.edu.cn

Academic Editor: Panajotis Agathoklis

According to the pros and cons of contourlet transform and multimodality medical imaging, here we propose a novel image fusion algorithm that combines nonlinear approximation of contourlet transform with image regional features. The most important coefficient bands of the contourlet sparse matrix are retained by nonlinear approximation. Low-frequency and high-frequency regional features are also elaborated to fuse medical images. The results strongly suggested that the proposed algorithm could improve the visual effects of medical image fusion and image quality, image denoising, and enhancement.

1. Introduction

As an analytical probe, there has been an ever-increasing interest in developing and applying medical imaging technique to problems in clinical diagnosis. The list of possible applications of X-ray, ultrasound, CT, MRI, SPECT, and PET in clinical diagnosis continues to grow and diversify. Although those imaging technologies have given clinicians an unprecedented toolbox to aid in clinical decision-making, advances in image fusion of comprehensive morphological and functional information retrieved from different imaging technologies could enable physicians to identify human anatomy, physiology, and pathology as well as diseases at an even earlier stage.

Recently, there has been active research using medical image fusion technology for clinical applications in the academic community. Many researchers have proposed various image fusion algorithms which have achieved good results, such as the Laplacian pyramid transform [1], the contrast pyramid transform [2, 3] techniques based on the morphological pyramid transform [4], techniques based on the pyramid gradient transform [5], wavelet transform [6–8], Ridgelet, and Curvelet. DO and Martin Vetterli proposed

the contourlet transform in 2002, which is a "real" two-dimensional image representation based on wavelet multiscale analysis and known as a Pyramidal Directional Filter Bank (PDFB). The multiscale geometric analytical tool used in contourlet transform demonstrates excellent spatial and frequency domain localization properties of wavelet analysis, as well as the bonus of multidirectional, multiscale characteristics and good anisotropy, demonstrating its suitability to describe the geometric characteristics of an image [9, 10]. Additionally, the contourlet wavelet transform with smaller contourlet coefficients is able to express abundant sparse matrices with depicting image edges, such as curves, straight lines, and other features. After contourlet transformation, the image becomes more focused, which is conducive to the tracking and analysis of important image features. Contourlet transform can decompose in any direction and on any scale, which is key to the accurate description of image contours and directional textural information. To date, many scholars have applied the contourlet transform to image fusion and reported good results, particularly when combined with the image characteristics of contourlet transform fusion [11, 12], nonsubsampled contourlet image fusion [13, 14], and nonlinear approximation of contourlet transform fusion [15, 16].

This paper proposes an image fusion algorithm based on the analysis of a large number of image fusion contourlet transform techniques, which combines nonlinear approximation of contourlet transform and regional image features. First, contourlet decomposition is employed to extract the high-frequency and low-frequency regions of an image. The low-frequency coefficients are retained, and nonlinear approximations of the most significant high-frequency coefficients are obtained. Then, the low-frequency coefficients and the most significant high-frequency coefficients are combined via image fusion. The coefficient matrix module is used to calculate the energy region near the center point of the low-frequency region, and a reasonable fusion coefficient is chosen. Based on the most significant high-frequency coefficients, this paper employs the fusion rule of salience/match measure with a threshold. CT and MRI image simulations and experimental results indicate that the proposed method achieves better fusion performance and visual effects than the wavelet transform and traditional contourlet fusion methods.

2. Nonlinear Approximation of Contourlet Transform Algorithm

A contourlet transform model of the filter group can be extended into a continuous function of square space $L^2(R^2)$ [17, 18]. In a continuous domain contourlet transform, $L^2(R^2)$ is decomposed into multiscale, multidirectional subspace sequence by the use of an iterative filter group, as shown the following equation:

$$L^2(R^2) - V_{j_0} \oplus \left(\bigoplus_{j \leq j_0} \left(\overset{2^{l_j}}{\underset{k=0}{\oplus}} W_{j,k}^{(l_j)} \right) \right). \tag{1}$$

The definition of space V_{j_0} and W_j is consistent with wavelet decomposition [19]. V_{j_0} is the approximate space. The scaling function ϕ provides an approximation component on the 2^J scale represented by $\{\phi_{J,n}(t) = \phi_J(t - 2^J n)\}_{n \in z^2}$, as generated by zooming and panning the scaling function orthogonal basis. W_j is decomposed into 2^j directional subspace $W_{j,k}^{(l_j)}$, expressed as $W_j = \bigoplus_{k=0}^{2^{l_j-1}} W_{j,k}^{(l_j)}$. The $W_{j,k}^{(l_j)}$ space is defined in the rectangular frame $2^{j+l_j-2} \times 2^j$ or $2^j \times 2^{j+l_j-2}$, which belongs to $\{\rho_{j,k,n}^{l_j}(t)\}_{n \in z^2}$, as shown in the following equation:

$$\rho_{j,k,n}^{l_j}(t) = \sum_{m \in Z^2} g_k^{l_j} \left[m - S_k^{l_j} n \right] u_{j,m}(t). \tag{2}$$

In Formula (2), $g_k^{l_j}$ is a low-pass analysis filter of PDB. The sampling matrix $S_k^{(l_j)}$ can be expressed as follows:

$$S_k^{(l_j)} = \begin{cases} \text{diag}\left(2^{l_j-1}, 2\right) & 0 \leq k < 2^{l_j-1} \\ \text{diag}\left(2, 2^{l_j-1}\right) & 2^{l_j-1} \leq k < 2^{l_j}. \end{cases} \tag{3}$$

In Formula (3), the k parameters directly determine the conversion of orientation, that is, the horizontal or vertical bias. According to multiresolution analysis theory, $\{\rho_{j,k,n}^{l_j}(t)\}_{n \in Z^2}$ can be obtained from the original function and its translation, as shown in the following equation:

$$\rho_{j,k,n}^{l_j}(t) = \rho_{j,k}^{l_j}\left(t - 2^{j-1}S_k^{(l_j)}n\right). \tag{4}$$

According to the theory described above, $\rho_{j,k,n}^{l_j}(t)$ is a continuous domain contourlet, while j, k, and n represent the scale, orientation, and position parameters of the contourlet, respectively.

Given a set of base functions $\{\phi_n\}_{n=1}^{\infty}$ in a nonlinear approximation of contourlet transform, the function can be expanded to $f = \sum_{n=1}^{\infty} c_n \phi_n$. Then the maximum absolute values of $M(c_n)$ coefficients are used to approximate the original function, expressed as $\tilde{f} = \sum_{n \in I_M} c_n \phi_n$, where I_M is the index of the maximum absolute value of the coefficient M and $\tilde{f}$ represents the nonlinear approximation of the function [20].

3. Feature Matching Algorithm

3.1. Low-Frequency Fusion Algorithm. The low-frequency subband retains the profile information of the original image; the low-frequency region is processed as much as possible in order to retain the profile characteristics. In this paper, the window coefficient matrix is employed to calculate the energy in the region near the image center point, which not only takes regional factors into account but also retains the characteristics of directivity and highlights the central pixel. The energy E of the low-frequency region can be defined as follows:

$$E_{j_0}(m, n) = \left\{ (x, y) \in \Omega(m, n) : \left(z, V_{j_0}(m, n) \right) \right\}. \tag{5}$$

$\Omega(m, n)$ represents the center of the neighborhood of (m, n), (x, y) represents the center of the proximity panel of (m, n), z is the area coefficient matrix, and V_{j_0} is the low-frequency subband coefficient of the fused image. According to the rule of the low-frequency region of energy fusion, the energy E of the low-frequency region must be calculated first. X is the center of the two adjacent subimages of the low-frequency region and the center region of the two adjacent low-frequency subimages of (m, n). Then, the absolute value of the regional energy E can be expressed as follows:

$$V_{j_0}(m, n) = \begin{cases} V_{j_0}^A(m, n) & E_{J_0}^A(m, n) > E_{J_0}^B(m, n) \\ V_{j_0}^B(m, n) & E_{J_0}^A(m, n) \leq E_{J_0}^B(m, n). \end{cases} \tag{6}$$

3.2. High-Frequency Fusion Algorithm. This paper utilizes high-frequency coefficients and the rules of the match measure with a threshold. The local energy of the high-frequency region [21] can be defined as follows:

$$S(i, j, k) = \sum_m \sum_n C(i + m, j + n, k)^2. \tag{7}$$

$C(i, j, k)$ represents the position of the high-frequency coefficients of (i, j) on the k decomposition level. The size of the image in a neighborhood of the window (typically 3×3 or 5×5 pixels) is defined by (m, n). The neighborhood of the sum of the square of the high-frequency coefficients is represented by the local energy of point (i, j, k). The match degree of point (i, j, k) is defined as follows:

$$M_{AB}(i, j, k)$$
$$= \frac{2 \sum_m \sum_n C_A(i + m, j + n, k) C_B(i + m, j + n, k)}{S_A(i, j, k) S_B(i, j, k)}. \quad (8)$$

The fusion rule of the high-frequency coefficients is defined by the following formula:

$$C(i, j, k) = W_A C_A(i, j, k) + W_B C_B(i, j, k). \quad (9)$$

Match degree, which is measured by the matching degree of the feature information in corresponding position of the two original images A and B, determines the proportion of the characteristic information of different original images. The point (i, j, k)'s match degree is determined by the rules as follows:

(1) If $M_{AB} \leq T$, then

$$W_A = 1,$$
$$W_B = 0,$$
$$S_A > S_B,$$
$$W_A = 0,$$
$$W_B = 1,$$
$$S_A \leq S_B. \quad (10a)$$

(2) If $M_{AB} > T$, then

$$W_A = 1 - W_B,$$
$$W_B = \frac{1}{2} - \frac{(1 - M_{AB})}{2(1 - T)},$$
$$S_A > S_B,$$
$$W_A = \frac{1}{2} - \frac{(1 - M_{AB})}{2(1 - T)},$$
$$W_B = 1 - W_A,$$
$$S_A \leq S_B. \quad (10b)$$

In the rules listed above, M_{AB} represents the match degree, and $T \in (0, 1)$ represents the matching threshold. When $M_{AB} \leq T$, we take the larger value of the local energy $C_A(i, j, k)$ and $C_B(i, j, k)$ as high-frequency coefficient. When $M_{AB} > T$, we take the value $W_A C_A(i, j, k) + W_B C_B(i, j, k)$, where the weight W_A and W_B have correlation with the degree of matching, and $W_A + W_B = 1$. Obviously, the calculation process of feature matching rules demonstrates good locality, because the fusion results of the high-frequency coefficient value at (i, j, k) are only determined by the coefficient values which are contained by the $m \times n$ neighborhood of point (i, j, k).

4. Experimental Results and Analysis

The CT and MRI image fusion experimental simulations were implemented on PIV 2.4 GHz, using a 4 GB RAM PC as the development platform of Matlab7.0. After nonlinear approximation contourlet transform was performed, a 3×3 feature region is calculated in the high-frequency and low-frequency regions, and the high-frequency region match threshold is 0.75 as proposed by Burt and Lolczynski [21].

Figure 1 depicts the results of nonlinear approximation contourlet transform performed on an MRI image. The various proportions of nonlinear approximation retain the most significant coefficients at high-frequency subbands. Table 1 describes the MRI image feature coefficients and the most significant coefficients at various approximation proportions.

Figure 2 depicts the matching fusion of MRI and CT image characteristics based on nonlinear approximation contourlet transform. A constant low-frequency region is maintained after nonlinear approximation of significant coefficients at high-frequency subbands, and the images are then fused according to their regional characteristics. This paper quantitatively analyzes the effects of fusion based on the indicators of standard deviation, correlation coefficients, entropy, and mutual information [22, 23].

4.1. Standard Deviation. The standard deviation (STD) reflects the contrast change of an image: the larger the value, the clearer the edge contour; the definition of STD is given as follows:

$$\text{STD} = \sqrt{\frac{\sum_{i=1}^{M} \sum_{j=1}^{N} \left[f(i, j) - \hat{f} \right]^2}{M \times N}}. \quad (11)$$

In the formula, $f(i, j)$ represents the result fusion image, while $M \times N$ represents the image f, and $\hat{f}$ represents the mean value of f.

4.2. Correlation Coefficients. Correlation coefficient (CC) is a measure of the similarity of two images: the greater the correlation coefficient, the better the fusion effect; CC is defined as

$$\text{CC}(X, Y)$$
$$= \frac{\sum_{i=1}^{M} \sum_{j=1}^{N} \left(X(i, j) - \overline{X} \right) \left(Y(i, j) - \overline{Y} \right)}{\sqrt{\left(\sum_{i=1}^{M} \sum_{j=1}^{N} \left[X(i, j) - \overline{X} \right]^2 \right) \left(\sum_{i=1}^{M} \sum_{j=1}^{N} \left[Y(i, j) - \overline{Y} \right]^2 \right)}}. \quad (12)$$

4.3. Entropy. Entropy (EN) measures the amount of information maintained by the fused image. The larger the entropy value is, the more information the result image has. EN is defined as

$$\text{EN} = -\sum_{0}^{255} P_i(x) \log_2 p_i(x), \quad (13)$$

in which $P_i(x)$ is defined as the normalized histogram of the variable x and $\sum_{0}^{255} P_i(x) = 1$.

TABLE 1: Significant coefficients.

	MRI image	10% coefficients	30% coefficients	50% coefficients
Significant coefficients	86016	6554	19661	32768

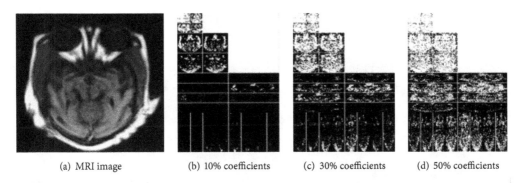

(a) MRI image (b) 10% coefficients (c) 30% coefficients (d) 50% coefficients

FIGURE 1: Nonlinear approximation of contourlet.

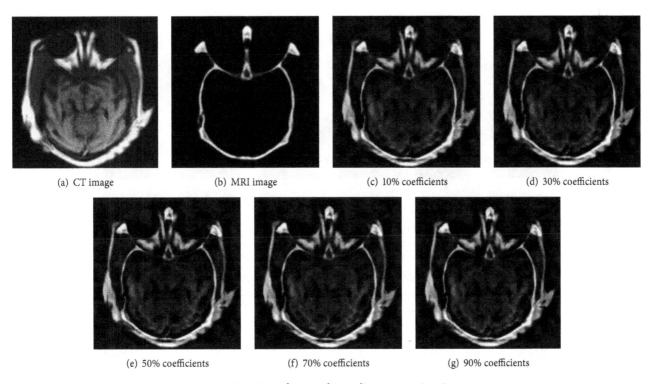

(a) CT image (b) MRI image (c) 10% coefficients (d) 30% coefficients

(e) 50% coefficients (f) 70% coefficients (g) 90% coefficients

FIGURE 2: Fusion of contourlet nonlinear approximation.

4.4. Mutual Information.

Mutual information (MI) can be used to measure the mutual correlation or similarity of the two input images. The higher the mutual information of the fused image, the more information extracted from the original images and the better the fusion effect. For the two input discrete image signals, MI is defined as

$$MI(x, y) = H(x) + H(y) - H(x, y), \qquad (14)$$

in which $H(x)$ is an entropy function; $H(x) = -\sum_0^{255} P_i(x)\log_2 p_i(x)$, while $H(x, y)$ is a joint entropy function; $H(x, y) = -\sum_0^{255} P_i(x, y)\log_2 p_i(x, y)$. $P_i(x, y)$ is defined as histogram of normalized distribution of x and y and $\sum_0^{255} P_i(x, y) = 1$.

As shown in Table 2, the maximum value of the standard deviation in the fused image can be obtained for less than 50% significant coefficients, which demonstrate sharper profile edges and the highest resolution at 50% nonlinear approximation. This may be the result of few significant coefficients which will in turn result in less extraction of edge contours; alternatively, too many significant coefficients will lead to the extraction of excess noise. Correlation coefficients, mutual information, and entropy have little effect on image fusion

TABLE 2: Indexes of performance evaluation.

	Standard deviation	Correlation coefficients	Entropy	Mutual information
10% significant coefficients	50.48	0.66	7.68	4.51
30% significant coefficients	56.32	0.69	7.68	4.53
50% significant coefficients	63.16	0.70	7.70	4.54
70% significant coefficients	59.32	0.71	7.70	4.55
90% significant coefficients	57.16	0.73	7.72	4.55

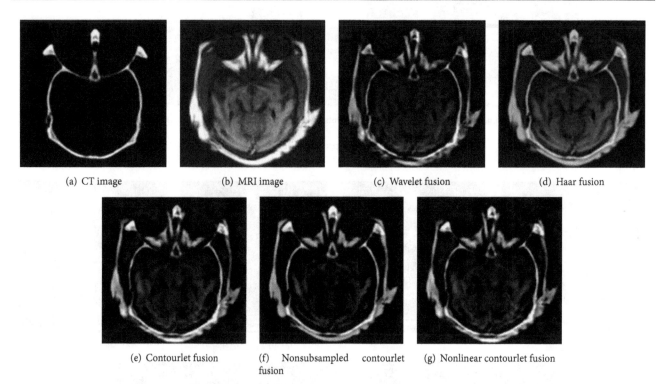

(a) CT image (b) MRI image (c) Wavelet fusion (d) Haar fusion

(e) Contourlet fusion (f) Nonsubsampled contourlet fusion (g) Nonlinear contourlet fusion

FIGURE 3: Fusion results' comparison.

with various proportions of significant coefficients. The primary reason for this is that the low-frequency subband retains the profile information of the original image, while fused images do not achieve nonlinear approximation in the low-frequency region. Results indicate that fusion image quality demonstrates a nonlinear relationship to the proportion of significant coefficients. When the significant coefficient is 50%, the quality of image fusion is highest.

In order to verify the effectiveness of the algorithm, we compare our result with others from different researchers. Figure 3 shows different fusion results for MRI and CT images with different algorithms, in which Figure 3(a) is the experimental result with fusion algorithm based on regional feature of wavelet coefficients [24], Figure 3(b) is experimental result based on Haar wavelet transform [25], Figure 3(c) is the result of coefficient weighted fusion algorithm after contourlet transform [19], Figure 3(d) is the fusion result based on the nonsubsampled contourlet transform (NSCT) and regional features [26], and Figure 3(e) is our experimental fusion result, which is an effect of regional image feature matching after 50% nonlinear estimation to the high-frequency coefficients by the contourlet transform. For

the visual assessment, the fusion images (Figures 3(a) and 3(b)) are based on the wavelet transform methods; the color is shallow, and edge profile is not clear enough, which cannot reflect the source CT and MRI images of the details of the information. In Figure 3(c), with contourlet transform, the fusion image effect is slightly better than the wavelet method and can more clearly reflect the content information of the source images. In Figures 3(d) and 3(e), the fusion image not only inherits the bone tissue of the CT image but also can keep the soft tissue of the MRI image; moreover, the image edge detail can be more obvious after image fusion.

Analyzing the results quantitatively with the indexes shown in Table 3, the corresponding STD, CC, EN, and MI of Figures 3(a) and 3(b), which are based on the wavelet transform methods, are relatively small, which shows that the information has been lost in the process of image fusion and also shows a notable difference between the fusion image and the source images. It has been demonstrated that the ability of wavelet transform method to extract information from the source image is poor, and the fusion effect is not good. Figure 3(c) gets more directions in the high-frequency part by using contourlet transform method and can better

TABLE 3: Indexes of performance evaluation.

	Standard deviation	Correlation coefficients	Entropy	Mutual information	Running time
Wavelet fusion	50.48	0.64	6.78	4.16	1.608
Haar fusion	58.60	0.66	7.59	4.47	1.901
Contourlet fusion	59.32	0.72	7.63	4.52	3.021
Nonsubsampled contourlet fusion	65.01	0.73	7.72	4.59	5.561
Nonlinear contourlet fusion	63.16	0.72	7.70	4.55	1.254

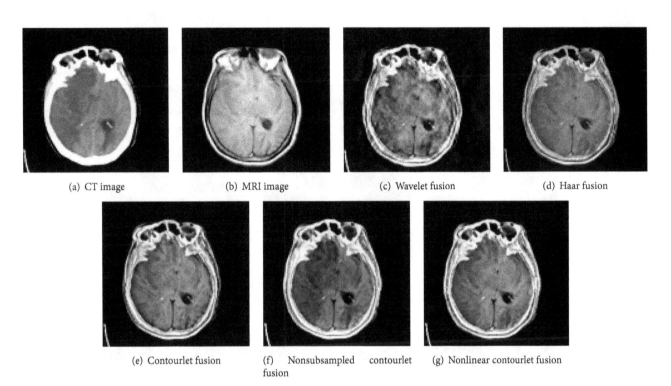

(a) CT image (b) MRI image (c) Wavelet fusion (d) Haar fusion

(e) Contourlet fusion (f) Nonsubsampled contourlet fusion (g) Nonlinear contourlet fusion

FIGURE 4: Fusion results' comparison.

deal with the direction of the details relative to the wavelet transform, so the coefficient of each index is superior to wavelet fusion. In Figure 3(d), both the coefficient of each index and the quality of image fusion are the highest, but the algorithm needs a large amount of computation and is too time-consuming. Figure 3(e) is the result of our nonlinear contourlet algorithm, in which index coefficients outperform wavelet transform and contourlet transform, and the fusion image quality is close to the NSCT; moreover, it greatly reduces the amount of calculation and has significant application value.

Figures 4, 5, and 6 are another group of fusion results of CT and MRI medical images using different algorithms; indexes of the performance evaluation are shown in Tables 4, 5, and 6, respectively. Both from the subject visual perspective and from the object standard of the fused image estimate, the experiment result of our algorithm is better than wavelet and contourlet fusion algorithm. When compared with the nonsubsampled contourlet fusion algorithm, our algorithm has greatly enhanced the computing speed, without losing the fusion quality.

5. Conclusions

This paper proposes an image fusion algorithm based on nonlinear approximation of contourlet transform and regional features applied to medical image processing, which combines nonlinear approximation of contourlet transform characteristics with the high-low frequency coefficient region feature algorithm. First, the algorithm retains the original low-frequency coefficients and then approximates high-frequency coefficients in order to extract the most nonlinear significant coefficients. Second, a coefficient matrix module is used in the low-frequency region to calculate the energy region near the center point and choose a reasonable fusion coefficient, which improves profile information retention of the original image. Finally, the rules of the salience/match measure with a threshold are used to calculate the center point of the region analysis feature and select the integration factor in the high-frequency region according to the most significant coefficients in order to better fuse image edge contours and texture. Via the experiment on CT and MRI images, the results show that the fusion image quality of our algorithm greatly outperforms the wavelet coefficients, Haar wavelet

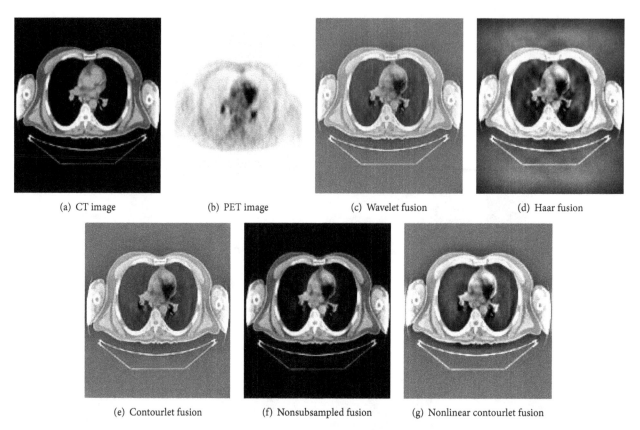

(a) CT image   (b) PET image   (c) Wavelet fusion   (d) Haar fusion

(e) Contourlet fusion   (f) Nonsubsampled fusion   (g) Nonlinear contourlet fusion

FIGURE 5: Fusion results' comparison.

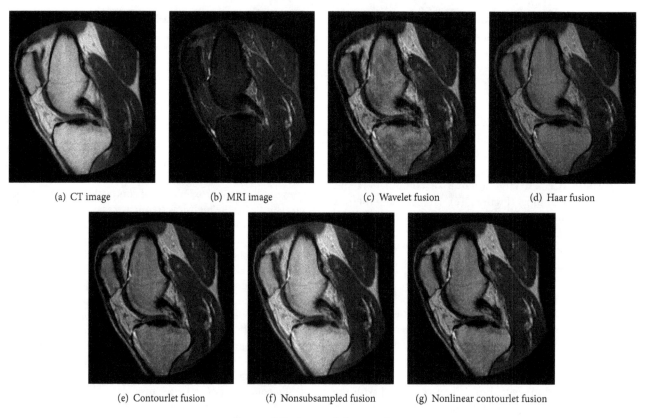

(a) CT image   (b) MRI image   (c) Wavelet fusion   (d) Haar fusion

(e) Contourlet fusion   (f) Nonsubsampled fusion   (g) Nonlinear contourlet fusion

FIGURE 6: Fusion results' comparison.

TABLE 4: Index of performance evaluation.

	Standard deviation	Correlation coefficients	Entropy	Mutual information	Running time
Wavelet fusion	80.14	0.75	2.24	2.15	2.013
Haar fusion	80.27	0.77	3.54	2.22	2.408
Contourlet fusion	81.30	0.80	4.39	2.27	4.211
Nonsubsampled contourlet fusion	81.48	0.84	5.23	3.32	9.054
Nonlinear contourlet fusion	81.39	0.81	5.14	2.91	1.701

TABLE 5: Index of performance evaluation.

	Standard deviation	Correlation coefficients	Entropy	Mutual information	Running time
Wavelet fusion	53.11	0.72	6.23	1.96	1.752
Haar fusion	57.84	0.75	6.30	2.03	1.805
Contourlet fusion	60.82	0.83	7.52	2.10	3.501
Nonsubsampled contourlet fusion	70.06	0.96	8.04	2.07	7.526
Nonlinear contourlet fusion	62.97	0.85	7.69	2.12	1.055

TABLE 6: Index of performance evaluation.

	Standard deviation	Correlation coefficients	Entropy	Mutual information	Running time
Wavelet fusion	44.97	0.73	5.78	4.80	2.805
Haar fusion	49.72	0.76	5.88	4.95	2.932
Contourlet fusion	51.26	0.80	6.35	5.42	4.921
Nonsubsampled contourlet fusion	59.06	0.88	6.60	5.67	10.594
Nonlinear contourlet fusion	52.33	0.82	6.42	5.44	1.824

transform, and coefficient weighted contourlet transform and is very close to NSCT. Moreover, our algorithm has greatly improved the computation efficiency. Nonlinear contourlet transform has a certain filter and noise removal function, which outperforms the contourlet transform, while high-frequency component nonlinear feature extraction method retains features to maximum and has greatly improved the computing speed, which outperforms NSCT. In short, the method has certain advantages in both image quality and computation efficiency, so it can provide more reliable information to doctors.

Competing Interests

The authors declare that there are no competing interests regarding the publication of this paper.

Acknowledgments

This work is supported by the Zhejiang Provincial Natural Science Foundation of China (Grant no. LY15F020033), the National Natural Science Foundation of China (Grant no. 61271414), and the Science and Technology Plan Project of Wenzhou, China (Grant no. Y20160070).

References

[1] T. Windeatt and R. Ghaderi, "Binary labelling and decision-level fusion," *Information Fusion*, vol. 2, no. 2, pp. 103–112, 2001.

[2] D. Rajan and S. Chaudhuri, "Data fusion techniques for super-resolution imaging," *Information Fusion*, vol. 3, no. 1, pp. 25–38, 2002.

[3] P. J. Burt and E. H. Adelson, "The laplacian pyramid as a compact image code," *IEEE Transactions on Communications*, vol. 31, no. 4, pp. 532–540, 1983.

[4] A. Toet, "Image fusion by a ration of low-pass pyramid," *Pattern Recognition Letters*, vol. 9, no. 4, pp. 245–253, 1989.

[5] A. Toet, L. J. Ruyven, and J. M. Valeton, "Merging thermal and visual images by a contrast pyramid," *Optical Engineering*, vol. 28, no. 7, pp. 789–792, 1989.

[6] A. Toet, "A morphological pyramidal image decomposition," *Pattern Recognition Letters*, vol. 9, no. 4, pp. 255–261, 1989.

[7] P. J. Burt, *A Gradient Pyramid Basis for Pattern Selective Image Fusion*, SID Press, San Jose, Calif, USA, 1992.

[8] T. Ranchin and L. Wald, "The wavelet transform for the analysis of remotely sensed images," *International Journal of Remote Sensing*, vol. 14, no. 3, pp. 615–619, 1993.

[9] L. J. Chipman, T. M. Orr, and L. N. Graham, "Wavelets and image fusion," in *Proceedings of the IEEE International Conference on Image Processing. Part 3 (of 3)*, pp. 248–251, Los Alamitos, Calif, USA, October 1995.

[10] H. Li, B. S. Manjunath, and S. K. Mitra, "Multisensor image fusion using the wavelet transform," *Graphical Models and Image Processing*, vol. 57, no. 3, pp. 235–245, 1995.

[11] L. Kun, G. Lei, and C. Weiwei, "Regional feature self-adaptive image fusion algorithm based on contourlet transform," *Acta Optica Sinica*, no. 4, pp. 681–686, 2008.

[12] K. Zhu and X.-G. He, "Remote sensing images fusion method based on morphology and regional feature of contourlet coefficients," *Computer Science*, no. 4, pp. 301–305, 2013.

[13] A. L. Da Cunha, J. Zhou, and M. N. Do, "The nonsubsampled contourlet transform: theory, design, and applications," *IEEE Transactions on Image Processing*, vol. 15, no. 10, pp. 3089–3101, 2006.

[14] F. Pak, H. R. Kanan, and A. Alikhassi, "Breast cancer detection and classification in digital mammography based on non-subsampled contourlet transform (NSCT) and super resolution," *Computer Methods and Programs in Biomedicine*, vol. 122, no. 2, pp. 89–107, 2015.

[15] Y. Wu, W. Hou, and S. Wu, "Fabric defect image de-noising based on contourlet transform and nonlinear diffusion," *Journal of Electronic Measurement & Instrument*, vol. 25, no. 8, pp. 665–670, 2011.

[16] H. Wang, Q. Yang, R. Li, and Z. Yao, "Tunable-Q contourlet transform for image representation," *Journal of Systems Engineering and Electronics*, vol. 24, no. 1, pp. 147–156, 2013.

[17] L.-C. Jiao and S. Tan, "Development and prospect of image multiscale geometric analysis," *Acta Electronica Sinica*, vol. 31, no. 12, pp. 1975–1981, 2003.

[18] H. Y. Patil, A. G. Kothari, and K. M. Bhurchandi, "Expression invariant face recognition using local binary patterns and contourlet transform," *Optik*, vol. 127, no. 5, pp. 2670–2678, 2016.

[19] Z. Xin and C. Weibin, "Medical image fusion based on weighted Contourlet transformation coefficients ," *Journal of Image and Graphics*, vol. 19, no. 1, pp. 133–140, 2014.

[20] X.-C. Xue, S.-Y. Zhang, H.-F. Li, and Y.-F. Gun, "Research on application of contourlet transform for image compression," *Control & Automation*, no. 25, 2009.

[21] P. J. Burt and R. J. Lolczynski, "Enhanced image capture through fusion," in *Proceedings of the 4th International Conference on Computer Vision*, pp. 173–182, IEEE, Berlin, Germany, May 1993.

[22] L.-M. Hu, J. Gao, and K.-F. He, "Research on quality measures for image fusion," *Acta Electronica Sinica*, vol. 32, pp. 218–221, 2004.

[23] G. Qu, D. Zhang, and P. Yan, "Information measure for performance of image fusion," *Electronics Letters*, vol. 38, no. 7, pp. 313–315, 2002.

[24] Z.-G. Zhou and X.-H. Wang, "Image fusion algorithm based on the neighboring relation of wavelet coefficients," *Computer Science*, vol. 36, no. 5, pp. 257–261, 2009.

[25] L. Min, "Multifocus image fusion based on morphological haar wavelet transform," *Computer Engineering*, vol. 38, no. 23, pp. 211–214, 2012.

[26] L. Chao, L. Guangyao, T. Yunlan, and X. Xianglong, "Medical images fusion of nonsubsampled Contourlet transform and regional feature," *Journal of Computer Applications*, vol. 33, no. 6, pp. 1727–1731, 2013.

18

Autofocus on Depth of Interest for 3D Image Coding

Khouloud Samrouth,[1] Olivier Deforges,[1] Yi Liu,[1] Mohamad Khalil,[2] and Wassim EL Falou[2]

[1]*UEB, CNRS UMR 6164, IETR Lab, INSA de Rennes 20, Avenue des Buttes de Coesmes, CS 70839, 35708 Rennes, France*
[2]*Faculty of Engineering I, Lebanese University, Tripoli, Lebanon*

Correspondence should be addressed to Khouloud Samrouth; khouloud.samrout@gmail.com

Academic Editor: Panajotis Agathoklis

For some 3D applications, one may want to focus on a specific depth zone representing a region of interest in the scene. In this context, we introduce a new functionality called "autofocus" for 3D image coding, exploiting the depth map as an additional semantic information provided by the 3D sequence. The method is based on a joint "Depth of Interest" (DoI) extraction and coding scheme. First, the DoI extraction scheme consists of a precise extraction of objects located within a DoI zone, given by the viewer or deduced from an analysis process. Then, the DoI coding scheme provides a higher quality for the objects in the DoI at the expense of other depth zones. The local quality enhancement supports both higher SNR and finer resolution. The proposed scheme embeds the Locally Adaptive Resolution (LAR) codec, initially designed for 2D images. The proposed DoI scheme is developed without modifying the global coder framework, and the DoI mask is not transmitted, but it is deduced at the decoder. Results showed that our proposed joint DoI extraction and coding scheme provide a high correlation between texture objects and depth. This consistency avoids the distortion along objects contours in depth maps and those of texture images and synthesized views.

1. Introduction

Recent studies in the 3D technology led to a growing development in 3D applications. Nowadays, next generations of highly advanced multimedia video systems, such as 3D television (3DTV), 3D cinemas, and free viewpoint television (FTV), provide depth perception for the viewers [1, 2] on both large TV screens [3] and mobile phones [4] and allow free navigation within a real-world scene [5, 6]. Such autostereoscopic systems, providing 3D viewing experience without special glasses or other head gear [7, 8], rely on depth maps to give the 3D impression and to synthesize intermediate views at an arbitrary view point [9, 10]. These depth maps can be considered as an additional semantic information on the scene, which can be exploited in a region of interest (RoI) context. Indeed, among advanced functionalities for image coding, such as scalability, lossy/lossless and security, RoI is useful for many applications [11]. In RoI-based image coding, some regions, that are of interest to the viewer, are encoded with a higher fidelity than the rest of the image. There are several 2D applications using the RoI coding such as compression of infrared or digital medical images [12,

13], segmentation [14], and accurate objects location [15]. However, for some 3D applications, the areas of interest can be partially or fully dependent on the depth information [16]. In this context, new research works have been devoted to the application of the RoI feature in the 3D domain [16–20]. In [17], Fan et al. proposed a digital watermarking algorithm for copyright protection of 3D images. The proposed watermarking scheme was based on Depth Perceptual Region of Interest (DP-RoI) [18] from the idea that the Human Visual System (HVS) is more sensitive to the distortion in foreground than background regions in 2D image. The DP-RoI extraction and tracking algorithms were proposed in [18] where Zhang et al. exploited the depth information beside the large contrast of illumination in the texture image to extract the RoI. In [19], Karlsson and Sjöström determined the foreground by using the information in the depth map. The foreground was defined as the RoI. It was used to reallocate bits from the background to the RoI by applying a spatiotemporal filter [21] on the texture image. This method achieved an improvement in the perceived quality of foreground at the expense of a quality reduction in background. In the method proposed by Karlsson, the RoI coding has only been used

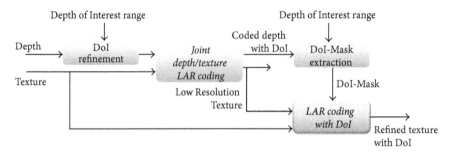

FIGURE 1: Block diagram of the proposed DoI scheme.

TABLE 1: Functional comparison for RoI coding.

Codec	RoI resolution unit	Different quality for background/foreground	RoI mask transmission
JPEG2K	Pixel	No	No
JPEGXR	Block	Yes (except lossless)	Yes
H.264	Block	Yes (except lossless)	Yes
HEVC	Block	Yes (except lossless)	Yes
LAR	Pixel	Yes	No

for the ordinary monoscopic texture video, part of the 2D plus depth representation, without the depth map. Zheng et al. [20] proposed a scheme for RoI coding of 3D meshes inspired by JPEG2000 [22]. In [16], Chamaret et al. adaptively adjusted the shift between the two views of a stereoscopic system in order to have a null disparity on the RoI area. This enhanced the visual quality of a given area in the rendered view scene. However, Chamaret et al.'s method was applied on stereoscopic and not on autostereoscopic systems.

Many different contributions have been proposed for the RoI extraction and coding schemes in the 3D domain, but only a few combine both extraction and coding. From a representation and coding point of view, three important criteria must be considered for the RoI coding system: (1) RoI spatial resolution, (2) the RoI-mask cost, and (3) the choice of quality levels between background/foreground. Most of the state-of-the-art codecs apply a block-based RoI coding scheme, where the coding unit is a block of a minimum 16×16 pixels, such as JPEGXR [23], H.264 [24], and HEVC [25]. When the RoI spatial resolution is block-based, the RoI-mask cost is reduced. However, it decreases the accuracy along the RoI contours. On the other hand, other state-of-the-art codecs, such as JPEG2000 [26, 27], apply RoI pixel-based scheme but impose the difference of quality between background and foreground. Table 1 gives a functional comparison of these different codecs. Indeed, for 3D applications, the resolution of objects contours in the depth map has to be very fine, in particular when rendering intermediate views. The reason is that 3D rendering software, such as VSRS [28], relies on depth maps to synthesize intermediate views. Several researches [29–32] highlight the influence of depth image compression and its implications on the quality of video plus depth virtual view rendering.

In this paper, we propose a so-called "Depth of Interest" (DoI) scheme for joint representation and coding of the region of interest in the 2D + Z autostereoscopic domain. The related application consists of an automatic focus on a given depth range for a better rendering in this area of interest. It offers a fine extraction of objects with well-defined contours in the depth map, inducing a low distortion among area of interest in the synthesized views. Contrary to the state-of-the-art methods, such a scheme better fits with the three criteria of a RoI coding scheme: (1) it relies on a pixel-based resolution, (2) the RoI-mask transmission is almost free as only the two values limiting the Depth of Interest range are transmitted, and (3) it allows freely choosing different qualities for the different regions in the scene (cf. Table 1). The proposed DoI coding scheme was tested on a large set of MPEG 3D reference sequences (*Balloons*, *Kendo*, *BookArrival*, *Newspaper*, *UndoDancer*, and *GTFly*).

This paper is organised as follows. In Section 2, the global coding scheme is presented. In Section 3, the 2D LAR coder framework and the 2D + Z coding scheme are described. In Section 4, the proposed DoI representation and coding scheme is explained. Section 5 provides the experimental results for DoI extraction, coding performance, and subjective quality tests for texture images and synthesized intermediate views. Finally, we conclude this paper in Section 6.

2. Global Coding Scheme

The proposed scheme embeds the Locally Adaptive Resolution (LAR) codec [33]. LAR is a global coding framework based on a content-based QuadTree partitioning. It provides a lot of functionalities such as *a unique codec for lossy and lossless compression*, resolution and quality scalability, partial/full encryption, 2D region of interest coding, rate control, and rate-distortion optimization [34]. Extensions to scalable 2D + Z coding have been presented in [35].

For 2D + Z applications, it can be assumed that the object of interest is located in a specific depth zone. This depth range which is provided as an input of our global coding scheme defines the Depth of Interest (DoI). First, the DoI representation scheme consists in defining, from the depth map, a binary mask covering the DoI zone. It leads to a fine extraction of objects located within a DoI zone. Then, the DoI coding scheme aims at ensuring a higher quality at DoI zone at the expense of other depth zones. Higher visual quality in the DoI is ensured for both depth and texture images (cf. Figure 1).

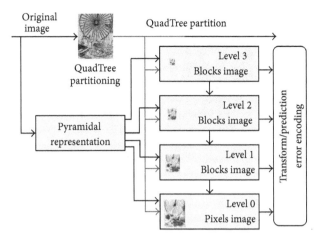

FIGURE 2: LAR multiresolution coder scheme.

For this purpose, firstly, a DoI refinement is applied on the depth map (Section 4.1). The QuadTree partition of the depth map is adapted to get a higher resolution at the DoI layer, and thus well-defined contours along the objects of interest are obtained. Secondly, a DoI coding is applied on the texture image (Section 4.2). The RoI-based scheme using the defined depth-based binary mask allows setting different qualities inside and outside the DoI. The benefits of the proposed DoI representation scheme are as follows: (1) it is content-based; (2) the DoI coding scheme is inserted as a preprocess, and thus we prevent modifying the coder which reduces the complexity of the coder; (3) the DoI-Mask is not transmitted to the decoder, and thus there is no over cost coding.

3. LAR Coder Framework

3.1. 2D LAR Coder. Locally Adaptive Resolution (LAR) [33] is an efficient multiresolution content-based 2D image coder for both lossless and lossy image compressions (cf. Figure 2).

3.1.1. QuadTree Partitioning. The LAR coder relies on a local analysis of image activity. It starts with the estimation of a QuadTree representation, conditioning a variable-size block partitioning ($1 \times 1, 2 \times 2, \ldots, 64 \times 64, 128 \times 128$ pixels). The block size estimation is performed by comparing the difference of the local maximum and minimum values within the block with a given threshold Th_{Quad}. Therefore, the local resolution defined by the pixel size depends on the local activity: the smallest blocks are located upon edges, whereas large blocks map homogeneous areas (cf. Figure 3). Then, the main feature of the LAR coder consists in preserving contours while smoothing homogeneous parts of the image. This QuadTree partition is the key structure of the LAR coder.

3.1.2. Transform and Prediction. The coder uses a pyramidal representation of the image. Starting from the upper level of the pyramid (lower resolution/larger blocks), a dyadic decomposition conditioned by the QuadTree is performed. Each level of the decomposition integrates a 2×2 block transform (interleaved S + P transform) stage and a prediction

one. The resulting prediction error is quantized using an input quantization factor Q_p and coded using an adapted entropy coder. The quantization value for each level is then given by $Q_l = Q_p/2^l$, with l being the pyramidal level (full resolution for $l = 0$). It has been found in [34] that the near optimal choice for the pair $(Q_p, \text{Th}_{\text{Quad}})$ is to set as $\text{Th}_{\text{Quad}} = (2/3)Q_p$. Thus Q_p is the only parameter of the codec, and $Q_p = 1$ induces a lossless compression.

3.2. Global 2D + Z LAR Coding Scheme. The proposed DoI coding scheme integrates a global 2D + Z coding scheme. The global scalable 2D + Z coding scheme has been proposed in [35] (cf. global scheme in Figure 4). In a first step, a QuadTree partition is built considering only the Z image, (Quad_Z). Based on Quad_Z, the 2D image, represented in a (Y, C_b, C_r) colour space, is encoded first at low bit rate and low resolution. Then, the Z image is encoded with an improved prediction stage using the Y component of the previously encoded 2D image. In a second step, the QuadTree partition is refined considering both 2D and Z images (Quad_{ZT}). Finally, based on Quad_{ZT}, the quality of the 2D image is improved by a new coding process at a finer resolution. This joint coding method preserves the spatial coherence between texture and depth images and reduces visual artefacts for synthesized views, especially upon edges. In terms of complexity, this coding scheme has a reduced one compared to JPEG2K and about the same one compared to JPEGXR. For objective efficiency compression point of view, the codec is close to JPEG2K and significantly outperforms JPEGXR (cf. Figure 5).

4. Proposed Depth of Interest (DoI) Representation and Coding Scheme

In this section, we present the proposed joint (Depth of Interest) DoI representation and coding scheme. Firstly, a DoI refinement of depth is presented in Section 4.1. Secondly, a DoI coding of texture is presented in Section 4.2.

4.1. DoI Refinement of Depth. As previously mentioned, quality of compressed depth map will be strongly linked to

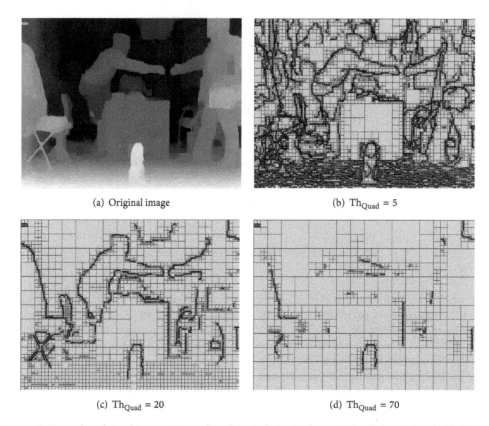

(a) Original image   (b) $Th_{Quad} = 5$

(c) $Th_{Quad} = 20$ (d) $Th_{Quad} = 70$

FIGURE 3: Examples of QuadTree partition of BookArrival view 10 frame 33 for different thresholds Th_{Quad}.

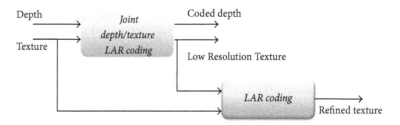

FIGURE 4: Global 2D + Z coding scheme.

the distortion introduced on contours. Thus, a local quality enhancement of depth inside a DoI should firstly aim at refining the spatial resolution. As the LAR initially considers a fix threshold to build the QuadTree, a possible solution would be to design a new QuadTree algorithm with an adaptive threshold. We opted for another solution preserving the QuadTree estimation stage but introducing a depth map preprocessing. This stage performs a dynamic range adjustment on the depth map so that the Depth of Interest (DoI) gets the largest dynamic range at the expense of the other depth zones (cf. Figure 1).

We introduce the following notations:

(i) In_Depth: input depth map.

(ii) Out_Depth: output depth map after dynamic range adjustment.

(iii) Z_{in_l}, Z_{in_h}: input low and high limits of Depth of Interest range.

(iv) W_{in}: input Depth of Interest window size, with $W_{in} = Z_{in\_h} - Z_{in\_l}$.

(v) W_{out}: adjusted Depth of Interest window size, with $W_{out} = F \times W_{in}$.

The input depth range $[Z_{in\_l}, Z_{in\_h}]$ and F coefficient can be considered as approximations of the focal distance and F-number (or relative aperture) in optical system, respectively. In particular, the F parameter will control the degree of image sharpness for the DoI. These parameters will be set by the user.

The proposed piecewise adjustment function is given in Figure 6 and the corresponding algorithm in Procedure 1. We set the constraint that the value of the middle point of the input depth range has to be unchanged.

The Out_Depth image is then used for the QuadTree estimation, whereas the input depth is encoded with the same quantization parameter for the whole image.

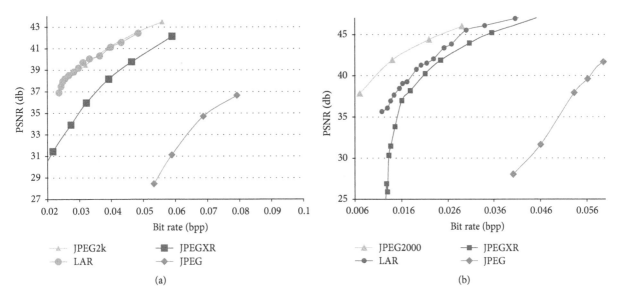

(a)   (b)

FIGURE 5: Rate-distortion curves of depth images for (a) GTFly frame 157 view 1 and (b) UndoDancer frame 250 view 1.

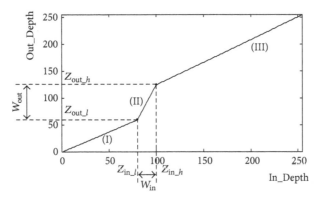

FIGURE 6: Output dynamic range adjustment of depth values as a function of input values.

FIGURE 7: Original input binary depth mask of Balloons view 5 frame 1 (1024×768 pixels) for foreground zone with $Z_{\text{in}\_l} = 128$, $Z_{\text{in}\_h} = 255$.

4.1.1. QuadTree Results after Depth Map Preprocessing.
Figures 7 and 10 represent the DoI zone within Z_{in_l} and Z_{in_h} in the original input depth map (original input binary depth mask). Figures 8(a) and 8(b) present the original and the adjusted depth maps, respectively. Indeed, after the dynamic range adjustment of the depth map, the DoI is mapped by smaller blocks. Thus, it leads to an increase of the local

resolution inside the DoI area in the QuadTree (cf. Figures 9 and 11).

4.1.2. Objective and Visual Results of Decoded Depth Maps in DoI Context.
In this section, we compare the depth map coding between the original 2D + Z LAR solution and the proposed one including the adjustment stage. For the same bit rate, the previous preprocessing step decreases the global objective quality of the depth image in comparison with the classic coding. However, it increases the local quality within the DoI with a gain up to 11 dB for the given configuration as the local resolution in the DoI is increased, (cf. Figures 12 and 14). Furthermore, we can notice a significant visual quality improvement in the DoI (cf. Figures 13 and 15). More precisely, it is obviously visible that edges of objects within DoI are more accurately encoded in comparison with the classic coding scheme.

4.2. DoI Coding of Texture.
The "DoI" coding of texture means that the texture image has to be compressed with unequal quality according to the given DoI (cf. Figure 1).

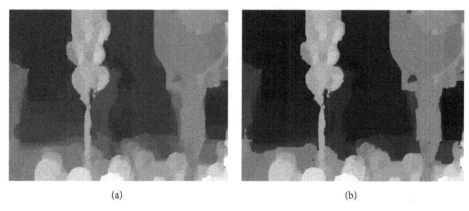

FIGURE 8: Depth map of Balloons view 5 frame 1: (a) original and (b) after dynamic range adjustment of foreground zone with $Z_{\mathrm{in}\_l} = 128$, $Z_{\mathrm{in}\_h} = 255$, $F = 1.3$.

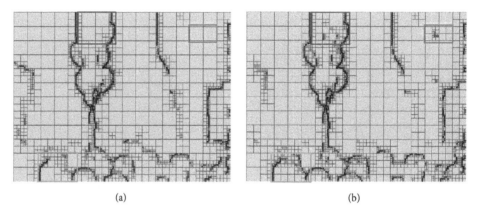

FIGURE 9: QuadTree results of depth map Balloons view 5 frame 1: (a) from original map with $\mathrm{Th}_{\mathrm{Quad}} = 28$ and (b) after dynamic range adjustment of foreground zone with $Z_{\mathrm{in}\_l} = 128$, $Z_{\mathrm{in}\_h} = 255$, $F = 1.3$, and $\mathrm{Th}_{\mathrm{Quad}} = 29$.

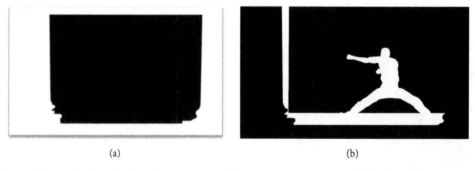

FIGURE 10: Original input binary depth mask of UndoDancer view 1 frame 250 (1920×1080 pixels) (a) for foreground zone with $Z_{\mathrm{in}\_l} = 128$, $Z_{\mathrm{in}\_h} = 255$ and (b) for depth zone within $Z_{\mathrm{in}\_l} = 100$, $Z_{\mathrm{in}\_h} = 121$.

The first step is the extraction of a binary mask image (DoI-Mask) that will be further used to define the region of interest, considering that only the depth range ($Z_{\mathrm{in}\_l}, Z_{\mathrm{in}\_h}$) is transmitted to the decoder. This extraction is simply performed by a binarization step of the coded depth image, with the depth range as input parameter. The considered depth image is the coded one for two main reasons. The first one is that the process has to be duplicated at the decoder side. The second reason is that the

binary mask has to be seen as a subset of the QuadTree partition.

The second step is the quality enhancement for the DoI for the texture. As mentioned in Section 3.2, the texture image is encoded in two passes: first, the 2D + Z images are compressed at low bit rate based on Quad_Z only, and then the 2D image is enhanced considering Quad_{ZT}. In this coding scheme, the same quantization factor Q_p is applied at both passes.

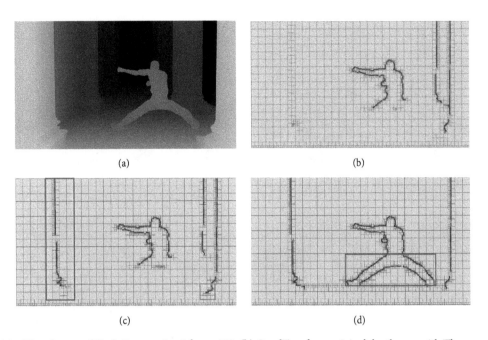

FIGURE 11: (a) Original Depth map of UndoDancer view 1 frame 250, (b) QuadTree from original depth map with $\mathrm{Th_{Quad}} = 47$, (c) QuadTree from depth map after dynamic range adjustment of foreground zone with $Z_{\mathrm{in\_l}} = 128$, $Z_{\mathrm{in\_h}} = 255$, $F = 1.3$, and $\mathrm{Th_{Quad}} = 60$, and (d) QuadTree from depth map after dynamic range adjustment of foreground zone with $Z_{\mathrm{in\_l}} = 128$, $Z_{\mathrm{in\_h}} = 255$, $F = 7.0$, and $\mathrm{Th_{Quad}} = 71$.

Input: In_Depth, $Z_{\mathrm{in\_l}}$, $Z_{\mathrm{in\_h}}$, F
Output: Out_Depth
$$\delta W = W_{\mathrm{out}} - W_{\mathrm{in}} = (F - 1) \times W_{\mathrm{in}}$$
$$Z_{\mathrm{out\_l}} = Z_{\mathrm{in\_l}} - \frac{\delta W}{2}$$
$$Z_{\mathrm{out\_h}} = Z_{\mathrm{in\_h}} + \frac{\delta W}{2}$$
for all i **do**
  if In_Depth$(i) \leq Z_{\mathrm{in\_l}}$ **then**
    $b = \dfrac{Z_{\mathrm{out\_l}}}{Z_{\mathrm{in\_l}}}$
    (I) Out_Depth$(i) = b \times$ In_Depth(i).
  end if
  if $Z_{\mathrm{in\_l}} <$ In_Depth$(i) < Z_{\mathrm{in\_h}}$ **then**
    $b = \dfrac{Z_{\mathrm{out\_h}} - Z_{\mathrm{out\_l}}}{Z_{\mathrm{in\_h}} - Z_{\mathrm{in\_l}}}$
    $c = Z_{\mathrm{out\_l}} - b \times Z_{\mathrm{in\_l}}$
    (II) Out_Depth$(i) = b \times$ In_Depth$(i) + c$.
  end if
  if In_Depth$(i) > Z_{\mathrm{in\_h}}$ **then**
    $b = \dfrac{Z_{\mathrm{out\_h}} - 255}{Z_{\mathrm{in\_h}} - 255}$
    $c = 255 \times (1 - b)$
    (III) Out_Depth$(i) = b \times$ In_Depth$(i) + c$.
  end if
end for
{return the adjusted depth map}
return Out_Depth

PROCEDURE 1: Dynamic range adjustment of input depth map.

We introduce two different ways of texture quality enhancement. The first one consists in a global SNR quality enhancement using the concept of region-level coding introduced in [33] for RoI coding: the image is represented by regions mapping the QuadTree, and each region is independently encoded at a SNR quality level. The original solution allowed only two regions (RoI and non-RoI); we extended it until eight regions with their own quantization parameter, starting from label 0 for the RoI. Thus, the DoI coding system now defines the DoI-Mask as the RoI-mask and implements at least three quantization parameters: $Q_{p\_Z\_LR\_T}$ for the depth and Low Resolution Texture images, $Q_{p\_\mathrm{Ref}\_T\_\mathrm{DoI}}$ for refined texture image inside the DoI, and $Q_{p\_\mathrm{Ref}\_T\_\mathrm{NDoI}}$ for the refined texture image outside it (cf. Figure 16). In this paper, we present results for this configuration only, but other scenarios are possible as a total of seven quantization levels are available for the non-DoI zones. For instance, a simple one consists of first dividing the non-DoI zones into N depth ranges ($N < 8$), defining N regions, and then applying a progressive quantization in such a way that the quantization factor is weighted by the distance of the region to the DoI.

The second enhancement way is to obtain a local resolution refinement for the texture image inside the DoI only. It simply consists of refining the Quad_Z only inside the DoI by masking the input texture image for the Quad_{ZT} estimation ($\mathrm{Quad}_{ZT\_\mathrm{DoI}}$). For this mode, no information has to be transmitted to the decoder, and a unique quantization factor is applied (cf. Figure 17).

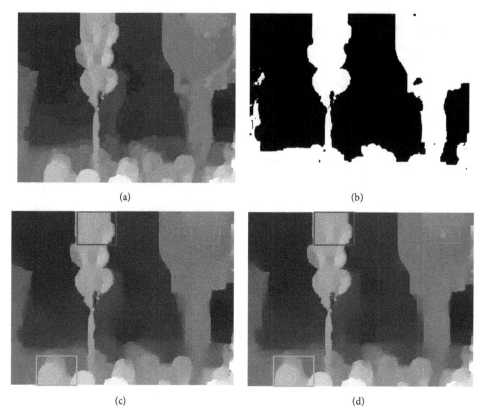

FIGURE 12: Visual quality comparison over depth map of Balloons view 5 frame 1 at 0.048 bpp: (a) original depth map, (b) input binary depth mask, (c) depth coded by classic LAR (Global PSNR = 36.75 dB), and (d) depth coded with DoI refinement of foreground zone with $Z_{\text{in}\_l} = 128$, $Z_{\text{in}\_h} = 255$, and $F = 1.3$ (Global PSNR = 36.53 dB).

A joint SNR enhancement and local resolution refinement solution also is feasible. Examples of the different solutions are presented in the next section.

The two proposed texture quality enhancement methods are both efficient, yet simple. Both methods are based on the LAR coder framework which has a low complexity as mentioned in Section 1. Thus, a relatively small additional computational cost is associated with both methods.

5. Experimental Results

5.1. Evaluation Methodology. After illustrating the preprocessing and encoding depth maps in Section 4.1, in this section, we focus on the texture coding aspects, with SNR quality and local resolution enhancement. Finally, we explore the results of the proposed coding scheme in synthesized views context. To the best of our knowledge, the proposed global representation and coding scheme is unique in terms of combined functionalities, so comparisons with state of the art are not feasible. However, we provide in the following comparative results for RoI with block instead of pixel accuracy. More details about the compression efficiency of the 2D + Z compared to the state of the art can be found in [35].

5.2. Objective and Visual Results of Decoded Texture Images in DoI Context. Some examples of DoI coding for texture

images are provided in the following. More particularly, Figures 18 and 21 show the original texture, the original input depth mask (defined from the original depth map of the DoI zone within Z_{in_l} and Z_{in_h}), and the DoI-Mask (defined from the decoded refined depth map) with different resolutions: full resolution as available for the proposed scheme and subsampled one by 8 × 8 or 16 × 16 block resolution, generally provided by state-of-the-art coders.

First, examples of SNR quality enhancement are provided. Figures 19 and 22 show a zoom on the visual quality of decoded texture image coded with classic LAR and with LAR-RoI using the full resolution DoI-Mask and a subsampled one. Results show that pixel accuracy on RoI contours gives a better visual quality (cf. Figures 20 and 23).

Then, Figure 24 shows an example of local resolution enhancement for DoI in the texture image. A higher resolution is accorded to the texture image in the DoI only which leads to an increase in the objective quality as well as in the visual quality in the DoI.

5.3. Visual Results of Synthesized Views in DoI Context. The final and most important issue in 2D + Z image coding is the visual quality of the resulting synthesized views. With the depth and texture information, intermediate views at an arbitrary view point can be synthesized with the View Synthesis Reference Software (VSRS 3.0) [28]. In this set of

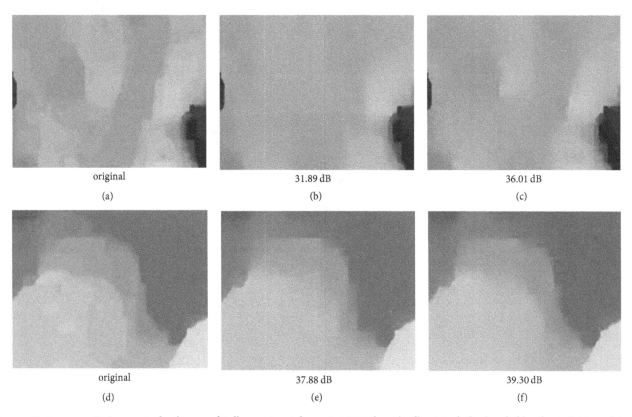

FIGURE 13: Zoom on DoI zones in depth map of Balloons view 5 frame 1 at 0.048 bpp: (a, d) original, (b, e) coded by classic LAR, and (c, f) coded with DoI refinement of foreground zone with $Z_{\text{in\_}l} = 128$, $Z_{\text{in\_}h} = 255$, $F = 1.3$.

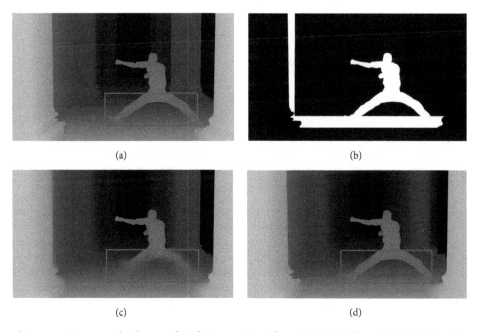

FIGURE 14: Visual quality comparison over depth map of UndoDancer view 1 frame 250 at 0.014 bpp: (a) original depth map, (b) input binary depth mask, (c) depth coded by classic LAR (Global PSNR = 35.66 dB), and (d) depth coded with DoI refinement of depth zone within $Z_{\text{in\_}l} = 100$ and $Z_{\text{in\_}h} = 121$ with $F = 7.0$ (Global PSNR = 32.88 dB).

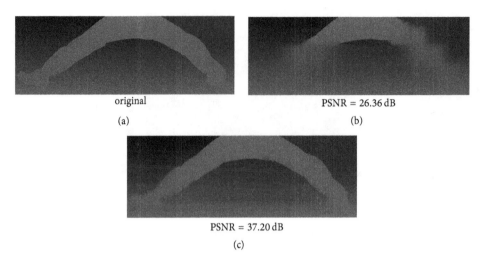

FIGURE 15: Zoom on DoI zones in depth map of UndoDancer view 1 frame 250 at 0.014 bpp: (a) original, (b) coded by classic LAR, and (c) coded with DoI refinement of depth zone within $Z_{in\_l} = 100$ and $Z_{in\_h} = 121$ with $F = 7.0$.

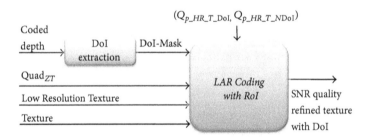

FIGURE 16: RoI coding based on DoI-Mask.

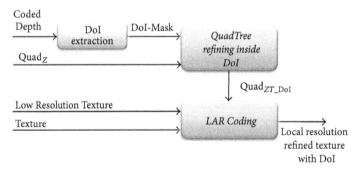

FIGURE 17: Local resolution refinement inside the DoI only.

experiments, we consider the texture images and the depth maps coded at low bit rate with and without the proposed DoI scheme, in order to evaluate the compression effect of the proposed technique on the synthesized views (cf. Figure 25). In order to compare the proposed DoI scheme with the RoI block-based approach (such as H264 and HEVC), we study the effect of RoI resolution on synthesized views by decoding texture images using DoI-Mask at different resolutions: full resolution and 8×8 and 16×16 block resolution. It is clearly noticeable that the quality within the DoI in the intermediate views synthesized from depth images decoded by the proposed DoI scheme is much better than the one synthesized from depth and texture images decoded by the

classic LAR at the same bit rate, (cf. Figures 26(c) and 26(d)). Moreover, the decoded texture images with block-based DoI scheme lead to a low quality synthesized views especially upon DoI contour, while the decoded texture images with our proposed pixel-based DoI scheme lead to a fine and accurate quality upon DoI contour in the synthesized views (cf. Figure 26).

6. Conclusion

In this paper a joint content-based scheme, called "Depth of Interest" (DoI) scheme, for representation and coding of the region of interest in the 3D autostereoscopic domain is

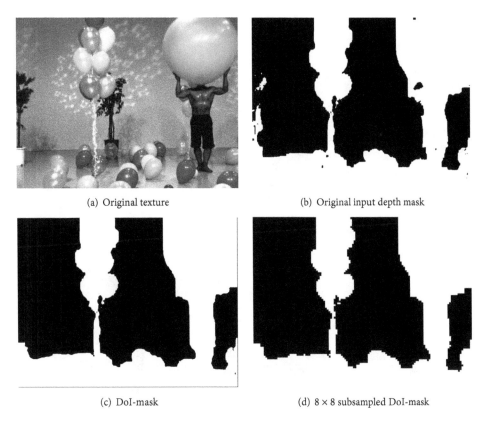

(a) Original texture   (b) Original input depth mask

(c) DoI-mask   (d) 8 × 8 subsampled DoI-mask

FIGURE 18: Mask of the Depth of Interest for foreground zone with $Z_{\text{in\_}l} = 128$ and $Z_{\text{in\_}h} = 255$ of (a) Balloons view 5 frame 1, extracted (b) from original depth, (c) from depth coded with DoI refinement scheme, and (d) from depth coded with DoI refinement scheme for 8 × 8 block resolution.

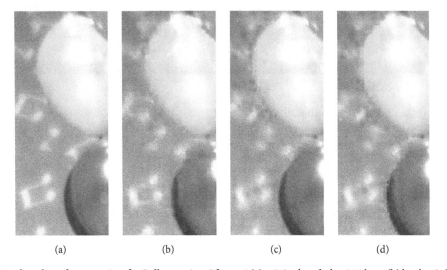

(a)   (b)   (c)   (d)

FIGURE 19: Zoom on visual quality of texture view for Balloons view 5 frame 1 (a) original, coded at 0.18 bpp, (b) by classic LAR (Global PSNR = 32.70 dB), (c) by applying the SNR quality enhancement ($Q_{p\_\text{Ref\_T\_DoI}} = 25$, $Q_{p\_\text{Ref\_T\_NDoI}} = 120$) using the full-resolution DoI-Mask of foreground zone with $Z_{\text{in\_}l} = 128$ and $Z_{\text{in\_}h} = 255$ (Global PSNR = 33.05 dB, DoI coded at 0.54 bpp, $\text{PSNR}_{\text{DoI}} = 36.87$ dB; non-DoI coded at 0.12 bpp, $\text{PSNR}_{\text{Non-DoI}} = 30.74$ dB), and (d) by applying the SNR quality enhancement for a 8 × 8 block resolution DoI-Mask.

presented. It ensures a higher quality in depth zones of the sequence that are of interest to the viewer. The proposed scheme embeds the LAR (Locally Adaptive Resolution) codec. The DoI representation scheme consists of defining, from the depth map, a binary mask covering the DoI zone.

Then, the DoI coding scheme is applied on both depth and texture images. For this purpose, a preprocess, consisting of a dynamic range adjustment, is applied on the depth map in order to increase the resolution in the QuadTree partition at the DoI zone. Then, for the texture image, we use a RoI-based

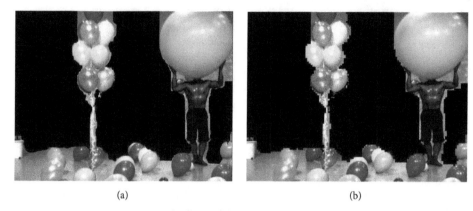

FIGURE 20: Extracted region of interest from texture coded with RoI using (a) the full-resolution DoI-Mask and (b) 8 × 8 block resolution DoI-Mask.

FIGURE 21: Mask of the Depth of Interest zone within Z_{in_l} = 100 and Z_{in_h} = 121 of (a) UndoDancer view 1 frame 255, extracted (b) from original depth, (c) from depth coded with DoI refinement scheme, and (d) from depth coded with DoI refinement scheme for 16 × 16 block resolution.

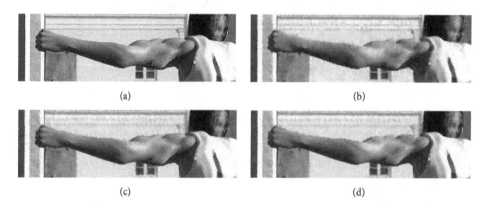

FIGURE 22: Zoom on visual quality of texture view for UndoDancer view 1 frame 250 (a) original, coded at 0.2 bpp (b) by classic LAR (Global PSNR = 24 dB), (c) by applying the SNR quality enhancement ($Q_{p\_Ref\_T\_DoI}$ = 25, $Q_{p\_Ref\_T\_NDoI}$ = 120) using the full-resolution DoI-Mask of depth zone within Z_{in_l} = 100 and Z_{in_h} = 121 (Global PSNR = 28.82 dB, DoI coded at 0.98 bpp, $PSNR_{DoI}$ = 36.06 dB, non-DoI coded at 0.17 bpp, $PSNR_{Non-DoI}$ = 28.1 dB), and (d) by applying the SNR quality enhancement for 16 × 16 block resolution DoI-Mask.

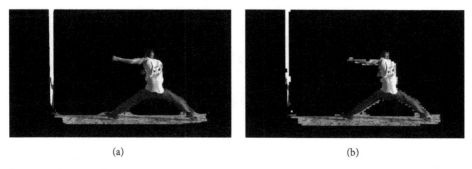

FIGURE 23: Extracted region of interest from texture coded with RoI using (a) the full-resolution DoI-Mask; (b) 16 × 16 block resolution DoI-Mask.

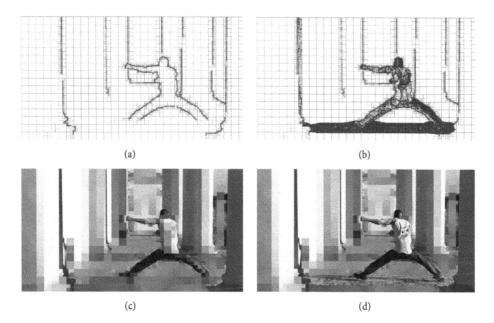

FIGURE 24: Visual quality comparison of texture view for UndoDancer view 1 frame 250 with $Th_{Quad} = 20, Q_p = 30$. (a) $Quad_Z$, (b) $Quad_{ZT\_DoI}$, (c) Low Resolution Texture at 0.06 bpp (Global PSNR = 17.2 dB), and (d) local resolution refined texture at 0.23 bpp ($PSNR_{DoI} = 32.24$ dB).

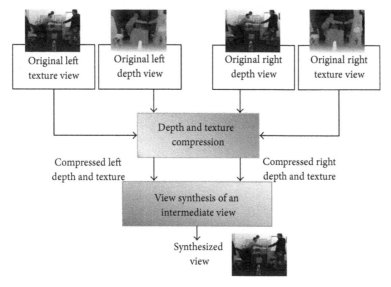

FIGURE 25: Synthesized view rendering framework.

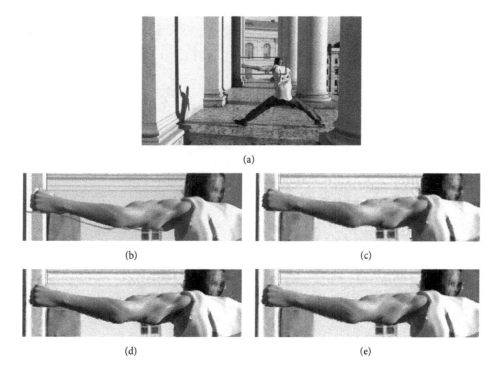

FIGURE 26: Visual quality comparison of synthesized view for (a) UndoDancer view 3 frame 250 using (b) uncompressed depth and texture; depth coded at 0.014 bpp and texture coded at 0.2 bpp (c) by classic LAR; (d) by the proposed DoI refinement of depth scheme and SNR quality enhancement of texture with a full-resolution DoI-Mask; (e) by the proposed DoI scheme with the 16×16 block resolution DoI-Mask.

scheme using the defined depth-based binary mask. The main strength of this scheme is that it provides a high correlation between texture objects and depth and allows high quality along objects contours in depth and texture images as well as in synthesized views. In future work, we will focus on a nonlinear adjustment of the dynamic range and we will also study multiple DoI zones.

Competing Interests

The authors declare that there is no conflict of interests regarding the publication of this paper.

References

[1] A. Smolic and P. Kauff, "Interactive 3-D video representation and coding technologies," *Proceedings of the IEEE*, vol. 93, no. 1, pp. 98–110, 2005.

[2] C. Fehn, R. de la Barré, and S. Pastoor, "Interactive 3-DTV-concepts and key technologies," *Proceedings of the IEEE*, vol. 94, no. 3, pp. 524–538, 2006.

[3] Phillips Research Press Information, "Philips 3d information display solution adds extra dimension to in-store messaging," 2005, http://www.research.philips.com/newscenter/archive/.

[4] J. Harrold and G. J. Woodgate, "Autostereoscopic display technology for mobile 3DTV applications," in *Proceedings of the Stereoscopic Displays and Virtual Reality Systems XIV*, San Jose, Calif, USA, January 2007.

[5] A. Smolic, K. Mueller, P. Merkle et al., "3D video and free viewpoint video—technologies, applications and MPEG standards," in *Proceedings of the IEEE International Conference on Multimedia and Expo (ICME '06)*, pp. 2161–2164, July 2006.

[6] M. Tanimoto, "Overview of FTV (free-viewpoint television)," in *Proceedings of the IEEE International Conference on Multimedia and Expo (ICME '09)*, pp. 1552–1553, New York, NY, USA, July 2009.

[7] N. A. Dodgson, "Autostereo displays: 3d without glasses," in *Proceedings of the Electronic Information Displays Conference (EID '97)*, vol. 38, pp. 31–36, November 1997.

[8] A. Vetro, S. Yea, and A. Smolic, "Toward a 3D video format for auto-stereoscopic displays," in *Applications of Digital Image Processing XXXI*, vol. 7073 of *Proceedings of SPIE*, pp. 1–12, September 2008.

[9] A. Smolic, K. Mueller, N. Stefanoski et al., "Coding algorithms for 3DTV—a survey," *IEEE Transactions on Circuits and Systems for Video Technology*, vol. 17, no. 11, pp. 1606–1621, 2007.

[10] P. Merkle, A. Smolic, K. Muller, and T. Wiegand, "Multiview video plus depth representation and coding," in *Proceedings of the 14th IEEE International Conference on Image Processing (ICIP '07)*, vol. 1, pp. 201–204, San Antonio, Tex, USA, 2007.

[11] I. Himawan, W. Song, and D. Tjondronegoro, "Automatic region-of-interest detection and prioritisation for visually optimised coding of low bit rate videos," in *Proceedings of the IEEE Workshop on Applications of Computer Vision (WACV '13)*, pp. 76–82, January 2013.

[12] G. Hu, M. Xiao, and S. Yuan, "Detecting automatically and compression algorithm for infrared image based on region of interest," in *Proceedings of the International Forum on Computer Science-Technology and Applications (IFCSTA '09)*, pp. 50–53, December 2009.

[13] M. Firoozbakht, J. Dehmeshki, M. Martini et al., "Compression of digital medical images based on multiple regions of interest," in *Proceedings of the 4th International Conference on Digital Society (ICDS '10)*, pp. 260–263, St. Maarten, Netherlands, February 2010.

[14] M. Nawaz, J. Cosmas, A. Adnan, and M. Ali, "Inter-intra frame segmentation using colour and motion for region of interest coding of video," in *Proceedings of the IEEE International Symposium on Broadband Multimedia Systems and Broadcasting (BMSB '11)*, Nuremberg, Germany, June 2011.

[15] Y. Li, W. Li, and Y. Ma, "Accurate iris location based on region of interest," in *Proceedings of the International Conference on Biomedical Engineering and Biotechnology (iCBEB '12)*, pp. 704–707, Macau, Macao, May 2012.

[16] C. Chamaret, S. Goddefroy, P. Lopez, and O. Le Meur, "Adaptive 3d rendering based on region-of-interest," in *Stereoscopic Displays and Applications XXI*, vol. 7524 of *Proceedings of SPIE*, pp. 1–12, February 2010.

[17] S.-L. Fan, M. Yu, G.-Y. Jiang, F. Shao, and Z.-J. Peng, "A digital watermarking algorithm based on region of interest for 3D image," in *Proceedings of the 8th International Conference on Computational Intelligence and Security (CIS '12)*, pp. 549–552, Guangzhou, China, November 2012.

[18] Y. Zhang, G. Jiang, M. Yu, Y. Yang, Z. Peng, and K. Chen, "Depth perceptual region-of-interest based multiview video coding," *Journal of Visual Communication and Image Representation*, vol. 21, no. 5-6, pp. 498–512, 2010.

[19] L. S. Karlsson and M. Sjöström, "Region-of-interest 3D video coding based on depth images," in *Proceedings of the 3DTV-Conference*, pp. 141–144, Istanbul, Turkey, May 2008.

[20] H. Zheng, B. Liu, and H. Zhang, "Region-of-interest coding of 3D mesh based on wavelet transform," in *Proceedings of the 3rd International Conference on Image and Graphics (ICIG '04)*, pp. 438–441, IEEE, Hong Kong, December 2004.

[21] L. S. Karlsson, *Spatio-temporal pre-processing methods for region-of-interest video coding [Licenciate Thesis 21]*, Department of Information Technology and Media, Mid Sweden University, Sundsvall, Sweden, 2007, http://urn.kb.se/resolve?urn=urn:nbn:se:miun:diva-51.

[22] JPEG 2000 Part I Final Committee Draft Version 1.0, ISO/IEC FCD15444-1: 2000, Annex H, March 2000.

[23] J. A. Raja, G. Raja, and A. K. Khan, "Selective compression of medical images using multiple regions of interest," *Life Science Journal*, vol. 10, no. 9, pp. 394–397, 2013.

[24] I. A. Fernandez, P. R. Alface, T. Gan, R. Lauwereins, and C. De Vleeschouwer, "Integrated H.264 region-of-interest detection, tracking and compression for surveillance scenes," in *Proceedings of the 18th International Packet Video Workshop (PV '10)*, pp. 17–24, December 2010.

[25] K. Misra, A. Segall, M. Horowitz, S. Xu, A. Fuldseth, and M. Zhou, "An overview of tiles in HEVC," *IEEE Journal on Selected Topics in Signal Processing*, vol. 7, no. 6, pp. 969–977, 2013.

[26] V. Sanchez, A. Basu, and M. K. Mandal, "Prioritized region of interest coding in JPEG2000," *IEEE Transactions on Circuits and Systems for Video Technology*, vol. 14, no. 9, pp. 1149–1155, 2004.

[27] C. Christopoulos, J. Askelöf, and M. Larsson, "Efficient methods for encoding regions of interest in the upcoming JPEG2000 still image coding standard," *IEEE Signal Processing Letters*, vol. 7, no. 9, pp. 247–249, 2000.

[28] M. Tanimoto, T. Fuji, K. Suzuki, N. Fukushima, and Y. Mori, "Reference softwares for depth estimation and view synthesis," Tech. Rep. M15377, ISO/IECJTC1/SC29/WG11, MPEG, Archamps, France, 2008.

[29] P. Merkle, Y. Morvan, A. Smolic et al., "The effect of depth compression on multiview rendering quality," in *Proceedings of the 2008 3DTV-Conference: The True Vision—Capture, Transmission and Display of 3D Video (3DTV-CON '08)*, pp. 245–248, May 2008.

[30] E. Bosc, M. Pressigout, and L. Morin, "Focus on visual rendering quality through content-based depth map coding," in *Proceedings of the 28th Picture Coding Symposium (PCS '10)*, pp. 158–161, Nagoya, Japan, December 2010.

[31] Y. Liu, S. Ma, Q. Huang, D. Zhao, W. Gao, and N. Zhang, "Compression-induced rendering distortion analysis for texture/depth rate allocation in 3D video compression," in *Proceedings of the Data Compression Conference (DCC '09)*, vol. 9, pp. 352–361, IEEE, Snowbird, Utah, USA, March 2009.

[32] A. Tikanmäki, A. Gotchev, A. Smolic, and K. Müller, "Quality assessment of 3D video in rate allocation experiments," in *Proceedings of the 12th IEEE International Symposium on Consumer Electronics (ISCE '08)*, April 2008.

[33] O. Deforges, M. Babel, L. Bedat, and J. Ronsin, "Color LAR codec: a color image representation and compression scheme based on local resolution adjustment and self-extracting region representation," *IEEE Transactions on Circuits and Systems for Video Technology*, vol. 17, no. 8, pp. 974–987, 2007.

[34] K. Samrouth, F. Pasteaua, and O. Deforgesa, "Quality constraint and rate-distortion optimization for predictive image coders," in *Image Processing: Algorithms and Systems XI*, vol. 8655 of *Proceedings of SPIE*, pp. 1–9, Burlingame, Calif, USA, February 2013.

[35] K. Samrouth, O. Deforges, Y. Liu, F. Pasteau, M. Khalil, and W. Falou, "Efficient depth map compression exploiting correlation with texture data in multiresolution predictive image coders," in *Proceedings of the IEEE International Conference on Multimedia and Expo Workshops (ICMEW '13)*, pp. 1–6, San Jose, Calif, USA, July 2013.

19

Image Encryption Algorithm based on a Novel Improper Fractional-Order Attractor and a Wavelet Function Map

Jian-feng Zhao,[1] Shu-ying Wang,[2] Li-tao Zhang,[3] and Xiao-yan Wang[1]

[1]*Department of Information Engineering, Henan Polytechnic, Zhengzhou, China*
[2]*Department of Minzu, Huanghe Science and Technology College, Zhengzhou, China*
[3]*Department of Mathematics and Physics, Zhengzhou Institute of Aeronautical Industry Management, Zhengzhou 450015, China*

Correspondence should be addressed to Shu-ying Wang; wsy0707@126.com

Academic Editor: Jucheng Yang

This paper presents a three-dimensional autonomous chaotic system with high fraction dimension. It is noted that the nonlinear characteristic of the improper fractional-order chaos is interesting. Based on the continuous chaos and the discrete wavelet function map, an image encryption algorithm is put forward. The key space is formed by the initial state variables, parameters, and orders of the system. Every pixel value is included in secret key, so as to improve antiattack capability of the algorithm. The obtained simulation results and extensive security analyses demonstrate the high level of security of the algorithm and show its robustness against various types of attacks.

1. Introduction

With rapid development of communications, network security of information has become increasingly important for many applications. While high redundancy for image and multimedia information is challenging traditional cryptography algorithms [1, 2], chaotic attractors have orbital pseudorandom properties, good unpredictability, highly sensitivity for initial conditions, topological transitivity features, and so on. These characters indicate that chaos-based cryptosystem is a research hotspot in multimedia security area [3]. In 1949, Shannon created confusion and diffusion in the world of cryptography [4]. To overcome high redundancies and strong correlations of digital images, chaos has been widely applied in traditional encryption algorithm [5–13]. Research proposed that one-dimensional chaotic system has low security [14, 15]. With higher dimension, chaotic attractor occupies more space and winding complexly. The most complex attractor has much more complex output signals so that encryption effect would be better, whereas three-dimensional autonomous chaotic systems with higher fractal dimension are rare [16].

Comparing with integer-order chaotic system, the fractional-order chaotic system is not only related to parameters of the system, but also closely linked with fractional orders of system. Improper fractional-order chaotic system, therefore, has strong nonlinear characters and complexity. In secret communication, it can enhance the density and security so as to enormously increase the difficulty of unmasking signals. The algorithm shows greater application value in communication field [17, 18].

The rest of this paper is organized as follows: Section 2 describes a novel complex attractor. In Section 3, the chaos-based encryption algorithm is proposed. The numerical experimental results of performance analysis are given in Section 4. Finally, Section 5 contains conclusion and perspectives.

2. Improper Fractional-Order Chaotic Flow

A new three-dimensional autonomous chaotic system with high fraction dimension is constructed, of which the governing fractional-order equation is

$$\frac{d^{q_1}x}{dt^{q_1}} = xz + b\sin(x + y + z),$$

$$\frac{d^{q_2}y}{dt^{q_2}} = az - by,$$

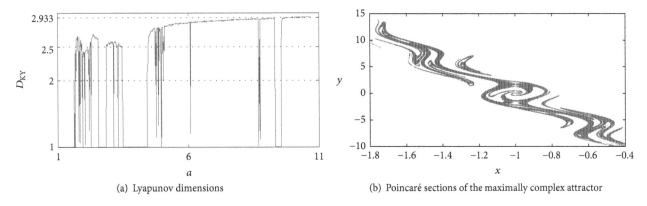

(a) Lyapunov dimensions

(b) Poincaré sections of the maximally complex attractor

FIGURE 1: Chaotic characters of the novel attractor with $q_1 = q_2 = q_3 = 1$.

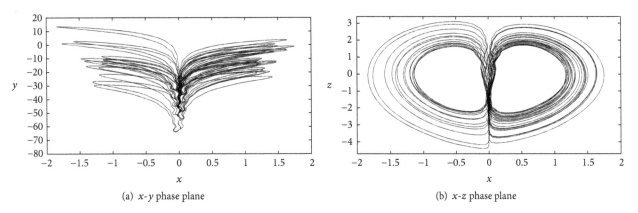

(a) x-y phase plane

(b) x-z phase plane

FIGURE 2: The fractional-order chaos with $q_1 = 1.01$, $q_2 = 1.1$, and $q_3 = 1.11$.

$$\frac{d^{q_3} z}{dt^{q_3}} = 1 - cx^2,$$

$$(1)$$

where $X = (x, y, z)^T$ are state variables and a, b, c are parameters. Three fractional orders are q_1, q_2, q_3; if $\max(q_1, q_2, q_3) < 1$, system (1) is a true fractional-order system, if $q_1 = q_2 = q_3 = 1$, system (1) is an integer-order system, and if $\max(q_1, q_2, q_3) > 1$, system (1) is an improper fractional-order system. Based on stability theory and numerical analysis of fractional-order system, when $(a, b, c) = (6, 5, 0.12)$ and $(q_1, q_2, q_3) = (1, 1, 1)$, the Lyapunov dimension D_{KY} is shown in Figure 1(a) with varying parameter a in interval $[1, 11]$. Almost all D_{KY} of chaotic attractors are larger than 2.5. With increasing control parameters, D_{KY} reaches as high as 2.9336 at some special parameters. As shown in Figure 1(b), the Poincaré section of the maximally complex attractor has hierarchical structure composed of dense points. When $(q_1, q_2, q_3) = (1.01, 1.1, 1.11)$, the improper fractional-order chaos presents interesting and complex dynamic behavior represented in Figure 2.

3. Image Encryption Algorithm

Algorithm process is shown in Figure 3.

Encryption Procedure. Image encryption algorithm mainly consists of two processes: confusion and diffusion.

Step 1 (pixel confusion). Suppose that the size of plaintext image is $L = M \times N$. Scanning the plaintext image line by line in order to obtain pixel matrix P is as follows:

$$P$$

$$= \begin{bmatrix} P(1) & P(2) & \cdots & P(N) \\ P(N+1) & P(N+2) & \cdots & P(2N) \\ \vdots & \vdots & \vdots & \vdots \\ P((M-1)N+1) & P((M-1)N+2) & \cdots & P(L) \end{bmatrix}. \quad (2)$$

In confusion procedure, the wavelet function map is taken as follows [21]:

$$x_{n+1} = k \cdot \left(1 - x_n^2\right) \cdot e^{-(x_n + \mu)^2 / 2}, \quad (3)$$

where $n \in N$ is the number of iterations. For numerical simulations, we take the initial value of the discrete system (3) as $x_0 = 0.3$, parameter $k = 1.33$, and $\mu = -0.6$. The chaotic characteristics of wavelet function map are shown in Figure 4(a), and its interesting bifurcation diagram varying with $\mu \in [-0.77, -0.29]$ is displayed in Figure 4(b).

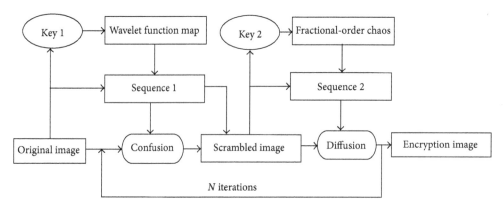

FIGURE 3: Encryption process.

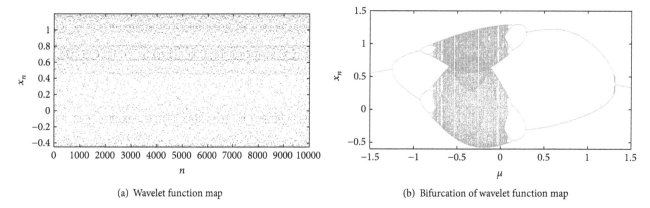

(a) Wavelet function map

(b) Bifurcation of wavelet function map

FIGURE 4: Wavelet function map.

To improve the sensitivity of original image to encryption image, secret keys are distracted by plain image. In confusion procedure, $T = \mathrm{mod}\left(\sum_{i=1}^{L} P(i), L\right)/(L-1)$ is initial vector of wavelet function map. Sequence $x(n)$ is rearranged by wavelet function map so as to engender position matrix $lx(n)$. Then $lx(n)$ is used to confuse position of image pixels and get matrix $\{C(i) \mid i = 1, 2, \ldots, L\}$. Finally matrix $\{C(i) \mid i = 1, 2, \ldots, L\}$ is transformed into permutation image C of size $M \times N$.

Step 2 (pixel diffusion). Confusion only changes the position of pixel point while the pixel value is fixed, so the attacker may break down the algorithm though the statistics.

In diffusion, T is used to disturb parameter $a = a + T$ of system (1). Then the chaos generates chaotic sequences and makes N_0 times preiteration to eliminate some harmful effect of chaos transient process. Matrix B is created and initialized as an empty sequence. State vector $\{x(1), x(2), x(3)\}$ is generated in every iteration and a parameter $m = \mathrm{mod}\,(\mathrm{abs}(x(1) + x(2) + x(3)), 3)$ is derived. Then, matrix B is assigned according to parameter m. When $m = 0$, $B = \{B, x_1, x_2\}$, when $m = 1$, $B = \{B, x_1, x_3\}$, and when $m = 2$, $B = \{B, x_3, x_1\}$.

In every interaction, sequence B has strong randomness after $2L + N_0$ times iteration. Then B is preprocessed in the following form:

$$K(i) = \mathrm{mod}\,(\mathrm{temp}, 256), \quad i = 1, 2, \ldots, L, \qquad (4)$$

where $\mathrm{Temp} = \mathrm{floor}\,((|B(i)| - \mathrm{floor}\,(|B(i)|)) \times 10^m)$, $|x|$ is absolution of x, and $\mathrm{floor}\,(x)$ expresses downrounding. The positive integer $m = 12$. The autocorrelation of sequence B focuses on the interval $[-0.1, 0.1]$ and is shown in Figure 5(a), whereas the autocorrelation of sequence K after the pretreatment focuses on a smaller interval $[-0.003, 0.003]$ processed in Figure 5(b).

During diffusion, first pixel of permutation image C is encrypted as follows:

$$C(1) = [C(1) + K(1)] \bmod 256$$
$$\oplus [C(L) + K(1 + L + T)] \bmod 256. \qquad (5a)$$

However, for pixel at position $i > 1$, pixel substitution is made according to

$$C(i) = [C(i) + K(i)] \bmod 256$$
$$\oplus [C(i-1) + K(i + L + T)] \bmod 256, \qquad (5b)$$
$$i = 1, 2, \ldots, L.$$

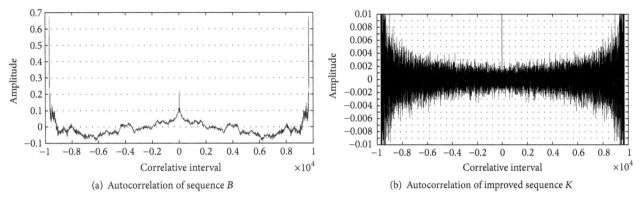

(a) Autocorrelation of sequence B (b) Autocorrelation of improved sequence K

FIGURE 5: Autocorrelation of sequences.

Then sequence $\{C(i), \; i = 1, 2, \ldots, L\}$ is conversed into matrix with size of $M \times N$.

Decryption is inverse operation of encryption process. Decryption image D is scanned line by line to get sequence $\{D(i) \mid i = 1, 2, \ldots, L\} \; (L = M \times N)$.

$$\text{temp} = C(i) \oplus [C(i-1) + K(i+L+T)] \bmod 256,$$
$$D(i) = [\text{temp} - K(i)] \bmod 256, \tag{6a}$$
$$i = L, L-1, \ldots, 2,$$
$$\text{temp} = C(1) \oplus [C(L) + K(1+L+T)] \bmod 256,$$
$$D(1) = [\text{temp} - K(1)] \bmod 256. \tag{6b}$$

Then, inverse scrambling operation for matrix $\{D(i) \mid i = 1, 2, \ldots, L\}$ is made. Firstly, sequence $x(n)$ is generated by wavelet function map to produce position matrix $lx(n)$. Then $lx(n)$ is arranged by the same law so as to get position matrix $llx(n)$. At last we use $llx(n)$ to confuse pixel position of image D to get matrix $\{E(i) \mid i = 1, 2, \ldots, L\}$ and change matrix E into $M \times N$ two-dimension matrix to observe final decrypted image.

4. Numerical Simulation and Performance Analysis

The proposed encryption technique is implemented in MATLAB 7.1. In the experiment, different types of digital images are tested, such as gray image, binary image, and color image.

4.1. 3D Histogram Analysis. Histogram is a graphical representation of the pixels intensity distribution of an image, and it can measure the capacity of resisting attack. The gray Lena image of size 256×256 is encrypted as shown in Figure 6(c) and the 3D histogram of the encrypted Lena image is shown in Figure 6(d). The binary image has only two colors and is sensitive to the change of pixel. 3D histograms of a binary image are encrypted and encrypted binary images are demonstrated in Figures 7(b) and 7(d), respectively. Figure 8(a) shows the color image and its RGB histograms; Figure 8(b) shows the encrypted color image of Figure 8(a) and its RGB histograms. The histogram of the encrypted image is fairly uniform and significantly different from that of the original image, so the information is unpredictable and histogram attack can be avoided.

4.2. Information Entropy. Information entropy, firstly proposed by Shannon in 1949, is a significant property that reflects the randomness and the unpredictability of an information source [4]. With bigger entropy image has more uniform gray distribution. The entropy $H(x)$ is defined by the following formula: $H(x) = -\sum_{i=1}^{n} p(x_i)\log_2 p(x_i)$, where $p(x_i)$ denotes the probability of symbol x_i. When $p(x_i) = 1/256$, the 256×256 gray image has maximum entropy of 8. Entropy of gray Lena image and binary image is 7.447144 and 0.593165, respectively, while its encryption is 7.988847 and 7.972069, respectively. Considering RGB components of color image Lena, average information entropy of the color Lena and encrypted color Lena is 7.198813 and 7.997281, respectively. It is obvious that the entropies of the cipher images are very close to the theoretical value of 8, which means that the encryption algorithm has ability of resisting statistical attack.

4.3. Correlation Coefficients of Adjacent Pixels. In the section, we aim at checking up the correlation of two adjacent pixels between the original image and encrypted image. In this simulation, randomly selected 1000 pairs of adjacent pixels (horizontally, vertically, and diagonally) are determined. The correlation coefficient between two adjacent pixels in an image is determined according to the following formula:

$$R_{xy} = \frac{\text{Conv}(x, y)}{\sqrt{D(x)}\sqrt{D(y)}}, \tag{7}$$

where

$$E(x) = \frac{1}{N}\sum_{i=1}^{N} x_i,$$
$$D(x) = \frac{1}{N}\sum_{i=1}^{N} [x_i - E(x)]^2, \tag{8}$$
$$\text{Conv}(x, y) = \frac{1}{N}\sum_{i=1}^{N} [x_i - E(x)][y_i - E(y)].$$

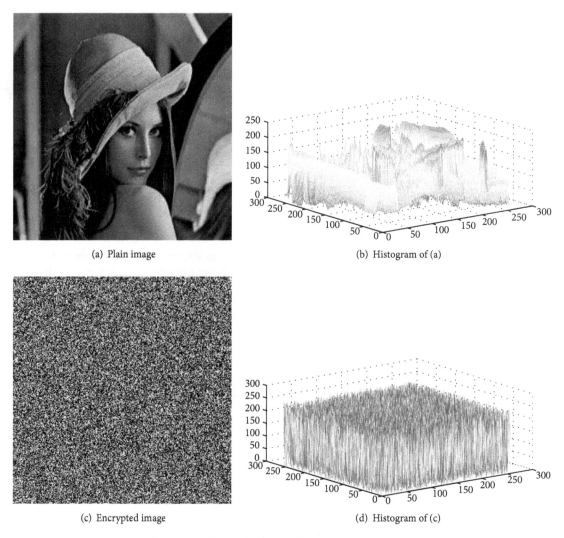

(a) Plain image

(b) Histogram of (a)

(c) Encrypted image

(d) Histogram of (c)

FIGURE 6: The gray Lena image.

Figure 9 displays correlation coefficients of adjacent pixels in four directions of Lena plain image and cipher image. The result emphasizes that there is hardly any correlation of adjacent pixels in encryption images. Correlation coefficients of the encrypted Lena image are smaller than other methods shown in Table 1. The statistical properties of original image have randomly spread to encryption image.

4.4. Resistance to Differential Attack. The attacker may observe the change of decryption by the tiny change of plaintext to find the correlation between plain image and cipher image. Based on principles of cryptology, a good encryption algorithm should be sensitive to plaintext sufficiently. In general, attacker makes a slight change (e.g., modify only one pixel) for plaintext to find out some relationships between plain image and encrypted image. If tiny change of original image can bring great changes to cipher image, the effect of differential attack will be reduced. Sensitivity of the plaintext encryption algorithm can be quantified by NPCR (number

of pixels changing rate) and UACI (unified average changing intensity). They are defined as follows:

$$D(i, j) = \begin{cases} 0, & C_1(i, j) = C_2(i, j), \\ 1, & C_1(i, j) \neq C_2(i, j), \end{cases}$$

$$\text{NPCR} = \frac{1}{M \times N} \sum_{i=1}^{M} \sum_{j=1}^{N} D(i, j) \times 100\%,$$

UACI

$$= \frac{1}{255 \times M \times N} \sum_{i=1}^{M} \sum_{j=1}^{N} |C_1(i, j) - C_2(i, j)| \times 100\%,$$

(9)

where $C_1(i, j)$ and $C_2(i, j)$ indicate pixel value of two encryption images at location (i, j). M and N present number of rows and columns of the original image.

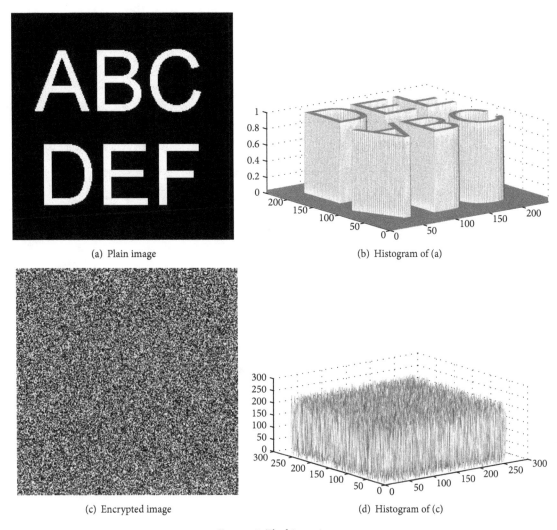

(a) Plain image

(b) Histogram of (a)

(c) Encrypted image

(d) Histogram of (c)

FIGURE 7: The binary image.

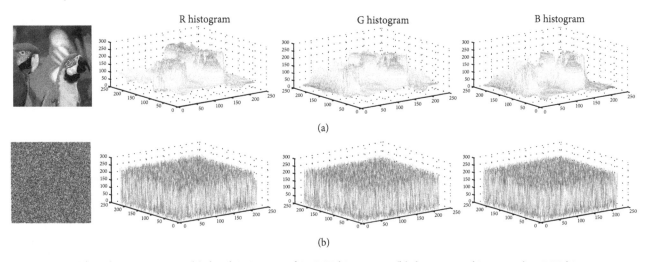

(a)

(b)

FIGURE 8: The color parrot image: (a) the plain image and its RGB histograms; (b) the encrypted image and its RGB histograms.

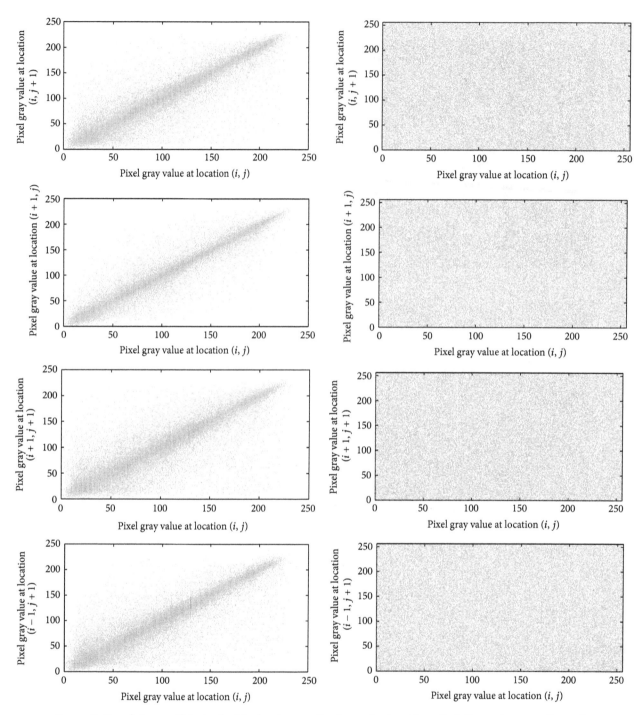

FIGURE 9: Correlation coefficients of original and encryption image: horizontal; vertical; diagonal; counterdiagonal.

The ideal expectations of NPCR and UACI can be calculated by the following simplified formulas:

$$\text{NPCR}_E = \left(1 - 2^{-n}\right) \times 100\%,$$

$$\text{UACI}_E = \frac{1}{2^{2n}} \frac{\sum_{i=1}^{2^n-1} i\,(i+1)}{2^n - 1} \times 100\% \qquad (10)$$

$$= \frac{1}{3}\left(1 + 2^{-n}\right) \times 100\%,$$

where n is the number of bits used to represent the different bit planes of an image. For gray scale image parameter $n = 8$ (8 bits per pixel). Hence expected NPCR and expected UACI are $\text{NPCR}_E = 99.6094\%$ (horizontal solid line in Figure 10(a)) and $\text{UACI}_E = 33.4635\%$ (horizontal solid line in Figure 10(b)), respectively. From the above formula we can see that relation $\text{NPCR}_E + 3\text{UACI}_E = 2$, so any value of the ideal expectations can illustrate the capability of algorithm to attack resisting plaintext.

TABLE 1: Correlation coefficient of different plain image and cipher image.

Plain image	Horizontal	Vertical	Diagonal	Counterdiagonal
Gray Lena				
Plain image	0.972953	0.970462	0.916925	0.938441
Encrypted image	-4.097226×10^{-5}	1.158832×10^{-4}	4.620716×10^{-5}	4.539076×10^{-4}
Encrypted image [19]	0.000417	-0.002048	-0.001554	
Encrypted image [20]	0.023	0.028	0.023	
Binary image				
Plain image	0.915352	0.922622291	0.868221	0.857255
Encrypted image	-3.811868×10^{-6}	-7.131676×10^{-4}	-9.372164×10^{-4}	-3.496642×10^{-4}
Color parrot				
R				
Plain image	0.945140	0.950725	0.919702	0.937272
Encrypted image	-0.001678	3.514572×10^{-4}	-9.329940×10^{-4}	-4.626904×10^{-5}
G				
Plain image	0.948746	0.941403	0.910118	0.929873
Encrypted image	-8.326210×10^{-4}	-4.626904×10^{-5}	1.484844×10^{-5}	6.479456×10^{-4}
B				
Plain image	0.956960	0.924891	0.924891	0.941023
Encrypted image	-7.902728×10^{-6}	1.1520873×10^{-4}	9.66501×10^{-4}	-1.766560×10^{-4}

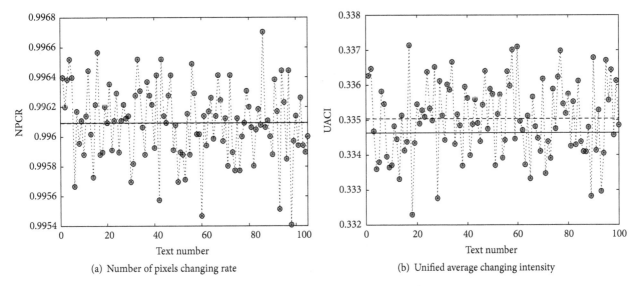

(a) Number of pixels changing rate

(b) Unified average changing intensity

FIGURE 10: Measured sensitivity of cipher image to plain image.

In this experiment, one hundred groups of Lena images are encrypted. In every group image, one is original image and the other is original image with only one changed pixel value (including border points and intermediate points, each time the changed amount is only 1). Then the test results are shown in Figure 10; every value fluctuates up and down near ideal value. The average values are $\overline{\text{NPCR}}$ = 99.6091% (horizontal dotted line in Figure 10(a)) and $\overline{\text{UACI}}$ = 33.5038% (horizontal dotted line in Figure 10(b)), respectively. Obviously the given encryption algorithm greatly improves the

sensitivity of plaintext, thereby enhancing capacity of resistance to differential attacks.

4.5. Key Sensitivity Test. Lena gray image is used to make experimental analysis. With right key, the decrypted image is clear and correct without any distortion in Figure 11(a). Decryption using keys with slight mismatch is performed so as to evaluate the key sensitivity. With a subtle change, the new key q_1 = 1.01000000001, and the decrypted image is incorrect, proposed in Figure 11(b). Subtle change of key

(a) Decrypted image

(b) Error decrypted image

FIGURE 11: The decrypted Lena image.

yields greatly different decrypted images. It is fully convincing that the algorithm has steady and superior secure performance in the first encryption round and will well resist differential attack.

4.6. Algorithmic Complexity Analyses. The time complexity of an algorithm quantifies the amount of time taken by an algorithm to run as a function of the size of the input to the problem. The time complexity is commonly described using the big-O notation, which suppresses multiplicative constants and lower order terms. Time complexity of generating key is $O(M \cdot N)$. The maximum complexity chaos and wavelet function map generate chaos sequences with time complexities $O(T_1^2)$ and $O(T_2^2)$, respectively. Pixel diffusion and substitution have the same time complexity $O(M \cdot N)$. At each step, the worst total time complexity is

$$O(M \times N) + O\left(T_1^2\right) + O\left(T_2^2\right) + O(M \times N)$$
$$= O(T),$$
(11)

where $T = \max\{M \cdot N, T_1^2, T_2^2\}$. T_1 and T_2 represent iterate numbers of maximum complexity chaos and wavelet function map, respectively.

5. Conclusion

This paper presents a novel fractional-order complex attractor with high fraction dimension, and the preprocessed chaotic sequence has good random character. Secret key is disturbed by every order and pixel value of plaintext; thus slight change of plaintext can bring vast differentness in encrypted image. Theoretical analysis and experimental results indicate that the encryption algorithm has some good characters, such as resistance for different attack, better information entropy, and low coefficient correlation. Comparing with some chaos-based algorithms, the estimated results demonstrate the strong capabilities and the effectiveness

of the proposed algorithm. The time complexity of the algorithm is proposed and an example is investigated to verify its validity and practicability. Our future works will focus on video encryption using fractional-order chaotic system.

Conflicts of Interest

The authors declare that they have no competing interests.

Acknowledgments

This research is supported by NNSFs of China (Grant no. 11501525), Science & Technology Innovation Talents in Universities of Henan Province (Grant no. 16HASTIT040), Teacher Education Curriculum Reform of Henan Province (Grant no. 2017-JSJYYB-190), Project of Youth Backbone Teachers of College and Universities in Henan Province (Grant nos. 2013GGJS-142 and 2015GGJS-179), and Basic & Advanced Technological Research Project of Henan Province (Grant no. 162300410261).

References

[1] B. Schneier, *Applied Cryptography: Protocols, Algorithms, and Source Code in C*, John Wiley & Sons, New York, NY, USA, 2nd edition, 1996.

[2] J. Daemen and V. Rijmen, *The Design of Rijndael: AES-The Advanced Encryption Standard*, Springer, Berlin, Germany, 2002.

[3] L. Kocarev, G. Jakimoski, T. Stojanovski, and U. Parlitz, "From chaotic maps to encryption schemes," in *Proceedings of the IEEE International Symposium on Circuits and Systems (ISCAS '98)*, pp. 514–517, IEEE, Monterey, Calif, USA, June 1998.

[4] C. E. Shannon, "Communication theory of secrecy systems," *The Bell System Technical Journal*, vol. 28, no. 4, pp. 656–715, 1949.

[5] N. K. Pareek, V. Patidar, and K. K. Sud, "Discrete chaotic cryptography using external key," *Physics Letters. A*, vol. 309, no. 1-2, pp. 75–82, 2003.

[6] X. Wang and L. Teng, "An image blocks encryption algorithm based on spatiotemporal chaos," *Nonlinear Dynamics. An International Journal of Nonlinear Dynamics and Chaos in Engineering Systems*, vol. 67, no. 1, pp. 365–371, 2012.

[7] S. Behnia, A. Akhshani, H. Mahmodi, and A. Akhavan, "A novel algorithm for image encryption based on mixture of chaotic maps," *Chaos, Solitons & Fractals*, vol. 35, no. 2, pp. 408–419, 2008.

[8] D. Xiao, X. Liao, and P. Wei, "Analysis and improvement of a chaos-based image encryption algorithm," *Chaos, Solitons & Fractals*, vol. 40, no. 5, pp. 2191–2199, 2009.

[9] X.-Y. Wang and X.-M. Bao, "A novel block cryptosystem based on the coupled chaotic map lattice," *Nonlinear Dynamics*, vol. 72, no. 4, pp. 707–715, 2013.

[10] G. Jakimoski and L. C. Kocarev, "Analysis of some recently proposed chaos-based encryption algorithms," *Physics Letters. A*, vol. 291, no. 6, pp. 381–384, 2001.

[11] S. Behnia, A. Akhshani, H. Mahmodi, and A. Akhavan, "A novel algorithm for image encryption based on mixture of chaotic maps," *Chaos, Solitons & Fractals*, vol. 35, no. 2, pp. 408–419, 2008.

[12] O. Mirzaei, M. Yaghoobi, and H. Irani, "A new image encryption method: parallel sub-image encryption with hyper chaos," *Nonlinear Dynamics*, vol. 67, no. 1, pp. 557–566, 2012.

[13] Y. Wang, K.-W. Wong, X. F. Liao, and G. R. Chen, "A new chaos-based fast image encryption algorithm," *Applied Soft Computing*, vol. 11, no. 1, pp. 514–522, 2011.

[14] A. I. Ismail, A. Mohammed, and D. Hossam, "A digital image encryption algorithm based a composition of two chaotic Wavelet function map," *International Journal of Network Security*, vol. 11, no. 1, pp. 1–10, 2010.

[15] R. Rhouma and S. Belghith, "Cryptanalysis of a new image encryption algorithm based on hyper-chaos," *Physics Letters, Section A: General, Atomic and Solid State Physics*, vol. 372, no. 38, pp. 5973–5978, 2008.

[16] X.-F. Li, K. E. Chlouverakis, and D.-L. Xu, "Nonlinear dynamics and circuit realization of a new chaotic flow: a variant of Lorenz, Chen and Lü," *Nonlinear Analysis. Real World Applications. An International Multidisciplinary Journal*, vol. 10, no. 4, pp. 2357–2368, 2009.

[17] J. F. Zhao, S. Y. Wang, Y. X. Chang, and X. F. Li, "A novel image encryption scheme based on an improper fractional-order chaotic system," *Nonlinear Dynamics*, vol. 80, no. 4, pp. 1721–1729, 2015.

[18] X. Wu, H. Wang, and H. Lu, "Modified generalized projective synchronization of a new fractional-order hyperchaotic system and its application to secure communication," *Nonlinear Analysis. Real World Applications*, vol. 13, no. 3, pp. 1441–1450, 2012.

[19] O. Mannai, R. Bechikh, H. Hermassi, R. Rhouma, and S. Belghith, "A new image encryption scheme based on a simple first-order time-delay system with appropriate nonlinearity," *Nonlinear Dynamics*, vol. 82, no. 1-2, pp. 107–117, 2015.

[20] Q. Liu, P.-Y. Li, M.-C. Zhang, Y.-X. Sui, and H.-J. Yang, "A novel image encryption algorithm based on chaos maps with Markov properties," *Communications in Nonlinear Science and Numerical Simulation*, vol. 20, no. 2, pp. 506–515, 2015.

[21] W.-B. Yu and X.-P. Wei, "Bifurcation diagram of a wavelet function," *Acta Physica Sinica*, vol. 55, no. 8, pp. 3969–3973, 2006.

20

Evolutionary Game Algorithm for Image Segmentation

Jin Zhong and Hao Wu

College of Computer Science, Hefei Normal University, Hefei 230601, China

Correspondence should be addressed to Jin Zhong; 952639879@qq.com

Academic Editor: Ping Feng Pai

The traditional two-dimensional Otsu algorithm only considers the limitations of the maximum variance of between-cluster variance of the target class and background class; this paper proposes evolutionary game improved algorithm. Algorithm takes full consideration of own pixel cohesion of target and background. It can meet the same of maximum variance of between-cluster variance. To ensure minimum threshold discriminant function within the variance, this kind of evolutionary game algorithm searching space for optimal solution is applied. Experimental results show that the method proposed in this paper makes the detail of segmentation image syllabify and has better antijamming capability; the improved genetic algorithm which used searching optimal solution has faster convergence speed and better global search capability.

1. Introduction

Image segmentation is the first step in image analysis, understanding, and pattern recognition, which is also one of the most important steps. Image segmentation is often used in medical image processing, such as nuclear magnetic resonance image, but it is also widely used in geographical space, environmental meteorology, and other fields. At present, there are many methods of image segmentation. Since each image has its own target and background, there is no general segmentation method for all images. Threshold segmentation is one of the most commonly used methods of image segmentation. Its essence is through the image histogram information to determine the threshold of image segmentation. Threshold segmentation method has the minimum error method, the maximum entropy method, and the maximum between-class variance methods. The traditional Otsu method is based on the statistical properties of the first-order histogram. It is widely used because of its simple algorithm and high real-time performance. Therefore, many literatures have improved the Otsu method and proposed a series of two-dimensional thresholding segmentation methods. In the literature [1], the statistical properties based on two-dimensional histogram are proposed to determine the

threshold value. It includes not only the gray information of the image pixels. But also the spatial information of the pixels. The effect is better than the one-dimensional Otsu method and has stronger antinoise performance. However, the traditional two-dimensional Otsu algorithm is complex and has long running time. And the effect of segmentation is vague on the contour. This paper is based on the evolutionary game algorithm of protein secretion mechanism. The two-dimensional thresholds are continuously optimized to obtain the two-dimensional thresholds that need to be image segmented. The algorithm has a good segmentation result and relatively good real-time performance and to a great extent solves the problem of local convergence.

2. The Principle of Two-Dimensional Maximum Between-Class Variance (Otsu) and Its Improvement

Otsu method Proposed by Japanese scholars in 1979 is the classic threshold segmentation methods. The basic idea is that it obtained the largest class difference of targets and background between the parties by image histogram statistics to determine the optimal threshold for image segmentation dynamically.

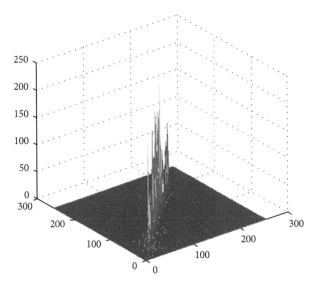

FIGURE 1: Two-dimensional histogram of an image histogram.

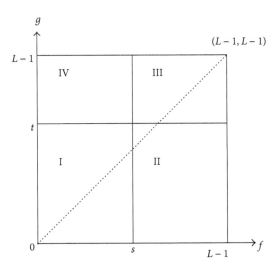

FIGURE 2: Two-dimensional projection plane.

2.1. Two-Dimensional Maximum Between-Class Variance Methods (Two-Dimensional Otsu Algorithm Method). Two-dimensional Otsu method is a two-dimensional correlation threshold method. The principle is as follows. Assume that the gray level of the original image f is L, size is $M * N$, and the value of each pixel in the image corresponds to a gray level. Scan the whole image. Calculating the neighborhood gray value of each pixel in the image, the size of the window neighborhood is usually odd. Get a smooth image g. Obviously g gray level is also L. Let m_{ij} be pixel value i of that image f. The number of pixels in the neighborhood gray value of j is the gray value and its binary group (i, j) of neighborhood pixels average. The result is two-dimensional histogram of point gray—neighborhood pixels gray. Then the two-dimensional joint probability density is

$$p_{ij} = \frac{m_{ij}}{M \times N}. \tag{1}$$

p_{ij} Meet $\sum_{i=0}^{L-1} \sum_{j=0}^{L-1} p_{ij} = 1$. It is $L * L$ matrix with size of $L * L$.

Figure 1 shows two-dimensional histogram of the schematic image. Figure 2 is the corresponding projection plane, f-axis represents the gray value of each pixel, and g-axis means neighborhood pixels' average of each pixel gray. Figures 1 and 2 show the peak of pixels intensity in the vicinity of the diagonal, because of the largest proportion of the target region and background region of the image. Distribution of the pixels gray level is uniform relatively.

Difference of point gray value and its neighborhood pixels gray average is not large, so they are concentrated near the diagonal.

Assume that value of the background and objectives in the image as two classes is C_b and C_o, respectively. (s, t) is two-dimensional threshold vector for images segmentation, and occurrence probability of the background is

$$\omega_b = p(C_b) = \sum_{i=0}^{s} \sum_{j=0}^{t} p_{ij} = \omega_b(s, t). \tag{2}$$

Occurrence probability of the target is

$$\omega_o = p(C_o) = \sum_{i=s+1}^{L-1} \sum_{j=t+1}^{L-1} p_{ij} = \omega_o(s, t). \tag{3}$$

In most cases, the occurrence probability of the noise and edge is very small. According to Figure 2, the probability of the regions II and IV can be regarded as 0 approximately.

According to Figure 2, the probability of the regions II and IV can be regarded as 0 approximately.

This can be considered as $\omega_b + \omega_o = 1$. The two classes of background and target correspond to the mean vector to be

$$\mu_b(s, t) = \left(\mu_{bi}, \mu_{bj}\right)^T$$

$$= \left[\frac{\sum_{i=0}^{s} \sum_{j=0}^{t} i p_{ij}}{\omega_b(s, t)}, \frac{\sum_{i=0}^{s} \sum_{j=0}^{t} j p_{ij}}{\omega_b(s, t)}\right]^T,$$

$$\mu_o(s, t) = \left(\mu_{oi}, \mu_{oj}\right)^T \tag{4}$$

$$= \left[\frac{\sum_{i=s+1}^{L-1} \sum_{j=t+1}^{L-1} i p_{ij}}{\omega_o(s, t)}, \frac{\sum_{i=s+1}^{L-1} \sum_{j=t+1}^{L-1} j p_{ij}}{\omega_o(s, t)}\right]^T.$$

Ensemble average is

$$\mu_{\text{all}}(s, t) = \left(\mu_{\text{all}i}, \mu_{\text{all}j}\right)^T = \left[\sum_{i=0}^{L-1} \sum_{j=0}^{L-1} i p_{ij}, \sum_{i=0}^{L-1} \sum_{j=0}^{L-1} j p_{ij}\right]^T. \tag{5}$$

Define discrete matrix

$$\sigma_B = \omega_b \left[\left(\mu_b - \mu_{\text{all}}\right)\left(\mu_b - \mu_{\text{all}}\right)^T\right]$$

$$+ \omega_o \left[\left(\mu_o - \mu_{\text{all}}\right)\left(\mu_o - \mu_{\text{all}}\right)^T\right]. \tag{6}$$

The trace of the discrete matrix class as the measure of dispersion of the background and objectives is

$$\mathrm{tr}\left(\sigma_B\right) = \omega_b \left[\left(\mu_{bi} - \mu_{\mathrm{all}i}\right)^2 + \left(\mu_{bj} - \mu_{\mathrm{all}j}\right)^2\right]$$
$$+ \omega_o \left[\left(\mu_{oi} - \mu_{\mathrm{all}i}\right)^2 + \left(\mu_{oj} - \mu_{\mathrm{all}j}\right)^2\right]. \tag{7}$$

When the trace of the dispersion matrix is the maximum value, we obtain the optimal segmentation threshold

$$\mathrm{tr}\left(s_{(s^*,t^*)}\right) = \max\left(\mathrm{tr}\left(s_{(s,t)}\right)\right), \quad 0 \le s, t \le L-1. \tag{8}$$

2.2. Two-Dimensional Maximum of Between-Class Variance Method. In the traditional two-dimensional Otsu method, the threshold discriminant function (trace of the dispersion matrix) takes into account only the variance of the target class and the background class; that is, the larger the variance between classes, the better the segmentation effect. However, the traditional two-dimensional Otsu algorithm does not take into account its own classified information of each type of pixels of target class and background class, that is, considering the cohesion within the classes. So, in this paper, the measure of the dispersion within the class is also introduced to the recognition function of threshold. This can reflect the efficiency of the overall classification, specifically, the following: two classes c_o and c_b existing in two-dimensional histogram and calculated variance of the center of the target class μ_o. The center of the background class μ_o with (i, j) is from each gray value and its neighborhood pixels average separately:

$$d_o = \frac{\sum_{i=0}^{s} \sum_{j=0}^{t} \left[\left(i - \mu_{oi}\right)^2 + \left(j - \mu_{oj}\right)^2\right] p_{ij}}{\omega_o},$$
$$\tag{9}$$
$$d_b = \frac{\sum_{i=s+1}^{L-1} \sum_{j=t+1}^{L-1} \left[\left(i - \mu_{bi}\right)^2 + \left(j - \mu_{bj}\right)^2\right] p_{ij}}{\omega_b}.$$

Obviously, the smaller the value of the variance of the target class and background class, the better its cohesion and the better the segmentation effect.

The definition of the measure of dispersion within class is

$$\rho_s = \omega_o d_o + \omega_b d_b. \tag{10}$$

Obviously, ρ_s is required smaller value, and cohesion within the classes gets the better effect.

We are considering the between-class variance and within the class variance. The threshold makes between-class variance the largest, and, at the same time, within the class variance meets the minimum value. A new discriminant function of the threshold is used in this article as follows:

$$\phi_s(s, t) = \frac{\omega_o \times \omega_b \times \mathrm{tr}\left(\sigma_B\right)}{\rho_s}. \tag{11}$$

Molecular $\omega_o \times \omega_b \times \mathrm{tr}(\sigma_B)$ shows the property of between-class variance and denominator ρ_s performance within the class cohesion; when $\phi_s(s, t)$ obtains the maximum value, effect of the image segment is best.

That is, when value of the discriminant function is the maximum, (s', t') is the best threshold for the segmentation threshold.

Now, the target class and background class are separated greatly, and the cohesion of target class and background is the best kind.

The optimal threshold vector to achieve the gray image banalization is got as follows:

$$f(i, j) = \begin{cases} 0, & i < t, j < s, \\ \\ 1, & i \ge t \text{ or } j \ge s. \end{cases} \tag{12}$$

3. Threshold Vector Evolutionary Game Algorithm

In this paper, the optimal solution of the threshold vector can be obtained by the evolutionary game algorithm. The new generation of each generation of the algorithm is randomly paired and repeated. Each individual is to optimize their objective function to the optimal value [2–8]. The target value is determined by the evolutionary game matrix. Set the objective function as $f_1(x, y)$, $f_2(x, y)$. The objective function has two mixed variables x and y. The game structure of evolutionary algorithm is designed as follows:

$$\begin{bmatrix} \text{Agent} & \text{Fitness} \\ V_1 = (x_1, y_1) & F_1 \\ V_2 = (x_2, y_2) & F_2 \\ \vdots & \vdots \\ V_k = (x_k, y_k) & F_k \end{bmatrix} \begin{array}{c} \text{Plays} \\ \leftrightarrow \\ \leftrightarrow \\ \vdots \\ \leftrightarrow \end{array} \begin{bmatrix} \text{Agent} & \text{Fitness} \\ G_1 = (x_1', y_1') & F_1' \\ G_2 = (x_2', y_2') & F_2' \\ \vdots & \vdots \\ G_k = (x_k', y_k') & F_k' \end{bmatrix}. \tag{13}$$

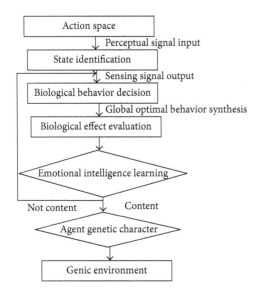

FIGURE 3: Architecture of population for the proliferation of evolution PEP.

The fitness of F_i is determined by the game matrix, $i = 1, 2, \ldots, k$. For the participants of the two random pairs of the game through the evolution game, the G_i of each participant's game payoff is the difference between the two objective functions:

$$
\begin{aligned}
G_1\left(V_i, V_i'\right) &= G_1\left(\left(x_i, y_i\right), \left(x_i', y_i'\right)\right) \\
&= f_1\left(x_i, y_i\right) - f_2\left(x_i', y_i'\right), \\
G_2\left(V_i, V_i'\right) &= G_2\left(\left(x_i, y_i\right), \left(x_i', y_i'\right)\right) \\
&= f_1\left(x_i', y_i'\right) - f_2\left(x_i, y_i\right).
\end{aligned}
\tag{14}
$$

According to this value, the fitness of each objective function is calculated by

$$
\begin{aligned}
F_i &= 100 \times \frac{G_1\left(\left(x_i, y_i\right), \left(x_i', y_i'\right)\right)}{\omega}, \\
F_i' &= 100 \times \frac{G_2\left(\left(x_i, y_i\right), \left(x_i', y_i'\right)\right)}{\omega}.
\end{aligned}
\tag{15}
$$

In the formula, a is B or C fitness scalar. ω is the maximum value of $G_k((x_i, y_i), (x_i', y_i'))$. Each generation of the subgame of the evolutionary algorithm is based on the fitness value.

3.1. Evolutionary Game Algorithm Based on Protein Secretion Mechanism.
Drawing on the main signal hypothesis in recent years, that is, the cooperative translation of protein secretion process [9], in this paper, based on the self-organization evolutionary game algorithm of protein secretion mechanism behavior, we use the method of signal peptide in the cell matrix to guide the synthesis of secreted protein synthesis as an algorithm to realize [9], as shown in Figure 3.

It is assumed that the state of the protein secretion system is discrete and the state, behavior, and emotional intelligence are represented by a collection of three-dimensional

sequences, represented by the I, I_{at}, I_t. The game matrix is described as

$$
\begin{bmatrix} I_{at}(t+1) \\ I_t \\ 1 \end{bmatrix} = \begin{bmatrix} I_{11} & -\omega & I_{13} \\ 1 & 0 & 0 \\ 0 & 0 & 1 \end{bmatrix} = \begin{bmatrix} I_t \\ I_{at}(t-1) \\ 1 \end{bmatrix}.
\tag{16}
$$

The line number of the matrix represents the behavior sequence. The value of the element of the matrix represents the corresponding behavioral states corresponding to the emotional intelligence value. I_{at} is expressed sentiment value a of behavior execution under state k. I_t represents the state of t intelligence. The high level regulation of protein secretion is achieved by evaluating the state of the system and by feedback learning based on the results of the evaluation. Here is the selection behavior of the algorithm steps in state recognition. Hypothetical selection behavior steps are as follows:

(1) After the behavior evolution of the state recognition, the state action selection rule is described by the formula, and all possible behaviors in the state can be represented by the "∗":

$$
A = A\text{function}\left(I_{*t}\right) = \max\left(I_{*t}\right).
\tag{17}
$$

(2) The rules of evaluation rules of emotional intelligence of the state of emotional intelligence factor are

$$
I_t = I\text{function}\left(I_{*t}\right) = \max\left(I_{*t}\right).
\tag{18}
$$

(3) The learning rules of emotional intelligence are described in formula, in which ω represents learning rate:

$$
\begin{aligned}
\left(I_{*t}(t+1)\right) &= U\text{function} = \left(I_*, I_{*t}\right) \\
&= (1-\omega)\, I_{*t}(t) + \omega I_{*t}.
\end{aligned}
\tag{19}
$$

Define the end condition of an emotional learning after the end of emotional learning. The self-adaptation of the subject to the behavioral environment is preserved in the protein secretion environment. These adaptive results are passed to the individual through the output of the protein secretion mechanism. Compared to the next generation, the next generation has a more adaptive behavior environment. Based on the mechanism of protein secretion, this paper designs the self-organization evolutionary game algorithm, as shown in Figure 4.

Here is the solving process for specific threshold vector.

(1) Coding. Gray level of an image is from 0 to 255, encoding binary. For one-dimensional Otsu method, the threshold is only one which can be represented by 8-bit binary.

The two-dimensional Otsu method has two threshold segmentations, so we use 16-bit (bit string length) method to achieve a binary encoding, that is $(x_0, x_1, \ldots, x_7, x_8, \ldots, x_{15})$, where top eight represent segmentation threshold s, and after eight they represent segmentation threshold t.

According to the improved two-dimensional histogram strategy proposed in Section 2.2 a strategy is that, in this test, N is 30, so $0 + 30 \leq s, t \leq 255 - 30$; that is, $0 + 30 \leq s, t \leq 255 - 30$.

(2) Initialization. Let the initial population be of popsize. Because the optimization parameters are two-dimensional

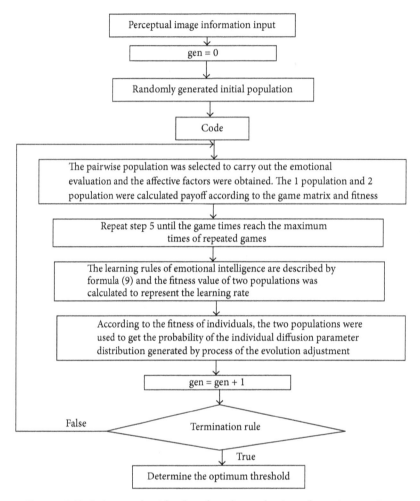

FIGURE 4: Evolutionary algorithm based on the mechanism of protein secretion.

threshold, so Initialize can randomly generate a pop size line, 16-column matrix by random number generator.

The following operations are for the targeted population initialized. Here process of decoding needs to take into account the range of s and t.

(3) Fitness Function. According to the analysis of Section 2.2, this new the threshold discriminant function $\phi_s(s, t)$ is the fitness function, and when $\phi_s(s, t)$ obtains the maximum, value of the parameters s and t is the optimal threshold for image segmentation.

(4) Select. The traditional genetic algorithm used in the roulette selection method usually leads to the loss of diversity of the population, and genetic algorithm will prematurely lose its evolutionary capacity.

This article takes the choice explained here. First of all, to retain some of the individuals with the highest fitness value of the parent directly into the offspring, for some suboptimal individuals after a certain mutation the excellent individuals can also enter the progeny; that is, through the evolution of different populations of the parent population, we get offspring.

This way not only ensures the outstanding individuals of the population structure into the next generation, but also ensures the diversity of the population. This makes the probability of having similar individual in the population reduced, increases the following crossover and mutation operation efficiency, and improves the convergence of the algorithm.

(5) Crossover. Crossover operation is the unique original characteristics [10] of genetic algorithm of evolutionary algorithm.

There is a problem about the traditional crossover operator; when Stocks evolve to the local optimum, many individuals are very similar, which is "close."

Cross-string of individuals is the same largely; the role of crossover operation does not work.

In order to avoid "close" cross, in this article, we selected individuals randomly for crossover Hamming distance judgments on the mating pool.

If we select the individual on the Hamming distance $H(s_i, s_j) \geq \lambda$ ($0 \leq \lambda \leq l$), according to the original the probability, we operate cross-cross.

TABLE 1: The threshold obtained from several algorithms.

Image	One-dimensional Otsu method is based on the traditional standards of GA	Threshold Method of literature 3	Traditional two-dimensional Otsu standards-based GA	This method
Horse	96	$(83, 145)$	$(83, 146)$	$(66, 143)$
Airplane	174	$(130, 209)$	$(131, 204)$	$(51, 218)$
Tank	116	$(175, 87)$	$(173, 85)$	$(34, 200)$

Conversely, if $H(s_i, s_j) < \lambda$, then we determine that the individuals are "close" and replace one of the individuals, until the conditions are met or all individuals in the group are tried to be replaced.

(6) Variation. The mutation operation in traditional genetic algorithm is based on a certain mutation probability for values of each individual bit string, that is, 1 to 0 or 0 to 1. Typically, the probability of mutation is relatively small. In the implementation process, some individuals could not have taken place to mutate, wasting a lot of computing resources. This article uses a dynamic mutation probability in order to increase the diversity of the population. The basic idea is to determine whether the current population is or not "mature"; if it is, then it mutates on a larger probability; otherwise, according to conventional mutation probability, $f_{\max}$ is defined as the best current population fitness; f_{avi} is the current population average fitness; if $kf_{\max} \geq f_{\mathrm{avi}}$, where $(0.5 \leq k \leq 1)$, as intensive factor, then our algorithm determines that the population does not "premature" and mutate on conventional probability. On the contrary, if the population is "premature" and mutates on much bigger than conventional probability to all individuals, it results in more individuals into the next generation, in order to ensure population out of local convergence.

4. Simulations and Analysis of Experiments

Image segmentation tests were carried out by the proposed image segmentation, that is, two-dimensional Otsu method based on improved genetic algorithm. We compared between segmentation of horse picture, airplane image, and tank image by the one-dimensional Otsu method, the traditional two-dimensional Otsu method, improved two-dimensional Otsu method based on the traditional GA, and the proposed algorithm.

Experiment hardware platform is 2.6 GHz Pentium 4, Capacity of memory is 512 MB, and operating environment is Matlab 7.0.

Various experimental parameters are set as follows

(1) one-dimensional Otsu method using the standard threshold of GA optimization, size of population: 10; number of iterations: 15; length of code: 8; probability of crossover: 0.7; probability of mutation: 0.05;

(2) traditional neighborhood of two-dimensional Otsu method, size of window neighborhood: 3;

(3) this method adopting an improved two-dimensional Otsu method and the improved GA, size of window neighborhood: 3; size of population: 10; number of iterations: 150; length of code: 16; probability of crossover: 0.7; Hamming discriminant distance: 2; larger mutation probability: 0.2; small mutation probability: 0.01; intensive factor: 0.8.

Various types of experimentally derived physical threshold are in Table 1, and result of one-dimensional Otsu method, traditional Otsu method based on the standards of GA, and this method is the average obtained for 30 independent experiments.

In the actual image acquisition process, images often will be affected by the external environment; the image will contain all kinds of noise; in the following example, horse pictures added a variety of noise; then this method deals with the results of noise.

Running time of one-dimensional Otsu method is shorter; however, from Figures 5, 6, and 7, the segmentation results show that traditional two-dimensional Otsu algorithm and out method are better; many details are not separated out, especially in Figure 6; the segmentation of the target aircraft is more accurate.

Figures 8, 9, and 10 show that various types of noise have a great impact on results of all one-dimensional Otsu algorithm. Its effects and antijamming capability are poorer than this method.

The traditional two-dimensional Otsu method is better than the one-dimensional Otsu method; the segmentation of images containing noise removal can be seen very clearly.

But its calculation is based on exponential growth because the algorithm has a double loop, a total of calculation times needed are $M \times N$, that is, $\mathrm{tr}(s_{(s,t)})$, and $M \times N$ is the total pixel number of times.

Every time it cumulates $s \times t + (L - s) \times (L - t)$ points; therefore, the algorithm complexity is $o(L^4)$.

This calculation is very large, and in practice such a long running time is unacceptable.

Relative to the one-dimensional Otsu method, the traditional two-dimensional Otsu method is the sacrifice of time in exchange for consideration of segmentation accuracy.

In this paper, an improved GA optimizes the threshold parameters; it is clear that the convergence for the calculation of $\phi_s(s, t)$ is product of the number of generations and size of population; Table 2 shows that the average convergence times of generation algebra of our algorithm are 15; therefore, it is also necessary to calculate $15 \times 10 = 150$ times. At the same

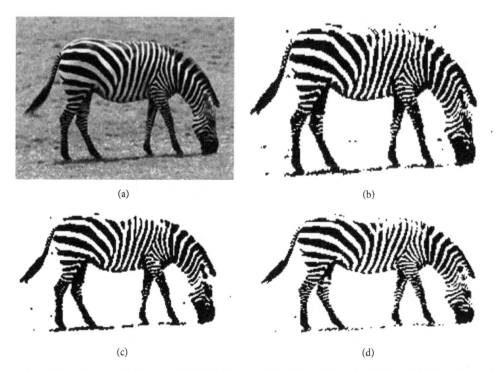

FIGURE 5: Segmentation of horse image. (a) Horse original. (b) Segmentation of one-dimensional Otsu. (c) The traditional two-dimensional Otsu method. (d) Our algorithm.

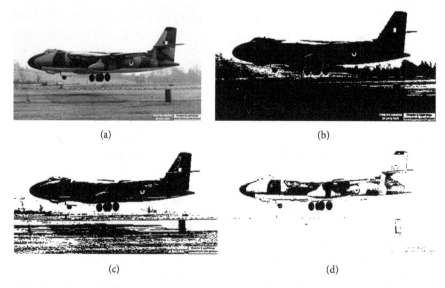

FIGURE 6: Segmentation of airplane image. (a) Horse original. (b) Segmentation of one-dimensional Otsu. (c) The traditional two-dimensional Otsu method. (d) Our algorithm.

time, it also needs to cumulate $s \times t + (L - s) \times (L - t)$ points. Thus, time complexity of the algorithm is $o(L^2)$.

For an image, the traditional Otsu method requires 256×256 calculating of $\text{tr}(s_{(s,t)})$. Out algorithm only needs to calculate 150 times of $\phi_s(s, t)$, 437 times faster.

In fact, the improved GA algorithm in this paper accelerates the convergence process; it is basically the average convergence times to twenty, saving the running time of this

algorithm greatly and avoiding local convergence problems from the traditional GA algorithm.

In order to verify that the improved GA has better convergence, the improved two-dimensional Otsu method also used standard GA parameters to do experiment and compared with our method.

Figures 11, 12, and 13 are the evolution curve of two algorithms about horse image, dragon image, and tank image, respectively.

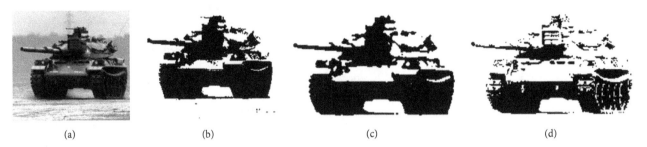

FIGURE 7: Segmentation of tank image. (a) Horse original. (b) Segmentation of one-dimensional Otsu. (c) The traditional two-dimensional Otsu method. (d) Our algorithm.

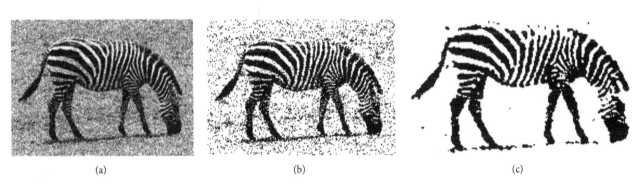

FIGURE 8: Horse image (0.02-degree encryption salt and pepper noise). (a) Original. (b) The results of one-dimensional Otsu method. (c) The results of our algorithm.

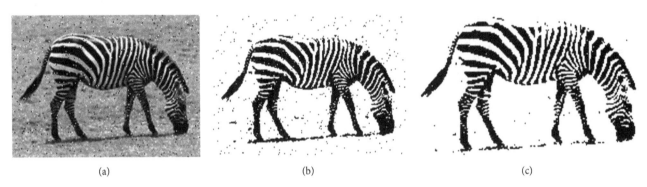

FIGURE 9: Horse image (mean of Gaussian noise is 0 and variance is 0.02). (a) Original. (b) The results of one-dimensional Otsu method. (c) The results of our algorithm.

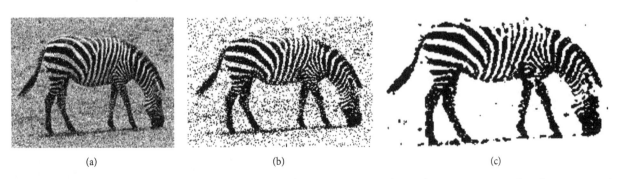

FIGURE 10: Horse image (mixed mean of Gaussian noise is 0 and variance is 0.02 and 0.02-degree encryption salt and pepper noise). (a) Original. (b) The results of one-dimensional Otsu method. (c) The results of our algorithm.

TABLE 2: Comparison of the running time of several two-dimensional Otsu algorithms.

Photo (specification)	Method of literature 3		The traditional method based on the traditional GA Otsu			This method (improved Otsu + improved GA)		
	Time complexity	Running time (/s)	Running time	The average convergence times of 30 times	The average convergence times of 30 times (/s)	Time multiplexing complex degree	The average convergence times of 30 times	The average convergence times of 30 times (/s)
Horse (158 * 228)	$o(L^4)$	6193	$o(L^2)$	137	14.3424	$o(L^2)$	15	4.1222
Airplane (230 * 500)	$o(L^4)$	8537	$o(L^2)$	113	17.4219	$o(L^2)$	14	5.9717
Tank (212 * 178)	$o(L^4)$	6723	$o(L^2)$	129	14.5323	$o(L^2)$	11	4.3312

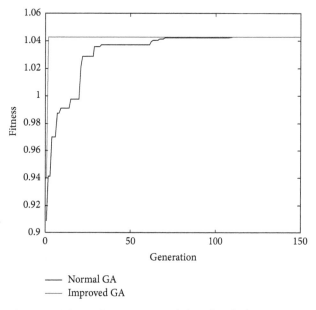

FIGURE 11: Two evolutionary curves' algorithm for horse image.

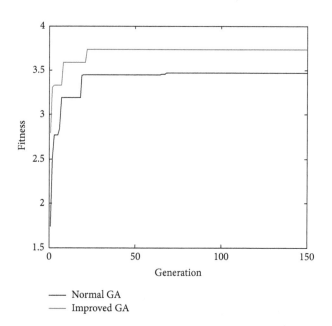

FIGURE 13: Two evolutionary curves' algorithm for tank image.

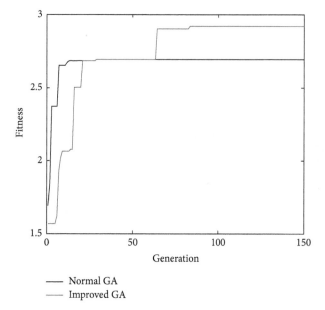

FIGURE 12: Two evolutionary curves' algorithm for airplane image.

According to Figures 11 and 12, we can get result of the improved GA algorithm and the traditional GA algorithm. In Figure 11, convergence times of the improved GA are 4, whereas convergence times of the traditional GA algorithm are 87; they have been the largest fitness value.

In Figure 12, convergence times of the improved GA is 22, convergence times of the traditional GA is 78, and the traditional GA get into a premature local convergence and did not reach maximum fitness value.

In Figure 13, convergence times of the improved GA is 13, convergence times of the traditional GA is 61, and there is no maximum fitness value.

Therefore, the improved genetic algorithm GA obtained the optimal threshold that is clearly better than the optimal solution traditional genetic algorithm obtained, but also it is closer to the optimal solution and overcomes "premature" problem from the traditional GA algorithm largely.

The horse figure, dragon figure, and tank image show the comparative results of running time of several algorithms from 30 figures of independent experiments, shown in Table 2.

Results of experimental show that the proposed improved genetic algorithm based optimization method to improve two-dimensional Otsu threshold vector is effective; it can both search the global optimal vector and get the cost of a very small amount of time, showing the higher robustness and real-time of algorithm.

5. Conclusion

The paper points out that the traditional two-dimensional Otsu method only considered deficiency of the largest variance between classes and proposes the threshold discriminant function which not only can reflect variance between classes, but also can reflect the variance within classes, and it obtained better segmentation than the traditional two-dimensional Otsu, while the genetic algorithm improved by this method has better population diversity and global search capacity.

Results of simulation show that the proposed method not only has better and faster segmentation effect, but also has some practical value.

Through a lot of pictures of other experiments, the results are generally better than the traditional two-dimensional Otsu method.

However, the relative algorithm GA based on the traditional standard two-dimensional Otsu method already has a very good time performance, but there are still some obstacles, because, in real-time applications, its running time is more than 4 seconds. So how to reduce running time and do not affect the segmentation result is an issue worthy of consideration.

Conflicts of Interest

There are no conflicts of interest in the publication of this article.

Acknowledgments

The authors acknowledge Anhui Province Commission, a major teaching reform project (2016jyxm0844). This paper is supported by the Natural Science Foundation of Anhui province (1708085qf157) and the Hefei Normal University Scientific Research Team (2015TD03).

References

[1] R. C. Gonzalez, *Digital Image Processing (2nd) [M]*, Publishing House of Electronics Industry, Beijing, China, 2003.

[2] Y. Min, *Digital Image Processing [M]*, China Machine Press, Beijing, China, 2006.

[3] J. Z. Liu and W. Q. Li, "Automatic thresholding using the otsu algorithm based on the two-dimensional gray image," *Journal of Electrical and Computer Engineering*, vol. 19, no. 1, pp. 101–105, 1993.

[4] K. Wei, T. Zhang, X. Shen, and J. Liu, "An improved threshold selection algorithm based on particle swarm optimization for image segmentation," in *Proceedings of the 3rd International Conference on Natural Computation, ICNC 2007*, pp. 591–594, August 2007.

[5] T. L. Huang and X. Bai, "An improved algorithm for medical image segmentation," in *Proceedings of the 2nd International Conference on Genetic and Evolutionary Computing, WGEC 2008*, pp. 289–292, September 2008.

[6] P. K. Sahoo and G. Arora, "A thresholding method based on two-dimensional Renyi's entropy," *Pattern Recognition*, vol. 37, no. 6, pp. 1149–1161, 2004.

[7] Q. Chang, L. Wang, C. Xing, and A. Liy, "Image threshold selection based on genetic algorithm," *Computer Engineering and Application*, vol. 38, no. 22, pp. 35–37, 2002.

[8] S. M. Bhandarkar and H. Zhang, "Image segmentation using evolutionary computation," *IEEE Transactions on Evolutionary Computation*, vol. 3, no. 1, pp. 1–21, 1999.

[9] W. Peizhen, D. Peiming, and C. Weinan, "A new mixed genetic algorithm for multilevel thresholding," *Chinese Journal of Image And Graphics*, vol. 5, no. 1, pp. 44–47, 2000.

[10] M. Q. Li, J. S. Kou, D. Lin, and S. Li, *Basic Theory and Application of Genetic Algorithm*, Science Press, Beijing, China, 2002.

21

Dynamically Predicting the Quality of Service: Batch, Online, and Hybrid Algorithms

Ya Chen and Zhong-an Jiang

University of Science and Technology, Beijing 100080, China

Correspondence should be addressed to Zhong-an Jiang; jza1963@263.net

Academic Editor: Jar Ferr Yang

This paper studies the problem of dynamically modeling the quality of web service. The philosophy of designing practical web service recommender systems is delivered in this paper. A general system architecture for such systems continuously collects the user-service invocation records and includes both an online training module and an offline training module for quality prediction. In addition, we introduce matrix factorization-based online and offline training algorithms based on the gradient descent algorithms and demonstrate the fitness of this online/offline algorithm framework to the proposed architecture. The superiority of the proposed model is confirmed by empirical studies on a real-life quality of web service data set and comparisons with existing web service recommendation algorithms.

1. Introduction

The quality of service or QoS has been exploited by many application domains as an importance metric for users to evaluate the quality of provided services. Especially when many providers offer similar services at the same time, this metric can be taken to identify reliable ones. The quality of service can be collected after user using a service and a user-service QoS matrix can be generated with these values. Once we have such a matrix, existing recommendation approaches [1–4] can be exploited to generate predictions for the missing values of the user-service QoS matrix. Because the QoS value is always related to the temporal/spatial information [5–7], other contextual information [8] has been used for improving the accuracy of QoS prediction. As the user-service QoS matrix is dynamic and increases with the usage of service, the model learned before may not be suitable for the current state. This fact requires us to rebuild a model after an increasing of data for a better model. Usually, it takes a long time when the user-service QoS matrix is huge. A dynamic model is needed for handling dynamics of available data.

As a concrete example, we will focus on one type of QoS prediction problem, the quality of web service prediction, to demonstrate the dynamic model of QoS prediction. Web service and APIs are very useful resources when developing Mashup applications. For example, ProgrammableWeb (ProgrammableWeb can be accessed at https://www.programmableweb.com/) provides over 11,000 collected web services and 12,000 open APIs [9]. The increasing number of services and APIs makes the effort of finding reliable services more difficult.

Since it is impossible for service users to make selection decisions without prior knowledge about service candidates, it is vital for researchers to develop quality of service (QoS) prediction approaches [10, 11] or service recommender systems [12, 13] to assist users or programs when dynamically choosing their services. In general, the problem of predicting the quality of web services may be abstracted in terms of a collection of services, a collection of users (programs), and each user's experiences (quality of services) on a subset of services. The objective for developing a QoS predicting system is to decide what level of quality a service can bring to a particular user or to a typical user.

Existing recommendation approaches have been applied in the web service discovering domain, for example, user-based collaborative filtering (CF) [14], item-base CF [15], and hybrid CF [16]. These web service and API prediction systems assume that all user-service invocation records are collected and the trained model will not change with the accumulation

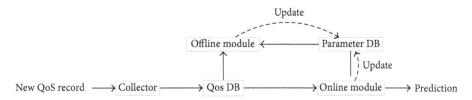

FIGURE 1: QoS prediction system architecture.

of new QoS value arriving to the system. In practice, this assumption is not always true and the QoS pattern may vary. A robust web service QoS prediction system should handle the dynamics. The training set for a batch algorithm or an offline algorithm must be available *a priori* and an online algorithm is required to update the learned model instead of retraining the whole model from scratch.

As mentioned before, context information is one of the most important information for QoS prediction, in web service or API recommendation scenarios; context-aware recommendation [17–20] is used to characterize the correlation between users' dynamic preferences and their contexts. Promising performance improvement has been achieved by these context-aware systems. However, these models can only handle the static data and the pattern dynamics are not able to be captured by these approaches.

Recently, with the success of matrix factorization and tensor factorization techniques on recommender systems [21–23], they have also been introduced to the web service QoS prediction domain [24]. The basic idea is to use a tensor factorization-based approach to evaluate time-aware personalized QoS values. These studies achieve performance improvements in comparison with traditional models; however, the temporal dynamics of user-service invocation records is not considered. We advocate that a 3-way tensor does not explicitly carry the necessary dynamics of user-side and service-side properties that may impact the web service quality. Therefore, we propose a timeSVD [25] based approach to characterize the dynamics of property change over time.

In this paper, we propose a general architecture and dynamic model which can update the learned model only based on the change of QoS values. Specifically, we design a hybrid model which jointly combines the online and offline algorithms. Such system is capable of monitoring the change of QoS values and adapting itself in real-time to the new arriving data. We conduct experiments on some real-life data and the empirical study confirms the effectiveness and efficiency of the proposed model.

The remainder of this paper is organized as follows. Section 2 gives the architecture of QoS prediction systems monitoring user-service invocation streams and incrementally predicting the quality of services. Section 3 presents a dynamic quality of service model and derives online, offline, and hybrid predictors resulting from a stochastic gradient descent algorithm. Section 4 presents an experimental evaluation of our approach. This paper ends with some discussion and brief conclusions.

2. Architecture

For a system which is capable of characterizing the dynamics of monitored services, one needs to instantaneously update the system parameters based on the newly available data. This fact indicates the most important feature of this system is the computing complexity. With the increasing of available data, it is impossible for a system to learn the model from all the collected historical data. This requires a system structure to simultaneously contain both offline and online training functions. The offline training module trains the model based on all available data. So the time cost of executing this part is relatively high. The offline training model updates the previously trained model parameters. Although training an online model is more efficient than the offline training module, the model accuracy may be lower than the offline model. When we collect enough data or the system is not busy, we can execute the batch algorithm or the offline model to improve the model accuracy of the online model. Note that we only keep one set of model parameters in the system; both online algorithm and offline algorithm will modify the same model. This requires us to design such an algorithm that supports this requirement. Figure 1 illustrates the architecture design of our system. Five components are involved in this architecture. Collector receives the new arrival QoS record and stores the incoming message to QoS DB. Then the online module, usually implemented by a light-weight algorithm, takes the existing model parameters from parameter DB and updates the parameters based on online algorithms. The updated parameters are then transferred to the parameter DB. The parameter DB stores the model parameters of the running systems. Online trainer and offline trainer will all start their process based on the model parameters saved in the parameter DB. If new prediction request comes, the online module will be executed to generate predictions based on the most recent learned model parameters. The offline module, which implements time costly training algorithms, is only invoked when the system is free loaded or has sufficient computation resources. The training of offline module also starts from the most recent model parameters and the updated ones are also saved in the parameter DB.

It can be seen that this architecture design is generic and can be suitable for many other QoS prediction scenarios based on user experiences. This fact shows the applicability of our proposed architecture.

From the architecture design, we can find that a profound algorithm framework is demanded to support the online and offline module together. That means that the online training algorithm is, on the one hand, capable of performing training "incrementally" based on the existing training results and, on the other hand, does so at a quick rate. In the next section, we introduce an algorithm framework based on stochastic gradient descent which can be transferred into online and also offline way.

3. Time-Dependent Quality of Web Service Prediction Model

In this section, we propose the formulation of the time-dependent quality of web service problem and a unified QoS prediction model.

3.1. Problem Statement. We use $\mathcal{I}$ and $\mathcal{U}$ to denote, respectively, the collection of all observed web services and the set of all users. We denote by $r_{u,i}$ the quality of web service i experienced by user u and by $r_{u,i}$ the estimate of this quantity is denoted by $\hat{r}_{u,i}$. In order to capture the temporal dynamics of the quality of a web service, time is slotted into intervals, and we use variable t to index the time interval in which the service is invoked. Then the quantities $r_{u,i}$ and $\hat{r}_{u,i}$ are augmented to the form of $r_{u,i,t}$ and $\hat{r}_{u,i,t}$ correspondingly. Let $\mathcal{T}$ denote the time index set $\{1, 2, \ldots, T\}$ for some positive integer T. The set of all observed $\{r_{u,i,t}\}$ across all users $\mathcal{U}$, all services $\mathcal{I}$, and all time-slots $\mathcal{T}$ is denoted by $\mathcal{R}$. We note that it is not the case that, for every $(u, i, t) \in \mathcal{U} \times \mathcal{I} \times \mathcal{T}$, service quality $r_{u,i,t}$ is observed; in fact for a quite significant fraction of $\mathcal{U} \times \mathcal{I} \times \mathcal{T}$, service quality is not observed. We denote by $\mathcal{K}$ the set of all (u, i, t) triples for which $r_{u,i,t}$ is not observed.

Let $\mathcal{H} \subset \mathcal{U} \times \mathcal{I} \times \mathcal{T}$ be a subset of (u, i, t) triples for which $r_{u,i,t}$ is not observed. The problem of predicting the quality of web services can then be phrased as for each $(u, i, t) \in \mathcal{H}$ obtaining an estimate $\hat{r}_{u,i,t}$ of $r_{u,i,t}$ based on $\mathcal{R}$. We note that $\mathcal{H}$ does not necessarily contain all unobserved (u, i, t) triples. The typical scenario is that it contains only the ones of practical interest. For example, if T indexes the present time-slot, $\mathcal{H}$ is the set of all (u, i, T) triples for which $r_{u,i,T}$ is not observed, or, alternatively, $\mathcal{H}$ could also be the set of all $(u, i, T + 1)$ triples. The two cases here correspond to predicting the unobserved service qualities in the current time-slot or predicting the service qualities in next time-slot.

3.2. Matrix Factorization Model and Its Variants. The matrix factorization model and its various modifications can be used to solve the service quality prediction problem of our interest. The key idea of matrix factorization is assuming a latent low-dimensional space $\mathbb{R}^D$ on which, for each user u, a user feature p_u is defined and for each item (i.e., service in the context of this paper) i, an item feature is defined. That is, p_u and q_i both belong to $\mathbb{R}^D$, and the estimated rating $\hat{r}_{u,i}$ is defined by the inner product of these two vectors: namely,

$$\hat{r}_{u,i} = q_i^T p_u. \tag{1}$$

We note that, in the original matrix factorization setting, the problem considered does not have temporal dynamic, or,

equivalently phrased, time index set $\mathcal{T}$ contains only a single time index, and as a consequence, index t is disregarded.

Representing the collection of q_i's as a $D \times |\mathcal{I}|$ matrix Q and the collection of $\{p_u\}$ as a $D \times |\mathcal{U}|$ matrix P, the estimation problem of interest then reduces to solve the following minimization problem: find (Q, P) that minimizes

$$\sum_{(u,i) \in \mathcal{K}} \left\| r_{u,i} - \hat{r}_{u,i} \right\|^2 + \lambda_Q \|Q\|^2 + \lambda_P \|P\|^2 \tag{2}$$

for some given positive values of λ_Q and λ_P. The notation $\| \cdot \|$ denotes either vector l-2 norm or matrix Frobenius norm, which should be clear from the context.

An extension of matrix factorization is regularized SVD with bias [26], which formulates the estimated $\hat{r}_{u,i}$ as

$$\hat{r}_{u,i} = \mu + b_i + b_u + q_i^T p_u, \tag{3}$$

where μ is the average of all QoS values on $\mathcal{K}$ and b_u and b_i are, respectively, user bias and item bias. Denote by $B_{\mathcal{U}}$ the collection of all b_u's and by $B_{\mathcal{I}}$ the collection of all b_i's. The estimation problem then reduces to the following minimization problem: find $(\mu, B_{\mathcal{U}}, B_{\mathcal{I}}, Q, P)$ that minimizes

$$\sum_{(u,i) \in \mathcal{K}} \left\| r_{u,i} - \hat{r}_{u,i} \right\|^2 \\ + \lambda \left(\|Q\|^2 + \|P\|^2 + \|B_{\mathcal{U}}\|^2 + \|B_{\mathcal{I}}\|^2 \right). \tag{4}$$

The optimization problems as stated in (2) and (4) can both be solved using gradient descent or stochastic gradient descent algorithms.

A further extension of the above SVD model is the so-called SVD++ model [25], in which the total number of entries in $\mathcal{R}$ that correspond to each user u is incorporated in defining $\hat{r}_{u,i}$. This leads to a revised form of the cost function in the optimization problem and further improved performance is obtained. Recently, [25] has introduced a timeSVD++, which builds upon SVD++ and considers incorporating time information in the definition of $\hat{r}_{u,i}$, that is, letting $\hat{r}_{u,i}$ vary with time.

We now restate the timeSVD++ model in the context of service quality prediction. It is worth noting that, in this problem, the number of times that a user invokes web services appears irrelevant, unlike in the typical application of SVD++ or timeSVD++, say Netflix movie-rating prediction problem, where the total number of times a user rates movies provides implicit information about their interest in the movie. For this reason, the version of timeSVD++ we present here drops the term relating the service invocation frequency of the users.

Moving time index t from subscript to a variable, the estimated quality is now defined as a function of time t as follows:

$$\hat{r}_{u,i}(t) = \mu + b_i(t) + b_u(t) + q_i(t)^T p_u(t), \tag{5}$$

where b_u, b_i, p_u, and p_i are all made time-dependent.

For further specification, let

$$\text{dev}_u(t) = (t - t_u) \cdot |t - t_u|^\beta,$$

$$\text{dev}_i(t) = (t - t_i) \cdot |t - t_i|^\beta,$$

$$b_u(t) = (b_u + \alpha_1 \text{dev}_u(t) + b_{u,t}) c_i(t),$$

$$b_i(t) = b_i + \alpha_2 \text{dev}_i(t) + b_{i,t}, \qquad (6)$$

$$p_u(t) = p_u + \alpha_3 \text{dev}_u(t),$$

$$q_i(t) = q_i + \alpha_4 \text{dev}_i(t).$$

Here user-centric bias $b_u(t)$ is modeled as a linear function of user-centric deviation $\text{dev}_u(t)$ at time t multiplied with $c_i(t)$, which models the time-varying rating scale service i receives at time t. The service-centric bias $b_i(t)$ is modeled as a linear function of service-centric deviation $\text{dev}_i(t)$ at time t. In the equations for $\text{dev}_u(t)$ and $\text{dev}_i(t)$, t_i is the time-slot in which the quality of service i is for the first time measured, and t_u is the time-slot in which user u invokes a service.

Similar to the previous settings, this model gives rise to a minimization problem with the following objective function:

$$\mathscr{L} = \sum_{(u,i,t) \in \mathscr{K}} \left\| r_{u,i,t} - \widehat{r}_{u,i,t} \right\|^2 \qquad (7)$$

$$+\lambda \left(\sum_u b_u^2 + \sum_i b_i^2 + \sum_u \left\| p_u(t) \right\|^2 + \sum_i \left\| q_i(t) \right\|^2 \right). \qquad (8)$$

The parameter set to minimize over in this optimization problem is the set of $\Theta = \alpha_1, \alpha_2, \alpha_3, \alpha_4,$ $b_u, b_i, \{b_{u,t}\}_t, \{b_{i,t}\}_t, p_u, q_i, \{c_i(t)\}_t$ and finding the parameter configurations that minimizes the objective function $\mathscr{L}$ defined above will allow us to predict service quality for unobserved (u, i, t) triples. This set of parameters to be optimized is denoted by θ in the following context.

At this point we have not only arrived at a sensible and well-defined notion of quality of web services, we also have translated the problem of QoS prediction to an optimization problem. In the remainder of this paper, we present a prediction algorithm based on stochastic grade descent algorithm [27].

4. Algorithm

Overall we take a stochastic gradient-based approach to minimize the objective function. Denoting $r_{u,i,t} - \widehat{r}_{u,i,t}$ by $err_{u,i,t}$, we have

$$\frac{\partial_L}{\partial_{b_u}} = \sum_{u,i,t} -err_{u,i,t} c_i(t) + \lambda b_u,$$

$$\frac{\partial_L}{\partial_{b_i}} = \sum_{u,i,t} -err_{u,i,t} + \lambda b_i,$$

$$\frac{\partial_L}{\partial_{p_u}} = \sum_{u,i,t} -err_{u,i,t} (q_i + \alpha_4 \text{dev}_i(t)) + \lambda p_u,$$

$$\frac{\partial_L}{\partial_{q_i}} = \sum_{u,i,t} -err_{u,i,t} (p_u + \alpha_3 \text{dev}_u(t)) + \lambda q_i,$$

$$\frac{\partial_L}{\partial_{b_{u,t}}} = \sum_{u,i,t} -err_{u,i,t} c_i(t) + \lambda (b_{u,t}),$$

$$\frac{\partial_L}{\partial_{b_{i,t}}} = \sum_{u,i,t} -err_{u,i,t} + \lambda b_{i,t},$$

$$\frac{\partial_L}{\partial_{\alpha_1}} = \sum_{u,i,t} -err_{u,i,t} \text{dev}_u(t) c_i(t) + \lambda \alpha_1,$$

$$\frac{\partial_L}{\partial_{\alpha_2}} = \sum_{u,i,t} -err_{u,i} \text{dev}_i(t) + \lambda \alpha_2,$$

$$\frac{\partial_L}{\partial_{\alpha_3}} = \sum_{u,i,t} -err_{u,i,t} \text{dev}_u(t) (q_i + \alpha_4 \text{dev}_i(t)) + \lambda \alpha_3,$$

$$\frac{\partial_L}{\partial_{\alpha_4}} = \sum_{u,i,t} -err_{u,i,t} \text{dev}_i(t) (p_u + \alpha_3 \text{dev}_u(t)) + \lambda \alpha_4. \qquad (9)$$

4.1. Offline/Batch Training Algorithm. Equation (8) allows a stochastic gradient ascent algorithm to optimize the objective function, in which the value of the objective function can be incrementally increased via updating the configuration of parameters. Referring to a generic element in the parameter set Θ by θ, for each $\theta \in \Theta$, we update each θ according to

$$\theta^{t+1} := \theta^t - \eta \frac{\partial_L}{\partial_\theta}, \qquad (10)$$

where η is a choice of step size. This update rule is applied iteratively in offline training, until convergence or upon reaching a prescribed number of iterations. As is well known, such gradient ascent algorithm monotonically increases the value of the objective functions over iterations.

We define a convergence condition so that if the gradient of the objective function becomes small, the parameter is then close to the optima. The algorithm is summarized as in Algorithm 1.

4.2. Online Training Algorithm. When the user-service invocation experiences arrive one at a time in sequence, the parameter update function of the previous stochastic gradient ascent algorithm is essentially our online training algorithm. More precisely, for each new invocation record $r_{u,i,t}^{\text{new}}$ that has just arrived, the online algorithm instantaneously updates θ according to (10). Such an update is only performed *once* in the online algorithm for each newly arrived invocation record. The simplicity of this computation, depending only on the current setting of θ, the incoming record is certainly remarkable.

> **Input:** invocation matrix $\mathcal{R}$, regularization parameter λ, learning rate η,
> number of latent factors d, max iterations itmax
> **Output:** parameter set Θ
> Initialize θ with random value
> **for** $it = 1$, $it <= it$max, $it + +$ **do**
>   **for** $u = 1$, $u <= |\mathcal{U}|$, $u + +$ **do**
>   **for** $s = 1$, $s <= |\mathcal{I}|$, $s + +$ **do**
>   **for** $t = 1$, $t <= |\mathcal{T}|$, $t + +$ **do**
>   update θ according to Eq. (9)
>   **end for**
>   **end for**
>   **end for**
> **end for**
> **return** Θ;

ALGORITHM 1: Offline algorithm.

> **Input:** The set of new available invocation records $\mathcal{R}^{new}_{u,i,t}$, regularization parameter λ,
> learning rate η, number of latent factors d, and the latest Θ^{old}
> **Output:** parameter set Θ^{new}
>   **for** $r^{new}_{u,i,t} \in \mathcal{R}^{new}_{u,i,t}$ **do**
>   update θ according to Eq. (9)
>   **end for**
>   **return** parameter set Θ^{new}

ALGORITHM 2: Online algorithm.

4.3. Hybrid Algorithm. As the online approach only takes into account current incoming invocation record, it is necessary to intermittently apply a batch algorithm within the online algorithm to collectively infer over the existing available data. As such, the convergence speed and the prediction precision are both increased. We introduce a hybrid approach that takes the best of Algorithms 1 and 2 and works in this way: at the beginning of each time step t, the online algorithm will process the incoming records and corresponding users and services between time step $(t - 1)$ and t. If a predefined number of data has arrived or if other criteria, such as additional computation resources, are met, a batch algorithm will be activated over all of the collected records during time step 0 and time step t. The batch phase can catch more detailed statistics of the overall QoS prediction model and improve the performance of the online prediction.

Note that when we take all available invocation records at a specific time t, denoted by $\mathcal{R}^t$ as the input of Algorithm 1, then this leads to a batch update rule which iteratively updates Θ until a predefined condition is achieved.

We articulate this algorithm as in Algorithm 3, where RBAC stands for run batch algorithm criteria.

It can be seen that this hybrid algorithm simulates the model updating process of our proposed architecture in Section 3.

5. Experimental Evaluation

In this section, we present the experimental evaluation of the time-dependent quality of web services prediction models.

5.1. Data Set. The dataset, real-world QoS evaluation results (response time and throughput), used for the experimentation is downloaded from http://www.wsdream.net/. This dataset includes 142 users on 4532 web services at 64 continuous time-slots. In this study, we choose the response time of user-service invocation to evaluate the performance of the algorithms. The provider of this dataset proposed a tensor factorization-based prediction approach in [24]. This method, referred as TF in the following context, is one of the baseline approaches compared in this study. Other baseline algorithms include traditional tensor factorization and traditional matrix factorization (MF) by compressing (averaging) the observed user-service pairs over different time periods.

As in practice, user-service invocation is typically quite sparse. Therefore, to evaluate the prediction performance over various data sparsity levels, we randomly choose 10%, 30%, and 50% of the data as the observed data to make the QoS prediction.

We examine the prediction precision of our proposed batch algorithm, online algorithm, and hybrid algorithm in our experiments. To validate the performance of our

---

Input: the set of new available invocation records $\mathscr{R}^{\text{new}}$, all available invocation records $\mathscr{R}^{t}$
    regularization parameter λ, learning rate η, number of latent factors d, max iterations itmax, and
    the latest Θ^{old}
Output: parameter set Θ
 while $R^{\text{new}}! = $ NULL **do**
  Update parameters by Algorithm 1, given $\mathscr{R}^{\text{new}}$, λ, η, d, and Θ^{old} as the input parameters;
  if RBAC == true **then**
   Update parameters by Algorithm 1, given $\mathscr{R}^{t}$, λ, η, d, itmax, and Θ^{old} as the input parameters;
  end if
 end while

ALGORITHM 3: Hybrid algorithm.

proposed models, we also consider TF [24, 28] and MF [26] for comparison.

As the traditional matrix factorization only predicts the quality of service for a specific time-slot, as in the scenario of time-dependent QoS prediction, the quality of a web service i can be characterized by the mean of $r_{u,i,\tau}$, where $r_{u,i,\tau}$ is the set of predicted QoS value for the observed time-slots. This measure, which we call the *average quality of web services* of service i, is formally defined follows:

$$r_{u,i} = \frac{\sum_{t \in \tau} r_{u,i,t}}{|\tau|}, \tag{11}$$

where $|\cdot|$ denotes the cardinality of a set. It is clear that this value is not able to characterize the dependencies and network performances over different time intervals.

5.2. Performance Evaluation. In this section, we present the experimental evaluation of the online incremental QoS prediction models in terms of RMSE, the prediction precision.

5.2.1. Evaluation Metric. As discussed in Section 3, the objective of our approach is to find a set of parameters to minimize the loss function of observing the web service invocation performance. Therefore, the loss function, RMSE, can naturally be used as the evaluation metric to compare the overall performance for the resulting model.

The definition of RMSE for the specific time-slot t is given by the following equation:

$$\text{RMSE} = \sqrt{\frac{\sum_{r_{i,j,t} \in \mathscr{T}} \sum_{u \in \mathscr{U}'} \left(\hat{r}_{i,j,t} - r_{i,j,t} \right)^2}{|T|}}, \tag{12}$$

where $r_{i,j,t}$ is the observed QoS of service i invoked by user u at time-slot t, $\hat{r}_{i,j,t}$ is the predicted corresponding QoS value, and T is the testing set.

5.3. Experimental Results. For comparison purpose, we also evaluate the performance of our proposed algorithm (TSVD) (a pure online version, a pure offline versio,n and the hybrid version the algorithm), MF, and TF on the collected data sets. We performed the following steps to demonstrate the performance of online algorithm and hybrid algorithm. At

the beginning, the experiments have no knowledge of user-service invocation records. At this point, the online algorithm operates every time an invocation record (or several records) arrives. We randomly choose one user-service invocation record and the performance of the algorithms is evaluated after each record arrives. After the incoming data arrives the parameters of online algorithm are updated and the performance on the testing set is evaluated. We also investigate the performance of the offline algorithm and other compared approaches with all the invocation records available. The results are constant when compared with the dynamic results from online algorithm and hybrid algorithm.

5.3.1. Batch Algorithm Performance. To show the impact of iteration rounds on the performance of our system, we evaluate the RMSE of the training set and the testing set with the increasing of the number of iterations. We first randomly choose 10% of the 64th time-slot as the testing set. To evaluate how training data sparseness affects algorithm performance, we then randomly choose 10%, 30%, and 50% of each time-slot of the original user-service invocation matrix as the training data, respectively. Figure 2 shows this impact at 10%, 30%, and 50%. We observe that our algorithm converges at around 100 to 300 iterations. In addition, the RMSE of the training set decreases when increasing the percentage of the training data. The RMSE of the testing set almost remains at the same level for all levels of sparseness. These two facts confirm the stability of our approach.

We investigate the effect of time-slots of data on the performance of different methods and the results are shown in Figure 3. When the sparsity of the user-service invocation matrix is great, 10% in this experiment, the performance of all three approaches increases when the number of observed time-slots increases. Our offline TSVD achieves the best performance when we choose 40 time-slot previous invocation records as the training set ($x = 40$). However, when the sparsity of the user-service invocation matrix decreases, 30% and 50%, the RMSE of the testing set becomes worse as the observed number of time-slots increases. For MF and TF, the RMSE increases with an increase of the observed time-slots of data. Also, when increasing the sparsity of the observed user-service invocation matrix, the performance of all three compared algorithms is increased in terms of RMSE.

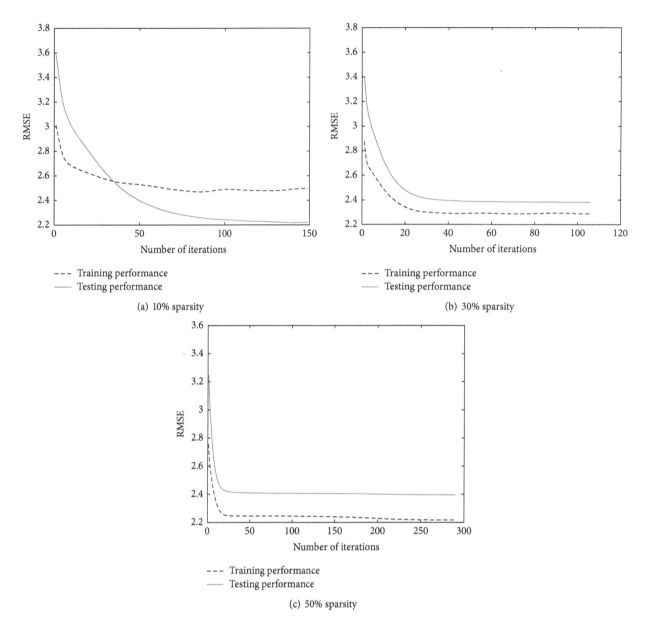

FIGURE 2: Performance dynamics of the offline TSVD over iteration rounds.

5.3.2. Online and Hybrid Algorithm Performance. We analyze the performance obtained from the offline algorithm, the online algorithm, and the hybrid algorithm to verify the superiority of our approach. To simulate the user-service invocation record arriving scenario, we randomly choose 10% of each time-slot records as the observed invocation record stream and take another 5% of each time-slot as the testing set. This experimental setup means that, for each 15 minutes' time-slot, there are about 20,000 invocation records arriving to the system. We evaluate the online and hybrid algorithms after the arrival of each 100 invocation records by calculating the RMSE of the testing set of the corresponding time-slot.

For the online algorithm, we merely keep updating the parameters with the incremental of records, for example, Algorithm 2. In the hybrid approach, the parameter update follows the same manner as the online algorithm except

at the end of each time-slot where a batch algorithm is executed on all the newly arrived data at the current time-slot.

Figure 4 demonstrates the performance of the online algorithm and the hybrid algorithm as user-service invocation records incrementally arrive. The RMSE performance of the testing set continues to increase as new data arrives. After accumulating enough invocation records, the online algorithm and the hybrid algorithm reach the similar level as the batch algorithm.

Moreover, as shown in Figure 4, the performance of the hybrid algorithm is always better than the online algorithm as the sequence of invocation records become available for the response time. At the end of the invocation record stream, the hybrid algorithm can perform the same level of performance as the offline algorithm.

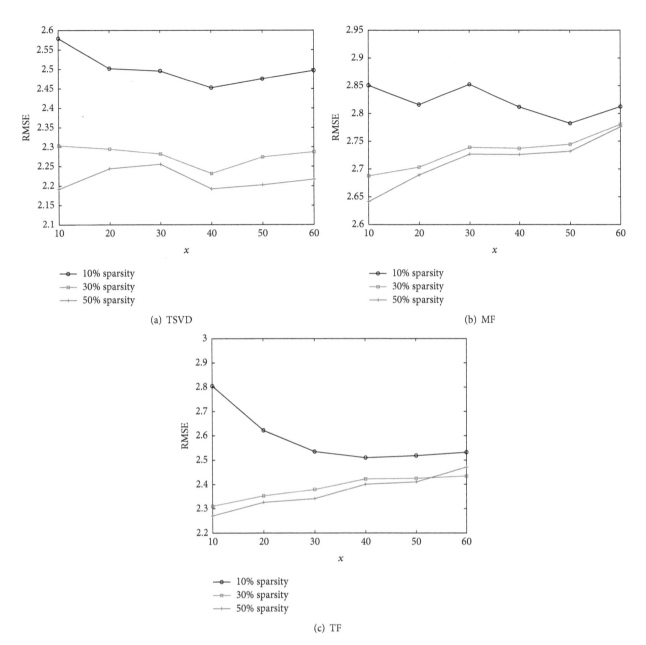

FIGURE 3: Performance comparison of the offline TSVD, MF, and TF.

This fact confirms that introducing a batch phase in the online algorithm improves the convergence rate of the online algorithm.

The user-service invocation records incrementally become available as shown in Figure 4. We see that the performance of our hybrid approach is close to the batch algorithm after observing the invocation records of the first few time-slots. This confirms the advantages of our quality of web service modeling approach.

Figure 4 also shows that the prediction performances of the hybrid algorithm are better than the online algorithm in terms of RMSE and reach the performance level of the offline algorithm much faster than the online algorithm. This is because the batch phase of the hybrid algorithm increases the prediction performance of the online time SVD. We can also observe that, as the observed data increases, the performance of both the online and the hybrid algorithms is improved.

Based on the above experiments, we have observed an improvement for the quality of web service prediction problem with both online and offline approaches. We conclude that our proposed model can effectively determine the quality of web services. In practice, the hybrid algorithm can begin by collecting a small amount of service invocation records and the parameters of the model can be initialized by the batch algorithm, so that the performance will be further improved.

6. Conclusion

In this paper, we propose a hybrid system designing framework for dynamic service quality prediction, which takes

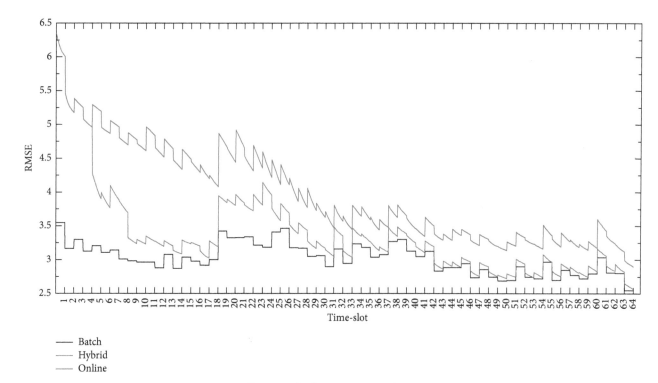

FIGURE 4: Performance comparison.

the best of both online and offline algorithms, gives a good tradeoff for the effectiveness of the offline algorithm, and is applicable to most real-life scenarios. We have also developed a quality of service predicting system that fits the proposed architecture and have introduced a factorization approach to formulate the quality of services which is a more generative model for quality assessment. An online algorithm and an offline algorithm have been developed under this generative model. Furthermore, we have designed a practical hybrid algorithm to simulate the process of the proposed architecture, which begins working with little or no knowledge of web services and user experiences. The model is refined as it goes along. Empirical studies have been conducted on a real web service invocation data set and experimental results show that the quality of services can be precisely predicted.

Although this paper provides a unified modeling approach for the quality of service prediction, the general factorization methodology presented is applicable to the algorithmic engines of other predictors from user experiences. We also note that the factorization modeling approaches allow the use of more advanced features, possibly encoded by tensor factorization, and other well-principled algorithms to develop both online and offline trainers for the proposed generic predictor architecture.

Competing Interests

The authors declare that they have no competing interests.

References

[1] B. Sarwar, G. Karypis, J. Konstan, and J. Riedl, "Itembased collaborative filtering recommendation algorithms," in *Proceedings of the 10th International Conference on World Wide Web*, pp. 285–295, ACM, Hong Kong, May 2001.

[2] G. Adomavicius and A. Tuzhilin, "Toward the next generation of recommender systems: a survey of the state-of-the-art and possible extensions," *IEEE Transactions on Knowledge and Data Engineering*, vol. 17, no. 6, pp. 734–749, 2005.

[3] J. Wang, A. P. De Vries, and M. J. T. Reinders, "Unifying user-based and item-based collaborative filtering approaches by similarity fusion," in *Proceedings of the 29th Annual International ACM SIGIR Conference on Research and Development in Information Retrieval*, pp. 501–508, ACM, Seattle, Wash, USA, August 2006.

[4] M. Balabanović and Y. Shoham, "Fab: content-based, collaborative recommendation," *Communications of the ACM*, vol. 40, no. 3, pp. 66–72, 1997.

[5] J. Liu, M. Tang, Z. Zheng, X. Liu, and S. Lyu, "Location-aware and personalized collaborative filtering for web service recommendation," *IEEE Transactions on Services Computing*, vol. 9, no. 5, pp. 686–699, 2016.

[6] Z. Li, J. Cao, and Q. Gu, "Temporal-aware QoS-based service recommendation using tensor decomposition," *International Journal of Web Services Research*, vol. 12, no. 1, pp. 62–74, 2015.

[7] S. Meng, Z. Zhou, T. Huang et al., "A Temporal-Aware Hybrid Collaborative Recommendation Method for Cloud Service," in *Proceedings of the IEEE International Conference on Web Services (ICWS '16)*, pp. 252–259, San Francisco, Calif, USA, June 2016.

[8] F. Sardis, G. Mapp, J. Loo, M. Aiash, and A. Vinel, "Investigating a mobility-aware qos model for multimedia streaming rate adaptation," *Journal of Electrical and Computer Engineering*, vol. 2015, Article ID 548638, 7 pages, 2015.

[9] P. C. Evans and R. C. Basole, "Revealing the API ecosystem and enterprise strategy via visual analytics," *Communications of the ACM*, vol. 59, no. 2, pp. 26–28, 2016.

[10] L. Li, M. Rong, and G. Zhang, "A web service QoS prediction approach based on multi-dimension QoS," in *Proceedings of the 6th International Conference on Computer Science & Education (ICCSE '11)*, pp. 1319–1322, IEEE, Singapore, August 2011.

[11] L. Chen, Y. Feng, J. Wu, and Z. Zheng, "An enhanced QoS prediction approach for service selection," in *Proceedings of the IEEE International Conference on Services Computing (SCC '11)*, pp. 727–728, July 2011.

[12] Y. Jiang, J. Liu, M. Tang, and X. Liu, "An effective Web service recommendation method based on personalized collaborative filtering," in *Proceedings of the IEEE 9th International Conference on Web Services (ICWS '11)*, pp. 211–218, July 2011.

[13] X. Chen, X. Liu, Z. Huang, and H. Sun, "RegionKNN: a scalable hybrid collaborative filtering algorithm for personalized web service recommendation," in *Proceedings of the IEEE 8th International Conference on Web Services (ICWS '10)*, pp. 9–16, IEEE, July 2010.

[14] L. Shao, J. Zhang, Y. Wei, J. Zhao, B. Xie, and H. Mei, "Personalized QoS prediction forweb services via collaborative filtering," in *Proceedings of the IEEE International Conference on Web Services (ICWS '07)*, pp. 439–446, IEEE, Salt Lake City, Utah, USA, July 2007.

[15] Q. Zhang, C. Ding, and C.-H. Chi, "Collaborative filtering based service ranking using invocation histories," in *Proceedings of the IEEE 9th International Conference on Web Services (ICWS '11)*, pp. 195–202, July 2011.

[16] Z. Zheng, H. Ma, M. R. Lyu, and I. King, "WSRec: a collaborative filtering based web service recommender system," in *Proceedings of the IEEE International Conference on Web Services (ICWS '09)*, pp. 437–444, IEEE, July 2009.

[17] A. Schmidt, M. Beigl, and H.-W. Gellersen, "There is more to context than location," *Computers and Graphics (Pergamon)*, vol. 23, no. 6, pp. 893–901, 1999.

[18] A. Karatzoglou, L. Baltrunas, K. Church, and M. Böhmer, "Climbing the app wall: enabling mobile app discovery through context-aware recommendations," in *Proceedings of the 21st ACM International Conference on Information and Knowledge Management (CIKM '12)*, pp. 2527–2530, Maui, Hawaii, USA, November 2012.

[19] Y. Xu, J. Yin, W. Lo, and Z. Wu, "Personalized location-aware QoS prediction for web services using probabilistic matrix factorization," in *Web Information Systems Engineering—WISE 2013*, vol. 8180 of *Lecture Notes in Computer Science*, pp. 229–242, Springer, Berlin, Germany, 2013.

[20] X. Fan, Y. Hu, R. Zhang, W. Chen, and P. Brezillon, "Modeling Temporal effectiveness for context-aware web services recommendation," in *Proceedings of the IEEE International Conference on Web Services (ICWS '15)*, pp. 225–232, IEEE, July 2015.

[21] B. Hidasi and D. Tikk, "Fast als-based tensor factorization for context-aware recommendation from implicit feedback," in *Machine Learning and Knowledge Discovery in Databases*, pp. 67–82, Springer, Berlin, Germany, 2012.

[22] H. Wermser, A. Rettinger, and V. Tresp, "Modeling and learning context-aware recommendation scenarios using tensor decomposition," in *Proceedings of the International Conference on Advances in Social Networks Analysis and Mining (ASONAM '11)*, pp. 137–144, IEEE, Kaohsiung, Taiwan, July 2011.

[23] Y. Shi, A. Karatzoglou, L. Baltrunas, M. Larson, A. Hanjalic, and N. Oliver, "TFMAP: optimizing MAP for top-n context-aware recommendation," in *Proceedings of the 35th Annual ACM SIGIR Conference on Research and Development in Information Retrieval (SIGIR '12)*, pp. 155–164, Portland, Ore, USA, August 2012.

[24] Y. Zhang, Z. Zheng, and M. R. Lyu, "WSPred: a time-aware personalized QoS prediction framework for Web services," in *Proceedings of the 22nd IEEE International Symposium on Software Reliability Engineering (ISSRE '11)*, pp. 210–219, IEEE, December 2011.

[25] Y. Koren, "Collaborative filtering with temporal dynamics," in *Proceedings of the 15th ACM SIGKDD International Conference on Knowledge Discovery and Data Mining (KDD '09)*, pp. 447–456, Paris, France, June 2009.

[26] Y. Koren, "Factorization meets the neighborhood: a multifaceted collaborative filtering model," in *Proceedings of the 14th ACM SIGKDD International Conference on Knowledge Discovery and Data Mining (KDD '08)*, pp. 426–434, Las Vegas, Nev, USA, August 2008.

[27] L. Bottou, "Stochastic learning," in *Advanced Lectures on Machine Learning*, O. Bousquet and U. von Luxburg, Eds., vol. LNAI 3176 of *Lecture Notes in Artificial Intelligence*, pp. 146–168, Springer, Berlin, Germany, 2004.

[28] M. Welling and M. Weber, "Positive tensor factorization," *Pattern Recognition Letters*, vol. 22, no. 12, pp. 1255–1261, 2001.

22

Self-Tuning Control Scheme based on the Robustness σ-Modification Approach

Nabiha Touijer,[1] **Samira Kamoun,**[1] **Najib Essounbouli,**[2] **and Abdelaziz Hamzaoui**[2]

[1]*Laboratory of Sciences and Techniques of Automatic Control and Computer Engineering (Lab–STA),
National School of Engineering of Sfax, University of Sfax, BP 1173, 3038 Sfax, Tunisia*
[2]*CReSTIC, IUT de Troyes, 9 Rue de Québec, BP 396, 10026 Troyes Cedex, France*

Correspondence should be addressed to Nabiha Touijer; nabiha_ettouijer@yahoo.fr

Academic Editor: James Lam

This paper deals with the self-tuning control problem of linear systems described by autoregressive exogenous (ARX) mathematical models in the presence of unmodelled dynamics. An explicit scheme of control is described, which we use a recursive algorithm on the basis of the robustness σ-modification approach to estimate the parameters of the system, to solve the problem of regulation tracking of the system. This approach was designed with the assumptions that the norm of the vector of the parameters is well-known. A new quadratic criterion is proposed to develop a modified recursive least squares (M-RLS) algorithm with σ-modification. The stability condition of the proposed estimation scheme is proved using the concepts of the small gain theorem. The effectiveness and reliability of the proposed M-RLS algorithm are shown by an illustrative simulation example. The effectiveness of the described explicit self-tuning control scheme is demonstrated by simulation results of the cruise control system for a vehicle.

1. Introduction

Adaptive control has been known since 1950 by Caldwell [1]. Different types of adaptive controls were discussed and used to design adaptive laws of the proposed control schemes. Various studies have been focused on the development of adaptive control theory [2–4]. Stability theory was introduced. In this context, several studies have been developed [5–15].

Egardt [16] noted that the application of adaptive laws could easily be unstable in the presence of small perturbations. In the early 1980s, the robust adaptive control behavior has become much discussed [17, 18]. Several researches developed and studied the robust adaptive control [19–29]. In continuous time, Ioannou and Sun [10] developed the robust adaptive control (pole placement control and model reference control) for dynamic systems in presence of unmodelled dynamics. The different developed control scheme has been based on algorithms with different robustness approach (dead zone, normalization...) to estimate the parameters of the systems. In discrete time, different robust adaptive control schemes have been developed and applied to the class of linear systems described by a mathematical model ARX

in the presence of unmodelled dynamics [30–32]. Different robust adaptive control of monovariable systems have been developed on the basis of the modified recursive least squares algorithm M-RLS with approach robustness dead zone [33–36]. The stability conditions of the different proposed estimation scheme have been demonstrated. A robust explicit scheme of self-tuning regulation using the modified filtering recursive algorithm with dead zone was applied to a temperature regulation system in the building [37]. The M-RLS algorithm was extended to a multivariable system, where the stability condition of estimation scheme has been shown and a robust self-tuning control has been developed [38]. The different parametric estimation algorithms were based on the knowledge of the bounds of the unmodelled dynamics.

This paper focuses on the regulation-tracking problem for the stochastic systems described by the ARX mathematical model, in the presence of unknown unmodelled dynamics in the parameters of the system. This problem consists of developing a control law (called the corrector) allowing the output of the system to follow a time-varying reference signal while reducing the effects of disturbances acting at different locations of the system to be controlled. An explicit scheme of self-tuning control has been designed with the assumptions that the norm of the vector of the parameters is known. A quadratic criterion is proposed to develop M-RLS algorithm with σ-modification that will be used in the estimation step of control scheme. The choice of parameter σ is given. The stability condition of the proposed parametric estimation scheme is proved using the small gain theorem [39] and based on the stability condition of the RLS algorithm [40].

The remainder of his paper is structured as follows. Section 2 describes the stochastic systems by ARX mathematical model in presence of unmodelled dynamics. Section 3, firstly, treats the RLS algorithm, and, secondly, a new quadratic criterion is proposed to develop M-RLS algorithm with σ-modification. Furthermore, the choice of σ is given. The stability condition of the developed parametric estimation scheme is shown on the basis of the concepts of the small gain theorem. Section 4 presents an explicit scheme of self-tuning control using the proposed recursive algorithm M-RLS with σ-modification to estimate the parameters of the system. Section 5 provides two simulation examples. Firstly, a simulation example is given to illustrate the reliability and the effectiveness of the proposed M-RLS algorithm with σ-modification which are compared to the RLS algorithm. And secondly the simulation results of the cruise control system for vehicles are given to show the performance of the explicit scheme of self-tuning control which is compared to the explicit scheme of self-tuning control based on the RLS algorithm. Finally, concluding remarks are given in Section 6.

2. System Description

This section describes a stochastic system by ARX mathematical model with unknown parameters and in the presence of unmodelled dynamics.

Let us consider a linear stochastic system, which can be described by the following discrete-time ARX mathematical model:

$$A\left(q^{-1}\right) y(k) = B\left(q^{-1}\right) u(k) + v(k), \qquad (1)$$

where $u(k)$ and $y(k)$ represent, respectively, the input and the output of the system at the discrete-time k, $v(k) = e(k) + m(k)$ is the noise acting on the system, where $e(k)$ is an independent random variable with zero mean and constant variance and $m(k)$ is unknown unmodelled dynamics, and $A(q^{-1})$ and $B(q^{-1})$ are polynomials, which are defined, respectively, as

$$\begin{aligned} A\left(q^{-1}\right) &= 1 + a_1 q^{-1} + \cdots + a_{n_a} q^{-n_a}, \\ B\left(q^{-1}\right) &= b_1 q^{-1} + \cdots + b_{n_b} q^{-n_b}, \end{aligned} \qquad (2)$$

where n_a and n_b are the orders of the polynomials $A(q^{-1})$ and $B(q^{-1})$, respectively.

We suppose that the orders n_a and n_b are known.

The output $y(k)$ of system (1) can be given by

$$\begin{aligned} y(k) = &-a_1 y(k-1) - \cdots - a_{n_a} y(k-n_a) + b_1 u(k-1) \\ &+ \cdots + b_{n_b} u(k-n_b) + v(k). \end{aligned} \qquad (3)$$

The mathematical model (3) can be written as follows:

$$y(k) = \theta^T \varphi(k) + v(k), \qquad (4)$$

where θ^T and $\varphi^T(k)$ are the parameters vector and the observation vector, respectively, such that

$$\theta^T = \left[a_1 \cdots a_{n_a} \ b_1 \cdots b_{n_b}\right], \qquad (5)$$

$$\begin{aligned} \varphi^T(k) = \big[&-y(k-1) - \cdots \\ &- y(k-n_a) u(k-1) \cdots u(k-n_b) \big]. \end{aligned} \qquad (6)$$

3. Parametric Estimation Algorithm

This section concerns solving the parametric estimation problem for the considered stochastic system (1) on the basis of the two following assumptions.

Assumption 1. The parameters intervening in vector θ (5) are bounded; an upper bound M_0 of θ is known, such that

$$0 < \|\theta\| \le M_0. \qquad (7)$$

Figure 1 represents the first area of θ.

Assumption 2. The parameters intervening in vector θ (5) are bounded; an upper bound and a lower bound, respectively, $M_{\max}$ and $M_{\min}$, are known, such that

$$0 < M_{\min} \le \|\theta\| \le M_{\max}. \qquad (8)$$

Figure 2 represents the second area of θ with

$$\|\theta\| = \sqrt{\sum_{i=1}^{n_a} a_i^2 + \sum_{j=1}^{n_b} b_j^2}. \qquad (9)$$

The aim of this section is the development of a robust recursive parametric estimation algorithm for uncertain dynamic system. Thus, we propose to use, in the parametric estimation algorithm RLS, a parameter of robustness which is known in the literature by σ-modification. The developed algorithm is called modified recursive least square (M-RLS) algorithm with σ-modification. However, before the formulation of this algorithm, we present, in the following subsection, the recursive least square algorithm RLS.

3.1. Recursive Least Square Algorithm RLS. To show the advantages of the proposed recursive parametric estimation algorithm RLS with σ-modification to be proposed later, the RLS algorithm is given to compare its performance to the performance of the proposed parametric estimation scheme, which is described in this subsection.

The recursive parametric estimation algorithm RLS is given by

$$\hat{\theta}(k) = \hat{\theta}(k-1) + P(k) \varphi(k) \varepsilon(k),$$

$$P(k) = P(k-1) - \frac{P(k-1) \varphi(k) \varphi^T(k) P(k-1)}{1 + \varphi^T(k) P(k-1) \varphi(k)}, \qquad (10)$$

$$\varepsilon(k) = y(k) - \varphi^T(k) \hat{\theta}(k-1).$$

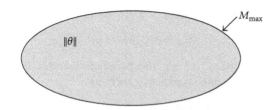

FIGURE 1: Representation of the first area.

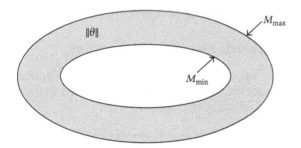

FIGURE 2: Representation of the second area.

Theorem 3 (see [40]). *Consider a linear system which can be described by input-output mathematical model (3) (without unmodelled dynamic). The estimation of the parameters intervening in the mathematical model can be made by using RLS algorithm (10). If the components of the vectors $\widehat{\theta}(0)$ and $\varphi(k)$ are finite, then the convergence of the RLS algorithm is ensured.*

Lemma 4 (see [40]). *Let us consider the RLS algorithm (10) to estimate the parameters intervening in (3). If the components of vectors $\widehat{\theta}(0)$ and $\varphi(k)$ are finite, and if again the adaptation gain $P(k)$ is decreasing, then the convergence of this algorithm is ensured.*

In the presence of unmodelled dynamics, the inconvenient of the RLS algorithm is that, at the computing of $\widehat{\theta}(k-1)$, the corresponding norm can exceed certain threshold. Then the effectiveness of this algorithm is not ensured.

The proposed key idea is based on the two following steps.

Step 1. If Assumption 1 (or Assumption 2) is verified, then $\widehat{\theta}(k)$ is given by the RLS algorithm (10).

Step 2. If Assumption 1 (or Assumption 2) is not verified, we propose to develop a parametric estimation algorithm such that

$$\widehat{\theta}(k) = f\left(\widehat{\theta}(k-1)\right) + P(k)\,\varphi(k)\,\varepsilon(k), \qquad (11)$$

where $0 < \|f(\widehat{\theta}(k-1))\| \le M_0$ or $M_{\min} \le \|f(\widehat{\theta}(k-1))\| \le M_{\max}$.

3.2. Modified Recursive Least Square Algorithm M-RLS with σ-Modification. In order to overcome the parametric estimation problem for the considered system, we will develop a modified algorithm M-RLS with σ-modification.

The following quadratic criterion is proposed to solve the parametric estimation problem for the considered system:

$$J(k) = \sum_{i=n_a+1}^{k} \frac{\left[y(i) - \widehat{\theta}^T(k)\,\varphi(i)\right]^2}{2}$$

$$+ \sum_{i=n_a+1}^{k} \widehat{\theta}^T(k)\,\zeta(i)\,\widehat{\theta}(i), \qquad (12)$$

where $\zeta(i)$ is a symmetrical matrix, whose choice is to give certain robustness to the developed estimation scheme with respect to the unmodelled dynamics.

The optimal of the estimated vector of parameters $\widehat{\theta}(i)$, which is given by the minimization of the quadratic criterion $J(k)$, can be obtained by the calculation of the derived of this criterion, such that

$$\frac{\partial(J(k))}{\partial\left(\widehat{\theta}(i)\right)} = -\sum_{i=n_a+1}^{k} y(i)\,\varphi(i) + \sum_{i=n_a+1}^{k} \varphi(i)\,\varphi^T(i)\,\widehat{\theta}(k)$$

$$+ \sum_{i=n_a+1}^{k-1} \zeta(i)\,\widehat{\theta}(i). \qquad (13)$$

In fact, the optimal of the vector of the estimated parameters $\widehat{\theta}(i)$ corresponds to the cancellation of (13). Thus, by cancelling expression (13) derivative of the $J(k)$ quadratic criterion considered, we can write the following expression:

$$P^{-1}(k)\,\widehat{\theta}(k) = \sum_{i=n_a+1}^{k} y(i)\,\varphi(i) - \sum_{i=n_a+1}^{k-1} \zeta(i)\,\widehat{\theta}(i), \qquad (14)$$

such that

$$P^{-1}(k) = \sum_{i=n_a+1}^{k} \varphi(i)\,\varphi^T(i). \qquad (15)$$

At the discrete-time $k+1$, (14) is written as follows:

$$P^{-1}(k+1)\,\widehat{\theta}(k+1) = \sum_{i=n_a+1}^{k+1} y(i)\,\varphi(i)$$

$$- \sum_{i=n_a+1}^{k} \zeta(i)\,\widehat{\theta}(i)$$

$$= \sum_{i=n_a+1}^{k} y(i)\,\varphi(i) \qquad (16)$$

$$- \sum_{i=n_a+1}^{k-1} \zeta(i)\,\widehat{\theta}(i)$$

$$+ y(k+1)\,\varphi(k+1)$$

$$- \zeta(k)\,\widehat{\theta}(k).$$

Using (14) and (15) and adding and subtracting $\varphi(k+1)\varphi^T(k+1)\widehat{\theta}(k)$ to the right member of (16), we obtain

$$P^{-1}(k+1)\widehat{\theta}(k+1) = P^{-1}(k+1)\widehat{\theta}(k)$$
$$+ \varphi(k+1)\varepsilon(k+1) \quad (17)$$
$$- \zeta(k)\widehat{\theta}(k).$$

with

$$\varepsilon(k+1) = y(k+1) - \varphi^T(k+1)\widehat{\theta}(k). \quad (18)$$

Multiplying (16) by $P(k+1)$, the estimated vector $\widehat{\theta}(k+1)$ is given as follows:

$$\widehat{\theta}(k+1) = \widehat{\theta}(k) - \zeta(k)P(k+1)\widehat{\theta}(k)$$
$$+ P(k+1)\varphi(k+1)\varepsilon(k+1). \quad (19)$$

Then, the deduced recursive parametric estimation algorithm RLS with σ-modification is defined by

$$\widehat{\theta}(k) = \widehat{\theta}(k-1) - \zeta(k-1)P(k)\widehat{\theta}(k-1)$$
$$+ P(k)\varphi(k)\varepsilon(k),$$

$$P(k) = P(k-1) - \frac{P(k-1)\varphi(k)\varphi^T(k)P(k-1)}{1 + \varphi^T(k)P(k-1)\varphi(k)}, \quad (20)$$

$$\varepsilon(k) = y(k) - \varphi^T(k)\widehat{\theta}(k-1).$$

The determination of the following function depends on the choice of parameter $\zeta(k-1)$:

$$f\left(\widehat{\theta}(k-1)\right) = \widehat{\theta}(k-1) - \zeta(k-1)P(k)\widehat{\theta}(k-1). \quad (21)$$

Based on Assumption 1, parameter $\zeta(k-1)$ is defined as follows:

$$0 < \left\|\widehat{\theta}(k-1) - \zeta(k-1)P(k)\widehat{\theta}(k-1)\right\| < M_0. \quad (22)$$

We propose to write matrix $\zeta(k-1)$ as follows:

$$\zeta(k-1) = \sigma(k-1)P^{-1}(k). \quad (23)$$

The following conditions permit determining parameter $\sigma(k-1)$:

(1) If the next condition satisfies $0 < \|\widehat{\theta}(k-1)\| \leq M_0$, then we take $\sigma(k-1) = 0$.

(2) if the next condition satisfies $\|\widehat{\theta}(k-1)\| > M_0$, then we must determine a value for the parameter $\sigma(k-1)$, while satisfying the following condition:

$$\sigma(k-1) < 1. \quad (24)$$

Using (23), (22) can be written as follows:

$$0 < (1 - \sigma(k-1))\|\widehat{\theta}(k-1)\| < M_0. \quad (25)$$

Using the second condition and dividing (25) by $\|\widehat{\theta}(k-1)\|$, (25) can be written as follows:

$$0 < 1 - \frac{M_0}{\|\widehat{\theta}(k-1)\|} < \sigma(k) < 1. \quad (26)$$

Then, there exists a finite scalar σ_0, such that

$$\sigma(k) = \sigma_0\left[1 - \frac{M_0}{\|\widehat{\theta}(k-1)\|}\right], \quad (27)$$

if $\|\widehat{\theta}(k-1)\| > M_0$, with $\sigma_0 > 1$.

Thus, the parameter $\sigma(k-1)$ is defined as follows:

$$\sigma(k-1)$$
$$= \begin{cases} 0, & \text{if } \|\widehat{\theta}(k-1)\| \leq M_0 \\ \sigma_{\max}(k-1) = \sigma_0\left[1 - \frac{M_0}{\|\widehat{\theta}(k-1)\|}\right], & \text{either, with } \sigma_0 > 1. \end{cases} \quad (28)$$

Based on Assumption 2, the parameter $\sigma(k-1)$ is defined as follows:

$$M_{\min} \leq \left\|\widehat{\theta}(k-1) - \sigma(k-1)P(k)\widehat{\theta}(k-1)\right\|$$
$$\leq M_{\max}. \quad (29)$$

We must consider the conditions intervening in the three following situations, in order to determine the parameter $\sigma(k-1)$:

(1) If the following condition satisfies $\|\widehat{\theta}(k-1)\| < M_{\min}$, then we must take

$$\sigma(k-1) = \sigma_{\min}(k-1). \quad (30)$$

(2) If the following condition satisfies $M_{\min} \leq \|\widehat{\theta}(k-1)\| \leq M_{\max}$, then we must take

$$\sigma(k-1) = 0. \quad (31)$$

(3) If the following condition satisfies $\|\widehat{\theta}(k-1)\| > M_{\max}$, then we must take $\sigma(k-1) = \sigma_{\max}(k-1)$, where $\sigma(k-1)$ is given by (27), with $M_0 = M_{\max}$.

By considering the first situation, we can define the parameter as $\sigma_{\min}(k-1)$ as follows:

$$\left\|\widehat{\theta}(k-1) - \sigma_{\min}(k-1)\widehat{\theta}(k-1)\right\| \geq M_{\min}. \quad (32)$$

Dividing (32) by $\|\widehat{\theta}(k-1)\|$, we can write the following inequality:

$$[1 - \sigma_{\min}(k-1)] > \frac{M_{\min}}{\|\widehat{\theta}(k-1)\|}. \quad (33)$$

In (33), adding $\sigma_{\min}(k-1)$ and subtracting $M_{\min}/\|\widehat{\theta}(k-1)\|$, we obtain

$$\sigma_{\min}(k-1) < 1 - \frac{M_{\min}}{\|\widehat{\theta}(k-1)\|} < 0. \quad (34)$$

Thus, we can affirm that there exists a finite scalar σ_1, such that

$$\sigma_{\min}(k) = \sigma_1 \left[1 - \frac{M_{\min}}{\left\| \hat{\theta}(k-1) \right\|} \right], \tag{35}$$

$$\sigma(k-1) = \begin{cases} \sigma_{\min}(k-1) = \sigma_1 \left(1 - \dfrac{M_{\min}}{\left\| \hat{\theta}(k-1) \right\|} \right) & \text{if } \left\| \hat{\theta}(k-1) \right\| < M_{\min} \\[3mm] 0, & \text{if } M_{\min} \le \left\| \hat{\theta}(k-1) \right\| \le M_{\max} \\[3mm] \sigma_{\max}(k-1) = \sigma_0 \left(1 - \dfrac{M_{\max}}{\left\| \hat{\theta}(k-1) \right\|} \right), & \text{either, with } \sigma_1, \sigma_0 > 1. \end{cases} \tag{36}$$

Consequently, the proposed recursive parametric estimation algorithm RLS with σ-modification is defined by

$$\hat{\theta}(k) = \hat{\theta}(k-1) - \sigma(k-1)\hat{\theta}(k-1)$$
$$+ P(k)\varphi(k)\varepsilon(k),$$
$$P(k) = P(k-1) - \frac{P(k-1)\varphi(k)\varphi^T(k)P(k-1)}{1 + \varphi^T(k)P(k-1)\varphi(k)}, \tag{37}$$
$$\varepsilon(k) = y(k) - \varphi^T(k)\hat{\theta}(k-1),$$

where $\sigma(k-1)$ is defined by (28) (or (36)).

If $\sigma(k-1) = 0$, then the RLS algorithm has been used.

In the next, the convergence condition of the RLS algorithm is used to demonstrate the sufficient condition of stability of the proposed estimation scheme.

3.3. Stability Analysis of the Proposed Parametric Estimation Scheme. Based on the small gain theorem, the stability analysis of the proposed parametric estimation scheme is established.

Consider the closed-loop system Figure 3, where H_1 and H_2 are causal operators. The small gain theorem gives a sufficient condition for stability of the closed-loop system below, using the notion of the gain operator defined later.

Theorem 5 (small gain theorem [39]). *Consider the closed-loop system Figure 3, where the operators H_1 and H_2 are bounded. Let the gains of the systems H_1 and H_2 are γ_1 and γ_2, respectively. If $\gamma_1\gamma_2 < 1$, then the closed-loop system is input-output stable.*

The a posteriori prediction error $\varepsilon_\circ(k)$ is given by

$$\varepsilon_\circ(k) = y(k) - \varphi^T(k)\hat{\theta}(k) = -\varphi^T(k)\tilde{\theta}(k) \tag{38}$$

with

$$\tilde{\theta}(k) = \hat{\theta}(k) - \theta. \tag{39}$$

where the following condition is supposed to satisfy $\|\hat{\theta}(k-1)\| < M_{\min}$, with $\sigma_1 > 0$.

Thus, the parameter $\sigma(k-1)$ is defined as follows:

Subtracting θ of the first equation in (37) and based on (39), (39) can be given by

$$\tilde{\theta}(k) = \tilde{\theta}(k-1) + P(k)\varphi(k)\varepsilon_\circ(k)$$
$$- \sigma(k-1)\hat{\theta}(k-1). \tag{40}$$

Using (40), the a posteriori prediction error $\varepsilon_\circ(k)$ is given by

$$\varepsilon_\circ(k) = -\varphi^T(k)\left[P(k)\varphi(k)\varepsilon_\circ(k) + \tilde{\theta}(k-1) \right.$$
$$\left. - \sigma(k-1)\hat{\theta}(k-1) \right]. \tag{41}$$

Let us consider parameter $w(k)$, which is defined as follows:

$$w(k) = -\varepsilon_\circ(k). \tag{42}$$

Using (41) and (42), the closed-loop system is shown in Figure 4.

Based on Lemma 4, we assume that the gain matrix $P(k)$ is decreasing and bounded and that the components of vector $\varphi(k)$ are finite. If $P(k)\varphi(k)$ and $\varphi(k)$ are bounded, then there exists $\gamma_1 \ge 0$, $\gamma_2 \ge 0$, β_1 and β_2, such that

$$\|P(k)\varphi(k)\varepsilon_\circ(k)\| \le \gamma_1 \|\varepsilon_\circ(k)\| + \beta_1,$$
$$\|\varphi(k)\tilde{\theta}(k)\| \le \gamma_2 \|\tilde{\theta}(k)\| + \beta_2. \tag{43}$$

Based on the closed-loop system shown in Figure 4, $\varepsilon_\circ(k)$ and $\tilde{\theta}(k)$ can be written, respectively, as follows:

$$\varepsilon_\circ(k) = -\varphi^T(k)\tilde{\theta}(k) + U_1 = -\varphi^T(k)\tilde{\theta}(k),$$
$$\tilde{\theta}(k) = P(k)\varphi(k)\varepsilon_\circ(k) + U_2(k) \tag{44}$$

with

$$U_1 = 0,$$
$$U_2(k) = \tilde{\theta}(k-1) - \sigma(k-1)\hat{\theta}(k-1). \tag{45}$$

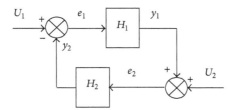

FIGURE 3: General closed-loop system.

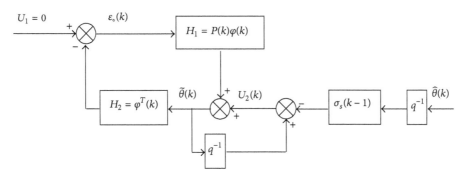

FIGURE 4: Closed-loop system of the parametric estimation scheme.

Based on (43) and using (44), we can write

$$\|\varepsilon_\circ(k)\| \le \gamma_2 \|\tilde\theta(k)\| + \beta_2, \tag{46}$$

$$\|\tilde\theta(k)\| \le \|U_2(k)\| + \gamma_1 \|\varepsilon_\circ(k)\| + \beta_1. \tag{47}$$

If

$$\gamma_1\gamma_2 < 1, \tag{48}$$

then

$$\|\varepsilon_\circ(k)\| \le \frac{1}{1 - \gamma_1\gamma_2} \left[\gamma_2 \|U_2(k)\| + \gamma_2\beta_1 + \beta_2\right], \tag{49}$$

$$\|\tilde\theta(k)\| \le \frac{1}{1 - \gamma_1\gamma_2} \left[\|U_2(k)\| + \gamma_1\beta_2 + \beta_1\right]. \tag{50}$$

So, if $U_2(k)$ is bounded, then the stability condition of the recursive parametric estimation scheme is ensured, such that

$$U_2(k) = \tilde\theta(k-1) - \sigma(k-1)\hat\theta(k-1)$$

$$= \hat\theta(k-1) - \theta - \sigma(k-1)\hat\theta(k-1) \tag{51}$$

$$= \hat\theta(k-1)[1 - \sigma(k-1)] - \theta.$$

The norm of $U_2(k)$ is given by

$$\|U_2(k)\| = \left\|\hat\theta(k-1)[1 - \sigma(k-1)] - \theta\right\|$$

$$\le \left\|\hat\theta(k-1)[1 - \sigma(k-1)]\right\| + \|\theta\|. \tag{52}$$

Based on (7) (or (8)) and (25), $U_2(k)$ is bounded, such that

$$\|U_2(k)\| \le 2M_0. \tag{53}$$

Based on (47), (48) and (49) are given by, respectively,

$$\|\varepsilon_\circ(k)\| \le \frac{1}{1 - \gamma_1\gamma_2} \left[2\gamma_2 M_0 + \gamma_2\beta_1 + \beta_2\right],$$

$$\|\tilde\theta(k)\| \le \frac{1}{1 - \gamma_1\gamma_2} \left[2M_0 + \gamma_1\beta_2 + \beta_1\right]. \tag{54}$$

Theorem 6. *The closed-loop system of the proposed recursive parametric estimation scheme shown in Figure 4 is stable; if the operator $P(k)\varphi(k)$ and $\varphi(k)$ are bounded and have positive gain, respectively, γ_1 and γ_2 are defined, such that $\gamma_1\gamma_2 < 1$.*

4. Explicit Scheme of Self-Tuning Control

This section discusses the regulation-tracking problem for the considered system, where an explicit scheme of self-tuning control will be developed. The following quadratic criterion $J(k+d+1)$ is used to design the controller:

$$J(k+d+1)$$

$$= \left[S\left(q^{-1}\right)\left[y(k+d+1) - y_r(k+d+1)\right]\right]^2 + \left[Q\left(q^{-1}\right)u(k)\right]^2, \tag{55}$$

where $y_r(k+d+1)$ represents the desired output signal, $u(k)$ is the control law, and $S(q^{-1})$ and $Q(q^{-1})$ are two polynomials, such that

$$S\left(q^{-1}\right) = 1 + s_1 q^{-1} + \cdots + s_{n_s} q^{-n_s},$$

$$Q\left(q^{-1}\right) = q_0 + q_1 q^{-1} + \cdots + q_{n_q} q^{-n_q}. \tag{56}$$

Note that the orders n_s and n_q of the polynomials $S(q^{-1})$ and $Q(q^{-1})$, respectively, are chosen by the designer.

The derivate of the criterion $J(k+d+1)$, which is described by (55), is given by

$$\frac{\partial J\left(k+d+1\right)}{\partial\left(u\left(k\right)\right)}$$

$$= 2b_1 S\left(q^{-1}\right) \left[y\left(k+d+1\right) - y_r\left(k+d+1\right)\right] \tag{57}$$

$$+ 2q_0 Q\left(q^{-1}\right) u\left(k\right)$$

with

$$S\left(q^{-1}\right) y\left(k+d+1\right) = qB\left(q^{-1}\right) F\left(q^{-1},k\right) u\left(k\right)$$

$$+ G\left(q^{-1},k\right) y\left(k\right) \tag{58}$$

$$+ F\left(q^{-1},k\right) v\left(k+d+1\right),$$

where $F(q^{-1},k)$ and $G(q^{-1},k)$ are solutions of the following polynomial equation:

$$S\left(q^{-1}\right) = A\left(q^{-1}\right) F\left(q^{-1},k\right) + q^{-d-1} G\left(q^{-1},k\right). \tag{59}$$

The polynomials $F(q^{-1},k)$ and $G(q^{-1},k)$ are given by

$$F\left(q^{-1},k\right) = 1 + F_1\left(k\right) q^{-1} + \cdots + F_d\left(k\right) q^{-d},$$

$$G\left(q^{-1},k\right) = G_0\left(k\right) + G_1\left(k\right) q^{-1} + \cdots \tag{60}$$

$$+ G_{n_a-1}\left(k\right) q^{1-n_a}.$$

Thus, the optimal control law $u(k)$ can be written by

$$u\left(k\right) = \frac{1}{Z\left(q^{-1},k\right)} \left[-G\left(q^{-1},k\right) y\left(k\right)\right.$$

$$\left. + \frac{1}{b_1} S\left(q^{-1}\right) y_r\left(k+d+1\right)\right], \tag{61}$$

where the polynomials $H(q^{-1},k)$ and $Z(q^{-1},k)$ are given by, respectively,

$$Z\left(q^{-1},k\right) = H\left(q^{-1},k\right) + \frac{1}{b_1} q_0 Q\left(q^{-1}\right),$$

$$H\left(q^{-1},k\right) = qB\left(q^{-1}\right) F\left(q^{-1},k\right). \tag{62}$$

4.1. Explicit Scheme of Self-Tuning Control.

The recursive algorithm of the explicit robust self-tuning control scheme is formulated by the following steps.

Step 1. Estimate the parameters intervening in the ARX mathematical model (1) using the M-RLS algorithm with σ-modification (37).

Step 2. Calculate the parameters intervening in the polynomials $F(q^{-1},k)$ and $G(q^{-1},k)$ by solving the polynomial equation defined as follows:

$$S\left(q^{-1}\right) = \widehat{A}\left(q^{-1}\right) F\left(q^{-1},k\right) + q^{-d-1} G\left(q^{-1},k\right). \tag{63}$$

Step 3. Calculate the control law $u(k)$ given by the following equation:

$$u\left(k\right) = \frac{1}{z_1\left(k\right)} \left[-\sum_{r=2}^{n_b+d-1} z_r\left(k\right) u\left(k-r+1\right)\right.$$

$$\left. - \sum_{t=0}^{n_a-1} g_t\left(k\right) y\left(k-t\right) + \frac{1}{\widehat{b}_1\left(k\right)} y_r\left(k+d+1-j\right)\right. \tag{64}$$

$$\left. + \sum_{j=1}^{n_s} \frac{s_t}{\widehat{b}_1\left(k\right)} y_r\left(k+d+1-j\right)\right].$$

Note that if $\widehat{b}_1(k) = 0$, then we take $h_1(k) = 0.01$.

5. Simulation Results

5.1. Simulation Example 1. Let us consider that the dynamic system can be described by the following mathematical model ARX:

$$y\left(k\right) = -a_1\left(k\right) y\left(k-1\right) - a_2\left(k\right) y\left(k-2\right)$$

$$+ b_1\left(k\right) u\left(k-2\right) + b_2\left(k\right) u\left(k-3\right) + e\left(k\right), \tag{65}$$

where $y(k)$ and $u(k)$ are the output and the input of the second-order system with time delay being one and $e(k)$ is white noise acting on the system.

The output of the system can be given as follows:

$$y\left(k\right) = \theta^T\left(k\right) \varphi\left(k\right) \tag{66}$$

with

$$\theta^T\left(k\right) = \left[a_1\left(k\right) \ a_2\left(k\right) \ b_1\left(k\right) \ b_2\left(k\right)\right], \tag{67}$$

$$\varphi^T\left(k\right)$$

$$= \left[-y\left(k-1\right) \ -y\left(k-2\right) \ u\left(k-2\right) \ u\left(k-3\right)\right], \tag{68}$$

where $\theta(k)$ and $\varphi(k)$ represent, respectively, the vector of the parameters and the vector of the observations.

The bounds of unmodelled dynamic presented in the system are unknown, but the norm of the vector of the parameters is given by the following inequality:

$$M_{\min} \leq \|\theta^*\| \leq M_{\max} \tag{69}$$

with $M_{\min} = 0.85$ and $M_{\max} = 1.05$.

In simulation, the nominal values of the uncertain parameters of system are defined by the following.

$a_1(k) = 0.79 + 0.1 \sin(0.1k)$, $a_2(k) = 0.2 + 0.1 \cos(0.1k)$, $b_1(k) = 0.4 + 0.1 \sin(0.1k)$, and $b_2(k) = 0.3 + 0.1 \cos(0.1k)$. The evolution curve of the norm of the vector of the nominal values of parameters is given Figure 5.

The objective of this simulation example is the demonstration of the performance of the robust recursive algorithm for parameter estimation M-RLS with σ-modification (37). A comparative study between the recursive algorithm RLS (10) and the proposed recursive algorithm (37) is treated. The more robust algorithm is the algorithm which can estimate the parameters such that the norm of the vector of the estimated parameters is inside the desired area.

The input signal is a square signal with amplitude that equals two and a period that equal 100, $\{e(k)\}$ is a sequence of random variables with zero mean and variance $\sigma^2 = 0.2$, and the gain matrix $P(0) = 1000I$.

We use the recursive algorithm RLS (10) to estimate the parameters involved in (67). Figure 6 shows the evolution curve of the variance of the prediction error $\sigma_\varepsilon^2(k)$ and Figure 7 shows the evolution curve of the norm of the vector of the estimated parameters $\|\hat{\theta}(k)\|$.

We use the proposed recursive algorithm M-RLS with σ-modification (37) to estimate the parameters involved in (67). Figure 8 represents the evolution curve of the variance of the prediction error $\sigma_\varepsilon^2(k)$ and Figure 9 represents the evolution curve of the norm of the vector of the estimated parameters $\|\hat{\theta}(k)\|$.

Based on the simulation results, we conclude that the proposed recursive algorithm M-RLS with σ-modification (37) is more robust than the recursive algorithm defined by (10).

5.2. Simulation Example 2: The Vehicle. We treat here an example of numerical simulation which is related to the control of a vehicle of laboratory, by using the described algorithm of the explicit scheme of the self-tuning control. Figure 10 represents the scheme of this vehicle, as considered by Sam Fadali [41], in which U is the input force, V is the velocity of this vehicle, and b is the coefficient of viscous friction.

Sam Fadali [41] determined the following transfer function $G(s)$ in open loop, such that describes the dynamic behavior of the vehicle:

$$G(s) = \frac{K}{s+3}. \tag{70}$$

The discrete transfer function $G(q^{-1})$ relating to (70) can be defined as follows, such that the used sampling period is $T_e = 0.02$ sec:

$$G\left(q^{-1}\right) = \frac{b_1(k) q^{-1}}{1 - 0.9418q^{-1}}. \tag{71}$$

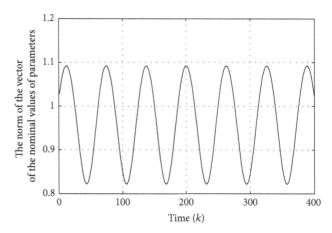

FIGURE 5: Evolution curve of the norm of the vector of the nominal values of parameters $\|\theta(k)\|$.

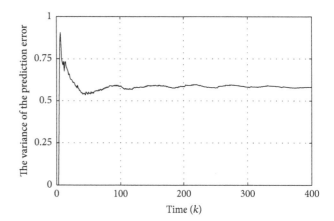

FIGURE 6: Evolution curve of the variance of the prediction error $\sigma_\varepsilon^2(k)$.

For the system to be stable, the closed-loop poles or the roots of the following characteristic equation

$$1 + G\left(q^{-1}\right) = 0 \tag{72}$$

must lie within the unit circle.

To ensure this condition of the stability of the system in closed loop, the parameter $b_1(k)$ must be defined as follows:

$$-0.054 < b_1(k) < 1.941. \tag{73}$$

This system can be described by the following mathematical model ARX:

$$y(k) = -a_1 y(k-1) + b_1(k) u(k-1) + v(k), \tag{74}$$

where $y(k)$ represents the velocity of vehicle, $u(k)$ represents the input force, a_1 and $b_1(k)$ are unknown parameters, and $v(k)$ is noise which can be given by the following equation:

$$v(k) = e(k) + m(k), \tag{75}$$

in which the element $m(k)$ designates the unmodelled dynamics related to the parameter $b_1(k)$.

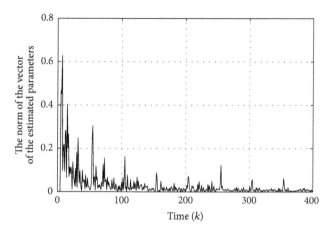

FIGURE 7: Evolution curve of the norm of the vector of the estimated parameters $\|\widehat{\theta}(k)\|$.

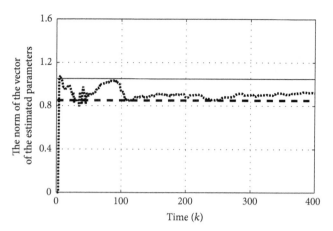

FIGURE 9: Evolution curve of the norm of the vector of the estimated parameters $\|\widehat{\theta}(k)\|$.

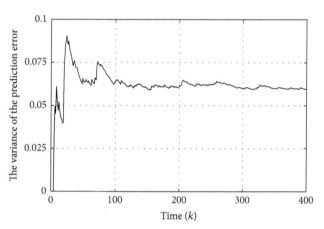

FIGURE 8: Evolution curve of the variance of the prediction error $\sigma_\varepsilon^2(k)$.

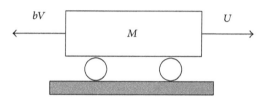

FIGURE 10: Schematic representation of the cruise control system for a vehicle.

The output of the vehicle can be defined as follows:

$$y(k) = \theta^T(k)\,\varphi(k) + v(k), \tag{76}$$

where the vectors of the parameters $\theta(k)$ and of the observation $\varphi(k)$ are given by the following expression, respectively:

$$\theta^T(k) = [a_1 \quad b_1(k)], \tag{77}$$

$$\varphi(k) = [-y(k-1) \quad u(k-1)]. \tag{78}$$

Thus, the data of the explicit scheme of the proposed robust self-tuning control are as follows:

(1) The different values of the parameters involved in (77) are chosen such that $a_1 = -0.9418$, $b_1(k) = 2 + 0.1\sin(0.2k)$, $m(k) = 0.05\sin(0.2k)u(k-1)$.

(2) The sequence of noise $\{e(k)\}$ is composed of independent random variables with zero mean and constant variance $\sigma^2 = 0.04$.

(3) We will take $\widehat{\theta}(0) = 0$ and $P(0) = 100I$ (where I is an identity matrix).

(4) The application of the recursive algorithm M-RLS with σ-modification is based on the knowledge of the region Σ where $\theta \in \Sigma$, such that

$$\Sigma = \{\theta \in \mathfrak{R}^n,\ 0 < \|\theta(k)\| < M_0 = 0.9433\} \cup \{a_1$$

$$\in \mathfrak{R}^n,\ b_1(k) > 0,\ M_{\min} = 0.9433 < \|\theta(k)\| \tag{79}$$

$$< M_{\max} = 2.1628\}.$$

(5) $s_1 = 0.51$, $q_0 = 2.6$, and $q_1 = -2.1$.

(6) The evolution curve of the reference velocity $y_r(k)$ is shown in Figure 11.

The tracking error is defined by

$$v(k) = y_r(k) - y(k). \tag{80}$$

Using the same initial conditions, we will compare the numerical simulation results of the explicit scheme of self-tuning based on the recursive algorithm RLS (10) (control scheme (1)) and of the robust explicit scheme of self-tuning control based on the robust recursive algorithm M-RLS with σ-modification (37) (control scheme (2)). Control laws are applied to the example of the vehicle in the presence of unmodelled dynamics.

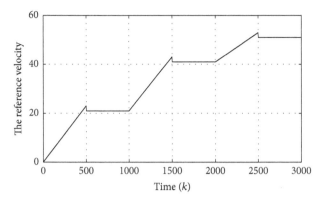

FIGURE 11: Evolution curve of the reference velocity $y_r(k)$.

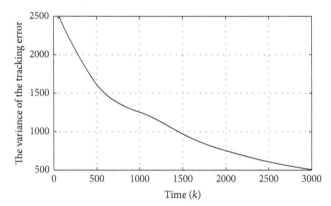

FIGURE 12: Evolution curve of the variance of the tracking error $\sigma_v^2(k)$ (control scheme (1)).

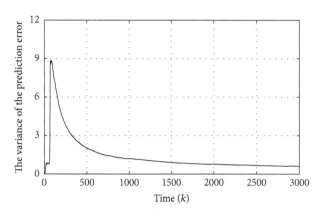

FIGURE 13: Evolution curve of the variance of the prediction error $\sigma_\varepsilon^2(k)$ (control scheme (1)).

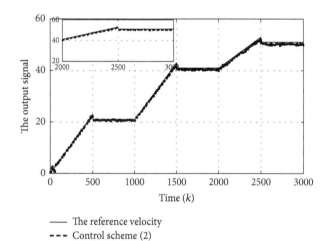

—— The reference velocity
- - - Control scheme (2)

FIGURE 14: Evolution curve of the output signal $y(k)$ and of the reference velocity $y_r(k)$.

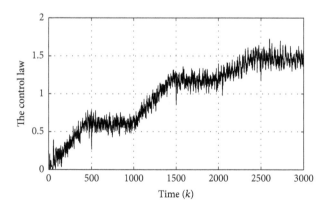

FIGURE 15: Evolution curve of the control law $u(k)$.

Figure 12 show the evolution curve of the variance of the tracking error and Figure 13 show the evolution curve of the variance of the prediction error in the control scheme (1) based on the recursive algorithm RLS (10) to estimate the parameters involved in (79) with considering (77).

In control scheme (2), Figure 14 shows the evolution curve of the velocity $y(k)$, Figure 15 shows the evolution curve of the input force $u(k)$ (or the control law), Figure 16 shows the evolution curve of the estimated parameter $\hat{a}_1(k)$, Figure 17 shows the evolution curve of the estimated parameter $\hat{b}_1(k)$, Figure 18 shows the evolution curve of the norm of the vector of the estimated parameters $\|\hat{\theta}(k)\|$, Figure 19 shows the evolution curve of the variance of the tracking error $\sigma_v^2(k)$, and Figure 20 shows the evolution curve of the variance of the prediction error $\sigma_\varepsilon^2(k)$.

The different illustrated simulation results in Figures 11–20 show the performance of the developed robust explicit self-tuning control scheme on the basis of the proposed M-RLS algorithm with the robustness σ-modification approach. This control scheme is robust, in the presence of unknown unmodelled dynamics, and allows the output to follow the desired velocity while reducing the effects of disturbances acting at different locations in the system. In addition, the estimated parameters are within the desired region.

6. Conclusion

In this paper, we have proposed the M-RLS algorithm with the robustness σ-modification approach. This approach was designed assuming that the bound of desired system parameters norm is known. The stability condition of the parametric estimation scheme was established using the concepts of

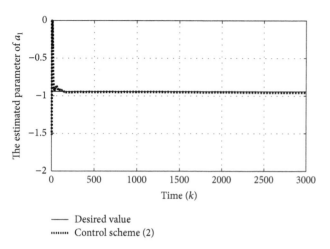

—— Desired value
········ Control scheme (2)

FIGURE 16: Evolution curve of the estimated parameter $\widehat{a}_1(k)$.

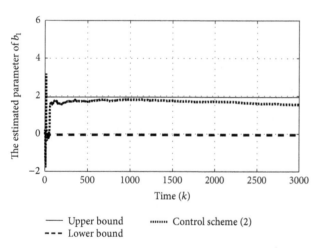

—— Upper bound   ········ Control scheme (2)
--- Lower bound

FIGURE 17: Evolution curve of the estimated parameter $\widehat{b}_1(k)$.

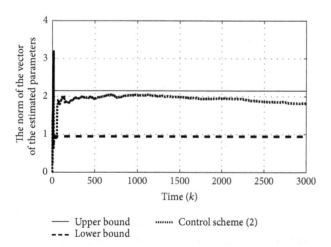

—— Upper bound   ········ Control scheme (2)
--- Lower bound

FIGURE 18: Evolution curve of the norm of the vector of the estimated parameters $\|\widehat{\theta}(k)\|$.

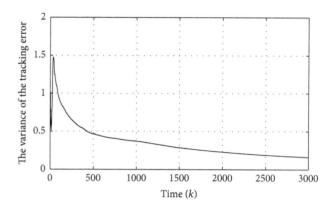

FIGURE 19: Evolution curve of the variance of the tracking error $\sigma_v^2(k)$.

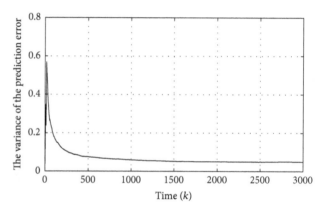

FIGURE 20: Evolution curve of the variance of the prediction error $\sigma_\varepsilon^2(k)$.

the small gain theorem. A numerical simulation example has shown the effectiveness and the performance of M-RLS algorithm with σ-modification.

An explicit scheme of self-tuning control was developed to solve the regulation-tracking problem for the linear systems in the presence of unknown unmodelled dynamics. This control scheme was based on the proposed M-RLS algorithm with σ-modification approach. The robustness of the proposed control scheme for the stochastic system, in the presence of unknown unmodelled dynamics, is shown using the simulation results of the cruise control system for the vehicle.

Competing Interests

The authors declare that there is no conflict of interests regarding the publication of this paper.

References

[1] W. I. Caldwell, "Control system with automatic response adjustment," American Patent, 2,517,081. Filed 25, 1950.

[2] K. J. Åström, "Theory and applications of adaptive control—a survey," *Automatica*, vol. 19, no. 5, pp. 471–486, 1983.

[3] K. J. Åström and B. Wittenmark, *Adaptive Control*, Addison-Wesley, New York, NY, USA, 1989.

[4] R. Isermann, K. H. Lachmann, and D. Matko, *Adaptive Control Systems*, Prentice-Hall, New York, NY, USA, 1992.

[5] T. R. Fortescue, L. S. Kershenbaum, and B. E. Ydstie, "Implementation of self-tuning regulators with variable forgetting factors," *Automatica*, vol. 17, no. 6, pp. 831–835, 1981.

[6] K. J. Åström and B. Wittenmark, "On self tuning regulators," *Automatica*, vol. 9, no. 2, pp. 185–199, 1973.

[7] S. Boyd and S. S. Sastry, "Necessary and sufficient conditions for parameter convergence in adaptive control," *Automatica*, vol. 22, no. 6, pp. 629–639, 1986.

[8] D. W. Clarke and P. J. Gawthrop, "SELF-tuning control," *Proceedings of the IEE*, vol. 126, no. 6, pp. 633–640, 1979.

[9] Z. Li, "Discrete-time adaptive control for time-varying systems subject to unknown fast time-varying deterministic disturbances," *IEE Proceedings. D. Control Theory and Applications*, vol. 135, no. 6, pp. 445–450, 1988.

[10] P. A. Ioannou and J. Sun, *Robust Adaptive Control*, Prentice-Hall, 1996.

[11] Z. Li and R. J. Evans, "Generalised minimum variance control of linear time-varying systems," *IEE Proceedings: Control Theory and Applications*, vol. 149, no. 1, pp. 111–116, 2002.

[12] R. Marino and P. Tomei, "Adaptive control of linear time-varying systems," *Automatica*, vol. 39, no. 4, pp. 651–659, 2003.

[13] A. Patete, K. Furuta, and M. Tomizuka, "Self-tuning control based on generalized minimum variance criterion," in *Proceedings of the 9th IFAC Workshop Adaptation and Learning in Control and Signal Processing (ALCOSP '07)*, pp. 411–416, August 2007.

[14] A. Patete, K. Furuta, and M. Tomizuka, "Stability of self-tuning control based on Lyapunov function," *International Journal of Adaptive Control and Signal Processing*, vol. 22, no. 8, pp. 795–810, 2008.

[15] A. Patete, K. Furuta, and M. Tomizuka, "Self-tuning control based on generalized minimum variance criterion for autoregressive models," *Automatica*, vol. 44, no. 8, pp. 1970–1975, 2008.

[16] B. Egardt, *Stability of adaptive controllers*, vol. 20 of *Lecture Notes in Control and Information Sciences*, Springer, Berlin, Germany, 1979.

[17] P. A. Ioannou and P. V. Kokotovic, *Adaptive Systems with Reduced Models*, vol. 47 of *Lecture Notes in Control and Information Sciences*, Springer, Berlin, Germany, 1983.

[18] C. E. Rohrs, L. Valavani, M. Athans, and G. Stein, "Robustness of continuous-time adaptive control algorithms in the presence of unmodeled dynamics," *IEEE Transactions on Automatic Control*, vol. 30, no. 9, pp. 881–889, 1985.

[19] P. A. Ioannou and A. Datta, "Robust adaptive control: design, analysis and robustness bounds," in *Grainger Lectures: Foundations of Adaptive Control*, Springer, New York, NY, USA, 1991.

[20] M. Kamoun, "Design of robust adaptive regulators for large-scale systems," *International Journal of Systems Science*, vol. 26, no. 1, pp. 47–63, 1995.

[21] V. J. Leite and P. L. Peres, "Robust control through piecewise Lyapunov functions for discrete time-varying uncertain systems," *International Journal of Control*, vol. 77, no. 3, pp. 230–238, 2004.

[22] C. W. Lim, Y. J. Park, and S. J. Moon, "Robust saturation controller for linear time-invariant system with structured real parameter uncertainties," *Journal of Sound and Vibration*, vol. 294, no. 1-2, pp. 1–14, 2006.

[23] K. El Rifai and K. Youcef-Toumi, "Switched systems," in *Robust Adaptive Control of Switched Systems*, chapter 2, pp. 35–50, Prentice Hall, 2009.

[24] S. Kamoun, "Design of optimal self-tuning regulators for large-scale stochastic systems," *International Journal of Information and Systems Science*, vol. 6, no. 2, pp. 201–219, 2010.

[25] M. Hedayati, N. Mariun, H. Hizam, and S. Bahari, "Design of robust controller for STATCOM applied to large induction motor using normalized coprime factorization approach," *Arabian Journal for Science and Engineering*, vol. 38, no. 10, pp. 2713–2723, 2013.

[26] M. B. Kadri, "Disturbance rejection in nonlinear uncertain systems using feedforward control," *Arabian Journal for Science and Engineering*, vol. 38, no. 9, pp. 2439–2450, 2013.

[27] Y. Chen, G. Mei, G. Ma, S. Lin, and J. Gao, "Robust adaptive inverse dynamics control for uncertain robot manipulator," *International Journal of Innovative Computing, Information and Control*, vol. 10, no. 2, pp. 575–587, 2014.

[28] C. Wang, "Adaptive tracking control of uncertain MIMO switched nonlinear systems," *International Journal of Innovative Computing, Information and Control*, vol. 10, no. 3, pp. 1149–1159, 2014.

[29] H. Sheng, W. Huang, T. Zhang, and X. Huang, "Robust adaptive fuzzy control of compressor surge using backstepping," *Arabian Journal for Science and Engineering*, vol. 39, no. 12, pp. 9301–9308, 2014.

[30] G. Feng and T. Fu, "Robust adaptive rejection of unknown deterministic disturbances," *Computers and Electrical Engineering*, vol. 21, no. 1, pp. 1–12, 1995.

[31] A. Jerbi and E. W. Kamen, "Robust adaptive control of discrete-time systems arbitrary rate of variation," *Journal of Mathematical Systems Estimation and Control*, vol. 6, no. 4, pp. 1–31, 1996.

[32] M. Makoudi and L. Radouane, "A robust model reference adaptive control for non-minimum phase systems with unknown or time-varying delay," *Automatica*, vol. 36, no. 7, pp. 1057–1065, 2000.

[33] X. Y. Gu and C. Shao, "Robust adaptive control of time-varying linear plants using polynomial approximation," *IEE Proceedings D: Control Theory and Applications*, vol. 140, no. 2, pp. 111–118, 1993.

[34] X. Wei, L. Del Re, and J. Tan, "Robust adaptive control of quasi-LPV systems," in *Proceedings of the IEEE/ASME International Conference on Advanced Intelligent Mechatronics (AIM '05)*, pp. 1617–1622, July 2005.

[35] S. Alonso-Quesada and M. De la Sen, "A discrete robust adaptive control to stabilize LTI plants by using multirate sampling," in *Proceedings of the IEEE International Conference on Control and Automation (ICCA '09)*, pp. 240–245, IEEE, Christchurch, New Zealand, December 2009.

[36] Y. Fu and T. Chai, "Robust self-tuning PID-like control with a filter for a class of discrete time systems," in *Proceedings of the 50th IEEE Conference on Decision and Control and European Control Conference (CDC-ECC '11)*, pp. 6783–6787, December 2011.

[37] N. Touijer and S. Kamoun, "Design of robust self-tuning control schemes for stochastic systems described by input-output mathematical models," *International Journal of Innovative Computing, Information and Control*, vol. 11, no. 3, pp. 1101–1112, 2015.

[38] N. Touijer and S. Kamoun, "Development of robust self-tuning control for MIMO linear systems with dead-zone approach," *International Journal of Circuits, Systems and Signal Processing*, vol. 8, pp. 101–108, 2014.

[39] G. Zames, "On the input-output stability of time-varying nonlinear feedback systems. Part I: conditions using concepts of loop gain, conicity, and positivity," *IEEE Transactions on Automatic Control*, vol. 11, pp. 228–238, 1966.

[40] M. Kamoun, *Modeling, identification and decentralized adaptive control of discrete-time large-scale systems [Thesis in Electrical Engineering—Automatic Control]*, University of Tunis 2, Tunis, Tunisia, 1994 (French).

[41] M. Sam Fadali, *Digital Control Engineering: Analysis and Design*, Prentice Hall, Upper Saddle River, NJ, USA, 2009.

Permissions

List of Contributors

Chunlei Li, Xiaowei Song, Zhoufeng Liu, Aihua Zhang and Ruimin Yang
School of Electronic and Information Engineering, Zhongyuan University of Technology, Zhengzhou 450007, China

Shu Fan and Honglin Zhao
Communication Research Center, Harbin Institute of Technology, Harbin 150080, China

Hengchi Liu and Yongxin Feng
School of Information Science and Engineering, Shenyang Ligong University, Shenyang 110159, China

Yuntao Zhao
School of Information Science and Engineering, Shenyang Ligong University, Shenyang 110159, China
College of Information Science and Engineering, Northeaster University, Shenyang 110819, China

Changjun Zha
Key Laboratory of Intelligent Computing & Signal Processing, Ministry of Education, AnhuiUniversity, No. 3 Feixi Road, Hefei 230039, China
Department of Electronic Information and Electrical Engineering, Hefei University, No. 99 Jinxiu Road, Hefei 230601, China

Yao Li, Jinyao Gui, Huimin Duan and Tailong Xu
Department of Electronic Information and Electrical Engineering, Hefei University, No. 99 Jinxiu Road, Hefei 230601, China

Xiaoyu Zhang, Jiusheng Chen and Quan Gan
College of Electronics, Information & Automation, Civil Aviation University of China, Tianjin 300300, China

Wei Sun and Xingyan Chang
Department of Business Administration, North China Electric Power University, Baoding 071003, China

Feng Wang, Guiling Sun and Tianyu Geng
College of Electronic Information and Optical Engineering, Nankai University, Tianjin 300350, China

Jianping Zhang
School of Electronic Information and Electrical Engineering, Shanghai Jiaotong University, Shanghai 200030, China

Radhey Shyam and Yogendra Narain Singh
Department of Computer Science & Engineering, Institute of Engineering and Technology, Lucknow 226 021, India

Fudong Liu, Zheng Shan and Yihang Chen
State Key Laboratory of Mathematical Engineering and Advanced Computing, Zhengzhou, Henan 450001, China

Valentin Smirnov, Dmitry Ignatov and Michael Gusev
Speech Drive LLC, Saint Petersburg, Russia

Mais Farkhadov
V.A. Trapeznikov Institute of Control Sciences of RAS, Moscow, Russia

Natalia Rumyantseva and Mukhabbat Farkhadova
RUDN University, Moscow, Russia

Xin Song, JinkuanWang and Jingguo Ren
Engineering Optimization and Smart Antenna Institute, Northeastern University at Qinhuangdao, Qinhuangdao 066004, China

Feng Wang
State Grid Ningxia Information & Communication Company, GreatWall East Road, No. 277, Xingqing District, Ningxia 750000, China

Zuocai Wang
Chengdu Institute of Computer Applications, Chinese Academy of Science, University of Chinese Academy of Sciences, Chengdu 610041, China

Bin Chen
Chengdu Institute of Computer Applications, Chinese Academy of Science, University of Chinese Academy of Sciences, Chengdu 610041, China
Guangzhou Electronic Science Inc. of Chinese Academy of Science, Guangzhou, China

Jin Wu
School ofAeronautics and Astronautics and School ofAutomation, University of Electronic Science and Technology of China (UESTC), Chengdu, China

Shu-Ying Wang
Department of Nationalities, Huanghe Science and Technology College, Zhengzhou 450053, China

Jian-Feng Zhao
Department of Information Engineering, Henan Polytechnic, Zhengzhou 450046, China

Xian-Feng Li
College of Mathematics and Science, Lanzhou Jiaotong University, Lanzhou 730070, China

Li-Tao Zhang
Department of Mathematics and Physics, Zhengzhou Institute of Aeronautical Industry Management, Zhengzhou 450015, China

Liming Duan
Engineering Research Center of Industrial Computed Tomography Nondestructive Testing of the Education Ministry of China, Chongqing University, Chongqing, China
College of Mechanical Engineering, Chongqing University, Chongqing, China

Wuli Wang
Engineering Research Center of Industrial Computed Tomography Nondestructive Testing of the Education Ministry of China, Chongqing University, Chongqing, China
College of Mechanical Engineering, Chongqing University, Chongqing, China
College of Information and Control Engineering, China University of Petroleum (East China), Qingdao, China

Yong Wang
Chongqing Huayu Heavy Machinery & Electrical Co., Ltd., Chongqing, China

Jan Kleine Deters
University of Twente, Enschede, Netherlands

Rasa Zalakeviciute and Mario Gonzalez
Intelligent & Interactive Systems Lab (SI2 Lab), FICA, Universidad de Las Américas, Quito, Ecuador

Yves Rybarczyk
Intelligent & Interactive Systems Lab (SI2 Lab), FICA, Universidad de Las Américas, Quito, Ecuador
DEE, Nova University of Lisbon and CTS, UNINOVA, Monte de Caparica, Portugal

Zhihao Wang, Junfang Wang, Yonghua Huo and Yanjun Tuo
Science and Technology on Information Transmission and Dissemination in Communication Networks Laboratory, Shijiazhuang, China

Yang Yang
State Key Laboratory of Networking and Switching Technology, Beijing University of Posts and Telecommunications, Beijing, China

Hui Huang and Xi'an Feng
School of Marine Science and Technology, Northwestern Polytechnical University, Xi'an 710072, China

Jionghui Jiang
Zhijiang College of Zhejiang University of Technology, Hangzhou 310024, China

Khouloud Samrouth, Olivier Deforges and Yi Liu
UEB, CNRS UMR 6164, IETR Lab, INSA de Rennes 20, Avenue des Buttes de Coesmes, CS 70839, 35708 Rennes, France

Mohamad Khalil and Wassim EL Falou
Faculty of Engineering I, Lebanese University, Tripoli, Lebanon

Jian-feng Zhao and Xiao-yan Wang
Department of Information Engineering, Henan Polytechnic, Zhengzhou, China

Shu-ying Wang
Department of Minzu, Huanghe Science and Technology College, Zhengzhou, China

Li-tao Zhang
Department of Mathematics and Physics, Zhengzhou Institute of Aeronautical Industry Management, Zhengzhou 450015, China

Jin Zhong and Hao Wu
College of Computer Science, Hefei Normal University, Hefei 230601, China

Ya Chen and Zhong-an Jiang
University of Science and Technology, Beijing 100080, China

Nabiha Touijer and Samira Kamoun
Laboratory of Sciences and Techniques of Automatic Control and Computer Engineering (Lab–STA), National School of Engineering of Sfax, University of Sfax, BP 1173, 3038 Sfax, Tunisia

Najib Essounbouli and Abdelaziz Hamzaoui
CReSTIC, IUT de Troyes, 9 Rue de Québec, BP 396, 10026 Troyes Cedex, France

Index

Printed in the USA
CPSIA information can be obtained
at www.ICGtesting.com
JSHW051437221024
72173JS00006B/1500

9 781632 409256